Making Endless War

Law, Meaning, and Violence

The scope of Law, Meaning, and Violence is defined by the wide-ranging scholarly debates signaled by each of the words in the title. Those debates have taken place among and between lawyers, anthropologists, political theorists, sociologists, and historians, as well as literary and cultural critics. This series is intended to recognize the importance of such ongoing conversations about law, meaning, and violence as well as to encourage and further them.

Series Editors: Martha Minow, Harvard Law School
                         Austin Sarat, Amherst College

MAKING ENDLESS WAR

*The Vietnam and Arab-Israeli Conflicts
in the History of International Law*

Edited by Brian Cuddy and Victor Kattan

University of Michigan Press
Ann Arbor

Published in the United States of America by the
University of Michigan Press
Manufactured in the United States of America
Printed on acid-free paper
First published August 2023

A CIP catalog record for this book is available from the British Library.

Library of Congress Control Number: 2023003902
LC record available at https://lccn.loc.gov/2023003902

ISBN 978-0-472-07587-4 (hardcover : alk. paper)
ISBN 978-0-472-05587-6 (paper : alk. paper)
ISBN 978-0-472-90319-1 (open access ebook)

DOI: https://doi.org/10.3998/mpub.12584508

An electronic version of this book is freely available, thanks in part to the support of libraries
working with Knowledge Unlatched (KU). KU is a collaborative initiative designed to make
high quality books Open Access for the public good. More information about the initiative
and links to the Open Access version can be found at www.knowledgeunlatched.org.

The University of Michigan Press's open access publishing program is made possible
thanks to additional funding from the University of Michigan Office of the Provost and
the generous support of contributing libraries.

Cover illustrations: Vietnam Army Pith Helmet on bamboo pole in rice field, courtesy
Shutterstock.com / Aaron Herron. Palestinian Intifada boy with rocks in hands ready for
fight, courtesy Shutterstock.com / Zurijeta.

For our children,
Lara, Gabrielle, and Rosemary,
and
Zachariah

Contents

viii Contents

Foreword

How International Law Evolves—
Norms, Precedents, and Geopolitics

Richard Falk

Prologue

We should understand that this volume devoted to the relevance of international law to these two geographically distinct war zones in the Middle East and Southeast Asia in the period after World War II is a very distinctive undertaking. I am not familiar with any similar search for comparisons and connections, either in relation to the Indochina or Arab-Israeli conflicts, with respect to lawmaking interactions and potentialities. What is notable about this inquiry is that it considers the interaction between regional scale conflicts to be both a source of new norms of international law and occasions for evasions and justifications of existing norms.

My point of departure is to take note of the motivation of the lead political actors in both conflict configurations to evade the constraints on the use of force imposed by the UN Charter, a constitutional framework for international law drafted under the primary influence of World War II and later made more urgent by the use of atomic bombs against Japanese cities. This influence expressed itself by the adoption of a war prevention rationale powerfully set forth in the opening words of the Charter Preamble, "to save succeeding generations from the scourge of war." This language was a response not only to the devastation associated with the thus concluded war with its 60 million deaths but to the fear that a future war of similar or greater proportions would bring even more catastrophic results for the entire world. The Charter norms on the use of force were designed to be very constraining, suggesting that recourse to force by states was to be legal only if undertaken in self-defense against a prior armed attack [Articles 2(4), 51 of the UN Charter] or in response to a decision of the Security Council. As the editors' opening chapter suggests, the Charter carried forward the transformational ambitions to prohibit international war-making and coercive diplomacy by constraining legally mandated recourses to international uses of force as comprehensibly as possible. It should be understood that these ambitions were always tied to the self-restraint of and harmony among the five permanent members of the Security Council who enjoyed a right of veto, which effectively exempted them from an obligatory connection with the international legal norms governing force set forth in the Charter. Even if the General Assembly attempted to fill this gap between international law and geopolitical privilege its authority was constitutionally limited to making "recommendations," nothing more.

The geopolitical condition of fragile and always partial harmony prevailed in 1945 as a result of the recent victory over fascism achieved by the Allied Powers. The UN was established with some hope, although contested by political realists from its inception, that the combination of these restraining norms and the collective security mechanisms of the Security Council could ensure a peaceful world. Such idealistic expectations were challenged by the Korean War (1950–53) and by the 1956 Suez Crisis and Operation, and above all by the outbreak of the Cold War. Nevertheless, until the decade of the 1960s there remained a superficial attachment by the geopolitical antagonists to the UN Charter framework constraining aggressive war-making as the focus continued to be on the avoidance of a third world war or any disregard of the taboo prohibiting recourse to nuclear weaponry.

This changed in the decade of the 1960s. It became clear that the victors in World War II were faced with significant geopolitical challenges that could not be addressed by adhering to the Charter norms. This was made apparent in the Indochina War, especially its Vietnam central arena. The Charter notion of self-defense was not applicable nor would the American extension of the war to North Vietnam in 1965 have enabled the Security Council to restore peace due to the veto power possessed by the geopolitical antagonists, the Soviet Union and the United States. For these reasons the Indochina War, despite its scale and level of destruction, was undertaken without heeding or seriously engaging the UN framework or contemporary international law.[1] The US government, in particular, issued elaborate documentary justifications for the forcible actions undertaken by invoking international law. Its legal rationalizations were partisan in nature and one-sided, and as such unconvincing to the scholarly community of international jurists.

As well, both in Indochina and the Middle East the warfare that resulted was not between political entities of symmetric technological capabilities and tactics. International law had been evolved to address wars fought between sovereign states of roughly equivalent technological capabilities and was concerned with limiting and regulating war rather than outlawing it. The experience of World War II convinced the victors that there was a gap in the legal framework concerning the protection of civilians living under military occupation, captured prisoners of war, and the treatment of wounded soldiers on the battlefield. This realization resulted in the negotiation of the four Geneva Conventions of 1949, a new corpus of law that became known as "international humanitarian law."

Yet these Geneva Conventions were still preoccupied with wars between sovereign states. What was shown by the Indochina and Middle East wars of the 1960s was the importance of extending international humanitarian law (IHL) to conditions of sustained warfare *within* sovereign states, especially when magnified in intensity by external interventions, proxy wars, and geopolitical alignments. Acknowledging the prevalence of this new type of violent conflict gave rise to the two 1977 Geneva Protocols that were deemed supplemental to the 1949 treaties. In particular, Protocol I dealing with the Protection of Victims in International Armed Conflicts was a tricky area for international law as it challenged the sovereign rights of the territorial government, and even trickier for the United States as it explicitly extended the protection of IHL to armed conflicts in which a people are fighting against colonial domination, alien occupation, or racist regimes.[2] This meant that Protocol I applied to foreign interventions in domestic armed conflicts that were struggles over the control of the state. Protocol II was somewhat less controversial as it extended IHL to non-international conflicts and did not have any bearing on interventionary diplomacy, although it did seek IHL accountability for purely internal wars, purporting to put legal limits on previously unlimited territorial sovereign rights.

By considering such conflicts as entitled to international protection it was perceived as weakening the sovereign authority of states to deal with insurgent opposition movements without being subject to international legal accountability. This resistance to the internationalization of anticolonial struggles pertains directly to the Vietnam and Palestinian experiences. Indeed, the diplomacy producing the Protocol was prompted by the tactics and experience of the Vietnam War, which exhibited gaps in the coverage of international humanitarian law as specified by the four Geneva Conventions of 1949.[3] The importance of exempting such armed conflicts from IHL is part of the geopolitical effort to retain freedom of geopolitical maneuver, as Cuddy and Kattan explain, in the momentous international shift from the earlier international law focus on total war to the new realities of endless wars. Protecting civilian populations in this new epoch of postcolonial warfare, as in Syria, Yemen, Afghanistan, Iraq, Libya, and Ukraine, are suggestive of the need for further renovation of IHL, and indeed the overall law of war framework. A merit of this volume is to frame this transition by reference to the Vietnam and Middle East experiences, with particular reference to the unresolved Palestinian struggle. This struggle has taken on a new relevance in the last six years as a result of an emergent civil society consensus that Israel's apartheid policies and practices are blocking the realization of the long denied basic rights of the Palestinian people.[4]

In assessing these legal developments two features of international political society are paramount and need to be kept in mind when discussing the two geographically and psycho-politically distinct war zones:

—the primacy of geopolitics vis-a-vis international law;
—the primacy of military necessity in combat situations.

These two realities, given the absence of centralized governmental institutions on a global level, have accentuated the marginality of international law in war/peace situations, both with respect to recourse to force and the behavior of the parties in the course of warfare.

Acknowledging these two definitive constraints on the role of international law in relation to war should not lead us to cynical conclusions that "law is irrelevant with respect to war" or that "international law does not matter." International law is relevant and matters for several reasons: it empowers civil society activism; it provides a channel for domestic dissent from war-making in democratic societies in both government circles and civil society; and it moderates behavior to the extent that reciprocal interests support compliance with international legal norms (e.g., treatment of prisoners of war).

During the Vietnam War, the US government was more eager than subsequently to retain its liberal image as a champion of a rule-governed international order, and so it went to great lengths to argue that its policies and practices in Vietnam accorded with international law and the UN Charter. Such eagerness also legitimated antiwar activism that could invoke international law to challenge Washington's behavior in Vietnam. It also emboldened critics in Congress to mount objections framed in legal and constitutional language, and allowed international law scholars like myself to be invited to testify before congressional committees or have opinion pieces published in mainstream media venues.[5]

Unfortunately, with the rightest drift in American politics and the lobbying leverage of the American Israel Public Affairs Committee (AIPAC) and other Zionist groups, the authority of international law and the UN have experienced sharp declines. The United States no longer invests diplomatic energy in upholding a liberal image and increasingly relies on coercive threats and militarism to pursue its foreign policy goals, especially in the Middle East. The reliance on unlawful threats of military attack has been at the core of US/Israeli/Saudi confrontational diplomacy directed at Iran for several decades. This trend has reached a symbolic climax of sorts by its imposition of sanctions on the former Prosecutor of the International Criminal Court (ICC) for recommending an investigation of US war crimes in Afghanistan. Israel also has responded with a furious denunciation of this international institution for daring to propose a limited investigation of its crimes in Occupied Palestine. Although the US government after a change in presidential leadership terminated its sanctions imposed on ICC officials, it did not accept the extension of ICC authority to investigate allegations against itself or Israel. Since the Ukrainian Crisis of 2022, the US government has displayed a mixture of hypocrisy and opportunism by urging ICC investigation of Russian war crimes in Ukraine.

The fury of these reactions suggests two opposite interpretations. The first, and most obvious, is the refusal of leading states to defer to international law in settings where national security issues or geopolitical alignments are paramount. And the second, that the fury of the reactions to legally framed allegations suggest how deeply sensitive the governments of such states become when accused of serious violations of international law by credible procedures. In response, such governments do not try to defend their behavior but move to discredit and weaken international procedures of accountability, in part, as a form of damage control to avoid any worsening of their international reputations. Even if the ICC were to prosecute and convict, there is almost no prospect that its judgments would be enforced, and so the whole pushback is about safeguarding legitimacy and opposing impingements by *symbolic politics* on traditional spheres of geopolitical and sovereign autonomy.

A Brief Comment on the Two War Zones

For the United States in Vietnam the Charter norms were perceived as inconsistent with the political mission of preventing a communist victory in South Vietnam and a subsequent unification of Vietnam under the control of Hanoi. It was believed in Washington that it was militarily necessary to extend the war zone beyond the boundaries of South Vietnam to punish North Vietnam for supplying weaponry and personnel to the anti-regime insurgency led by the National Liberation Front (NLF). Similarly, the extensions of the war to Laos and Cambodia were prompted by calculations associated with disrupting the support of the war in South Vietnam by keeping a base area in and maintaining supply chains that passed through Cambodia. Similar reasoning produced sustained air attacks on Laos, unlawfully abusing diplomatic privileges by orchestrating this military campaign from within the American Embassy in the Laotian capital city of Vientiane. In other words, the Cold War priorities prevailed over efforts to constrain recourse to war and tactics in war. On the other side, the priorities of national liberation and anticolonial legitimacy also prevailed over legal constraints.

In the Middle East there were similar factors at work, although tempered by some balancing considerations. The United States was still in the 1960s seeking to balance its commitment to Israel with its vital strategic interests in retaining favorable access to regional oil supplies at affordable prices situated in Arab countries. In this respect, contrary to Israel's wishes at the time, the United States, along with European countries, sought to affirm international law with respect to the acquisition of territory by force, the major premise of the unanimous UN Security Resolution 242 adopted after the 1967 war. Yet even then there was insufficient political will to implement the rhetoric, by an insistence on a timely Israeli withdrawal.

Of even greater relevance to the focus of this volume is the degree to which antagonists in the Middle East with respect to Israel/Palestine evaded the Charter norm on recourse to war. Israel in 1967 and Egypt in 1973 both sought to gain military advantage by striking first, and thus apparently violating the requirement of a prior armed attack contained in Article 51, although there are respectable legal counterarguments in both settings.[6] Both governments defended their actions by claiming security imperatives as providing a convincing "legal" rationale for preemption.

As far as interconnections are concerned, both war zones produced conflicts that ignored the fundamental framework of international law and institutional accountability that was the hallmark of the war prevention efforts after World War II. The asymmetric nature of the wars also strained the law of war during combat, especially in Indochina, but also in the Middle East to the extent that warfare after 1967 shifted to Palestinian temporary efforts to pursue an armed struggle strategy that was designated as "terrorism" by Israel and its supporters.[7] Such a rationale had been used by the United States in Vietnam, but with less impact due to the outcome of the struggle and the absence of widespread support for the war in the West, including even in the United States in its last stages.

International Law Evolves

Against this background it becomes possible to get a better appreciation of how international law evolves. It is important to realize that in some sense all of international law is "soft law" because of the absence of regular procedures of authoritative interpretation and enforcement, not to mention "the geopolitical exemption" of the winners of World War II implicit in the right of veto conferred by the Charter. Added to this, international law in relation to peace and security issues suffers from the special issues previously mentioned—essentially the primacy of geopolitics and of military necessity. Geopolitics manipulates the law governing *recourse* to force, while military necessity by its priority under combat circumstances is constantly reshaping the law involving the *use* of force.

A major interconnection between Indochina and the Middle East is illustrative. In Indochina, the United States created a strong precedent for disregarding the Charter conceptions governing the law on the recourse to force. It put forward some legal justifications to the effect that North Vietnam was guilty of "indirect aggression" by its support of the insurgency in the South, creating a legal foundation for extending the war beyond the confines of South Vietnam. After the 1964 Gulf of Tonkin alleged attack on American naval vessels in international waters and the February 1965 NLF attack on a US military camp near Pleiku, the US government shifted its legal rationale to one of collective self-defense against a prior armed attack.[8] It also contended that Cambodia and Laos violated the laws of war governing neutrality by allowing their territories to be used for hostile purposes associated with North Vietnam's belligerent activities.

Although Israel in 1967 and Egypt in 1973 did not specifically invoke the American precedents set in the Vietnam War, their conduct was shielded from critical scrutiny by the combination of a weakening of the geopolitical commitment to the Charter conception of permissible recourse to force, and by the sense that these specific recourses to force were within their context "reasonable." Because of the geopolitical alignment with Israel, the Egyptian surprise attack on Israel was legally condemned by Western countries, but in a manner that made it appear to be more an expression of alliance diplomacy than a pronouncement of allegiance to international law. Such a view gains weight from the pattern of practice in years subsequent to 1973.

It was also evident that the West controlled international legal discourse on permissible and impermissible uses of force. In this way the violence of nonstate actors and liberation movements was demonized as "terrorism" while state violence, even if directed at civilian targets, was treated under rubrics of security and self-defense rather than delimited as "state terror." Such a discourse gained wider impacts after the 9/11 attacks on the United States, and through the launch of the so-called War on Terror. It has impacted strongly in the Middle East contexts, especially allowing Israel to validate its excessive force and collective punishment as security measures or as the exercise of the right of every sovereign state to defend itself. To some extent, especially in recent years, the UN has challenged this discourse by issuing many reports on Israeli violations of the Geneva Conventions and international humanitarian law more generally. This tension between the geopolitical discourse and the UN discourse is what leads the United States and Israel, in particular, to make accusations about UN bias when it comes to violations of international law. It is this tension, however, that enables civil society initiatives to claim the legitimacy of international law, as is the case with support for the Boycott, Divestment, and Sanctions Campaign (BDS) or by mounting challenges to Israeli apartheid.

It should be noted, in passing, that when Western interests are engaged, as by Russia's 2022 attack on Ukraine, the Charter framework is again invoked as if it is as authoritative and constraining as when adopted in 1945. In other words, the fate of norms is tied to the control of the international normative discourse, and especially in relation to the geopolitics of propaganda.[9]

Conclusion

The main conclusion reached is that the Charter framework established in 1945 was greatly weakened, if not altogether rendered somewhat anachronistic, by the combined impact of geopolitical opportunism and military circumstances in the wars taking place in Indochina and the Middle East in the decades after World War II. To some extent, it can be asserted that the Charter framework was always unrealistic given the character of a state-centric world order system that included hegemonic actors recognized as such by their right of veto in the UN Security Council, a disempowering reality that was fully disclosed after the onset of the Cold War. The nature of the conflicts, which consisted of nationalist movements, was also not anticipated by the kind of legal order envisioned for the post–World War II era, which was not able to cope with the normative challenges of asymmetric warfare or wars of national liberation.

There is also an important tension with regard to the orientation toward normative discourse. The West seeks a statist discourse with unrestricted discretion for geopolitical actors, excepting of course its rivals who are held fully accountable by reference to the UN Charter framework. The South, and the UN General Assembly, is generally favorable to the claims of nationalist movements and anticolonialist struggles, especially if directed toward liberation from European or Western control. In this regard, this subaltern discourse is supportive of the situation of the Vietnamese and Palestinian national liberation struggles, given concreteness in international law by the wide consensus supporting the inalienable right of self-determination as enshrined in Article 1 of both International Covenants on Human Rights, and more broadly reaffirmed in the influential Declaration on Principles of International Law concerning Friendly Relations and Co-operation among States in Accordance with the Charter of the United Nations.[10]

NOTES

1. Indeed, the flaunting of international law was so notorious and the failure of the UN to respond so pronounced that the celebrated British philosopher Bertrand Russell convened a civil society tribunal composed of leading public intellectuals, presided over by Jean-Paul Sartre, which produced a full documented set of conclusions relating to US violations of the laws of war. See John Duffett, ed., *Against the Crime of Silence: Proceedings of the Russell International War Crimes Tribunal* (Flanders, NJ: O'Hare Books, 1968). See also Tor Krever's chapter in this volume for a more detailed discussion of the Russell Tribunal.

2. On the reasons for the US refusal to ratify the Additional Protocols, see the chapter by Victor Kattan in this volume.

3. On the influence of the Vietnam and Arab-Israeli conflicts on the drafting of Additional Protocol I, see the chapter by Amanda Alexander and the chapter by Ihab Shalbak and Jessica Whyte in this volume.

4. See "Israel's apartheid against Palestinians: Cruel system of domination and crime against humanity," Amnesty International, February 1, 2022; "A Threshold Crossed: Israeli Authorities and the Crimes of Apartheid and Persecution," Human Rights Watch, April 27, 2021; "A regime of Jewish supremacy from the Jordan River to the Mediterranean Sea: This is apartheid," B'Tselem, January 12, 2021; Richard Falk and Virginia Tilley, "Israeli Practices towards the Palestinian People and the Question of Apartheid," UN Economic and Social Commission for West Asia, 2017.

5. On the significance of international law for civil society activism and domestic dissent during the Vietnam War, see the chapter by Madelaine Chiam and Brian Cuddy in this volume.

6. See John Quigley's chapter in this volume for a differing legal characterization of responsibility for initiating the 1973 War. See also John B. Quigley, *The Six-Day War and Israeli Self-Defense: Questioning the Legal Basis for Preventive War* (Cambridge: Cambridge University Press, 2013).

7. On the development of "operational law" in the United States and Israel, which appears to have been developed partly in response to the conflict conditions in Vietnam and the Middle East as well as the new IHL rules of the 1977 Additional Protocols, see the chapter by Craig Jones in this volume.

8. For further analysis, see Brian Cuddy's chapter in this volume. Both the Gulf of Tonkin and Pleiku attacks were used to justify plans to expand the combat zone in Vietnam to the north of the country, across the boundary between North and South.

9. General Assembly Resolution ES-11/1, March 18, 2022, A/RES/ES-11/1.

10. General Assembly Resolution 2625, October 24, 1970, A/RES/2625.

ONE

The Transformation of International Law and War between the Middle East and Vietnam

Brian Cuddy and Victor Kattan

International Law in Relief

War, as a concept as much as a set of practices, occupies a central place in the development of international law. But not all wars have had an equal effect on the shape and pace of legal change. This volume is built on the premise that any attempt to understand how the content and function of international law changed in the second half of the twentieth century should consider two armed conflicts, fought on opposite edges of Asia, and the legal pathways that link them together across time and space. The Arab-Israeli conflict (including both the wars between Israel and the Arab states and the ongoing Israel-Palestine conflict) and the Second Indochina War (called the American War in Vietnam, but known more commonly in the United States and around the world as the Vietnam War) are each the product of their own particularities, dynamics, and histories. But considered closely, and especially taken together, these two armed conflicts can also help us to tell a story of the transformation of international law, and its relationship to war, since 1945.

This claim of significance is contestable. The legal scholars Oona Hathaway and Scott Shapiro agree "that the defining feature of an international system is how it regulates armed conflict," but they want to push these two regional conflicts (and others like them) to the margins of our understanding of the development of international law. For them, the great story of international law in the twentieth century is the outlawing of war and territorial conquest.[1] A series of initiatives—centering for Hathaway and Shapiro on the Paris Peace Pact of 1928 but culminating in the United Nations Charter of 1945—did away with an "old world order" in which war was legal and conquest a corollary right of war. The resulting "new world order" turned international law on its head, and the intertwined acts of aggressive war, territorial conquest, and annexation all became illegal. This legal transformation was remarkably successful. Hathaway and Shapiro find that "for every 100 square kilometers taken through sticky conquests before 1929, just 6 square kilometers were thus obtained after 1948." With their "bird's-eye view, it is possible to see what observers on the ground too often miss: that what was once frighteningly common is now thankfully infrequent, because what was once seen as the embodiment of international law is now understood as its repudiation."[2]

While conquest and territorial annexation became rare after 1945, wars did not cease. Hathaway and Shapiro therefore qualify their argument by noting that the prohibition on acquiring territory by conquest worked where sovereignty was clear and borders were accepted. "But if sovereignty is disputed and the lines hazy, the legal situation gets complicated very quickly." Hathaway and Shapiro attribute the residual violence of the transformed legal order to "clumsy decolonization" resulting in "botched handoffs" from empire to nation and "blurry lines" on the world map that engender uncertainty and contestation over sovereignty. The outlawry of aggressive war and territorial conquest also works paradoxically to prop up weak states that then become, for Hathaway and Shapiro, a source of violence. "Those weak states sometimes become failed states," they write (with little attention to the agency of the United States and other major powers such as Russia in the making of weak and failed states). "And those failed states too often become breeding grounds for internal conflict and terrorism." The messy wars of decolonization and the internal violence of weak or failed states together make up what Hathaway and Shapiro label "the dark side of the New World Order."[3]

In order to make their argument, Hathaway and Shapiro push the conflicts in the Middle East and Indochina (and other places) to the margins of the development of international law. They become side-stories to the main narrative of an end to conquest and annexation. To get up close—to be "on the ground"—with these conflicts is to distract from a full appreciation of this grand transformation, suggest Hathaway and Shapiro. Acknowledging that the acquisition of territory by Israel in 1967 and North Vietnam in 1975 were "events of great significance to those involved," they nonetheless insist that to focus on these (and eight other similar cases of post-1928 conquests that stuck) "risks missing the forest for the trees, or more accurately failing to see that the forest *has so few trees*."[4] Hathaway and Shapiro acknowledge the incredible violence of these events but do not want it to overshadow the bigger picture. "Without minimizing this pain and distress, the broad perspective provided by our data makes clear that these conquests were, in historical terms, both relatively rare and comparatively small." To focus on the exceptions, such as with Israel-Palestine and Vietnam, is to miss the broader rule.[5]

Where attention is given to the violence of these exceptions, the finger is pointed at botched handoffs and blurry lines. The British Mandate of Palestine is "perhaps the most infamous example of a botched handoff," write Hathaway and Shapiro, noting that "at least one reason the conflict has proven so intransigent is that the British mandate expired with no clear plan for the territory it had governed." Minimizing the extent to which the United Nations Partition Plan for Palestine in UN General Assembly Resolution 181 (II) *did* provide a clear—if unenforced—plan for the territory of the British Mandate, Hathaway and Shapiro declare that "Palestine became a legal black hole, a territory in which the chain of sovereignty had been broken."[6] They offer a similar analysis for the violence visited on the people of Indochina after 1945. "Much the same happened in Vietnam, where the sudden end of Japanese rule left uncertainty—and then war— over who was the rightful sovereign after Japan relinquished control."[7] For Hathaway and Shapiro, the wars in the Middle East and Indochina are not productive of international legal order in any meaningful sense. They are aberrations, to be regretted and corrected, but of little consequence for the development of international law.

Starting from positions marginal or diagonal to that narrative, however, allows for the possibility that international law has not developed in spite of the conflicts in the Middle East and Indochina but because of them.[8] On closer examination, the "legal black holes" (Hathaway and Shapiro's words) or the "crevices" of international law (Ihab Shalbak and Jessica Whyte's words from their chapter in this volume) are not simply unfortunate byproducts of historical progress but are themselves crucial drivers of change in the international legal order. This volume, then, examines the development of international law in relief. It *begins* with the crevices, black holes, and other recesses that make up the so-called dark side of the international legal order, allowing a different story about the transformation of legal order in the twentieth century to emerge. Our approach recasts the outlawry of aggressive war, as important as it is, as the background to legal change. We instead foreground attempts to develop legal rationales for the continued waging of war after 1945—not the total, industrialized warfare of the sort the UN Charter signatories sought to avert, but more limited and diffuse forms of warfare. Examining international law in relief allows us to move beyond explaining the end of war as a legal institution and toward understanding the attempted institutionalization of endless war.

From Total War to Endless War

The Vietnam and Middle East conflicts are not, of course, the most marginal places from which to gain a different perspective on the development of international law since the mid-twentieth century. As major regional conflicts they occupy a much more prominent position in the history and practice of international law than places such as Nauru, Nagaland, and Namibia.[9] Both conflicts were—and in the case of the Israel-Palestine conflict, continue to be—very much in the public spotlight. They made headline news. They were debated passionately in the newspapers, on radio, and in universities all over the world. Nor did these debates ignore the legal dimensions of these two conflicts. On the contrary, both conflicts were highly visible international law conflicts, in which all sides invoked international rules, procedures, and institutions.

In the case of the Vietnam War, Americans both for and against US involvement developed international law rationales to make their cases. The US government and its supporters put significant effort into making the argument that North Vietnam was engaged in armed aggression against South Vietnam for the purposes of conquest, making the case in public speeches, films, and two white papers released in 1961 and 1965.[10] This official narrative of North Vietnamese aggression was challenged by antiwar activists, clergy, scholars, and lawyers. To them, the United States was the aggressor, violating the 1954 Geneva Accords, unjustly intervening in a civil war, and waging war inhumanely.[11] Guenter Lewy, an early postwar scholarly voice arguing for the necessity and justness of the American effort in Vietnam, noted that "the impact of the antiwar movement was enhanced by the widely publicized charges of American atrocities and lawlessness."[12] The weight of public opinion eventually followed the antiwar movement and shifted against the American war effort.

This shift in public opinion was, in turn, a key prompt for Congress to stop funding the war. South Vietnam—and by proxy the United States—lost the war when Saigon fell to North Vietnamese troops in 1975. The United States had won most of the major military battles of the war, but losing the battle for public opinion at home mattered more in determining the war's ultimate outcome.[13]

In the Middle East conflicts, too, legal arguments have been offered and rebutted by all sides. The Israeli government and its supporters developed international law rationales for its use of force in 1948, 1956, and 1967, and its displacement of the Palestinian people from their homes, which were contested by the Arab states and their Palestinian supporters.[14] Israel's settlements in Palestinian territories have been widely condemned as contrary to international law, most notably by the principal judicial organ of the United Nations.[15] Israel has invested a lot of resources into countering legal narratives articulated by international organizations and anti-occupation activists that its annexation of East Jerusalem, the settlements, and its prolonged occupation of the West Bank and the Gaza Strip violate international law.[16] Israel has employed public spokesmen well versed in the law of war to vigorously challenge claims that its armed forces might have committed war crimes in the West Bank and Gaza. Its reaction to the Goldstone report of 2011 is a case in point.[17]

Despite (or perhaps because of) the vast quantity of pages devoted to the legal aspects of the Vietnam and Middle East conflicts, there is little sense that international law played much of a role in the initiation or conduct of these wars, or in ensuring just outcomes. "It is a humbling realization of no small moment," Richard Falk wrote of the Vietnam War in 1973, "to acknowledge that only international lawyers have been paying attention to the international law arguments on the war."[18] The legal historian Samuel Moyn adds that "it will be obvious to anyone who has studied or lived through the period that none of the legal monuments in an American landscape roiled by the Vietnam war were terribly prominent in the scheme of things."[19] The place of legal argument in the antiwar movement should not be overplayed, in other words, and nor should the effect of international law on the Middle East conflicts. The human rights attorney and legal scholar Noura Erakat notes that "few conflicts have been as defined by astute attention to law and legal controversy" as the Palestinian-Israel conflict. "Enumerating a comprehensive list of the legal questions surrounding this conflict could span the pages of an entire book," she adds, before observing that "none of these issues has been resolved by legal fiat, even as all parties have availed themselves of the law's moral, political, and intellectual logic." For all the legal arguments advanced against Israel's occupation of Palestinian territories, "international law has seemed futile, if not irrelevant."[20]

If law's effect on these wars seems marginal, early assessments of the effect of these conflicts on the development of international law were also underwhelming. Writing five years after the fall of Saigon, Geoffrey Best, a leading historian of the laws of war, had "nothing" to say about the Vietnam War "because it raised few new questions of principle." On the Middle East, Best added only that "the amount of writing about the Arab-Israeli conflict is by now enormous, and exceptionally controversial."[21] The debates over international law in Vietnam and the Middle East seemed to generate much heat but little light. This sense of international law's stasis was only intensified by the Cold War. The standoff between the United States and the Soviet Union formed the backdrop to both conflicts and ensured that international law arguments were as often as not advanced (and certainly perceived) as propaganda and psychological warfare rather than genuinely held legal opinions. In the standard telling, the Cold War stunted the development of international law after 1945, and the regional conflicts waged within the context of the Cold War did not change that narrative.[22]

Several other factors also worked to obscure the ways in which the Vietnam and Middle East conflicts transformed the relationship between war and law. The turn to a politics of human rights in the 1970s helped Americans draw a line under their Vietnam War experience. Human rights, in the words of Barbara Keys, "helped Americans make sense of the new global terrain . . . not as a means of coming to terms with the Vietnam War but as a means of moving past it."[23] Moving past both the lawless and law-bending aspects of the war Washington waged in Vietnam included latching on to "just war" theory, which served to pull a medieval mask over the novelties of the 1960s and 1970s.[24] After the war, too, as Anthea Roberts notes, American international lawyers turned inwards, prioritizing American interests and interpretations in a way the previous generation of multilingual, often émigré, lawyers did not.[25] Naz Modirzadeh argues similarly that the "passion-filled Vietnam-era scholarship" in international law has given way to "an aridly technical, acontextual, and ahistorical" mode of international law scholarship in the early twenty-first century.[26] Part of that process has involved losing any sense that the Vietnam and Middle East conflicts of the twentieth century have relevance to the armed conflicts of today. Having always assumed that contemporary analyses of war and law were "far more law-rich and technical" than anything previous generations of lawyers could offer—that "the forms of legal argumentation and available legal doctrines prior to our present moment were not sophisticated enough to imagine questions like the notion of extraterritorial non-international armed conflict or the outer limits of the geographic scope of non-international armed conflict"—Modirzadeh herself was "astonished" to find precedents and parallels from the 1960s and 1970s that spoke directly to twenty-first-century concerns.[27]

Revisiting the Vietnam and Middle East conflicts today, and foregrounding them in a study of the development of international law, shows that they were not merely unfortunate exceptions to a larger narrative of progress. Nor did the international law arguments proffered and rebutted during those conflicts amount to only a fiery but ultimately vacuous, insignificant, and unsophisticated debate. The Vietnam and Middle East conflicts of the twentieth century were themselves productive of new approaches to, and interpretations of, international law. As Richard Falk notes in the foreword to this volume, the Vietnam and Middle East conflicts were not merely exceptions to the intended legal order of 1945 but were also "a source of new norms of international law." Whether or not anyone except for international lawyers was paying attention to the legal arguments of the 1960s and 1970s, some of those arguments nevertheless contributed to particular interpretations of international law, which were then advanced by certain states attempting to control the normative discourse for employing force in international law. This new discourse was not so much prompted by total wars of the sort that had motivated the war-prevention rationale of the UN Charter, as it was by smaller-scale regional wars, including wars of national liberation, that motivated attempts to *reinterpret* the Charter and the post–World War II international legal order more generally. This, then, is not a story about the outlawry of "total war" but the rise and attempted legitimation of the "endless war" that characterizes our current age.

The armed conflicts fought in the first decades of the twenty-first century, especially those waged by the United States and its allies, seem to many like a new form of war, in which the old lines that circumscribed, particularized, and regulated war seem to have blurred. The persistent wars in Afghanistan and Iraq, the use of force beyond those war zones, potently symbolized by the remotely piloted drone, and the sense that the conduct of hostilities now increasingly sits outside the old rules of war all form the backdrop to renewed interest in the history of the international law of war and peace. The perceived lack of a horizon is particularly troubling. "This is an endless war without boundaries, no limitation on time or geography," suggested US senator Lindsay Graham in early 2018. "We don't know exactly where we're at in the world militarily and what we're doing."[28] At about the same time, Samuel Moyn noted that "the literature of endless war has crystallized into an identifiable genre."[29] Despite the ahistorical and universalist assumptions embedded within the language of "endless" and "everywhere" war, contemporary armed conflict and the legal logics that argue for its legitimacy do have a history. An important element in the emergence and contingent development of this history can be located in the Middle East and Indochina conflicts.

The wars fought in Vietnam and the Middle East were not just physical confrontations. They were also battles of ideas, including legal ideas. To justify their decisions to resort to the use of military force and to use that force in particular ways, Americans, Vietnamese, Israelis, Egyptians, Syrians, Jordanians, Palestinians, their supporters in the West, and other parties to these conflicts appealed widely to international laws and customs. These appeals rested not only on settled understandings of the relevant international law but also on legal interpretations that attempted to shift those understandings. Those novel legal interpretations did not always arise in each conflict independently, however, but were often the product of migrations and mutations of legal knowledge between the two war zones. New understandings of both legal substance (e.g., the right of self-defense, the distinction between civilians and combatants) and legal process (e.g., the legal authority of the UN versus unilateral legal authority) arose out of the conversations, comparisons, and commonalities that connected these two conflicts.

None of this is to downplay the significant differences between the two conflicts—especially the obvious one that whereas the Vietnam War is history, the annexation of occupied Palestinian lands, and the blockade of Gaza, is very much still with us. While recognizing the distinctiveness of each of the two conflicts examined, this volume also considers them in tandem. The migration of legal ideas between these two conflicts helped establish legal precedents and interpretations for the justification of violence that changed the face of armed conflict, and these precedents and interpretations matter for why and how war is waged today.

Connected Histories

The material aid postwar Vietnam provided to revolutionaries around the world was quite meagre. Focused internally on the political and economic development of their now-unified country, and externally on fraught relations with Cambodia and China (leading to the Third Indochina War launched in late 1978), Vietnamese leaders had little to offer revolutionary groups in terms of hardware and training. The historian Lien-Hang Nguyen notes that in the early 1980s, at the request of the Sandinista government of Nicaragua, Vietnam sent two dozen personnel to train Nicaraguan soldiers in overcoming American-style counterinsurgency. But with international attention on the presence of Vietnamese troops in Cambodia, the Nicaraguan mission was kept a secret. "Though committed to passing on the torch of revolution, Hanoi did not advertise its forays into foreign terrain as the Soviets, Chinese, and Cubans had done earlier in the Cold War," writes Nguyen. "Even though revolutionary groups throughout the Third World appealed to Hanoi for guidance and support during and after the Vietnam War, Vietnam was in neither the economic nor the political position to assist other national liberation struggles."[30]

Rather than a source of material support, then, Vietnam would provide intellectual and moral support for other such struggles around the world. Le Duan, general secretary of the Communist Party of Vietnam and architect of North Vietnam's strategy in the American War, described the Vietnamese revolution as "the bridge between socialism and the revolutionary world, the spearhead for the people's movement as well as for national liberation struggles in Asia, Africa, Latin America." The Vietnamese experience served as the "model" of a successful national liberation struggle, and Nguyen observes that "the revolutionary Third World pored over the translated writings of Ho Chi Minh and Vo Nguyen Giap while they listened intently to the speeches of Madame Nguyen Thi Binh."[31]

The Vietnamese and Palestinian liberation movements saw themselves as connected—as partners in the same broad political and legal project.[32] "The Vietnamese and Palestinian people have much in common," Giap told a delegation from the Palestine Liberation Organization visiting Hanoi in 1970, "just like two people suffering from the same illness."[33] Two historians of the Palestinian national movement, Yezid Sayigh and Paul Chamberlin, both highlight how Palestinian liberation groups looked to the Vietnamese model (as well as the Chinese, Algerian, and Cuban examples) in their own struggle. Different Palestinian groups diverged in how they invoked the Vietnamese experience depending on their understanding of the connection between armed struggle and social and economic revolution. The Popular Front for the Liberation of Palestine (PFLP), led by George Habash, "argued that the Vietnamese revolution had demonstrated that by mobilizing the masses, studying the art of revolutionary warfare, and building international alliances, a movement could achieve victory over imperialism."[34] Given Israeli military power, the PFLP called for turning the Middle East into "a second Vietnam" and the establishment of an "Arab Hanoi" (possibly Amman or Beirut) as a base area that could support the war effort in a way North Vietnam had done for the southern National Liberation Front.[35] Fatah, led by Yasser Arafat, was less invested than the PFLP in the precise social theories that underlay Vietnam's model of people's war, but it nonetheless still paired the Palestinian and Vietnamese struggles in general terms, consciously connecting the Deir Yassin and My Lai massacres, for example, and using the Vietnamese association "as a way of accessing international networks of Third World radicals."[36] In his inaugural address to the UN General Assembly in November 1974, Arafat reminded the world that Israel had backed "South Viet Nam against the Vietnamese revolution."[37]

The links between the United States and Israel go well beyond the sphere of ideas, of course, with Israel getting more US foreign aid (US$150 billion as of 2021) than any other country since World War II. Almost all American aid to Israel is in the form of military assistance, with Washington currently pledged to give Israel $3.8 billion in military aid per year until 2028.[38] There is a blunt material difference in the links between the Vietnamese and Palestinian national movements on the one hand and the American and Israeli states on the other. Yet the heft of the aid transfers should not obscure the important intellectual transfers that also occur. Like the Vietnamese-Palestinian relationship, the exchange of ideas matters in the US-Israel relationship.

The Israeli soldier-politician Moshe Dayan's 1966 visit to South Vietnam to observe US and South Vietnamese operations is emblematic of the exchange of ideas in the realm of military strategy and tactics. No longer on active service in the military, and in between stints as a cabinet minister, Dayan arranged to report on the American war effort for the Israeli newspaper *Maariv*. He later wrote that "I wanted to see for myself, on the spot, what modern war was like, how the new weaponry was handled, how it shaped up in action, whether it could be adopted for our own use." In Dayan's words, he visited Vietnam because it was "the best, and only military 'laboratory' at the time."[39]

This idea of America's Vietnam War as a laboratory was widely acknowledged well before Dayan visited the country. "Defense officials do not like the terminology, but they readily concede that Vietnam has given the United States armed forces a 'laboratory for war,'" reported Jack Raymond for the *New York Times* in May 1965. "Tactical theories are being tried, men trained and weapons tested."[40] The development of counterinsurgency theories and practices in Vietnam and elsewhere further ensured that the idea of a laboratory was not confined to a conventional military domain. Tracing the connections between foreign counterinsurgency and domestic policing, the historian Stuart Schrader observes that Vietnam and other Third World countries in the early and mid-1960s were a "laboratory of professionalization" for American policing, boosting the War on Crime back home in the United States and contributing to new forms of "racially invidious policing and incarceration."[41] But the "laboratory" image as a link between Vietnam and the Middle East is particularly resonant. For just as Dayan saw America's Vietnam War as a laboratory that might provide lessons for Israel, so the Israel-Palestine conflict has come to be seen as a laboratory for modern military and paramilitary techniques and technologies.

As Rhys Machold observes, "the concept of the laboratory is employed in making sense of Israel's perceived centrality in global patterns of violence and militarism." It has gained increasing traction in recent times in part as a (not always helpful) explanation "for addressing how Israel has emerged as a major exporter of weapons, security technology and expertise"—including back to the United States via the "Israelification" of American military and police forces.[42] But the idea of Palestine as a laboratory has deep historical roots. Laleh Khalili has both described the "horizontal circuits" in which "officials and foot soldiers, technologies of control, and resources travel not only between colonies and metropoles but also between different colonies of the same colonial power and between different colonial metropoles," and identified Palestine's crucial role in these circuits—"as either a point of origin or an intermediary node of transmission."[43] The suppression of the Palestinian Revolt (1936–39) was a crucial temporal link in the British counterinsurgency knowledge chain that connected pre–World War I campaigns in Ireland, Bengal, the North-West Frontier Province, and South Africa to the post–World War II wars of decolonization in Malaya, Cyprus, Kenya, and other colonies.

Khalili identifies the movement of personnel, the sharing of training programs and doctrines, and the creation of think-tanks and other transnational epistemic communities as key vectors in the transmission of knowledge around the horizontal circuits. We believe that lawyers, legal doctrine, and other juridical concepts also deserve significant attention in the transnational circuits that connect the Vietnam and Middle East conflicts.[44] "Gaza is a laboratory in more than one sense," observes Eyal Weizman. "Most significantly of all, it is the thresholds that are tested and pushed: the limits of the law, and the limits of violence that can be inflicted by a state and be internationally tolerated."[45] But these thresholds are not solely the result of Israel's use of force in Gaza in the twenty-first century. The circuits of legal knowledge that push—and resist—these new thresholds cut across history and geography. The circuit that connects the Vietnam and Middle East conflicts is, we believe, particularly worthy of attention.

Without minimizing the particularities of each conflict—and the chapters that follow flesh out differences as well as connections—we suggest that to consider the Vietnam and Middle East conflicts in tandem allows for a fresh perspective on the history of international law since World War II. Examining the circuits of state, revolutionary, and antiwar knowledge and practice allows us to trace, for example, the diminution over time of what Richard Falk in his foreword terms the "war-prevention rationale" of the UN Charter. The conflicts in Indochina and the Middle East loomed large as states and antiwar activists debated and reinterpreted the meanings of "aggression," "armed attack," and "self-defense" in the legal prohibition on the use of force in international life. The Vietnam War and Middle East conflicts were similarly central to the renegotiation of *who* could fight in wars, and *how* they could fight. Saigon fell in 1975, in between sessions of the Diplomatic Conference on the Reaffirmation and Development of International Humanitarian Law Applicable in Armed Conflicts (1974–1977), giving the Vietnamese Communists a powerful voice in Geneva to advocate for the idea of "people's war." The legitimation given national liberation movements and their fighters in the 1977 Additional Protocols to the Geneva Conventions served as post facto vindication of the Vietnamese struggle, a milestone in the Palestine Liberation Organization's turn to international law and institutions, and a prompt for the United States and Israel to increasingly craft their own legal interpretations and innovations. The subsequent juridification of war in the twenty-first century—more laws, more lawyers, more legal controversies—owes much to the Vietnam and Middle East conflicts.

Background and Volume Outline

The Vietnam War and Arab-Israeli conflicts are also connected by their colonial origins, and especially through the violent end to formal European imperialism in Indochina and the Middle East in the middle of the twentieth century. France secured colonial control of Vietnam in the late nineteenth century, but during World War II the Vichy-aligned colonial regime lacked sufficient armed forces to preserve its dominance and so it allowed Japanese troops into the country—an occupying force in all but name. In 1941, Vietnamese nationalists formed the Revolutionary League for the Independence of Vietnam, known as the Viet Minh, to contest both French formal and Japanese informal rule. Their campaign intensified after Japan overthrew the colonial French government in March 1945, and when Japan surrendered in August the Viet Minh moved to take power. On September 2, 1945, Ho Chi Minh proclaimed Vietnamese independence. Postwar France insisted on its right to return to power in Indochina, however, and with the help of British occupation forces regained control of southern Vietnam. Negotiations between France and the Viet Minh broke down in late 1946, and the First Indochina War commenced, lasting until 1954.

After initially supporting the Viet Minh against the Japanese, the United States increasingly put its weight behind the French effort to reestablish its empire in Indochina. The ascension of Harry Truman to the presidency, and the onset of the Cold War, led to greater suspicion of the Viet Minh's communist core, and to more support for France, especially from 1949. The newly proclaimed People's Republic of China threw its support to the Viet Minh around the same time. Despite significant amounts of American aid, France's military and political position in Vietnam deteriorated. Defeated in battle at Dien Bien Phu in May 1954, France relinquished its rule in Indochina as part of the July 1954 Geneva Accords. The Accords temporarily divided Vietnam in two to allow for the regrouping of military forces. But the unification elections planned for 1956 never happened, and two Vietnamese regimes emerged, each styled as a state—the Democratic Republic of Vietnam in the north and the Republic of Vietnam in the south.[46]

The administration of US president Dwight Eisenhower backed the anticommunist nationalist Ngo Dinh Diem in South Vietnam, pouring money into his nation-building efforts. Hanoi's leadership initially focused on its own nation-building efforts in the north, too, but from the late 1950s increasingly turned to bringing about unification through support to southern revolutionaries. Hanoi prompted the formation of the southern National Liberation Front (NLF), often referred to as the Viet Cong, in December 1960 and the insurgency against the Diem regime intensified.[47] Increased support from the new administration of John F. Kennedy bolstered Diem for a time, but domestic opposition and loss of American faith eventually led to Diem's overthrow. A string of shaky successor governments in Saigon saw Kennedy's successor, Lyndon Johnson, continue to increase aid to South Vietnam, culminating in 1965 with the decision to fight the war with American military might directly.

The colonial origins of the Middle East conflicts are similarly complex. The region known as the Middle East (or the Levant or West Asia) was partitioned into mandates after World War I and divided between the British and French Empires. France secured control of Syria and Lebanon, while Britain took Palestine, Transjordan, and Mesopotamia (Iraq). Native opposition to British and French rule led to serious uprisings in all these places, which were brutally crushed. Iraq remained a client state of Great Britain even after it was admitted to the League of Nations in 1932, as did Egypt, which joined in 1937. Egypt had been colonized by British forces since the late nineteenth century when British and Indian troops were sent to Egypt and Sudan to put down a revolt that threatened the empire's commercial and strategic interests. During World War II, the French government recognized the independence of Syria and Lebanon, and Britain progressively transferred power to the Emir of Transjordan until Jordan was recognized as an independent state in 1946.

In Palestine, the political situation was more complex due to British support for the establishment of a Jewish national home, which was opposed by Palestine's indigenous community, the majority of whom comprised Arabic-speaking Muslims and Christians of various denominations and sects. The Jewish community in 1917 formed less than 10 percent of the population, but the League of Nations supported their emigration from Europe to Palestine, which was to alter the demographic balance of the country considerably. Palestine's Arab community feared they would lose the economic and political privileges they had enjoyed as Ottoman citizens and opposed British rule and Jewish immigration, often violently. Between 1936 and 1939, a major Arab uprising in Palestine was crushed by British troops and the leaders of the Arab community's political parties were either killed or sent into exile. In 1947, following a revolt by Palestine's Jewish community, which now formed one-third of the population of the country, Britain announced that it would leave Palestine. The UN adopted General Assembly resolution 181 (II) that envisaged a transfer of power from the British authorities to a commission that would supervise the establishment of Arab and Jewish states in Palestine with a special international regime established for the City of Jerusalem, but the plan was never enforced as originally envisaged due to the outbreak of the First Arab-Israeli War of 1948. During the war, two-thirds of Palestine's Arab population were evicted or fled from their homes, and the armies of Egypt, Transjordan, and Iraq occupied sections of the country that had been allotted to the Arab state in resolution 181 (II), except for the City of Jerusalem that was divided between Jewish forces and the Jordanian Arab Legion.

The First Arab-Israeli War concluded with several armistice agreements between Israel and the Arab states, signed between February and July of 1949. The demarcation line (the "Green Line" or pre-1967 borders) established by the armistice agreements allowed for the cessation of major hostilities but also set the scene for seven years of low-intensity conflict as Arabs, principally Palestinian refugees with economic, social, and emotional motivations to return to the lands they had been expelled or fled from in 1948, sought to cross the new lines. Infiltration across the new boundaries from the Arab states (especially Jordan and, from 1954, Egypt) into Israeli territory and Israel's responses—particularly its reprisal operations—were the major sources of friction in the years from the armistice agreements to the Second Arab-Israeli War (or Suez Crisis) of 1956.

In chapter 2, Brian Cuddy traces both the evolution of Israel's reprisal policy in the years 1949–1956 and the concurrent emergence of a key Israeli justification for its reprisal operations: the idea that a string of small-scale provocations justifies a single, more significant strike in return. The United States government not only condemned Israeli reprisals but also rejected this argument, now often referred to as the "accumulation of events" doctrine, when it was advanced by Israel in the 1950s. A decade later, however, Washington's attitude shifted. After some internal debate, the administration maintained its formal opposition to reprisals, but State Department lawyers nonetheless reproduced elements of Israel's "accumulation of events" doctrine in the official US justification for bombing North Vietnam. Government lawyers integrated the argument more fully into a justification based on self-defense and, later, made clear that the doctrine allowed for anticipatory self-defense rather than retaliatory punishment. Like Israel, then, albeit by a somewhat different legal route, the United States challenged the conventional understanding of an "armed attack" in international law, borrowing (although not acknowledging) for Southeast Asia what it had once rejected in the Middle East.

In chapter 3, Madelaine Chiam and Brian Cuddy turn from the internal US government debates over the legal justification for bombing North Vietnam to the public reception of, and reaction to, the justifications offered by the United States. In March 1965, the State Department issued a memorandum laying out the legal case for its actions against North Vietnam, sparking debate within the American legal profession over the lawfulness of Washington's war in Southeast Asia. The participants in the debate, first generalist lawyers then specialist international lawyers, mobilized their legal expertise and the American ideological commitment to the rule of law to argue both for and against the legality of US actions. This elite-level debate over law received less attention from 1967 as a larger, more activist antiwar movement—with its own, more popular, understanding of international law—came to dominate the American conversation regarding the war. But the debate nonetheless gained enough public and political traction to have a significant impact on the way the US government and American legal profession subsequently engaged with questions of law and war. The participants took different lessons from the debate and moved along different pathways from 1967—some toward more solidarity with activist and anticolonial interpretations of international law, others toward improving the establishment's facility with incorporating law into national security policymaking—but the debate remains an important moment in the development of American international law.

The year 1967 was a critical time in America's Vietnam War. It saw renewed commitment to General Westmoreland's pacification strategy—what he called "the other war"—but also represented the height of the big unit war, which involved search and destroy operations in rough terrain along the Demilitarized Zone and in the jungles of the highlands. According to American statistics, in 1967 alone, US troops killed 25,564 Vietnamese communist guerrilla fighters. American scorch earthed tactics also produced huge refugee flows, with the number of internally displaced Vietnamese reaching one million by the end of 1967. American military strategy also soaked up precious American combat manpower by exacting a heavy price in American lives. During the first half of 1967, American casualties reached an average of 816 killed in action per month, compared with a monthly average of 477 in 1966.[48] Opposition to America's war increased at home and abroad, which together with the war's drain on American resources made 1967 a key inflection point in America's global position.[49]

That same year, 1967, was also a key turning point in the Middle East, with the Six-Day War, also known as the June 1967 War, marking a number of new features in regional politics: the beginning of Israel's occupation of East Jerusalem, the West Bank, the Gaza Strip, the Golan Heights, and the Sinai Peninsula; a revived Palestinian national movement called the Palestine Liberation Organization (PLO), which sought to liberate all parts of the country by commando action; and Washington's more direct diplomatic, military, and legal support for Israel.

In chapter 4, John Quigley provides an assessment of the legality of military action by Egypt and Syria in October 1973. Reversing its usual argument for *expanding* the temporal frame of reference upon which to judge the use of force, in October 1973 Israel argued the narrow point that Egypt and Syria were aggressors because they initiated hostilities. Egypt and Syria did indeed strike first on October 6, but in attacking into their own territory in the Sinai Peninsula and the Golan Heights they were taking a course of action that had been legally available to them since the occupation of those territories by Israel in 1967 and in the face of UN Security Council inaction. As with its war in Vietnam, the United States was able to use its position as a veto-wielding member of the Security Council to steer discussion away from questions of legality from 1967 through 1973. But this support for Israel in the face of international sentiment that favored the territorial rights of the Arab states only added to the increasingly unfavorable international political context that faced the United States as a result of its war in Southeast Asia and the changed composition of the United Nations. Even though Washington withdrew combat troops from South Vietnam six months prior to the October 1973 war, it continued to be challenged over its wartime practices, most notably at a series of diplomatic conferences that renegotiated the laws of war between 1974 and 1977.

In chapter 5, Amanda Alexander shifts the frame of legal analysis from the use of force to the conduct of hostilities. The 1977 Additional Protocols to the 1949 Geneva Conventions established the principle of distinction between civilians and combatants and the protection of civilians as perhaps the central precepts of international humanitarian law. But the easy acceptance of those precepts today masks how their particular features emerged as flawed compromises from the 1974–1977 negotiations. The United States and the Vietnamese communists (both the government of North Vietnam and the National Liberation Front in South Vietnam) took different legal and spatial understandings of armed conflict into the Second Indochina War. Those differences between Western conventional war and revolutionary war played out both on the battlefields of Vietnam and around the conference tables of Geneva. Diplomatically outnumbered in Geneva, the United States and its Western allies were forced to accept the proposition that wars of national liberation—wars fought to free a country from imperial control—were legitimate international conflicts, and that guerrilla fighters could be legitimate combatants. The guerrilla fighter question put the principle of distinction front and center at the conference, with long and complex debates eventually leading to a compromise: combatants only needed to distinguish themselves from the civilian population during a military engagement and the preceding deployment. Thus the principle of distinction was enshrined in law only by accepting the lack of any absolute difference between combatant and civilian.

In chapter 6, Ihab Shalbak and Jessica Whyte continue to examine the question of the relation between irregular fighters and the civilian population, but from a Palestinian perspective. As one of the few national liberation movements that had not achieved statehood by the time the Additional Protocols were finalized, the stakes of the debate were crucial for the Palestinians, touching as they did on the existential question of who constituted a people. In the years between the 1967 War and the Diplomatic Conference, armed struggle played a central role in the self-constitution of a Palestinian identity. The essential unity of civilian and combatant—fighter and farmer—was the foundation upon which the Palestinian national movement reconstituted the Palestinian people, with a right to self-determination and a right to return to their land. The cause of combatant status for irregular fighters, then, was central to the Palestinian participation in the negotiations for the Additional Protocols. The Palestinian delegation stressed that giving status to irregular fighters was actually a means of protecting civilians, given the harm inflicted on civilians by counterinsurgency campaigns and pacification. Winning recognition for guerrilla fighters and protections for civilians, however, came at the cost of operating within the strictures of international law—of substituting state-building for nation-building.

What did not change as a result of concluding the Additional Protocols was Israel's continued treatment of the civilian population of Palestine with suspicion, irrespective of its newly defined and protected status within international law. But diplomatic and political relations between Israel, the Arab states, and the PLO did undergo some significant changes from the late 1970s. In 1982, Israel completed its withdrawal from the Sinai Peninsula after concluding a peace treaty with Egypt, although the PLO was less successful in its attempt to liberate Palestine by armed struggle, and its leadership was exiled to Tunisia during Israel's 1982 siege of Beirut. From Tunis, the PLO embarked on discussions with peace activists close to Israel's Labor Party, and in 1993, following the formation of a government led by Labor after the 1992 general election, the PLO recognized the State of Israel, and in exchange Israel allowed the PLO's leadership to return from exile and govern the West Bank and the Gaza Strip.

In chapter 7, Victor Kattan returns the focus to the United States, revisiting critiques of the laws of war among lawyers serving in the US government following the fall of Saigon in 1975 that viewed the emergence of a Third World bloc in the UN as a problem. A marriage of convenience was also taking place between the United States and Israel, whose interests became increasingly entwined in the 1970s as they saw themselves as liberal democracies fighting insurgents that hid amidst civilian populations only to invoke the law of war to their advantage. Disconcerted by the "Third Worldism" of the Carter administration, the interests of neo-conservatives with close links to members of the Israeli government and Vietnam War veterans became aligned after the drafting of the Additional Protocols to the 1949 Geneva Conventions. Bitterness over the loss of the Vietnam War, the success of national liberation struggles in influencing the drafting of Additional Protocol I, and a spate of high-profile terrorist attacks against US citizens between 1983 and 1985, persuaded Ronald Reagan to refuse to send the treaty to the Senate for advice and consent for ratification. For the Reagan administration, certain provisions of API were considered too constraining on US power in the global confrontation with the Soviet Union and too accommodating to the interests of the national liberation movements that were supported by the Soviet Union in undermining US interests in the Third World. To win the Cold War, the United States wanted to go on the offensive and in order to accomplish this objective international law needed to be interpreted flexibly.

In chapter 8, Craig Jones looks at the mechanics of how this flexible interpretation of the laws of war came about in practice. As a result of the Vietnam War, and in an attempt to overcome the negativity toward the laws of war felt by many US commanders who had fought in Vietnam, the United States invented and developed a new military-legal discipline called "operational law." A mix of domestic and international law, operational law was designed to give military commanders the tools they needed for "mission success." US military lawyers first consciously used the approach in Panama (1989) and the First Gulf War (1990–91), and it was then picked up and developed by the Israeli military during the Second Intifada beginning in September 2000. Applying the idea of operational law has allowed the United States and Israeli militaries to domesticate international law, which combined with the creative interpretive legal work of military lawyers has seen the expansion of the scope and space of a permissible target and other controversial policies that push at the boundaries of international law.

In chapter 9, Tor Krever looks not at how international law has been used to advance American and Israeli policies and practices in Vietnam and Palestine but at how it has been used to contest and condemn those policies and practices. In both the Vietnamese and Palestinian struggles, law has been used as a tool of resistance. A prominent form of such resistance has been peoples' tribunals—bodies set up by private citizens but modeled on legal courts for the purpose of judging and condemning state behavior with reference to law. The British philosopher Bertrand Russell was the inspiration behind two sessions of the International War Crimes Tribunal that heard testimony and issued verdicts against US actions in Vietnam in 1967. Subsequent "Russell Tribunals" have periodically been conducted since, including the Russell Tribunal on Palestine, which held six sessions between 2010 and 2014. All peoples' tribunals navigate a tension between legal form and political purpose, but the way they do so has changed over time. The Vietnam War tribunal attempted to mobilize international law tactically in service to a broader practice of resistance against imperialism. Four decades later, the Palestine tribunal had a greater tendency to invoke international law, and compliance with the law, not just tactically but as an end in itself. Just as legalism has become more prominent in American and Israeli military practices since the Vietnam War, then, so too has it become more prominent in opposition to those practices. With its potential to obscure larger political goals, this juridification of resistance has not come without cost.

In chapter 10, we close the volume with a chapter on how the wars in Vietnam and the Middle East shaped the rationalization for various uses of armed force by the United States and Israel between the Cold War and the "War on Terror." We suggest that America's culture wars and the impact of English-language media, cinema, and other forms of popular culture have had an oversized impact on the language of war. This is supported by the quantity of literature devoted to these two conflicts in specialized international law journals as well as official government publications. We trace the roots of the special relationship between the United States and Israel to their common enemies, and the two wars fought against international terrorism, declared by the Reagan administration after the 1983 Beirut bombings, and then following 9/11 by the Bush administration. Resistance to these rationalizations for the permissive use of force by the American and Israeli governments, together with criticism from the scholarly community, led to the establishment of smaller groups of like-minded ideologically committed lawyers associated with Tel Aviv and Washington who embarked on a process of "reform." This reform process involved persuading the governments of powerful states in North America, Europe, and Australasia to revise the prohibition on the use of force in Article 2(4) of the UN Charter to enable military action against novel types of threats, especially those emanating from ungoverned spaces. The permissive interpretations of international law held by these like-minded lawyers were shaped by their common threat perceptions, which in turn had been largely shaped by the conflicts in Vietnam and the Middle East. A consequence of these rationalizations has been the legitimization of endless wars and the novel technologies that sustain them. Even if these lawyers have not been as successful in advancing their new interpretations of the law beyond the Anglosphere, scholars should nevertheless remain vigilant about the sources and origins of these arguments because they risk further estranging the international community, by which we mean *all* members of the United Nations and not just "the West" or a "concert of democracies," from the UN Charter's war-prevention rationale.

The Vietnam and Middle East conflicts were fundamental to the development of our current international legal order. They shaped both prominent public lawmaking moments, especially the Diplomatic Conference leading to the Additional Protocols in 1977, and also the slower behind-the-scenes accretion of interpretation and practice, the significance of which was often difficult to discern at the time and is only readily apparent in historical perspective. Bringing such a perspective to the study of the Vietnam and Middle East conflicts, and studying these two regional conflicts in tandem, allows this volume to provide the beginnings of a framework for better appreciating the development of international law and war since 1945. The changes wrought to the international legal order and to the character of war during, and as a result of, the Vietnam and Middle East conflicts were important and enduring.

NOTES

1. Oona A. Hathaway and Scott J. Shapiro, *The Internationalists: How a Radical Plan to Outlaw War Remade the World* (New York: Simon and Schuster, 2017), xix.

2. Hathaway and Shapiro, *The Internationalists*, 321, 329. "Sticky" conquests are those that have not been reversed by later events. Historians who are sympathetic to Hathaway and Shapiro's argument still question the suddenness of the shift they describe, and they suggest that ideas about the outlawry of war have a longer and more complex history than Hathaway and Shapiro acknowledge. Isabel Hull, for example, questions Hathaway and Shapiro's portrayal of the Paris Peace Pact as "almost magical in its transformative capacities," preferring instead to see a "long and uneven history of legal change" going back to the seventeenth century. Isabel V. Hull, "Anything Can Be Rescinded," review of *The Internationalists: How a Radical Plan to Outlaw War Remade the World*, by Oona Hathaway and Scott Shapiro, *London Review of Books* 40, no. 8 (April 26, 2018); see also Sharon Korman, *The Right of Conquest: The Acquisition of Territory by Force in International Law and Practice* (Oxford: Clarendon Press, 1996). These ideas have a more diverse history, too, including not just Hathaway and Shapiro's four "internationalists"—all men, all European or American—but extending the cast of characters much wider to socialists, feminists, conservatives, and other groups who articulated an internationalist vision.

3. Hathaway and Shapiro, *The Internationalists*, 353, 355, 368, 365.

4. Hathaway and Shapiro also gloss over the acquisition of territory in 1948 by Israel in areas allotted to the Arab State in the UN Partition Plan following the

adoption of General Assembly Resolution 181 (II) on November 29, 1947, which purported to establish two states in Palestine.

5. Hathaway and Shapiro, *The Internationalists*, 328, 329.

6. Hathaway and Shapiro, *The Internationalists*, 355–57.

7. Hathaway and Shapiro, *The Internationalists*, 357.

8. Mary Beth Norton, "History on the Diagonal," *American Historical Review* 124, no. 1 (February 2019): 1–19.

9. Cait Storr, *International Status in the Shadow of Empire: Nauru and the Histories of International Law* (Cambridge: Cambridge University Press, 2020); Lydia Walker, "Decolonization in the 1960s: On Legitimate and Illegitimate Nationalist Claims-Making," *Past and Present* 242 (February 2019): 227–64. Storr begins her work on Nauru from the premise "that the international order one perceives is radically determined by the place in which one stands" (8) and rejects "any presumption of Nauru as anomaly" (10). Walker's comparison of Naga and Namibian nationalist claims-making excavates "a layer of international relations, usually unseen" that "worked within the UN's fissures" (228).

10. See, for example, Lyndon B. Johnson, Address at Johns Hopkins University: "Peace Without Conquest," April 7, 1965, reprinted in *The American Presidency Project* by Gerhard Peters and John T. Woolley, https://www.presidency.ucsb.edu/node/241950; Department of Defense, "Why Vietnam?" documentary film, 1965, https://archive.org/details/gov.archives.arc.2569861; Department of State, "A Threat to the Peace: North Viet-Nam's Effort to Conquer South Viet-Nam," December 1961; Department of State, "Aggression from the North: The Record of North Viet-Nam's Campaign to Conquer South Viet-Nam," February 1965; Roger H. Hull and John C. Novogrod, *Law and Vietnam* (Dobbs Ferry, NY: Oceana Publications, 1968); John Norton Moore, *Law and the Indo-China War* (Princeton: Princeton University Press, 1972).

11. See, for example, Consultative Council of the Lawyers Committee on American Policy Towards Vietnam, *Vietnam and International Law: The Illegality of United States Military Involvement*, rapporteur John H. E. Fried (Flanders, NJ: O'Hare Books, 1967); Clergy and Laymen Concerned About Vietnam, *In the Name of America: The conduct of the war in Vietnam by the armed forces of the United States as shown by public reports compared with the Laws of War binding on the United States Government and on its citizens*, director of research Seymour Melman (Annandale, VA: The Turnpike Press, 1968); John Duffett, ed., *Against the Crime of Silence: Proceedings of the Russell International War Crimes Tribunal* (Flanders, NJ: O'Hare Books, 1968); Richard A. Falk, Gabriel Kolko, and Robert Jay Lifton, eds., *Crimes of War: A legal, political-documentary, and psychological inquiry into the responsibility of leaders, citizens, and soldiers for criminal acts in wars* (New York: Vintage Books, 1971); Richard A. Falk, ed., *The Vietnam War and International Law*, 4 vols. (Princeton: Princeton University Press, 1968–1976). The latter series included a variety of viewpoints on the conflict but overall tended to favor antiwar perspectives.

12. Guenter Lewy, *America in Vietnam* (New York: Oxford University Press, 1978), 434.

13. There are still scholars who argue that the United States could have won the Vietnam War had Congress, responding to public opinion, not cut funds for the war. For an overview of this literature, see Gary R. Hess, *Vietnam: Explaining America's Lost War* (Malden, MA: Blackwell, 2009), 179–206.

14. See, for example, Colloquium of Arab Jurists, *The Palestine Question: Seminar of Arab Jurists on Palestine, Algiers, 22–27 July, 1967* (Beirut: Institute for Palestine Studies, 1968); Nathan Feinberg, *The Arab-Israel Conflict in International Law: A Critical Analysis of the Colloquium of Arab Jurists in Algiers* (Jerusalem: The Magnes Press, 1970); Faris Yahya, *The Palestine Question and International Law* (Beirut: PLO Research Center, 1970); Henry Cattan, *Palestine and International Law: The Legal Aspects of the Arab-Israeli Conflict* (London: Longmans, 1973); Nathan Feinberg, *Studies in International Law, with Special Reference to the Arab-Israeli Conflict* (Jerusalem: The Magnes Press, 1979); W. Thomas Mallison and Sally V. Mallison, *An International Law Analysis of Major United Nations Resolutions Concerning the Palestine Question* (New York: United Nations, 1979); Julius Stone, *Israel and Palestine: Assault on the Law of Nations* (Baltimore: Johns Hopkins University Press, 1981).

15. Legal Consequences of the Construction of a Wall in the Occupied Palestinian Territory, Advisory Opinion, ICJ Reports 2004, 136 at 184, para 120.

16. On the settlements, see, for example, the writings of Eugene Rostow (also a prominent figure in the Vietnam War), which continue to be cited in contemporary polemics: Eugene Rostow, "'Palestinian self-determination': Possible Futures for the Unallocated Territories of the Palestine Mandate," *Yale Studies in World Public Order* 5 (1978–1979): 147–72; Douglas Feith and Eugene Rostow, *Israel's Legitimacy in Law and History: Proceedings of the Conference on International Law and the Arab-Israeli Conflict* (New York: Center for Near East Policy Research, 1993). Another figure who wrote prolifically on the Vietnam War was John Norton Moore. His four-volume tome on the Arab-Israeli conflict remains essential reading: John Norton Moore, ed., *The Arab-Israeli Conflict*, 4 vols. (Princeton: Princeton University Press, 1973). See also, M. Cherif Bassiouni and Shlomo Ben Ami, eds., *A Guide to Documents on the Arab-Palestinian/Israeli Conflict, 1897–2008* (Leiden: Martinus Nijhoff, 2009).

17. See Human Rights in Palestine and Other Occupied Arab Territories: Report of the United Nations Fact-Finding Mission on the Gaza Conflict, UN Doc. A/HRC/12/48, September 25, 2009. For reactions see the documents listed on the website of Israel's Ministry of Foreign Affairs: https://www.gov.il/en/Dep artments/General/goldstone-fact-finding-report-a-challenge-to-democracies-fig hting-terror. See also Adam Horowitz, Lizzy Ratner, and Philip Weiss, eds., *The Goldstone Report: The Legacy of the Landmark Investigation of the Gaza Conflict* (New York: Nation Books, 2011).

18. Richard A. Falk, review of *Fire in the Lake: The Vietnamese and the Americans in Vietnam* by Frances Fitzgerald, *Texas Law Review* 51, no. 3 (March 1973): 618.

19. Samuel Moyn, "From Antiwar Politics to Antitorture Politics," in *Law and War*, ed. Austin Sarat, Lawrence Douglas, and Martha Merrill Umphrey (Stanford: Stanford University Press, 2014), 155.

20. Noura Erakat, *Justice for Some: Law and the Question of Palestine* (Stanford: Stanford University Press, 2019), 3, 2.

21. Geoffrey Best, *Humanity in Warfare* (New York: Columbia University Press, 1980), 371n44, 371n46.

22. For another recent challenge to this narrative, see Matthew Craven, Sundhya Pahuja, and Gerry Simpson, "Reading and Unreading a Historiography of Hiatus," in *International Law and the Cold War*, ed. Matthew Craven, Sundhya Pahuja, and Gerry Simpson (Cambridge: Cambridge University Press, 2020).

23. Barbara J. Keys, *Reclaiming American Virtue: The Human Rights Revolution of the 1970s* (Cambridge, MA: Harvard University Press, 2014), 3. See also *Samuel Moyn, The Last Utopia: Human Rights in History* (Cambridge, MA: The Belknap Press of Harvard University Press, 2010), esp. chap. 5, "International Law and Human Rights."

24. Michael Walzer, *Just and Unjust Wars: A Moral Argument with Historical Illustrations* (New York: Basic Books, 1977). See also Jessica Whyte, "The 'Dangerous Concept of the Just War': Decolonization, Wars of National Liberation, and the Additional Protocols to the Geneva Conventions," *Humanity* 9, no. 3 (Winter 2018): 313–41.

25. Anthea Roberts, *Is International Law International?* (New York: Oxford University Press, 2017), 50, 104–5.

26. Naz K. Modirzadeh, "Cut These Words: Passion and International Law of War Scholarship," *Harvard International Law Journal* 61, no. 1 (Winter 2020): 1.

27. Modirzadeh, "Cut These Words," 5–6.

28. Cited in Rukmini Callimachi, Helene Cooper, Eric Schmitt, Alan Blinder, and Thomas Gibbons-Neff, "'An Endless War': Why 4 U.S. Soldiers Died in a Remote African Desert," *New York Times*, February 20, 2018, https://www.nytimes.com/interactive/2018/02/17/world/africa/niger-ambush-american-soldiers.html

29. Samuel Moyn, "American Peace in an Age of Endless War," *Raritan* 37, no. 3 (Winter 2018): 153.

30. Lien-Hang T. Nguyen, "The Vietnam Decade: The Global Shock of the War," in *The Shock of the Global: The 1970s in Perspective*, ed. Niall Ferguson, Charles S. Maier, Erez Manela, and Daniel J. Sargent (Cambridge, MA: Belknap Press of Harvard University Press, 2010), 168.

31. Nguyen, "The Vietnam Decade," 169.

32. Evyn Lê Espiritu, "Cold War Entanglements, Third World Solidarities: Vietnam and Palestine, 1967–1975," *Canadian Review of American Studies* 48, no. 3 (2018): 352–86.

33. Cited in Paul Chamberlin, *The Global Offensive: The United States, the Palestine Liberation Organization, and the Making of the Post-Cold War Order* (New York: Oxford University Press, 2012), 1.

34. Chamberlin, *The Global Offensive*, 26. Habash was a key figure in the establishment of both the Arab Nationalist Movement in 1953 and the PFLP in 1967.

35. Yezid Sayigh, *Armed Struggle and the Search for State: The Palestinian National Movement, 1949–1993* (Oxford: Oxford University Press, 1999), 200; Chamberlin, *The Global Offensive*, 26.

36. Sayigh, *Armed Struggle and the Search for State*, 196–202; Chamberlin, *The Global Offensive*, 27.

37. Agenda item 108, Question of Palestine, United Nations General Assembly, 29th Session, Official Records, UN Doc. A/PV.2282 and Corr. 1, November 13, 1974, para. 41.

38. Jeremy M. Sharp, "U.S. Foreign Aid to Israel," Congressional Research Service Report RL33222, February 18, 2022.

39. Marc Leepson, "Moshe Dayan Sounds the Alarm in Vietnam," https://www.historynet.com/moshe-dayan-sounds-the-alarm-in-vietnam-3.htm. While Dayan came away impressed with American firepower and personnel, he expressed con-

cern at both the search-and-destroy and hearts-and-minds strategies of US forces, writing that "the Americans are winning everything—except the war."

40. Jack Raymond, "Vietnam Gives U.S. 'War Laboratory,'" *New York Times*, May 3, 1965, 12. Explaining the Pentagon's aversion to laboratory terminology, Raymond added that "officials hesitate to discuss Vietnam as a military proving ground because they fear it might be taken out of context—the Spanish Civil War 30 years ago was regarded by military experts as the Nazis' laboratory for World War II."

41. Stuart Schrader, *Badges Without Borders: How Global Counterinsurgency Transformed American Policing* (Oakland: University of California Press, 2019), 11, 2.

42. Rhys Machold, "Reconsidering the Laboratory Thesis: Palestine/Israel and the Geopolitics of Representation," *Political Geography* 65 (2018): 89, 88, 90.

43. Laleh Khalili, "The Location of Palestine in Global Counterinsurgencies," *International Journal of Middle East Studies* 42 (2010): 413–14.

44. Khalili does note the important historical continuity in the laws and regulations operating in Palestinian lands before and after 1948, which helps to account for "the striking isomorphism of British techniques of suppression during the Arab Revolt and the Israeli methods of population control since 1948 and especially in the last two decades." But she treats this as something of an exceptional feature of the Palestinian context, stating that "it is one of the very few loci—if not the only site—of asymmetric warfare where one counterinsurgent force has explicitly inherited and adapted not only the practices and doctrines of its preceding counterinsurgent army but also its laws and regulations." Khalili, "The Location of Palestine in Global Counterinsurgencies," 427. Different conclusions can be reached if *international* law is taken into account.

45. Eyal Weizman, *The Least of All Possible Evils: Humanitarian Violence from Arendt to Gaza* (London: Verso, 2011), 96. See also Machold, "Reconsidering the Laboratory Thesis," 90.

46. Whether or not North and South Vietnam were actually states was a question that aroused considerable legal controversy. Neither regime was admitted to the United Nations as a member state during the war—only in 1977 was Vietnam admitted as a single, unitary state. The United States argued, however, that South Vietnam had achieved de facto if not de jure statehood, and while it did not bestow diplomatic recognition on Hanoi it implicitly acknowledged North Vietnam's independence, too. Hanoi did not recognize the legitimacy of the Saigon regime's rule in the south.

47. For a discussion of the history and politics of naming the NLF, see Brett Reilly, "The True Origin of the Term 'Viet Cong,'" *The Diplomat*, January 31, 2018, https://thediplomat.com/2018/01/the-true-origin-of-the-term-viet-cong/

48. Lewy, *America in Vietnam*, 65, 73.

49. See, for example, Mark Atwood Lawrence, "America's Case of 'Tonkin Gulfitis,'" *New York Times*, March 7, 2017, https://www.nytimes.com/2017/03/07/opinion/americas-case-of-tonkin-gulfitis.html

TWO

From Retaliation to Anticipation

Reconciling Reprisals and Self-Defense
in the Middle East and Vietnam, 1949–65

Brian Cuddy

Beginning in December 2019, for several months the United States, Iran, and an Iranian-backed militia, Kataib Hezbollah, embarked on a cycle of tit-for-tat military violence within Iraq. The initial militia attack killed an American civilian contractor, resulting in the United States striking five bases held by Kataib Hezbollah, which in turn prompted a group of protesters to storm the US embassy in Baghdad. An American airstrike in early January 2020 that killed Qassim Suleimani, the leader of Iran's Quds force, was followed several weeks later by an Iranian missile attack on bases in Iraq that housed US forces. In March, after a Kataib Hezbollah-attributed rocket attack killed one British and two American soldiers, the United States hit five militia targets. A Department of Defense official described the latter raid as "specifically designed to be punishing and retaliatory."[1] In contrast, the Pentagon's top lawyer insisted that the motivation for the Suleimani attack was defensive, not punitive. Subjected to "an escalating series of armed attacks by Iran and Iran-supported militias," the United States used both classified intelligence and more general knowledge of "the larger context of continuing armed attacks by Iran" to assess that further attacks on US forces and interests were "likely to continue in the absence of a military response in self-defense to restore deterrence."[2] The rationale for American action swung from retaliation to anticipation.

The use of varying language to describe the aim of American airstrikes was not unique to the Trump administration, with the same mixed messages being delivered by the Biden administration after it initiated similar airstrikes in February and June of 2021.[3] After the February strikes, the Pentagon press secretary told reporters that "the American retaliation was meant to punish the perpetrators" of a prior rocket attack.[4] After the June strikes, however, the same press secretary used more considered language, justifying the "defensive precision airstrikes" as a means to "disrupt and deter" an "ongoing series of attacks."[5] The US government's rhetoric of retaliation and its legal argument of anticipation—recognizing a pattern of armed attacks, expecting future attacks in the pattern, and initiating the use of military force in self-defense to forestall those attacks—exist in uneasy relation to each other.

The confusion over the official purpose of recent American airstrikes is perhaps unsurprising given the longer history of retaliation in international law. Reprisals, in particular, have long been one of the most complicated and controversial features of international law, with Geoffrey Best, a historian of the law of war, labeling *reprisals* "the most deceptive and shifty word in the whole vocabulary of the subject."[6] Best was writing about belligerent reprisals used during wartime—otherwise illegal acts only allowed if they respond proportionally to a prior illegal and harmful act, and are intended to force the original lawbreaker back into conformity with international law. The scope of belligerent reprisals was successively narrowed over the twentieth century, but they were never made outright illegal. Armed reprisals used during peacetime, however, were seemingly outlawed altogether in 1945. The United Nations (UN) Charter's prohibition on the use of force (unless approved by the UN Security Council or used in self-defense) put peacetime reprisals outside the bounds of law.[7] But if the legal logic of armed reprisals disappeared, their strategic logic persisted, ensuring continued debates after 1945 about the value of, and justification for, peacetime reprisals.

This chapter considers American understandings of peacetime armed reprisals in the first two decades of the Charter era. It considers a series of debates over law and strategy that took place within the US government in the 1950s and 1960s across the dual contexts of the Arab-Israeli conflict and the Vietnam War. From 1945, the US government tended to accept the idea that reprisals were no longer a legitimate tool of statecraft. Washington held this line against the new state of Israel's insistence on using armed reprisals against its Arab neighbors in the 1950s. But this stance had consequences for how the United States framed its own recourse to force against North Vietnam in the first half of the 1960s. Pressured into accepting the implications of its antireprisal position in the Middle East for its war in Southeast Asia, the United States nonetheless also adapted some of Israel's reprisal justifications for its own use in, and since, the Vietnam War. How American military force is used and rationalized in the world today, then, owes something to the legal ideas that emerged in the 1950s and 1960s, and to the way those ideas migrated from one edge of Asia to the other.

The Emergence of Israel's Reprisal Policy, 1949–1953

The First Arab-Israeli War concluded with several armistice agreements between Israel and the Arab states, signed between February and July of 1949. The demarcation line (the "Green Line" or pre-1967 borders) established by the armistice agreements allowed for the cessation of major hostilities but also set the scene for seven years of low-intensity conflict leading up to the Second Arab-Israeli War (or Suez Crisis) in late 1956. Infiltration across the new boundaries from the Arab states (especially Jordan and, from 1954, Egypt) into Israeli-held territory, and Israel's responses, were the major sources of friction in the years from the armistice agreements to the Suez Crisis—"the core phenomenon of the Israeli-Arab conflict in the years 1949–1956," according to the historian Benny Morris.[8] In early 1951, Roger Tyler, the American consul in Jerusalem, acknowledged "the nearly endemic and often uncontrolled infiltration across the border" in the previous two years. The Arab Legion (the Jordanian army) had made some effort to restrain infiltration, "but lack of troops, popular condonement of infiltration as a justified excursion, and a long, poorly demarcated frontier have hindered the Legion," Tyler reported.[9] A significant share of the infiltration was inspired by local economic, social, and emotional concerns, as Palestinian refugees (particularly those in Jordan, including at this time the West Bank) sought to return to, and harvest from, their traditional lands.[10]

Israel introduced a series of defensive measures to counter infiltration, such as establishing a border police presence, instituting a shoot-to-kill policy, building fortifications, and laying mines and booby traps. Rather than remove the economic incentives of infiltration, these measures tended to prompt more organized, and armed, forays across the boundaries. "As Israeli counter-infiltration measures improved," writes Morris, "so did the organization and sophistication of the infiltrators."[11] Organized economic infiltration was also joined by politically motivated raiding for reasons of revenge, sabotage, or murder, including from 1954 or 1955 state-sponsored infiltration in the form of the Egyptian-backed *Fedayeen*.[12] While these armed raids from the Arab states "were only a small proportion of all infiltration," notes Morris, "they provided the cutting edge that turned the phenomenon into a major military-political problem for Israel."[13] Defensive measures alone were deemed insufficient to address this problem, and so Israel also developed a more assertive, and controversial, response to infiltration: reprisals.

Early reprisal operations tended to be small-scale and localized. From 1949 to early 1951, "the usual sequence of events," according to John Glubb, the British commander of the Arab Legion, was "a party of Jewish soldiers appears on the demarcation line and suddenly opens fire on a group of civilians, killing or wounding a number of them."[14] This system of localized collective punishment was occasionally supplemented by cross-border raids that made more of an attempt to find and punish the actual perpetrators of infiltrator attacks.[15] The first major shift in Israel's reprisal policy became apparent in early 1951, highlighted by an Israeli reprisal raid on the village of Sharafat in the early morning of February 7, killing nine Palestinian villagers. With the Sharafat raid, reprisal actions became noticeably more militarized, with regular (albeit unacknowledged) Israel Defense Forces (IDF) units now taking the lead, and assertive, as these units began to cross the border with Jordan more frequently and deliberately. "Formerly they fired normally from their own side of the line," wrote Glubb. "Recently a new factor has arisen—namely carefully planned raids by Israel soldiers into Jordan territory, resulting in the killing of a number of civilians. These planned raids by Israel soldiers into Arab territory are a new development." The direction of the reprisal operations also became more centralized. Glubb perceived "that orders to carry out these raids have been issued by some very high authority, which has even laid down the exact technique to be used. The object in every case seems to be merely to kill Arabs indiscriminately."[16]

Civilians, or at least civilian dwellings, were targeted directly in this phase of the reprisal policy, from early 1951 to late 1953. In planning the Sharafat raid, Israel's prime minister, David Ben-Gurion, explicitly rejected a retaliatory measure aimed at the Jordanian army in favor of "blow[ing] up the adjacent village responsible for the crime."[17] This "rigid enforcement of a reprisal-with-heavy-interest rule," in Glubb's words, was partly motivated by perceptions of Arab mentality.[18] Israeli officials speaking "off the record" often "state contemptuously that Arabs understand no argument but force," reported Glubb in early 1953. "They claim that an occasional 'punitive expedition' against the natives is the only way to teach them a lesson and keep them in their places."[19] The purpose of civilian targets also moved beyond collective punishment at the local level to a strategy of deterrence at the national level. Moshe Sharett, Israel's foreign minister, characterized this as "energizing the [Arab] government to take action," and Moshe Dayan, IDF chief of staff from late 1953, reasoned that the Egyptian and Jordanian governments would be driven "to prevent such incidents, because their prestige is [assailed], as the Jews have opened fire."[20]

Israel's more deliberate, militarized, and centralized policy of hitting civilian targets across the 1949 demarcation line in order to prompt Jordan to do something about infiltration—a policy of "active defense," as some Israeli officials termed it—was opposed by the United States. After Israeli raids against the West Bank villages of Rantis and Falama on the night of January 28–29, 1953, Tyler urged the State Department to issue the "strongest warnings to Israel that such attacks on innocent people are looked on with horror by official and public opinion" in the United States, and to remind Israel that "her brutal aggressions across frontiers becoming known will lessen sympathy for her and make it difficult for Congress to appropriate the needed funds."[21] The American ambassador in Tel Aviv, Monnett Davis, likewise reported that "our horror at deliberate acts of reprisal involving the killing of innocent people should be restated."[22] An aide memoire was duly delivered, warning Israel that its reprisal raids were "a grave danger to the stability and security of the region," and that if they continued the United States "must reserve its right to take appropriate action . . . possibly under the procedures of the United Nations."[23] Responding to the aide memoire, Ben-Gurion suggested there was no other way to protect Israeli lives and property. "I confess I do not know how we can do it without fighting back." Urging the United States to consider its own frontier history, Ben-Gurion insisted that in certain circumstances, reprisals were the "only effective means of self-defense."[24]

On the night of October 12–13, 1953, infiltrators attacked the Israeli village of Yehud (formerly an Arab town, known as Yahudia, before it was depopulated), killing a woman and two children. Israel responded two nights later by assaulting the West Bank village of Qibya, killing 69 people. Accounts differ as to whether the soldiers checked the buildings for civilians before destroying them. Arab Legion reporting on the raid labeled it a "'punitive' expedition" and noted that most of the bodies had gunshot or grenade wounds, suggesting the systematic killing of civilians.[25] Ze'ev Drory's careful parsing of the chain of orders that preceded the Qibya raid similarly suggests that civilians were directly targeted. At each level in the chain of command, from high political to boots-on-the-ground military, the targeting directive was ratcheted up until the final iteration, handwritten by the unit commander, Ariel Sharon, specified "the intention: attack Qibya village, occupy it, and inflict maximum damage on human life and property."[26] The reaction in Jordan and around the world was swift and severe. Ben-Gurion tried to obscure the IDF's role in the raid, telling the nation by radio that "a searching investigation" had made it "clear beyond doubt that not a single army unit was absent from its base on the night of the attack."[27] But few believed these obfuscations. An American diplomat in Tel Aviv told Sharett that a "policy of deliberate reprisals involving the killing of innocent persons inevitably created revulsion among the American people and was a violation of every moral standard."[28] The United States followed through on the ultimatum it had given Israel after the Rantis and Falama raids and, together with the United Kingdom and France, called on the Security Council to take up the matter.

In the face of international condemnation and Security Council consideration, Israel did not so much attempt to justify the Qibya raid as to contextualize it. Since early 1953, Israel had developed a rudimentary set of rationales for its cross-border retaliatory operations. It was sometimes suggested that patrols crossed the border in "hot pursuit" of infiltrators caught in the act, although as some observers noted, the carefully planned nature of the major IDF cross-border operations suggested they could not be "simple pursuit of Arab infiltrators."[29] In any case, while its appeal would persist for years to come, an asserted right of hot pursuit had no foundation as a standalone justification for resort to force in international law. Perhaps given this limitation, Israel also began to develop justifications based on the idea of necessity.

In February 1953, Davis reported from Tel Aviv that recent raids were thought to reflect a "major policy decision based on the conviction that the volume of infiltration was intolerable and that the Arab authorities concerned could not or would not cooperate in keeping it in check."[30] A few days later, Sharett framed this not merely as a policy decision but also as a legal justification. Telling Davis that Israel held Jordan responsible for "negligence, connivance, or even instigation" in connection with the border violence, Sharett declared that unless the Jordanian authorities showed themselves "ready and able" to control the situation, Israel "would consider itself entitled, and in duty bound, to use all measures in exercise of legitimate self-defense to put an end to attacks, protect life and property and ensure the security of traffic."[31] Sharett's language prefigured an "unwilling or unable" doctrine that would be floated in the 1970s, and promoted in the decades thereafter, but much like hot pursuit this rationale lined up with neither the facts nor the law.[32] Israel's reprisal raids did not target the armed bands responsible for the more serious forms of infiltration but civilians with no established connection to infiltration and, from 1954, state agents. Striking nonstate actors on the territory of another state without first gaining the permission of that state was, moreover, difficult to square with the UN Charter.

The most enduring argument that Israel advanced throughout 1953, however, was to suggest that the scale and intensity of infiltration had reached a point that excused an armed response. Israel began the systematic collection and collation of infiltration statistics from 1952, and it began to exploit that data in early 1953.[33] In a late January 1953 letter to the local UN commander, a senior IDF officer conveyed figures for infiltration across 1952 and highlighted six villages that Israel judged to be the source of most marauders and the sites of thieves' markets.[34] When two of those villages, Rantis and Falama, were struck two days later, the message implicit in the letter became clear: a series of minor incidents could invite a single major blow in return. In mid-1953, Abba Eban, Israel's representative to both the United States and the United Nations, made the case to State Department officials "that what was previously infiltration with predominant intent to steal has turned into a guerrilla pattern with intent to kill."[35] Political and editorial rhetoric extended this logic into a general claim that the magnitude of infiltration as a whole amounted to a form of warfare, with Israel having an attendant right to respond. "Most Israeli politicians came to regard the continual infiltration," suggests Morris, "as a type of undeclared 'guerrilla war' designed to weaken and perhaps even destroy Israel."[36]

It was this line of reasoning that came to the fore after the Qibya raid, as defenders of Israel encouraged the world to see the raid not merely in the context of the Yehud murders but in light of the whole pattern of infiltration into Israel. Sharett told American officials that he "did not wish to say a word in justification" for the Qibya raid, but he nonetheless insisted that the raid had to be seen against the "rising tide of border lawlessness." To treat the Qibya raid in isolation would "distort the picture," claimed Sharett.[37] Israeli newspapers reinforced this message, editorializing that it "would be a crying injustice and perversion of the facts if the Security Council were to concentrate on the events of the last days only," rather than addressing the "whole complex of small scale border war" or the "blood-soaked chain of incidents" that preceded the Qibya raid.[38] In a private meeting with US officials, Eban spoke of "a long series of incidents and provocations" to make the case that the attack on Qibya "was not an isolated incident."[39] In the Security Council, he declared that "violent marauding from Jordan is the origin of the sequence of bloodshed," and that what is "politely called infiltration is actually a campaign of murder, robbery, theft and sabotage which has increased in intensity since the latter part of 1952." No other UN member state faced "such cumulative and constant pressure" to its security.[40]

The legal character of this line of reasoning was left open, but two basic claims can be read into Israel's argument: that while each individual instance of infiltration might not have warranted a military response, several minor incidents were cumulatively enough to trigger a right to respond; and that high voltage but infrequent responses were equivalent or proportionate to a series of less destructive but more frequent events. Israel challenged the idea that its actions were both precipitous and excessive.

Israel's attempts to soften the blow of condemnation did little to influence the drafting of the Security Council resolution on the Qibya affair. Whereas an early draft of the resolution had the Security Council expressing "its deep concern" at the Qibya raid, the final resolution had the council more forthrightly expressing "the strongest censure."[41] Resolution 101 found that "the retaliatory action at Qibya taken by armed forces of Israel on 14–15 October and all such actions . . . are inconsistent with the parties' obligations under . . . the Charter of the United Nations."[42] The resolution was adopted by a vote of nine to zero, with abstentions from Lebanon and the Soviet Union.[43] (Lebanon's delegate, Charles Malik, had argued in the drafting deliberations for removing the word "retaliatory" from the resolution altogether so as to avoid the impression that the Qibya raid had been provoked.)[44] Of particular note, the resolution made no mention of the Israeli suggestion to consider the Qibya raid in the context of the whole pattern of infiltration. Washington did this deliberately, writing to its Middle Eastern posts that that the effect of the censure was "accentuated by ignoring suggestions advanced by Eban that the Security Council consider the Qibya raid in the context of the border situation as a whole."[45] The United States rejected not merely Israel's reprisal policy but also any suggestion that a pattern of preceding minor incidents could justify the use of military force across borders.

Moderating and Justifying Israel's Reprisal Policy, 1954–1956

The Qibya raid "had brought Israel's international standing to the edge of the abyss," reported Abba Eban to the Israeli government. "Even Deir Yassin did not evoke such nausea."[46] In response, Israel doubled down on the idea that the overall pattern of infiltration should be considered in making any assessment of the legitimacy of the Qibya raid. Even before Resolution 101 had been finalized, Eban was insisting to State Department officials that one of Israel's "fundamental objections" to the resolution was that "the censuring of Israel for its actions at Kibya was unprecedented in the annals of UN history and unwarranted in view of the disproportionate emphasis which was placed on Israel's misdemeanors as opposed to those of the Arabs."[47] In a Knesset foreign affairs debate, Sharett declared that "Qibya must be seen in terms of unceasing acts of aggression and murder over the years."[48] Israel increased the number of complaints it made to the Israel-Jordan Mixed Armistice Commission (MAC), as did Jordan, both governments "anxious to establish for the record . . . as impressive a mass of evidence condemning the other party as possible."[49] In his report to the Security Council mandated by Resolution 101, the chief of staff to the United Nations Truce Supervision Organisation (UNTSO) wrote of the "psychological warfare" being waged by Israel and Jordan.[50]

Israel's public relations push in late 1953 and early 1954 was in part an intensification of the efforts made since early 1953 to embed a sense of equivalency or proportion between ongoing infiltration from Jordan and Israel's less frequent but more lethal retaliatory blows. It was also indicative of new leadership, as Ben-Gurion stood down as prime minister in December 1953 and Sharett assumed the top job. More moderate than Ben-Gurion and attuned to the importance of diplomacy, Sharett emphasized political rather than military offensives. His rise to the top of Israel's government made its internal factions more visible as he battled "activists" like Dayan over the proper course of Israeli security policy. But it would be a mistake to exaggerate the importance of this divide for Israel's reprisal operations. The difference between Sharett and Ben-Gurion was one of "style more than substance," writes one of Ben-Gurion's biographers, Tom Segev. "Sharett also believed that the conflict with the Arabs could not be solved and that all that could be done was to manage it," suggests Segev, noting that the new prime minister "did not reject reprisal operations in principle."[51]

Believing that reprisal operations were ineffective tools in advancing Israel's security, Sharett nonetheless accepted that Israel's infiltration-induced "rage must be defused" from time to time—that "there is a need to let off steam."[52] Reporting six months into Sharett's premiership on "a good deal of private discussion here about the policy of retaliation," the American embassy in Tel Aviv underscored Sharett's political instincts.

Despite the public and government recognizing that the reprisal policy was "an international liability to Israel," the embassy assessed that the policy was likely to remain operational. "Retaliation constitutes an emotional outlet for most of the public and is responsive to the widely-held concept that the Arabs understand only force."[53] After the Qibya raid, therefore, Sharett worked not to end the reprisal policy but to better balance it with Israel's wider foreign policy. He sought greater civilian control over the military and consideration of a wider array of local and international factors in the decision process that approved reprisal operations. He desired a more finely calibrated reprisal policy in which the "dimensions" and "magnitude" of an operation could be adjusted "according to circumstances," and with appropriate "intermissions in the reprisals process."[54]

If Sharett and the moderates accepted the idea that reprisals were necessary, Dayan and the hardliners accepted the reality that the reprisal policy needed to change given the international backlash to the Qibya raid, including Resolution 101. Dayan, in Drory's words "the moving spirit behind the policy of retaliation," acknowledged "that a military operation had to be seen as justified by international public opinion." He did so begrudgingly, arguing that "what is permitted to the Arabs—and even to other peoples—will not be forgiven and pardoned if done by Jews or Israelis." But he accepted the essential lesson from the Qibya affair: that "even when the Arabs harm peaceful citizens we must direct our responses to military targets." The IDF issued new standing orders, and operational instructions now included a clear requirement to avoid harming women and children. Civilian targets would no longer be selected for reprisal operations, with objectives now limited to army camps, military posts, and police stations.[55]

Israel's new look reprisal policy would soon get its first test. On March 17, 1954, an Israeli bus was ambushed in a pass, Ma'ale Akrabim, in the Negev, with 12 people killed. The Israel-Jordan MAC, with no clear evidence as to the culprits, reached no decision on the massacre. Israeli officials asserted "that the Jordanian Government is directly implicated, since it does not guard the frontier and has been careless in its attitude towards infiltration," and stopped attending MAC meetings in protest.[56] Sharett withstood political and public pressure to retaliate immediately, but he relented when a watchman in the Israeli settlement of Kessalon was killed shortly afterwards. Ostensibly in reply to the Kessalon murder, but with the Ma'ale Akrabim attack also a motivating factor, Israeli forces struck a National Guard (Jordanian militia) outpost in the village of Nahhalin on the night of March 28–29, killing nine people. A significant number of

the casualties were national guardsmen or Arab legionnaires sent to rein-
force the outpost after the battle broke out.[57] While Sharett followed Ben-
Gurion's lead in denying official involvement in the raid—the new prime
minister publicly described it as a "local affair"—the American embassy in
Tel Aviv noted that the "nature" of the Nahhalin raid was "some substan-
tiation" of reports that Sharett had applied new conditions to the reprisal
policy to ensure they were "(a) selective and limited, (b) against the community in the vicinity of the crime for which the reprisal takes place, and
(c) that no women and children were to be killed but only members of local
defense force or others who resist."[58]

In his 1972 reflection on reprisals, the international law scholar Derek
Bowett pondered the absence of a Security Council condemnation of the
Nahhalin raid and suggested it was due to the "reasonableness" of the
Israeli reprisal measure. Bowett was struck by "the equation—or proportionality—of the damage: the guerrilla attack from Jordan on an Israeli
bus in the Negev killed eleven, the Israeli attack on the Jordanian village
killed 9 and wounded 14."[59] But this assessment is misleading. It is true that
the United States, along with France and the United Kingdom, wanted
the Security Council to consider the two incidents together (each was the
subject of a separate formal complaint), with the aim of providing a "safety
valve" for the relief of immediate tensions in the region and, the larger
prize, better mechanisms for peace between Israel and its neighbors.[60]
But this "remedial approach" did not entail equating the two attacks. The
United States was not moved by the "reasonableness" of the Nahhalin raid
and indicated its "complete disapproval of Israel's act."[61]

Nor was the United States moved by Eban once again trying to place
Israeli raids within "the context of preceding events." It was "fantastic and
grotesque," Eban told the Security Council, to isolate the Nahhalin "event
from the long and somber succession of Jordan aggressions and violations
which preceded it." Eban stated that 58 "armed attacks" upon Israel had
originated from the vicinity of Nahhalin in 1953, resulting in 4 people
killed, with a further 11 "armed attacks" in 1954 to date, including the
killing at Kessalon. "The problem," Eban summarized, "is one of constant
military attack," and he was determined to "bring to the notice of the Security Council these trends and tendencies of armed attack which have made
the State of Israel the chief casualty of the violence which has taken place
in the last four months."[62] The invocation of "armed attack" was a subtle
reference to Article 51 of the UN Charter, which allows for self-defense "if
an armed attack occurs," suggesting that perhaps Eban was trying to place
this now familiar Israeli argument on firmer legal ground.

A draft resolution prepared by the British government and supported by Washington, however, gave no indication that the Nahhalin raid was somehow more appropriate because of its military-hued target, low level of civilian casualties, or proportionality either to the Ma'ale Akrabim provocation or to the whole pattern of prior infiltrator attacks. If passed, the draft resolution would have expressed, in the same language as the Qibya resolution, "the strongest censure" of the attack on Nahhalin village, which was "inconsistent with Israel's obligations under . . . Article II, paragraph 4 of the Charter."[63] The Security Council debate on the Nahhalin and Ma'ale Akrabim incidents stalled because of procedural wrangles, a change of government in Jordan, attention shifting from the Israel-Jordan boundary to the Israel-Egypt boundary, and concerns around Soviet obstructionism, not because of any assessment, formal or informal, that the Nahhalin raid had reached some kind of threshold standard of "reasonableness" or because the pattern of preceding infiltration amounted to an armed attack thereby justifying an Israeli response.

The new look reprisal policy may have resulted in fewer civilian casualties, but it also required more soldiers and less obfuscation. "The new strategy," writes Morris, "necessitated far larger raiding forces (battalions and brigades rather than squads, platoons, and companies), [and] also usually called for official admission of responsibility." Attacking state facilities such as army barracks and police stations also invited greater state sponsorship of infiltration in return, and as the weight of Israel's reprisal policy shifted from Jordan to Egypt—as attention turned "from the West Bank to the Gaza Strip as the problematic heart of the Israeli-Arab conflict," in the words of Morris—the new policy therefore encouraged the rise of the Egyptian-backed *Fedayeen*.[64] The epitome of the new direction in the reprisal policy was the Black Arrow operation of February 1955, in which the IDF struck a small Egyptian army camp near Gaza city, killing 37 Egyptian soldiers and two civilians.

Israel offered divergent justifications for the Black Arrow raid. Ben-Gurion, back as defense minister and effectively prime minister in waiting, instructed the IDF to concoct a story of "hot pursuit," but the more serious justifications were offered by foreign ministry officials, who "explained the raid as a response to the previous six months of Egyptian border attacks," complete with detailed figures for infiltration going back a year.[65] In the Security Council, Eban noted "the persistent toll of human life, and to a lesser extent of property, which results from this purposeful, constant and mounting tide of illegal crossings," and decried the number of Israeli "graves which have mounted, one by one and two by two, across the years as a result of illegal crossings of the armistice demarcation line."[66] Despite Eban's arguments, the Security Council condemned the attack without citing any provocations.[67]

The appeal to a pattern of infiltrator attacks was by now a foundational Israeli argument for both the use of reprisal measures and the proportionality of those measures. Israel advanced this rationale in the wake of multiple reprisal raids throughout 1955 and 1956.[68] Officials even used it to justify Israel's Sinai campaign in the Suez Crisis—"in a sense the ultimate and largest retaliatory strike," according to Morris. On October 29, 1956, as an IDF offensive against Egypt was in progress, the foreign ministry issued a statement declaring Israel's objective was "to eliminate the Egyptian *Fedayeen* bases in the Sinai Peninsula," and claiming 24 Israeli casualties over the previous week from *Fedayeen* mines. As Morris notes, the idea was to plant a seed "that the IDF attacks were limited reprisals, not part of an unfolding war" concocted by the United Kingdom, France, and Israel working together in a secret partnership.[69] But even as its value as a tool of deception was waning, Israel continued to advance the general argument in support of its actions in the Sinai Peninsula.

At a special session of the UN General Assembly on the Suez Crisis, Eban noted that with the advent of the Nasser regime and the *Fedayeen*, Israel's boundary with Egypt had been "violated with consistency and with special frequency and intensity during the past two years." Refuting the idea that Israel's "obligations under the United Nations Charter require it to resign itself to . . . armed units practicing open warfare against it," Eban declared that Israel had "been forced to interpret Article 51 of the Charter as furnishing both a legal and a moral basis for . . . defensive action." Noting that the "inherent right of self-defence is conditioned in the Charter by the existence of armed attacks against a Member State," Eban asked rhetorically if anyone could "say that this long and uninterrupted series of encroachments did not constitute in its totality the essence and the reality of an armed attack?"[70]

Israel's defense of its actions in the Suez Crisis marked the culmination of the argument it had developed since early 1953 regarding the pattern of infiltration, or "series of encroachments." First offered merely to contextualize but not excuse Israeli reprisal actions, it had now morphed into a full-fledged argument under the international law of self-defense. In the UN debate over the Suez Crisis, Eban identified the "fundamental concept of reciprocity" that underlay Israel's attitude to the use of force but was otherwise careful to avoid the terminology of retaliation or reprisal.[71] The United States opposed the actions of Israel (and the United Kingdom and

France) in the Suez Crisis, just as it had opposed Israel's reprisal policy and the rationales given for it over the previous half-decade. As it intensified its support for South Vietnam in the 1960s, however, Washington would be forced to reckon with its opposition to reprisals and to reconsider its rejection of the idea that a pattern of minor events could help discern the existence of an armed attack and the appropriate level of response.

The US Policy Debate over the Use of Reprisals in Vietnam, 1961–1965

The 1960s brought new challenges for Washington, and new leadership determined to address those challenges in new ways. Soviet leader Nikita Khrushchev's early 1961 pledge to support wars of national liberation around the world heightened concerns within the incoming administration of John Kennedy over subversion, infiltration, and other methods of "indirect aggression" from Latin America to Southeast Asia. Devising legitimate ways to counter these perceived trends, including through the use of force, was a key concern for US officials engaged in national security affairs in the first half of the 1960s. The conflict in Vietnam increasingly became the context for developing these measures and their justifications, but in doing so American policy advisers and lawyers had to grapple with Washington's stance on Israeli reprisals in the 1950s.

As the American-supported regime of Ngo Dinh Diem came under increasing pressure in 1961, Kennedy sent his aides Maxwell Taylor and Walt Rostow to investigate the situation in South Vietnam. Their report of November 1961 recommended bolstering American aid to Saigon, but they also looked forward to a time when more forceful measures would be contemplated. "The United States must decide how it will cope with Khrushchev's 'wars of liberation,'" wrote Taylor and Rostow in a covering letter to the main report. "This is a new and dangerous Communist technique which bypasses our traditional political and military responses." They suggested that "the time may come in our relations to Southeast Asia when we must declare our intention to attack the source of guerrilla aggression in North Viet-Nam and impose on the Hanoi Government a price for participating in the current war which is commensurate with the damage being inflicted on its neighbors to the south."[72] As one perceptive reader of the Pentagon Papers noted of the Taylor-Rostow report, "the logic of reprisal was present in Vietnam well before the decision to bomb the North."[73]

The State Department's Office of the Legal Adviser, led in the Kennedy years by Abram Chayes, reviewed the Taylor-Rostow report for its international law ramifications. Chayes and his team described two kinds of "retaliatory attacks" that might be contemplated against North Vietnam. One kind of retaliatory attack was small-scale shallow raids into North Vietnamese territory to hit those places the southern insurgent National Liberation Front (NLF) was using for resupply and sanctuary, but not to attack North Vietnamese targets per se. "It would seem justifiable under international law principles relating to hot pursuit to follow the enemy across the border," Chayes wrote, "and attempt to destroy his bases of operations adjacent to the border."[74] One of the varied justifications that Israel offered in the early 1950s for its raids on Jordan, and would continue to offer in the years to come, hot pursuit was also offered as an excuse by American officials throughout the Vietnam War. Despite its 1961 advice, the Office of the Legal Adviser would come to recognize the legal deficiencies of any standalone hot pursuit doctrine and oppose its use in justifying US operations that crossed into the territory of South Vietnam's neighboring states, particularly Cambodia.[75] Self-defense would become the only acceptable public standard by which the legitimacy of American strikes outside South Vietnam could be assessed. Moreover, the doctrine had strategic as well as legal deficiencies, as shallow raids across the border to hit southern guerrillas hiding in North Vietnam were unlikely to impose enough of a price on Hanoi—to pack enough of a retaliatory punch—under the Taylor-Rostow logic.

The second kind of retaliatory attack described by Chayes—"direct attacks against Hanoi and similar strategic centers deep inside North VietNam"—was more aligned with the Taylor-Rostow logic of striking the source of the problem. But Chayes denied the legality of such attacks. Noting that the right to self-defense stipulated in Article 51 of the Charter could be invoked only in the event of an armed attack, Chayes argued that North Vietnamese infiltration into South Vietnam did not meet the standard of armed attack, which was "generally understood as a direct external attack upon one country by the armed forces of another such as the German invasion of Poland in 1939 or the North Korean attack on South Korea in 1950." With regard to direct attacks against strategic targets in North Vietnam, Chayes concluded that in "the absence of such overt aggression by means of armed attack against South VietNam, such action would go beyond permissible self-defense under general international law and would be contrary to the United Nations Charter."[76] Chayes and his team undermined the Taylor-Rostow logic on legal grounds, which may have made some small contribution to the lack of discussion about overtly striking North Vietnam in the administration's policy debates of 1962 and 1963. But the temptation to "attack the source" would remain, and in August 1964, when two US destroyers reported coming under fire from North Vietnamese torpedo boats in international waters, the United States responded.

On August 2, North Vietnamese torpedo boats fired upon the USS *Maddox* in the Gulf of Tonkin after the *Maddox* had first fired several warning shots. Two days later, the *Maddox* and USS *Turner Joy* reported—mistakenly it is now generally believed—coming under fire again. The president, now Lyndon Johnson, ordered air strikes on sites in North Vietnam associated with the torpedo boats. In his address to the nation on the evening of August 4, Johnson avoided the explicit language of reprisal or retaliation, but in a press conference Secretary of Defense Robert McNamara did call the US airstrikes "retaliation for this unprovoked attack on the high seas." Critics jumped on both the language and logic of retaliation evident in the US airstrikes. "Contemporary international law categorically denies and rejects a right of retaliation," declared the Soviet delegate to the Security Council. "The recognition of the right of self-defense in Article 51 of the United Nations Charter *ipso iure* precludes the right of retaliation." In the same meeting, Czechoslovakia's delegate reminded everyone of a statement the US ambassador to the United Nations, Adlai Stevenson, made to the council only four months previously reiterating the US government's "emphatic disapproval of provocative acts and retaliatory raids, wherever they occur and by whomever they are committed."[77]

While critics attacked the American airstrikes of August 1964 because of their retaliatory nature, others praised them for precisely the same reason. The strategic theorist Thomas Schelling thought that "it was as an act of reprisal—as a riposte, a warning, a demonstration—that the enterprise appealed so widely as appropriate."[78] Schelling was especially influential in national security officialdom at this time, including with key figures in the 1964 and early 1965 policy discussions on launching a more regularized bombing campaign against North Vietnam. It may not be surprising, therefore, that the language of reprisal was even more prominent in the next set of airstrikes against North Vietnam. On February 7, 1965, after an NLF attack on US and South Vietnamese military positions near Pleiku in the Central Highlands, Johnson ordered airstrikes against North Vietnam. The White House statement described the "retaliatory attacks against barracks and staging areas in the southern area of North Vietnam," codenamed Operation Flaming Dart, as "appropriate reprisal action against North Vietnamese targets."[79]

The antiwar Lawyers Committee on American Policy Towards Vietnam later condemned both the reliance on an implied right of reprisal
in the White House statement of February 7 and the fact that the official
justification from the State Department's Legal Adviser, a memorandum
prepared by Chayes's successor, Leonard Meeker, and released in March
1966, neglected to mention the initial US reliance on a reprisal rationale.[80]
But the Lawyers Committee's criticism was somewhat misplaced. Washington's official justification went in two directions on February 7. At the
same time as the White House and Pentagon were using the language of
retaliation and reprisal, Adlai Stevenson was using the language of self-
defense. The air attacks against North Vietnam were "a justified measure of
self-defense," wrote Stevenson to the president of the Security Council.[81]
Where the White House described "appropriate reprisal action," Stevenson wrote of "prompt defensive action." Meeker's March 1966 memo did
not ignore the rhetoric of reprisal and retaliation out of an oversight, as
the Lawyers Committee implied. It was rather a deliberate rejection of
that rhetoric and a vote of support for Stevenson's language of self-defense.

The March 1966 memo was the second of two major memos that
Meeker issued as legal adviser defending the position of the United States
in Vietnam on the basis of international law. The first memo, prepared in
the immediate wake of the air raids of February 7, 1965, similarly did not
mention justifications of retaliation or reprisal. But a covering note Meeker
wrote in forwarding the memo to National Security Adviser McGeorge
Bundy *did* explicitly address the language used by the White House on
February 7. In his covering note, dated February 11, Meeker took aim at
the language of reprisal and retaliation used by the administration over
the preceding days. He recommended that the United States avoid "reliance on theories of reprisal or retaliation, which are less readily available
under contemporary international law than they were before the Charter."
Instead of relying on an outmoded right of reprisal, Meeker wanted the
United States to base its justifications, as Stevenson had, on the right of
collective self-defense under the UN Charter. This would be "politically
more appealing in presenting our case to other governments and in the
court of public opinion around the world."[82] Read alongside this covering
note, the memo's lack of attention to the subject of reprisals makes more
sense. The memo did not mention reprisals because it sought to bury the
very idea that the United States could base its actions on a right of reprisal.
The memo was designed not merely, or even principally, to justify American actions to the world but to win a point in the internal debate over the
shape of that justification.

Of particular significance, in his covering note to Bundy, Meeker argued the "inconsistency in US reliance on reprisal or retaliation with respect to Vietnam when we have been publicly critical of such justifications in other circumstances—for example, in the Near East in situations involving Israel and the Arab states."[83] Washington's strong stance against Israel's reprisal policy and operations in the 1950s was now circling back to influence the policy—or at least the language justifying the policy—of the United States in Vietnam. Meeker's argument, backed up by the precedent of Washington's condemnation of Israeli reprisal operations in the 1950s, prevailed and the explicit language of reprisal and retaliation was dropped from Washington's official Vietnam War vocabulary.

This rejection of retaliation as a rationale for US actions against North Vietnam was confirmed later in 1965. In December, State Department officials objected to the rhetoric of reprisal in a request from the US ambassador in South Vietnam, Henry Cabot Lodge, Jr., to launch airstrikes against a new North Vietnamese target in retaliation for the NLF bombing of Saigon's Metropole Hotel, which served as a billet for US personnel. Secretary of State Dean Rusk wrote to Lodge, approving a strike on the Uong Bi thermal power plant but mandating that it "not be represented as 'reprisal' for [the] Metropole incident." Rehearsing Meeker's arguments from February, Rusk wrote, as "background," that the United States government "has repeatedly joined in denunciation of specific reprisal actions as in Yemen, Algeria, and Israel." The "basic reason" to avoid an "explicit reprisal rationale," concluded Rusk, was "to avoid serious international repercussions for action that we believe is in fact distinguishable from cases we have denounced but that could not easily be separated in face of criticism."[84] Rusk did not specify how he thought American actions in Vietnam in 1965 were distinguishable from Israeli actions against the Arab states, but whatever differences existed there were also striking similarities. Whether wittingly or not, the United States adopted some of the techniques that Israel had developed to justify its reprisal operations.

Repurposing the Pattern of Aggression, 1964–1965

The United States launched its not-a-reprisal airstrike on the Uong Bi thermal power plant on December 15, 1965. Rusk instructed the US embassy in Saigon to tell any inquiring media "that the target is directly related to military installations in the area being used in support of continuing infiltration and aggression in the South by the North Vietnamese regime" and that the "whole targeting pattern of bombings in the North is of course related to level of VC [Viet Cong] action in the South." The Metropole incident was only "one of the acts indicating a continued high level of terrorism" and infiltration, noted Rusk.[85] McNamara toed the same line, declaring publicly that the attack was "representative of the type we have carried out and will continue to carry out. I would not characterize it as retaliatory, but I think it is appropriate to the increased terror activity."[86] Whereas in February 1965, administration spokesmen were offering divergent rationales for the American use of force, by the end of that year the messaging was more consistent. Meeker had won his point, partly by recalling American opposition to Israeli reprisals, and the United States was now justifying its actions against North Vietnam not on any supposed right of retaliation but on the right of self-defense.

In his statement notifying the Security Council of the American response to the claimed attacks on US ships in the Gulf of Tonkin, Stevenson was careful to frame the American use of force as a defensive measure. The action US military forces "took in self-defense is the right of all nations and is fully consistent within the provisions of the Charter of the United Nations," Stevenson told the council. He explained that the American response against torpedo boats and their support facilities on the North Vietnamese coast was "limited in scale—its only targets being the weapons and facilities against which we had been forced to defend ourselves."[87] But to wait for a Gulf of Tonkin-like incident—real or imagined—before launching each "limited" response was an inefficient means of pressuring North Vietnam to stop its support for the southern insurgency. The Taylor-Rostow logic—striking the (northern) source of the (southern) problem—had lain dormant over 1962 and 1963, but it reemerged in the policy debates of 1964 and early 1965. As it reemerged, the justification for strikes against North Vietnam also shifted from the direct provocation of North Vietnamese gunboats to the pattern of North Vietnamese-directed violence in South Vietnam.

Even as Stevenson was carefully establishing a precise connection between the American airstrikes of August 4, 1964, and the alleged North Vietnamese provocation in the Gulf of Tonkin, he was also laying the groundwork for a more indeterminate justification based on the pattern of small-scale NLF attacks in South Vietnam. This rationale would, in turn, allow for a much more expansive and regular use of force against North Vietnam than the airstrikes of August 4. In the Gulf of Tonkin debate in the Security Council, Stevenson argued that the alleged North Vietnamese attacks on the US destroyers "defy rational explanation except as part of a larger pattern with a larger purpose." An attack on "United States destroyers in international waters is much more spectacular than the attempt to murder the mayor of a village in his bed at night," noted Stevenson, "but they are both part of the pattern," and it was "only in this larger view that we can discuss intelligently the matter that we have brought to this Council."[88]

The legal logic planted by Stevenson in August 1964 was operational-ized in conjunction with the Flaming Dart strikes of February 7, 1965. In notifying the Security Council of the US airstrikes, Stevenson did not make a precise connection between the attack at Pleiku and the American response, as he had between the Gulf of Tonkin provocation and the US airstrikes of August 1964. Instead he identified the target simply as "one of the major staging areas for the infiltration of armed cadres of North Viet-Namese troops into South Viet-Nam in violation of international law." A particular attack had, in Stevenson's reasoning, invited a general response. This was made possible by framing Pleiku as one point in a lon-ger sequence. The insurgent attacks on Pleiku "related directly to the cen-tral problem in Viet-Nam," which was "a pattern of military operations directed, staffed, and supplied in crucial respects from outside the country," wrote Stevenson. After detailing some aspects of the infiltration of soldiers and military equipment since 1959, and especially since 1964, Stevenson wrote that what "we are witnessing is a sustained attack for more than six years across a frontier set by international agreement." The United States was helping South Vietnam to resist "this systematic and continuing aggression," and because "reinforcement of the Viet Cong by infiltrators from North Viet-Nam is essential to this continuing aggression, counter-measures to arrest such reinforcement from the outside are a justified mea-sure of self-defense."[89]

The Office of the Legal Adviser's first memorandum laying out the pre-ferred justification for the Flaming Dart strikes (and implicitly rejecting a justification based on retaliation) used much the same language as Ste-venson's letter to the Security Council. The memo insisted that the insur-gent attacks of February 7 were not "an isolated occurrence" but were part of a "continuing armed aggression." Meeker and his team wrote that the "attacks against South Viet-Nam have mounted in intensity since August," and that "the whole course of conduct of North Viet-Nam, particularly as it has evolved in recent months, adds up to open armed attack within the meaning of Article 51—armed aggression carried on across international frontiers." In the absence of Security Council action to maintain an effec-tive peace in the area, the United States could continue its strikes against North Vietnamese targets until "the regime in Hanoi decides to cease its aggressive intervention in South Viet-Nam."[90]

In his second memo of March 1966, Meeker emphasized that "the external aggression from the North is the critical military element of the insurgency." According to the United States, the violence in South Vietnam was no longer merely state-sponsored, as in 1961, but now directly perpetrated by North Vietnam. Meeker made special note that since 1964 "the greater number of men infiltrated into the South have been native-born North Vietnamese," including regular units of the North Vietnamese army. While in a guerrilla war, "an 'armed attack' is not as easily fixed by date and hour as in the case of traditional warfare," wrote Meeker, "the infiltration of thousands of armed men clearly constitutes an 'armed attack' under any reasonable definition." While there "may be some question as to the exact date at which North Viet-Nam's aggression grew into an 'armed attack,'" concluded Meeker, "there can be no doubt that it had occurred before February 1965."[91]

The US rationale for using military force against North Vietnam from February 1965 did not (after some initial confusion) rely on an imagined right of retaliation. But its favored argument of self-defense did nonetheless owe something to the 1950s debates over reprisals, and in particular to Israel's claim that its reprisal raids should be considered within the whole context or broader pattern of infiltration from its Arab neighbors. While rejecting this argument in the 1950s, Washington came to embrace a version of it in the mid-1960s in defense of its actions in Vietnam. Highlighting the whole pattern of aggression in South Vietnam—along with public messages about hitting only military targets and minimizing civilian casualties—helped to signal American actions as proportional and reasonable. But more immediately in February 1965 (and later, when reflecting upon February 1965), it was put to work as a claim that, when taken as a whole, North Vietnamese violence in South Vietnam had reached sufficient intensity or "tempo" to qualify as an "armed attack" under the meaning of Article 51 of the UN Charter.[92]

A pattern of events in South Vietnam that proved "systematic and continuing" aggression from North Vietnam provided the legal justification for the White House to move beyond tit-for-tat airstrikes such as the Gulf of Tonkin response ("a short-term stimulant" to South Vietnamese morale, but "a long-term depressant," complained Bundy) and toward regularized bombing of North Vietnam. On February 7, 1965, the same day as the Pleiku attack and Flaming Dart response, Bundy wrote a memo to Johnson recommending a policy of "sustained pressure" against North Vietnam "in which air and naval action against the North is justified by and related to the whole Viet Cong campaign of violence and terror in the South."

Bundy, at this point still using the language of retaliation, characterized his recommendation as a policy of "graduated and continuing reprisal" or "sustained reprisal."[93] Meeker would ensure that the language of self-defense was substituted for Bundy's rhetoric of reprisal. But in identifying North Vietnam's actions as an "armed attack"—arguing, in effect, that the whole pattern of violence in South Vietnam was more than the sum of its parts—he also provided the legal justification for the implementation of Bundy's proposed policy. Operation Rolling Thunder, a massive aerial bombardment of North Vietnam, began within a month of February 7 and continued for nearly four years.

Conclusion

In the 1950s and 1960s, the governments of Israel and the United States (the latter via its support of South Vietnam) wrestled with the problems associated with infiltration, subversion, and guerrilla warfare. They each relied on a variety of rationales for targeting the groups involved in these activities outside the territorial bounds of Israel and South Vietnam. Both Israel and the United States at times justified their actions as "hot pursuit," although eventually both governments would accept that the so-called right of hot pursuit had no independent standing in international law.[94] More enduring was the argument advanced in rudimentary form by Israeli foreign minister Moshe Sharett in early 1953 that Israel needed to act against infiltration because Jordan was, if not complicit in the violence, then at least unwilling or unable to address it. This "unwilling or unable" argument would gain more extensive legal articulation in 1970 as the United States attempted to justify the Cambodian Incursion. From there, the doctrine circled back to the Arab-Israeli conflict, where the United States offered it first as a rationale for Israel's Entebbe rescue operation in 1976 and Israel then relied on it beginning in the late 1970s and early 1980s for its operations against the Palestine Liberation Organization in Lebanon.[95]

But Israel and the United States did not merely seek to act against nonstate actors in the territories of other states—infiltrators in Jordan, *Fedayeen* in Egypt, and Vietnamese communist forces in North Vietnam and Cambodia. They also sought to "strike at the source," as they saw it, of the aggression in order to punish the states of Jordan, Egypt, and North Vietnam for assisting or organizing the infiltration or subversion and to compel them to cease their actions. Despite this common underlying logic of reprisal, Israel and the United States would differ substantially on their public attitudes to retaliatory measures in the two decades after the UN Charter came into force.

Israel deemed reprisals a necessary and legitimate tool—even a moral imperative—of its security policy, and its reprisal policy only became more explicit over time. The Security Council generally condemned Israel's reprisal policy as inconsistent with the UN Charter's prohibition on the use of force, but some legal scholars have sought to reconcile it with the right of self-defense. Yoram Dinstein, one of Israel's leading international lawyers, argues that "defensive armed reprisals" are a justified form of self-defense, including against "a cluster of pin-prick assaults" that "form a distinctive pattern." The key test according to Dinstein for an armed reprisal being "defensive, and therefore lawful," is that its motivation be "future-oriented, and not limited to a desire to punish past transgressions." The crux of the issue, therefore, is "whether the unlawful use of force by the other side is likely to repeat itself."[96] The logic of a lawful armed reprisal, for Dinstein, must be anticipatory not retaliatory.

The United States also came to embrace both ideas—that a pattern of "pin-prick assaults" could justify a significant response and that legitimate force was anticipatory not retaliatory—but arrived at them via a different pathway. The US government opposed reprisals for reasons of both principle and national interest in the 1950s and regularly criticized Israel's reprisal operations. When Washington policymakers sought to rest the American use of force against North Vietnam on a right of reprisal, the Department of State Legal Adviser forced them to reconsider, in part by referencing the earlier American position on Israel's reprisal policy. But Meeker did not similarly reference, and was probably unaware of, the American rejection—most notably in the debates preceding UN Security Council Resolution 101 on the Qibya raid—of Israel's argument that the whole pattern of prior incidents should be considered in determining the legitimacy of any use of force. Instead he (and others) used a version of that argument to justify significant and ongoing armed measures against North Vietnam. Meeker did not explicitly extend his argument regarding the pattern of North Vietnamese aggression to make a claim for the anticipatory use of force—the idea is implicit in the concept of a "continuing" armed attack. But in the years after the Vietnam War, the "accumulation of events," as Bowett coined the doctrine, would increasingly and more explicitly be used to demonstrate future intent.[97]

Faced with sporadic terrorist attacks from the 1980s, the US government did not make the argument—as it had in the mid-1960s regarding North

Vietnam—that these incidents amounted to a continuing "armed attack" as specified in Article 51 of the UN Charter. Washington argued instead that such state-based "armed attacks" were not the only provocation covered by the inherent right of self-defense (also specified in Article 51), and that states could also respond with (proportional) force to individual acts of terrorism. But to be an act of self-defense, rather than mere reprisal, the recourse to force had to be intended to anticipate and prevent future terror attacks rather than punish past ones. Given the reluctance of governments to disclose classified information, the "accumulation of events" justification therefore retained its importance as a means of signaling respect for international rules and restraint.[98] Even if the pattern itself is barely discernible—a few measly points connected by dashed rather than solid lines—the *idea* of the pattern can imply that another attack in the sequence is likely to occur absent preventive measures. Playing on the assumption that past behavior is the best predictor for future behavior, the "accumulation of events" doctrine is now used to justify tat-to-forestall-tit operations such as the 2020 US airstrike on Qassim Suleimani that for all the world look like reprisals but for their proclaimed anticipatory rather than retaliatory motive.

NOTES

1. Eric Schmitt and Thomas Gibbons-Neff, "U.S. Carries Out Retaliatory Strikes on Iranian-Backed Militia in Iraq," *New York Times*, March 12, 2020, https://www.nytimes.com/2020/03/12/world/middleeast/military-iran-iraq.html

2. Paul C. Ney (General Counsel, Department of Defense), "Legal Considerations Related to the U.S. Air Strike Against Qassem Soleimani" (speech, BYU Law School, Provo, UT, March 4, 2020), https://assets.documentcloud.org/documents/6808252/DOD-GC-Speech-BYU-QS.pdf

3. There were some notable differences between the 2019–2020 and the 2021 cycles of violence, including the additional controversy about a possible US assassination policy sparked in 2020 by targeting the high-profile Suleimani, and that most of the February and June 2021 strikes took place on Syrian territory.

4. Helene Cooper and Eric Schmitt, "U.S. Airstrikes in Syria Target Iran-Backed Militias That Rocketed American Troops in Iraq," *New York Times*, February 25, 2021, https://www.nytimes.com/2021/02/26/us/politics/biden-syria-airstrike-iran.html

5. John Kirby, "Statement by the Department of Defense," news release, June 27, 2021, https://www.defense.gov/News/Releases/Release/Article/2672875/statement-by-the-department-of-defense/. See also United Nations Security Council, "Letter dated 29 June 2021 from the Permanent Representative of the United States of America to the United Nations addressed to the President of the Security Council," June 30, 2021, UN Doc. S/2021/614, Official Document System of the United Nations, https://documents.un.org/prod/ods.nsf/home.xsp

6. Geoffrey Best, *Humanity in Warfare* (New York: Columbia University Press, 1980), 108.

7. See, respectively, Article 2(4), Article 42, and Article 51 of the United Nations Charter, June 26, 1945 (entered into force October 24, 1945), https://www.un.org/en/charter-united-nations/

8. Benny Morris, *Israel's Border Wars, 1949–1956: Arab Infiltration, Israeli Retaliation, and the Countdown to the Suez War* (Oxford: Clarendon Press, 1993), v.

9. Jerusalem (S. Roger Tyler, Jr.) to State, Despatch 333, "Transmittal of Article in *Es-Sarih* Entitled 'Why Not Fight Infiltration,'" February 21, 1951, file 684a.85/2–2151, Department of State Central Decimal Files 1950–1954, Record Group 59, National Archives, College Park, Maryland, United States.

10. Fred J. Khouri, *The Arab-Israeli Dilemma*, 3rd ed. (Syracuse: Syracuse University Press, 1985), 183; Naseer H. Aruri, *Jordan: A Study in Political Development, 1921–1965* (The Hague: Martinus Nijhoff, 1972), 49–50.

11. Morris, *Israel's Border Wars*, 412.

12. Morris, *Israel's Border Wars*, 116–72; Fred J. Khouri, "The Policy of Retaliation in Arab-Israeli Relations," *Middle East Journal* 20, no. 4 (Autumn 1966): 439.

13. Morris, *Israel's Border Wars*, 54.

14. J. B. Glubb Pasha to unnamed correspondent, letter, February 8, 1951, enclosure 1, Amman (John F. Rogers) to State, Despatch 189, "Deterioration of Public Security on Jordanian-Israeli Armistice Line," February 15, 1951, file 684a.85/2–1551, Department of State Central Decimal Files 1950–1954.

15. Morris, *Israel's Border Wars*, 175–76, 192–93, 419.

16. Enclosure 1, Amman to State 189, February 15, 1951.

17. Cited in Tom Segev, *A State At Any Cost: The Life of David Ben-Gurion*, trans. Haim Watzman (London: Head of Zeus, 2019), 508.

18. Enclosure, Amman (Andrew G. Lynch) to State, Despatch 165, "Arab Legion Note on Jordan-Israel Border Relations, June 1952–October 1953," November 7, 1953, file 684a.85/11–753, Department of State Central Decimal Files 1950–1954.

19. "A Note on Refugee Vagrancy," February 11, 1953, enclosure, Amman (Joseph C. Green) to State, Despatch 255, "Report by Glubb Pasha on Jordan-Israel Border Infiltration," March 2, 1953, file 684a.85/3–253, Department of State Central Decimal Files 1950–1954.

20. Cited in Morris, *Israel's Border Wars*, 176, 177.

21. Jerusalem (Tyler) to State, Telegram 91, January 29, 1953, file 684a.85/1–2953, Department of State Central Decimal Files 1950–1954; Jerusalem (Tyler) to State, Telegram 110, February 12, 1953, file 684a.85/2–1253, Department of State Central Decimal Files 1950–1954.

22. Tel Aviv (Monnett B. Davis) to State, Telegram 1224, January 30, 1953, file 684a.85/1–3053, Department of State Central Decimal Files 1950–1954.

23. Tel Aviv (Davis) to State, Despatch 761, "Transmitting Text of Aide Memoire on Israel-Jordan Border Relations," February 16, 1953, file 684a.85/2–1653, Department of State Central Decimal Files 1950–1954.

24. Tel Aviv (Davis) to State, Telegram 1348, February 20, 1953, file 684a.85/2–2053, Department of State Central Decimal Files 1950–1954.

25. Amman (Lynch) to State, Despatch 136, "Arab Legion Report on Qibya Attack, October 14, 1953," October 19, 1953, file 684a.85/10–1953, Department of State Central Decimal Files 1950–1954. See also Morris, *Israel's Border Wars*, 247.

26. Ze'ev Drory, *Israel's Reprisal Policy, 1953–1956: The Dynamics of Military Retaliation* (London: Frank Cass, 2005), 109–10.

27. Tel Aviv (Francis H. Russell) to State, Telegram 492, October 20, 1953, file 684a.85/10–2053, Department of State Central Decimal Files 1950–1954.

28. Tel Aviv (Russell) to State, Telegram 472, October 17, 1953, file 684a.85/10–1753, Department of State Central Decimal Files 1950–1954.

29. Jerusalem (Tyler) to State, Despatch 128, "Israel-Jordan Border Relations (Jan 26–Feb 2)," February 3, 1953, file 684a.85/2–353, Department of State Central Decimal Files 1950–1954; Jerusalem (Tyler) to State, Telegram 97, February 5, 1953, file 684a.85/2–553, Department of State Central Decimal Files 1950–1954.

30. Tel Aviv (Davis) to State, Telegram 1231, February 2, 1953, file 684a.85/2–253, Department of State Central Decimal Files 1950–1954.

31. Tel Aviv (Davis) to State, Telegram 1247, February 5, 1953, file 684a.85/2–553, Department of State Central Decimal Files 1950–1954.

32. Ashley S. Deeks, "'Unwilling or Unable': Toward a Normative Framework for Extraterritorial Self-Defense," *Virginia Journal of International Law* 52 (2012): 549. Israel's cross-border raids of the 1950s are not listed.

33. Morris, *Israel's Border Wars*, 28n4.

34. Jerusalem (Tyler) to State, Telegram 92, January 30, 1953, file 684a.85/1–3053, Department of State Central Decimal Files 1950–1954.

35. Department of State, Memorandum of Conversation, "Alleged Jordan Border Violations," June 12, 1953, file 684a.85/6–1253, Department of State Central Decimal Files 1950–1954.

36. Morris, *Israel's Border Wars*, 411.

37. Tel Aviv to State 472, October 17, 1953.

38. Cited in Tel Aviv (Russell) to State, Telegram 497, October 21, 1953, file 684a.85/10–2153, Department of State Central Decimal Files 1950–1954.

39. Department of State, Memorandum of Conversation, "Israel's Security Situation; Israel's Policy toward Water Development," October 19, 1953, file 684a.85/10–1953, Department of State Central Decimal Files 1950–1954.

40. United Nations Security Council, Official Records, 637th Meeting, November 12, 1953, UN Doc. S/PV.637, pars. 57, 55, 64.

41. State to Amman, Telegram 206, November 10, 1953, file 330/11–1053, Department of State Central Decimal Files 1950–1954; State to Beirut, Telegram 568, November 18, 1953, file 684a.85/11–1853, Department of State Central Decimal Files 1950–1954.

42. United Nations Security Council, Resolution 101, November 24, 1953, UN Doc. S/RES/101.

43. Before 1966 there were only 11 members of the Security Council—5 permanent members and 6 elected members.

44. New York (James J. Wadsworth) to State, Telegram 267, November 21, 1953, file 684a.85/11–2153, Department of State Central Decimal Files 1950–1954.

45. State to Baghdad, Telegram 283, November 16, 1953, file 330/11–1453, Department of State Central Decimal Files 1950–1954.

46. Cited in Morris, *Israel's Border Wars*, 254.

47. Department of State, Memorandum of Conversation, "The Kibya Resolution in the Security Council," November 24, 1953, file 330/11–2453, Department of State Central Decimal Files 1950–1954.

48. Tel Aviv (Davis) to State, Telegram 644, December 2, 1953, file 330/12–253, Department of State Central Decimal Files 1950–1954.

49. Jerusalem (Slator C. Blackiston, Jr.) to State, Despatch 123, "Jordan-Israel Mixed Armistice Commission Consideration of Border Incidents During the Month of December 1953," January 7, 1954, file 684a.85/1–754, Department of State Central Decimal Files 1950–1954.

50. United Nations Security Council, "Report by the Chief of Staff of the Truce Supervision Organization to the Security Council Pursuant to the Council's Resolution of 24 November 1953," March 1, 1954, UN Doc. S/3183.

51. Segev, *A State At Any Cost*, 518; see also Morris, *Israel's Border Wars*, 235; cf. Drory, *Israel's Reprisal Policy*, 58.

52. Cited in Morris, *Israel's Border Wars*, 173; Drory, *Israel's Reprisal Policy*, 58.

53. Tel Aviv (Ivan B. White) to State, Telegram 1190, May 12, 1954, file 684a.85/5–1254, Department of State Central Decimal Files 1950–1954.

54. Drory, *Israel's Reprisal Policy*, 53–58, 112, 135; Morris, *Israel's Border Wars*, 236; Khouri, "The Policy of Retaliation in Arab-Israeli Relations," 437.

55. Drory, *Israel's Reprisal Policy*, 113, 115, 125.

56. Department of State, Memorandum of Conversation, "Mounting Tension on the Israel-Jordan Border," March 23, 1954, file 684a.85/3–2354, Department of State Central Decimal Files 1950–1954.

57. Drory, *Israel's Reprisal Policy*, 127; Jerusalem (Tyler) to State, Despatch 195, "HJK-Israel Border Relations in March," April 8, 1954, file 684a.85/4–854, Department of State Central Decimal Files 1950–1954.

58. Tel Aviv (Russell) to State, Telegram 1016, April 2, 1954, file 684a.85/4–254, Department of State Central Decimal Files 1950–1954; Tel Aviv (Russell) to State, Telegram 1020, April 3, 1954, file 684a.85/4–354, Department of State Central Decimal Files 1950–1954.

59. Derek Bowett, "Reprisals Involving Recourse to Armed Force," *American Journal of International Law* 66, no. 1 (1972): 11.

60. State to New York, Telegram 450, March 31, 1954, file 330/3–2954, Department of State Central Decimal Files 1950–1954.

61. State to New York, Telegram 460, April 2, 1954, file 330/4–254, Department of State Central Decimal Files 1950–1954.

62. United Nations Security Council, Official Records, 670th Meeting, May 4, 1954, UN Doc. S/PV.670, pars. 131, 134, 140, 141; cf. Jerusalem (Blackiston) to State, Despatch 227, "Allegations of Israel UN Representative Concerning HJK-Israel Border Relations and Pertinent UNTSO Statistics," May 31, 1954, file 684a.85/5–3154, Department of State Central Decimal Files 1950–1954.

63. New York (Henry C. Lodge, Jr.) to State, Telegram 705, May 7, 1954, file 330/5–754, Department of State Central Decimal Files 1950–1954; State to New York, Telegram 551, May 10, 1954, file 330/5–1054, Department of State Central Decimal Files 1950–1954.

64. Morris, *Israel's Border Wars*, 420, 312; Khouri, "The Policy of Retaliation in Arab-Israeli Relations," 440.

65. Morris, *Israel's Border Wars*, 327, 327n13.

66. United Nations Security Council, Official Records, 696th Meeting, March 30, 1955, UN Doc. S/PV.696, par. 81.

67. United Nations Security Council, Resolution 106, March 29, 1955, UN Doc. S/RES/106.

68. For a summary, see Bowett, "Reprisals Involving Recourse to Armed Force," 5–6.

69. Morris, *Israel's Border Wars*, 421, 403, 403n2.

70. United Nations General Assembly, Official Records, 562nd Plenary Meeting (First Emergency Session), November 1–2, 1956, UN Doc. A/PV.562, pars. 115, 134, 145, 146.

71. United Nations General Assembly, Official Records, 562nd Plenary Meeting (First Emergency Session), November 1–2, 1956, UN Doc. A/PV.562, par. 150.

72. Letter From the President's Military Representative (Taylor) to the President, November 3, 1961, in *Foreign Relations of the United States, 1961–1963*, vol. 1, *Vietnam, 1961*, ed. Ronald D. Landa and Charles S. Sampson (Washington, DC: Government Printing Office, 1988), Doc. 210.

73. Perry L. Pickert, "American Attitudes Toward International Law as Reflected in 'The Pentagon Papers,'" in *The Vietnam War and International Law*, ed. Richard A. Falk, vol. 4, *The Concluding Phase* (Princeton: Princeton University Press, 1976), 78.

74. Memorandum From the Legal Adviser (Chayes) to the Secretary of State, November 16, 1961, in *Foreign Relations of the United States, 1961–1963*, vol. 1, *Vietnam, 1961*, Doc. 261.

75. Brian Cuddy, "Was It Legal for the U.S. to Bomb Cambodia?," *New York Times*, December 12, 2017, https://www.nytimes.com/2017/12/12/opinion/america-cambodia-bomb.html

76. Memorandum From the Legal Adviser (Chayes) to the Secretary of State, November 16, 1961.

77. United Nations Security Council, Official Record, 1141st Meeting, August 7, 1964, UN Doc. S/PV.1141, pars. 79, 83, 31.

78. Thomas C. Schelling, *Arms and Influence* (New Haven: Yale University Press, 2008), 145. First published 1966.

79. "United States and South Vietnamese Forces Launch Retaliatory Attacks Against North Viet-Nam," *Department of State Bulletin* 52, no. 1339 (February 22, 1965): 238.

80. Consultative Council of the Lawyers Committee on American Policy Towards Vietnam, *Vietnam and International Law: The Illegality of United States Military Involvement*, rapporteur John H. E. Fried (Flanders, NJ: O'Hare Books, 1967), 53.

81. United Nations Security Council, "Letter dated 7 February 1965 from the representative of the United States of America to the President of the Security Council," February 8, 1965, UN Doc. S/6174.

82. Leonard C. Meeker (State Department Legal Adviser) to McGeorge Bundy (National Security Advisor), memorandum, "Legal Basis for United States and South Vietnamese Air Strikes," February 11, 1965, Doc. 214, Folder 4 (Vol. XXVIII, 2/9–19/65, Memos [2 of 2]), Box 13 [2 of 2], Vietnam Country File, National Security File, Lyndon Baines Johnson Library, Austin, Texas.

83. Meeker, "Legal Basis for United States and South Vietnamese Air Strikes," February 11, 1965.

84. State to Saigon, Telegram 1602, December 9, 1965, Doc. 81, Folder 5 (Vol. XLIII, 11/23–12/19/65, Cables [1 of 2]), Box 24, Vietnam Country File, National Security File, LBJ Library. The distinction, of course, was not obvious to outside observers. As Fred J. Khouri observes, US condemnations of Israel's October 28, 1965, retaliatory assault on Lebanon were undermined by its Vietnam War policies: "the Israelis were fully aware of the contradiction between Washington's request for restraint by Israel and America's failure to employ any appreciable restraint in her own actions in Vietnam, where the United States did not hesitate to employ the weapon of retaliation. Consequently, American ability to influence Israel's policies towards the Arabs was greatly weakened." Khouri, "The Policy of Retaliation in Arab-Israeli Relations," 450.

85. State to Saigon 1602, December 9, 1965.

86. Cited in Jacob Van Staaveren, *Gradual Failure: The Air War Over North Vietnam, 1965–1966* (Washington, DC: Air Force History and Museums Program, 2002), 204.

87. United Nations Security Council, Official Records, 1140th Meeting, August 5, 1964, UN Doc. S/PV.1140, pars. 46, 44.

88. United Nations Security Council, Official Records, 1140th Meeting, August 5, 1964, UN Doc. S/PV.1140, pars. 47, 49.

89. UN Security Council, "Letter dated 7 February 1965 from the representative of the United States of America to the President of the Security Council," February 8, 1965.

90. Memorandum, "Legal Basis for United States Actions Against North Viet-Nam," n.d. [February 11, 1965], Doc. 214, Folder 4 (Vol. XXVIII, 2/9–19/65, Memos [2 of 2]), Box 13 [2 of 2], Vietnam Country File, National Security File, LBJ Library. This internal government memo was finalized on February 11. An amended version of the same memo, dated March 8, was later made available to Congress and the public. See the chapter by Madelaine Chiam and Brian Cuddy in this volume for a discussion of the public debate regarding the March 8 memo.

91. Leonard C. Meeker, "The Legality of United States Participation in the Defense of Viet-Nam," *Department of State Bulletin* 54, no. 1396 (March 28, 1966): 475.

92. For the reference to "tempo," see Leonard C. Meeker, "Viet-Nam and the International Law of Self-Defense," *Department of State Bulletin* 61, no. 1437 (January 9, 1967): 59.

93. Memorandum From the President's Special Assistant for National Security Affairs (Bundy) to President Johnson, February 7, 1965, in *Foreign Relations of the United States, 1964–1968*, vol. 2, *Vietnam, January–June 1965*, ed. David C. Humphrey, Ronald D. Landa, and Louis J. Smith (Washington, DC: Government Printing Office, 1996), Doc. 84.

94. Yoram Dinstein, *War, Aggression and Self-Defence* (Cambridge: Grotius Publications, 1988), 224–25; Cuddy, "Was It Legal for the U.S. to Bomb Cambodia?"; Norman Menachem Feder, "Reading the U.N. Charter Connotatively: Toward a New Definition of Armed Attack," *New York University Journal of International Law and Politics* 19, no. 2 (Winter 1987): 395–96.

95. Cuddy, "Was It Legal for the U.S. to Bomb Cambodia?"; Mary Ellen O'Connell, "Self-Defence, Pernicious Doctrines, Peremptory Norms," in *Self-

Defence against Non-State Actors, Mary Ellen O'Connell, Christian J. Tams, and Dire Tladi (Cambridge: Cambridge University Press, 2019), 225; Ashley Deeks, "'Unwilling or Unable,'" 549; Dinstein, *War, Aggression and Self-Defence*, 225–29.

96. Dinstein, *War, Aggression and Self-Defence*, 211–12, 208; Feder, "Reading the U.N. Charter Connotatively," 414–17.

97. Bowett, "Reprisals Involving Recourse to Armed Force," 5ff.

98. Christopher Greenwood, "International Law and the United States' Air Operation Against Libya," *West Virginia Law Review* 89 (1987): 942, 954–56; cf. O'Connell, "Self-Defence, Pernicious Doctrines, Peremptory Norms," 223.

THREE

Public Discourses of International Law

US Debates on Military Intervention in Vietnam, 1965–67

Madelaine Chiam and Brian Cuddy

Between 1965 and 1967, a public debate took place in the United States over the legality, under international law, of the US military intervention in Vietnam. The participants in this debate were generally leading political, professional, and academic figures, including State Department officials, a group called the Lawyers Committee on American Policy Towards Vietnam, the American Bar Association (ABA), and scholars such as Richard Falk and John Norton Moore. The debate took place through a range of forums, including legal memoranda released to the public by the State Department and the Lawyers Committee, articles published in scholarly journals such as the *Yale Law Journal* and popular outlets such as *Dissent* magazine, and public and media statements by the various participants. The fact of the debate, and the nature of its arguments, were given prominence through government channels such as the Senate Foreign Relations Committee, some of whose hearings were broadcast on television, and garnered media coverage in newspapers such as the *New York Times*.

This chapter gives an account of this public debate with two aims. The first is simply to bring the debate into contemporary academic and public consciousness.[1] There is a narrative in international law scholarship that the public debates over the 2003 Iraq War were singular because of the prominence of international legal argument in those debates.[2] As

Madelaine Chiam argues elsewhere, this narrative obscures the role that international law played in a range of earlier public debates, including the arguments described in this chapter over the legality of the US intervention in Vietnam.[3] The debates of the 1960s complicate the assumption of "hiatus" that traditionally underpins accounts of international law during the Cold War, and they unsettle the idea that international law experienced a resurgence in the 1990s—an idea that came to its zenith in the ways that international law was deployed in the Iraq War debates.[4] Indeed, the active background role of the Lyndon B. Johnson administration in the Vietnam War debates suggests that some officials were worried about the capacity of the international legal arguments to undermine the administration's public positions on Vietnam. International law has a history as a public and popular language, and this chapter is an account of one part of that longer history.

The second aim of this chapter is to examine how the participants in this public debate understood this public language of international law, and what effect the public debate had on the subsequent trajectory of American international law. What kinds of legal arguments did they make? What did they seem to expect from their employment of legal argument? What can we learn about international law from how it was used in these debates? How did the public debate change the way international law operated in the American context? We argue that the speakers in this chapter use international legal language variously as a public claim to limit government action, as a language of government justification, and as a language of critique, of resistance and of solidarity. Some experts used international legal language in an attempt to control exercises of political power, and others dismissed these uses of international law as misguided or mere polemic.[5] The public prominence of debates over the legality of the conflict surprised some public commentators.

This chapter thus explores international legal arguments made in the public sphere in these debates of 1965–67 by asking who used international legal arguments, in what forums, and how those speakers characterized the international legal language that they used. To do so, the chapter proceeds as follows. The first part gives a chronological account of how the debate unfolded—who spoke in the debate, when and where they spoke, and the broad positioning of their argument. The second part examines the doctrinal arguments made by the participants—what were the legal arguments supporting and contesting US actions in Vietnam? The third part examines the ways in which the participants in the debate characterized international law—how did they understand the role of international law in public debate and government decision-making, and how did their understanding change as a result of their participation in the 1965–67 public debate over the Vietnam War? While the chapter does explore the doctrinal arguments in order to contextualize the debates, the focus is on understanding the roles that international law played, and was perceived to be able to play, by the actors in the public debates. We hold that approaching international law as a public language, rather than merely a set of doctrines, generates important understandings of law's changing role in both international and domestic affairs.

How the Debate Unfolded

The Johnson administration's initial legal justification for its military intervention in Vietnam was primarily intended for an international rather than domestic audience. Washington's first public defense of its sustained aerial bombing campaign against North Vietnam, initiated in February 1965, was prompted by the United Nations Charter's requirement that UN members notify the Security Council of any armed measures taken in self-defense.[6] US ambassador to the United Nations Adlai Stevenson wrote to the council's president on February 7 denouncing not just the immediate prompt for the American airstrikes but also North Vietnam's "sustained attack for more than six years across a frontier set by international agreement." As such, declared Stevenson, South Vietnamese and US actions were "a justified measure of self-defense."[7]

After further US airstrikes on February 11, a memorandum was prepared in the State Department's Office of the Legal Adviser laying out in more detail than Stevenson had the legal basis for the American actions. This memo, prompted at least in part by press inquiries to the White House on the subject,[8] was intended to put a stop to the use of reprisal rhetoric in the administration's public statements in favor of the language of self-defense.[9] On March 8, an amended version of this short memo was finalized for public release and sent abroad to all US diplomatic posts. It was no doubt intended to support the case laid out in a State Department white paper, "Aggression from the North: The Record of North Viet-Nam's Campaign to Conquer South Viet-Nam," released two weeks prior. While the legal memorandum was intended primarily for international and diplomatic audiences—that is, foreign governments—domestic audiences were not entirely forgotten. A copy of the March 1965 memo was also sent to the Senate Foreign Relations Committee,[10] which duly published it in a June 1965 update of the committee's documentary compilation on the war.[11]

Some readers were dissatisfied with the reasoning contained in the March 1965 memorandum. "A careful reading of the document convinced a group of American lawyers that our military involvement in Vietnam was in violation of international law, including the United Nations Charter," wrote one of those lawyers, William Standard, leading to the organization of the Lawyers Committee on American Policy Towards Vietnam and the commencement of the domestic public debate over the legality of Washington's actions in Vietnam.[12] The small group of lawyers who collected under the banner of the Lawyers Committee—"never more than ten or twelve really active participants at one time," recalled one of those active members[13]—were mostly from private practice, engaging, in historian Samuel Moyn's words, in "a fully elite model of agitation."[14]

Formed out of dissatisfaction with the State Department's formal legal justification for the war, the Lawyers Committee released their own memorandum, "American Policy Vis-à-Vis Vietnam," in September 1965, arguing that US intervention in Vietnam was contrary to international law. The memo was entered into the *Congressional Record* on September 23 by Senator Wayne Morse, Democrat of Oregon, on behalf of himself and Senator Ernest Gruening, Democrat of Alaska.[15] The drafting of the memorandum was driven by two New York lawyers, Standard and Joseph Crown, respectively chairman and secretary-treasurer of the Lawyers Committee.[16] The drafters of the memo do not appear to have been specialists in public international law as it relates to the use of force. Standard himself was an expert in the law of the sea, but his legal practice in that field focused mostly on maritime law. Crown was a tax lawyer. Prior to its publication, the memo received the endorsement of several prominent American legal authorities, none of whom were primarily international law experts.[17] The intellectual and professional origins of the Lawyers Committee and its approach, then, lay less in the so-called invisible college of international lawyers than in various traditions of the American legal profession, notably the National Lawyers Guild (NLG) and the "world peace through law" movement.[18]

Although there was no formal connection between the Lawyers Committee and the NLG, many of the committee's early members and supporters were affiliated with the guild, a progressive association of lawyers established in 1937 to counter the ABA's conservative and anti-New Deal orientation.[19] Support for the Republicans during the Spanish Civil War was a key (and divisive) issue within the NLG in its early years, and was also the inspiration for the Lawyers Committee's founders a quarter century later.

Taking as their model the Lawyers Committee on American Relations with Spain, whose "unique contribution had been a hard-hitting memorandum of law demonstrating the illegality and unwisdom of the embargo against Loyalist Spain," the new Lawyers Committee "paralleled this approach" with their own memo on Vietnam.[20] For Crown, the mode of legal activism was not the only parallel. "In a fundamental historical sense, Vietnam was a second Spain," he wrote in 1976. "The birth of Republican Spain had been strangled by Franco and his henchmen, Hitler and Mussolini. Independent Vietnam was sought to be strangled by Diem the American puppet, supported by his sponsors, Presidents Kennedy and Johnson."[21]

If the NLG and Lawyers Committee on American Relations with Spain provided some of the professional networks and intellectual impetus for the new Lawyers Committee, this genesis was not widely publicized. In an effort to appeal to the wider profession, the Lawyers Committee instead framed its contribution within the more mainstream peace through law tradition of the American bar.[22] Encompassing various strains of American legalist thought since the late nineteenth century—including arbitration, adjudication, and world federalism—the principal binding agent in the peace through law tradition was a commitment to peaceful settlement of international disputes. Indeed, the project of placing limits on the right of states to use force was often understood as a quintessentially *American* project. In 1958, Grenville Clark and Louis Sohn first published *World Peace through World Law*. Around the same time, president of the ABA Charles Rhyne pushed for the establishment of "Law Day," World Peace through Law conferences, and a World Rule of Law Center at Duke University directed by Dwight Eisenhower's former speechwriter, Arthur Larson.[23] Not all lawyers understood the tradition in the same way, but in the years before 1965 the American legal profession and its organized bar were committed to the idea of peace through law.

The Lawyers Committee targeted two main audiences. The first was Washington policymakers and legislators, and the committee soon formed a mutually supportive relationship with antiwar senators Morse and Gruening, who had been the only two members of Congress to vote against the Tonkin Gulf Resolution in August 1964. The second audience was members of the American legal profession, whom they tried to enlist as another means of pressuring decision-makers in Washington. After its publication in the *Congressional Record*, reprints of the Lawyers Committee memorandum, endorsed by Morse and Gruening, were distributed to 173,000 lawyers and 3,750 law professors across the United States in an attempt to rally the American legal profession to the antiwar cause. Only 700 lawyers signed on initially, but by January 1966 the Lawyers Committee counted 4,100 members.[24]

The outreach efforts of the Lawyers Committee also attracted some attention from the Johnson administration. White House counsel, Harry McPherson, was sufficiently concerned about the Lawyers Committee memorandum that he arranged for a response to be prepared by a professor of law at the University of Texas, E. Ernest Goldstein,[25] who drafted a one-paragraph statement affirming the legality of American actions in Vietnam. The Goldstein statement was ultimately signed or endorsed by 30 other professors of law, including Neill Alford of the University of Virginia, Myres McDougal of Yale University, Louis Sohn and Richard Baxter of Harvard University, and William Bishop of the University of Michigan. The statement was sent to the president in November 1965 and read into the *Congressional Record* in January 1966 by Senator Russell Long, Democrat of Louisiana.[26] Beyond this flurry of activity from lawmakers, law professors, and the White House, there was little attention given to the Lawyers Committee memorandum in 1965.

The somewhat flippant dismissal of the Lawyers Committee memorandum proved unsustainable, however, as the public debate over the war's legality heated up in early 1966. In January of that year, the Lawyers Committee revived its campaign by sending a letter and the memorandum to President Johnson. The timing of this new push allowed the Lawyers Committee's legal arguments against the war to gain more traction due to their airing in the Senate during a debate over financing additional spending on the war. The Lawyers Committee memorandum thus acted as the spur for a much longer and more public debate over the legalities of US uses of force in Vietnam.

The Lawyers Committee memorandum became one basis of argument for Morse and Gruening during speeches on the Senate floor and, especially, over the course of Senate Foreign Relations Committee hearings that took place in January and February 1966.[27] The senators drew on the work of the Lawyers Committee to question Secretary of State Dean Rusk in particular about the justifications for, and legality of, the US military intervention in Vietnam. This public questioning gave the Lawyers Committee memorandum—which was printed as an appendix to the published version of the committee hearings, as well as inserted twice into the *Congressional Record* around the same time[28]—and the legal arguments more generally both political momentum and public traction. Morse was blunt in his appreciation of the legal factors, denouncing "this illegal war of ours in Vietnam" and urging more attention be paid to "the great debate that is going on among international lawyers."[29]

On the final day of the hearings, Rusk declared that "the law officers of the Government ought to be permitted to file a legal brief on these questions."[30] The following month, the State Department duly issued such a brief. Much longer than the first memorandum of a year earlier, this second attempt aimed to systematically rebut the Lawyers Committee memorandum while presenting more fully the administration's position on the legality of its Vietnam intervention. "For the first time in modern history a Government had been compelled to 'reply' to a citizens' 'Brief' that its war activities were illegal," wrote Crown in his short history of the Lawyers Committee. "We had succeeded in projecting the illegality of the war onto the national scene. No small feat for a Gideon's Band!"[31] The 1966 State Department memorandum, "The Legality of United States Participation in the Defense of Vietnam," was submitted to the Senate Foreign Relations Committee on March 8, 1966.[32] It was also republished in both the *Yale Law Journal* and the *American Journal of International Law*, two academic journals that had continued to feature opposing views on the legality of US actions in Vietnam. The 1966 memorandum differed from the first in that it presented its arguments in far greater detail and contained significantly more legal authority, in what appeared to be an attempt to match the form and substance of the Lawyers Committee memorandum.

The 1966 State Department memorandum was also distinctive because its authorship was explicitly attributed to Leonard C. Meeker, the State Department legal adviser. The 1965 memorandum was released with generic State Department authorship.[33] Adjusting that practice and identifying Meeker—one of Rusk's top "law officers of the Government"—as the author of the 1966 State Department memorandum appears aimed at matching the claims to expertise that underpinned the authorship of the other legal statements by professors of international law. If the plausibility of the Lawyers Committee memorandum's arguments were bolstered by the endorsement of professors of international law, then making explicit Meeker's role in the 1966 State Department memorandum provided a counterpoint to that form of expertise and the arguments the Lawyers Committee was making.

The Johnson administration also called again on the professors of international law who had participated in the Goldstein statement of November 1965. In an indication of the administration's concern about the growing visibility of the Lawyers Committee memorandum and its critique of the legality of US policy on Vietnam, McPherson framed his 1966 request to the professors carefully. "It would be desirable," he wrote, "though not essential, to reject the position expressed in the Lawyers' Committee letter."[34] This time, Alford and McDougal led the response, drafting an opinion that was also signed by Bishop, Baxter, and Sohn. It was sent to the president on February 14, 1966, and read into the *Congressional Record* on February 23, 1966.[35]

The short opinion of the five professors affirmed and expanded upon the Goldstein statement and rebutted key points made by the Lawyers Committee to the president while expressly noting that the authors had not, as a group, read the memorandum on which the Lawyers Committee letter to the president was based. The five professors declared their shared interest with the Lawyers Committee in "attaining world peace through law" but differed from their fellow lawyers in suggesting that the American legal position regarding Vietnam was compatible with that goal. In May 1966, again at the urging of the Johnson administration, this group released a much longer brief outlining their position on the legality of US actions in Vietnam, authored this time by two younger scholars, John Norton Moore and James Underwood, with the support of McDougal.[36] This brief was effectively a long rebuttal to the Lawyers Committee memorandum, and it was distributed by the American Bar Association to all members of Congress.[37]

The ABA's role in prosecuting the Johnson administration's case for war in the public domain was not confined to the quasi-sponsorship and distribution of Moore and Underwood's brief. On February 21, 1966, the House of Delegates of the ABA passed a unanimous resolution supporting the legality of US actions in Vietnam. "The position of the United States in Vietnam is legal under international law, and is in accordance with the Charter of the United Nations and the South East Asia Treaty," the resolution concluded.[38] The resolution had been quietly encouraged by the White House and jointly recommended by the ABA Standing Committee on Peace and Law through United Nations and its Section of International and Comparative Law.[39] The ABA continued to publicly support US actions in Vietnam through 1966 and to openly reject the arguments of the Lawyers Committee. In May 1966, for example, Eberhard P. Deutsch, writing as the chair of the ABA Committee on Peace and Law through United Nations, published a further defense of US actions in Vietnam in the *American Bar Association Journal*.[40] In his article, Deutsch explicitly challenged the arguments of the Lawyers Committee memorandum and accused the members of the Lawyers Committee of taking an "emotional attitude opposed to United States policy" rather than a position based "on law."[41]

The fact and contents of this debate over the international legality of US actions in Vietnam, which occurred primarily among lawyers, was covered as an ongoing news item in the *New York Times*.[42] Articles included, for example, a story on February 5, 1966, that described the Lawyers Committee memorandum as an example of where the "legality of the war in Vietnam has been challenged by a group of lawyers."[43] In late February, the *Times* reported on the ABA's unanimous resolution, describing it as "unusual in its rapidity" and "amount[ing] to support of the Administration's Vietnam policy generally."[44] In early March, the *Times* included a story on the Meeker memorandum, describing it as a "rebuttal" to Senator Morse and the Lawyers Committee and giving a succinct summary of the memorandum's contents.[45] Five days after the Meeker memorandum article, the *Times* headlined a story, "ABA Under Attack on Vietnam Stand," and quoted the Lawyers Committee leadership, Standard and Crown, as calling the ABA resolution "a disservice to the bar" because it relied on "a minuscule analysis consisting of a distorted excerpting of a few phrases out of context, from Articles 51 and 52 of the United Nations Charter."[46]

With the preponderance of American lawyers expressing support for the legality of US actions in Vietnam, the Lawyers Committee and its supporters continued to write and advocate individually and in groups for their positions. Particularly notable was the establishment of the Consultative Council of the Lawyers Committee, consisting primarily of academic specialists in international law rather than the nonspecialist private practice lawyers that mostly comprised the parent committee. In its mass mailout to the American legal profession in late 1965, the Lawyers Committee had attracted endorsements for its memorandum from a number of prominent international lawyers.[47] In an effort to bolster both the legal authority and the legal analysis of the Lawyers Committee in the face of the pro-administration position, some of those same lawyers came together in 1966 to form the Consultative Council.

John H. E. Fried led the Consultative Council in drafting a lengthy legal brief that systematically dissected and contested Meeker's March 1966 Memorandum of Law. Published in 1967 as *Vietnam and International Law: The Illegality of United States Military Involvement*, it was the Consultative Council's primary contribution to the public debate over international law and the Vietnam War.[48] In a 1990 reissue of the Consultative Council's legal brief, Richard Falk, chairman of the Consultative Council, recalled that *Vietnam and International Law* "was actively discussed in academic and government circles" where it "lent credibility to the international law argument against the Vietnam policies."[49] But it had little wider appeal within the United States. As historian Luke Stewart notes, "the book had difficulty in finding a receptive audience in the national newspapers," and so its "chief contribution was to bolster the legal arguments in draft and military resister cases."[50]

Aside from the collective effort, individuals associated with the Consultative Council independently promoted the antiwar position. Falk was a particularly prominent critic, publishing in June 1966 two pieces that responded to these events: one in *Dissent* magazine and one in the *Yale Law Journal*.[51] The *American Journal of International Law* published multiple articles on the legal questions arising from the Vietnam conflict in 1966 and 1967, including two by John Norton Moore contesting the arguments of illegality made by Falk, Quincy Wright, and others.

The muted reception of the Consultative Council's legal brief is indicative of how the public debate over international law changed from 1967 as the war progressed and the antiwar movement grew. Members of the Lawyers Committee and the Consultative Council noticeably adjusted their tactics. No longer appealing solely to political leaders, they now also turned to supporting draft resisters and others arguing cases in American courts on the basis of the illegality and unconstitutionality of the US war in Vietnam.[52] Members of the Lawyers Committee also changed tack rhetorically, becoming more willing to label American actions as criminal and demand Nuremberg-like accountability, following the lead of the Europe-based Russell Tribunal.[53] But to have an open mind on the Russell Tribunal—widely condemned in the United States[54]—would only deepen the isolation from their professional colleagues. In this later phase of their work, the Lawyers Committee and the Consultative Council informed more widely read antiwar books that made the case for criminal conduct more explicitly, notably *In the Name of America*, sponsored by Clergy and Laymen Concerned About Vietnam.[55] But as the use of legal language became more popularized—"a war crimes movement from below," in Luke Stewart's phrasing[56]—the Lawyers Committee, and the elite-level debate more generally, declined relative to its height in 1966.

While it never generated the popular appeal of the later antiwar protests, the 1965–67 public conversation on international legality still generated some astonishment among commentators. Reflecting on the debates in 1969, scholar Jaro Mayda registered both surprise and dismay at the ways in which the international legal arguments had played out in the public domain. "Among the new dimensions which the strange and frustrating

warfare in Vietnam has projected into . . . government and society," Mayda
wrote, "is the fierce public polemic about the legality or illegality of the
United States participation in the conflict."[57]

The Terms of the Debate

The international legal debate revolved around two main issues: whether
the US intervention could be characterized as assisting South Vietnam
in collective self-defense against aggression from North Vietnam, and
whether the US action was justified as part of its treaty commitments under
either or both the Geneva Accords and the treaty creating the Southeast
Asia Treaty Organization (SEATO).

The US legal position at first centered only on the question of self-
defense. Rusk made this clear in a 1965 speech to the American Society
of International Law, where he described the US military action as "the
exercise of the right of collective self-defense under the United Nations
Charter."[58] The 1965 State Department memorandum similarly provided
justifications based only on collective self-defense. The four-page memorandum devoted two pages to setting out "The Facts," which were based
on the February 1965 State Department white paper, "Aggression from
the North." With this as its source document, the 1965 State Department
memorandum claimed—as a question of *fact*—that North Vietnam was
"carrying out a carefully conceived plan of aggression against the South."[59]

The legal arguments were contained in the remaining two pages of the
memorandum. First, the memorandum argued that the aggression from
the North amounted to an armed attack in response to which South Vietnam could act in self-defense under Article 51 of the UN Charter. The
United States, the memorandum claimed, was acting on requests from
assistance from South Vietnam, and its actions were thus justified as the
collective defense of South Vietnam. In the discussion of self-defense
and armed attack, no mention was made of the Southeast Asia Collective
Defense Treaty or SEATO.

Second, the memorandum argued that North Vietnam had repeatedly
violated the 1954 Geneva Accords in a manner that amounted to a material
breach of treaty obligations. This breach then gave rise to South Vietnam's
right to withhold compliance with parts of the Accords that "limit its ability
to protect its very existence."[60] That is, South Vietnam was justified in taking actions in its self-defense, including inviting assistance from the United
States, because North Vietnam had not complied with its obligations under

the Geneva Accords. The Geneva Accords had intended the division of Vietnam to be temporary, but South Vietnam had long assumed de facto statehood in American eyes—so much so that the international status of North and South Vietnam as states within the international system did not warrant any comment in this initial State Department memo. The memo was careful not to refer to the North-South frontier as an international border, however, instead labeling it "the internationally agreed demarcation line of 1954 between North and South Viet-Nam."[61]

The 1965 State Department memorandum included no supporting legal authorities for either of its arguments. The interpretations of the UN Charter and of treaty law on which the memorandum relied were presented as clear and uncontested. Further, the brevity of the memorandum suggests a State Department that was confident that the reasoning included in the memorandum was sufficient for the purposes of both public and political justification. This is, in many ways, unsurprising. As John Norton Moore noted after the release of the Pentagon Papers, the "*Realpolitik* planning" and "contemporary decision theory" favored by successive US administrations had created a national security process that was "poorly structured to take international-legal considerations into account."[62] It seems unlikely that Rusk, the lawyers in the State Department, or any others expected the legal issues around US military action in Vietnam to become an especially prominent part of public debate. Mayda's observation above about the "public polemic on legality" being a "new dimension" in the debate underscores this expectation.

That international law featured in the public debate about Vietnam seems largely a consequence of the second push made by the Lawyers Committee in early 1966, and the momentum given it by the Senate Foreign Relations Committee hearings and related publicity. In contrast to its reception in September 1965, the Lawyers Committee memorandum began to be more closely read (and critiqued) from early 1966. More densely written and comprehensively referenced than the 1965 State Department memo, the Lawyers Committee memorandum provided significant fodder for specialist international lawyers once they turned their attention it.

The departure point for the Lawyers Committee was not Southeast Asia but the Middle East—namely the breach by Israel, France, and the United Kingdom of their UN Charter commitments in the Suez Crisis of 1956, and the US position upholding the role of the United Nations in securing peace in the region and around the world. In both rejecting the justification offered by Israel for its advance into Egypt—the need to eliminate *Fedayeen* bases in the Sinai Peninsula—and praising the American stand against its own allies, the Lawyers Committee established the Second Arab-Israeli War as something of a legal and policy baseline from which to assess American actions in Vietnam.

The memorandum then rebutted the State Department arguments about collective self-defense on two bases. First, the Lawyers Committee adopted a strict reading of the Charter requirement that self-defense was justified only after an "armed attack" had occurred.[63] The Lawyers Committee briefly asserted that the American claim of North Vietnamese aggression against South Vietnam—a claim central to the 1965 State Department memorandum—failed to reach the threshold of armed attack as implied by this strict reading of Article 51, writing at one point that "the infiltrations from North Vietnam cannot be deemed to constitute an 'armed attack' within the purview of Article 51."[64] But no further explanation was given as to why the infiltrations did not meet the standard and, as a result, why the State Department's position on armed attack was problematic.

The Lawyers Committee most likely spent so little time parsing whether the actions of North Vietnam amounted to an armed attack on South Vietnam because, for the memo's drafters, the nature of the attack was secondary to the status (or lack thereof) of North and South Vietnam. If no such separate legal entities existed, in the Lawyers Committee's logic, no cross-border armed attack in the sense of Article 51 could have occurred. The Lawyers Committee argued that under the Geneva Accords of 1954, North and South Vietnam were a single state, albeit temporarily partitioned. The conflict between the two regimes was thus "civil strife," meaning "foreign intervention is forbidden, because civil strife is a domestic question—a position insisted upon by the United States in its civil war of 1861."[65] With no international conflict in existence, Article 51 could not be triggered. North Vietnamese actions "cannot be considered an armed attack by one nation on another."[66] Moreover, South Vietnam was not a member of the United Nations—a prerequisite for the operation of Article 51, according to the Lawyers Committee.[67] This argument that the war in Vietnam was a civil, not an international, war also offered a repudiation of the "material breach" of a treaty argument that the State Department had presented in its first memorandum in relation to the Geneva Accords. "The United States is in fact a foreign nation vis-à-vis Vietnam," stated the Lawyers Committee; "North Vietnam is not."[68]

In a further critique of Washington's understanding of the law of self-defense, the Lawyers Committee argued that "the right of collective self-defense under Article 51 presupposes that the nations invoking such right are properly members of a regional collective security system within the purview of the United Nations Charter." The Lawyers Committee memorandum rejected the argument that the collection of disparately located members of SEATO could act as a regional defense arrangement. "If artifices like SEATO were sanctioned," the memorandum stated, "the path would be open for the emasculation of the United Nations organization and the world system of international security assiduously developed to prevent the scourge of war."[69]

Even if SEATO could somehow act legitimately under Article 51 (collective self-defense) and Article 53 (regional organizations) of the UN Charter, the Lawyers Committee further argued, the Manila Pact itself did not allow the United States to defend South Vietnam because "our right to intervene is limited . . . by the requirement for unanimity among all eight of the treaty nations."[70] This directly contradicted the US government position—that the United States had an obligation to defend South Vietnam under SEATO, which it could exercise unilaterally. Rusk made this argument, for example, in his February 18 appearance before the Senate Foreign Relations Committee, where he stated that the United States had sent troops because South Vietnam had, "under the language of the SEATO Treaty, been the victim of aggression by means of armed attack."[71]

The second State Department memorandum, formally issued by Leonard Meeker as the department's legal adviser, echoed the arguments from the 1965 memorandum but presented them in far greater depth and with more detailed legal authority. For example, the memorandum repeated the arguments that the United States was justified in acting in collective self-defense to protect South Vietnam, but this time it specified the extent of the infiltration that it argued amounted to an "armed attack" by North Vietnam.[72] Meeker further expanded on the administration's arguments with regard to the applicability of the right of self-defense. This inherent right was not, argued Meeker, limited to members of the United Nations or to regional organizations. Moreover, the right applied regardless of whether or not South Vietnam was formally an independent sovereign state.[73]

The Meeker memorandum also provided detailed justifications for the administration's claims that its actions were justified under SEATO. According to Meeker, the American interpretation that SEATO authorized members to act unilaterally, rather than collectively, to protect other states under the treaty was accepted by the other SEATO member states.[74] It is clear from the events surrounding the release of the Meeker memorandum that these arguments were crafted in such detail in order to rebut specifically the arguments raised by the Lawyers Committee.

The other key contributions to the public debate on international law were also designed to rebuff the advocacy of the Lawyers Committee and, to the extent that they relied on the Lawyers Committee memorandum, Senators Morse and Gruening. The letter from the five international law professors of February 1966, for example, described the Lawyers Committee memorandum as containing "such egregious errors that we consider necessary an immediate refutation of the most significant of these." The professors argued that the Lawyers Committee had adopted an "excessively narrow" construction of Article 51 of the UN Charter and had effectively ignored the wide scope given to UN members to exercise a collective right of self-defense when invited by another state. South Vietnam, the authors argued, had been widely recognized as a state and the United States could thus exercise collective self-defense on its behalf, either as part of its inherent right protected under Article 51 or as part of the SEATO treaty.[75] The ABA's position was best summarized by Deutsch's May 1966 article in the *ABA Journal*. In that piece, Deutsch provided an account of the separation of North and South Vietnam under the Geneva Accords, described the history of the SEATO Treaty and characterized North Vietnam as having "violated continuously" the Geneva Accords and committed ongoing acts of aggression against South Vietnam.[76]

From around mid-1966, as academic specialists began to write at much greater length about the international law questions involved in America's war in Vietnam, the terms of the doctrinal debate shifted. Both pro-administration and antiwar writers were now willing to critique their own side's earlier arguments from late 1965 and early 1966. Moore and Underwood's book-length response to the Lawyers Committee barely mentioned Meeker's memorandum. Studied neglect of the administration position turned into more open criticism in early 1967, as Moore expressed some concerns about the State Department view on North Vietnamese aggression. For Moore, "the White Paper model of 'aggression from the North' . . . never captured the complex reality of the Viet Nam problem."[77]

Falk likewise distanced himself from the doctrinal arguments of his antiwar allies. Implying significant weaknesses in the Lawyers Committee analysis—analysis that he had signed onto in late 1965 "with alacrity," and that had his public endorsement[78]—Falk wrote in his 1966 *Yale Law Journal* article that it was "persuasive but trivial" for Meeker "to demonstrate that international law recognizes the right of individual and collective self-defense against an armed attack; that nonmembers of the United Nations enjoy the same rights of self-defense as do members; that South Viet Nam is a political entity entitled to claim the right of self-defense despite its origin as a 'temporary zone'; and that the right of collective self-defense may be exercised independent of a regional arrangement organized under Chapter VIII of the United Nations Charter."[79] The crux of the doctrinal question for Falk—armed attack—had been given short shrift by the Lawyers Committee, and so he quietly dismissed the majority of the committee's original legal analysis.

As the debate shifted from the halls of Congress and ABA gatherings to academic journals, the tone also changed from New York law firm to New Haven seminar room.[80] While the Consultative Council's legal brief proceeded along fairly conventional lines of doctrinal argument, other legal scholars took the debate, at least in their own minds, to a more sophisticated level—beyond "formalistic," "legalistic," and "trivial" points (Falk's words) and arguments "legalistic in the extreme" (Moore's words).[81] The doctrinal disagreements became subsumed within a policy-oriented legal vernacular of "requirements of world order" and "principal community values."[82]

The New Haven-style discussions of authority, control, values, and order eventually led to Falk editing a four-volume series, *The Vietnam War and International Law*, that reprinted key parts of the academic and public debate, including the Falk-Moore exchange in the *Yale Law Journal*. Moore then did the same for the Middle East, editing multiple volumes of *The Arab-Israeli Conflict*. As Moore wrote in a related study, "*The Vietnam War and International Law* and *The Arab-Israeli Conflict* bring together the principal readings and documents on the legal aspects of two of the major world-order issues of our time, both of which have mixed features of internal and international conflict."[83]

A significant share of *The Arab-Israeli Conflict* was devoted to the Third Arab-Israeli War (or Six-Day War) of June 1967. Moore was a supporter of the idea that Israel acted legitimately in self-defense in 1967.[84] Falk, too, came around to the view "that Israel was entitled to strike first in June of 1967, so menacing and imminent was the threat of aggression being mounted against her."[85] The 1967 war and subsequent Israeli reprisal raids became another important setting, alongside the Vietnam War, for building schemas regarding the legitimate use of force. To his (initially) tripartite model of intervention developed for the Vietnam War,[86] Falk added a 12-point framework for assessing claims to use retaliatory force based on Israel's late 1968 attack on Beirut International Airport.[87] Moore developed a typology of intervention that incorporated 22 categories upon which to assess the initiation of hostilities.[88] If the elite-level public debate of 1965–67 began with the Lawyers Committee setting one Middle East conflict—the Suez Crisis—as a baseline for assessing the legality of the Vietnam War,

it ended as legal scholars turned to another Middle East conflict—the 1967
war and its aftermath—to determine how and when to shift that baseline.

The Characterizations of International Law

Legality seemed to matter in the debate of 1965 to 1967, at least to the
members of the Lawyers Committee, some in the State Department and
the Senate, some members of the American legal profession, and perhaps
even to some members of the wider public. Unlike later Vietnam War
debates, this debate was not an example of "ordinary people" deploying
international legal language as a means to speak to those in power. It was
rather an example of already powerful members of an elite class of lawyers
attempting to influence American policy by using international law in the
public sphere. Nevertheless, the debate had an impact, not least in prompt-
ing important changes in the way the American legal profession engaged
with questions of US national security and foreign policy.

The key players in the public debate of 1965–67 explicitly engaged in
the debate as legal professionals and experts. The Lawyers Committee
memorandum implored its audience to take the authors' arguments seriously because of who they were. "[W]e, *as lawyers*," they wrote, "have been
compelled to reach [this conclusion]. We, *as lawyers*, urge our President to
accept the obligations for international behavior placed upon us by our
signature on the United Nations Charter."[89]

For the Lawyers Committee, international law offered both a way to
critique the Vietnam policies of the Johnson administration and a model
for how better to address the situation. Framing the Vietnam War as "illegal" allowed the Lawyers Committee to harness what they characterized
as the power of an international law that was both transcendent (designed
to "banish from the earth the 'scourge of war'") and standard-setting ("the
rule of law"). By emphasizing that it was lawyers authoring the memorandum, the Lawyers Committee called on professional expertise to add
weight to their claims.

The responders to the Lawyers Committee memorandum also relied
on their professional expertise as lawyers, but they crafted this expertise in
slightly different ways. The first shift was that all the responses—the ABA's
and all the permutations of the pro-administration groups—made much of
the numbers of legal professionals who supported their views: "thirty-one
professors of international law" had supported the Goldstein statement;
the ABA resolution had been "adopted unanimously."[90] The majority of

legal opinion in the United States sided with the Johnson administration and, in a field where there is no authoritative arbiter of international legality, the preponderance of professional opinion can carry significant weight. It mattered, in this sense, that the individuals who considered US policy on Vietnam to be consistent with international law were experts in international law. And here the second shift in the presentation of expertise becomes relevant.

It is significant that the authors of both the Goldstein statement and the opinion of the five international law professors described themselves as "teachers of international law."[91] In his work on expertise in international law, David Kennedy makes the case that "[a]rguments about who is and is not within the discipline, whose arguments are and are not plausible, or what expert work has what consequences in the world are all part of expert practice."[92] The Lawyers Committee had described themselves as "lawyers" as a way to establish their credentials, albeit as generalists rather than specialists. One way to combat the arguments of the Lawyers Committee was to combat the expertise of the people who wrote the memorandum. For the field of international law, generalist lawyers do not have the knowledge or authority of specialists, and in all manifestations the pro-administration group's statements were couched as the views of experts in international law. Similar motivations no doubt spurred the Consultative Council of the Lawyers Committee, which included significant figures of international law academia such as Richard Falk and Quincy Wright, to prepare their own legal brief over and above the original Lawyers Committee memorandum. Joseph Crown admitted as much, writing that "the refutation of the State Department's rebuttal memorandum, at certain points, called for sophisticated expertise in the field of International Law," with the establishment of the Consultative Council leading to "a qualitative enhancement" of the Lawyers Committee's "capability."[93]

Perceptions of authority and expertise also drove the administration's response to the Lawyers Committee. The perceived need to undermine the claim of the Lawyers Committee to authority during the public debate of 1965–67 helps to explain the shift in the State Department approach from releasing a general, unattributed memorandum in 1965, to releasing a second memorandum in 1966 explicitly attributed to Leonard Meeker, who enjoyed significant professional standing as the State Department legal adviser. The explicit attributions of Meeker's authorship sought to assert that the administration's view of the law must have been superior precisely because it was Meeker who developed that view. The two State Department memos point also to a shift in the Johnson administration's view of the importance of international legality. The 1965 memorandum came across as perfunctory. The administration was forced into releasing the 1966 Meeker memorandum to rebut the arguments made by the Lawyers Committee memorandum. This sequence suggests an administration for whom international law was an afterthought—a nuisance to be managed rather than standards to be taken into account from the outset.

But the events of the public debate suggest that the role of international legal argument, at least as a public language, was more potent than the Johnson administration anticipated. It is in many ways remarkable that the Lawyers Committee memorandum gained public and political traction in the first place. Senators Morse and Gruening placed the legal arguments at the center of their opposition to US policy on Vietnam, and once Rusk was questioned on this basis in the widely broadcast Senate Foreign Relations Committee hearings, the legal arguments became impossible to dismiss without a response. International law had enough public valence in 1965–1967 that the Johnson administration made multiple attempts to generate opinions that supported its policy and opposed the Lawyers Committee position. The Johnson administration did not want its intervention in Vietnam to be portrayed, or to be able to be portrayed, as contrary to international law. Washington's sensitivity to legal criticism exhibited in the public debate of 1965–67 at least partly explains subsequent government efforts to better perform its "duty to explain."[94]

Commitment to law mattered not only in the production of the various legal opinions in the 1965–67 debate but also in the expected reception to arguments framed in terms of law. Implicit in the Lawyers Committee memorandum was the belief that exercises of government power could be restrained by law in the United States, and even though drafted by generalists rather than specialists, the memorandum wielded its international legal arguments in the conviction they would be taken seriously. Sometimes, however, the confident tone of the legal arguments slipped, and the wording of the memorandum indicated a concern that the Johnson administration would not take seriously its international legal obligations. The second paragraph of the memorandum, for example, reads as almost an apologia for the Lawyers Committee advocacy:

> Observance of the rule of law is a basic tenet of American democracy. Hence it is fitting that American lawyers examine the action pursued by our Government to determine whether our Government's conduct is justified under the rule of law mandated by the United Nations Charter—a Charter adopted to banish from the earth the "scourge of war."[95]

Even though the members of the Lawyers Committee were in the minority of American lawyers regarding the Vietnam War, and were generally aligned with the NLG rather than the conservative mainstream of the American legal profession, they nonetheless fell within that profession's strong tradition of equating the rule of law in world affairs with the peaceful settlement of disputes and, since 1945, specifically with the UN Charter. Indeed, both sides of the 1965–67 debate claimed links to various strands of the American "world peace through law" tradition that was the most prominent expression of the organized bar's commitment to the rule of law in world affairs in the two decades after World War II.

If the peace through law tradition—of whichever stripe—was the primary intellectual site of public debate among lawyers in the early years of heavy American involvement in the war, the debate, and the war more generally, also effectively helped to eclipse that tradition within the American legal profession. Arthur Larson's World Rule of Law Center at Duke University "increasingly became a casualty of the Vietnam War," notes Larson's biographer, and "the grant money that had sustained the Rule of Law Center's personnel and programs gradually dried up during the second half of the 1960s."[96] The ABA's Standing Committee on Peace and Law through United Nations, which was a locus of the 1965–67 public debate, similarly declined.

The American world peace through law tradition may have declined as a result of the Vietnam War, but the American legal profession's ideological commitment to the "rule of law" did not. It remained constant throughout and after the war. The expression of that commitment *did* change, however, which in turn hinted at deeper shifts in American understandings of its role vis-à-vis law in the world. The American turn to human rights was the major manifestation of this change coming out of the Vietnam War,[97] but it was not the only one. The rise of the field of "national security law," which can be traced in important ways to the public debate over the legality of America's involvement in Indochina, was also emblematic of the new ways in which the United States sought to pursue its understanding of the rule of law in international affairs after the Vietnam War.[98]

The origins of the field of national security law have not been comprehensively traced. "The lineage is murky, there is still no published intellectual history, and there is no general template for field evolution," note three lawyers closely associated with the field.[99] The rise of national security law can be partly explained by generational change, as an international law community strongly influenced by foreign-language speaking European refugees and the experience of World War II was steadily replaced by a more monolingual community driven to promote narrower American interests.[100] But the beginnings of national security law can also be clearly traced to the public debate over the legality of the Vietnam War. Several of the protagonists of the 1965–67 debate were at the forefront of the development of this new field of law, including John Norton Moore and the American Bar Association.

In the wake of the Pentagon Papers release, Moore expressed his disquiet at how Washington's Vietnam War decision-making process did not take international legal considerations into account. He followed this up by writing a key intervention on the subject in the establishment journal *Foreign Affairs* just as Washington was finalizing its exit from Vietnam. More attention to law in policymaking would make for well-implemented and appropriately justified policy, argued Moore, while avoiding the high costs of failing to take law into account during the policy process. But just as important, for Moore, was the potential of law to formulate "a coherent and intellectually powerful foreign policy" for the United States "to recoup its leadership" after the Vietnam War. A renewed commitment to the idea of law could help combat "the present neo-isolationist tendencies within the United States" and "revive domestic support for a more active international policy."[101]

In support of this more active, law-based foreign policy approach, Moore later set up the nation's first university institute dedicated to national security law; coauthored a case book, *National Security Law*; and contributed to the field's establishment and growth in the American legal profession through the American Bar Association's Standing Committee on Law and National Security. First established in 1962 as the ABA Committee on Education about Communism, and renamed by Moore in 1978,[102] the ABA Standing Committee on Law and National Security quickly became the organized bar's focal point for the emerging field of practice.[103] In its early days, the committee was chaired by Morris Leibman, one of the lesser Wise Men of the post-World War II Democratic foreign policy establishment. According to longtime director of the committee, Holly McMahon, Leibman "appreciated the importance of integrating the rule of law and lawyers into the national security process."[104] He was also, according to Johnson administration aide Chester Cooper, "instrumental in pushing . . . through" the ABA resolution of February 1966 supporting the administration's position on the legality of the Vietnam War.[105] The link between the public debate of 1965–67 and the rise of national security law, then, is quite direct. In Moore's own words, the debate over the legality of US involvement in Vietnam "was really the starting point of my involvement in what became national security law."[106]

The lesson Moore's protagonist in the public debate of 1965–1967, Richard Falk, took from the debate was that citizens needed to be better organized to hold their government to account. In 1967, Falk labelled the Consultative Council of the Lawyers Committee's legal brief a "citizens' white paper" that might help "avoid future Vietnams,"[107] and the debate over the war was central to Falk's own journey of, as he calls it, "engaged citizenship."[108]

Falk's journey began and ended in very different places. During the public debate of 1965–67, he recollected more than 50 years later, "my work still fell within the mainstream liberal paradigm of legitimate debate on controversial issues." He received no pushback for his role as academic critic of US policy and was a sought-after speaker, including for war colleges, congressional committees, and judicial proceedings. At this stage in his career, Falk still felt "reasonably comfortable situated at this interface between the organized bar of practicing lawyers and the academic world."[109] Falk's "willingness to respect the boundaries of liberal dissent" changed in the middle of 1968 as a result of a visit to North Vietnam, which made "a permanent impact on my moral, legal, and spiritual consciousness."[110] It also affected how others in the legal profession perceived him, altering his "prior identity as a respected international law critic." As Falk recalls it, "the trip, highly publicized, made me, if not a pariah, at least situated on the far left, and no longer a promising, and more importantly, reliable young scholar with top echelon public service potential."[111]

Falk's departure from the American legal profession's mainstream was also precipitated by his increased willingness to take his understanding of the Vietnam War as illegal to its logical but unwelcome conclusion: that US political leaders and military commanders were criminally liable for their choices regarding the Vietnam War. Other lawyers, notably Telford Taylor, also gestured toward this argument.[112] But while Taylor "stretched his liberalism to the limit," he did not break with it as Falk did, preferring ultimately to condemn American policy as ill-judged rather than criminal.[113] Of course, the value of "Nuremberg thinking," as Falk came to call it, had more to do with activism than correct legal doctrine. The Lawyers Committee's turn toward the courts from 1967 had, for Falk, given rise to a political reform project that sought an acknowledgment "that every U.S. citizen has a constitutional right to a lawful foreign policy that can be tested by independent inquiry in a domestic court."[114]

Falk's visit to Vietnam in 1968 also crystalized another change in his approach to the Vietnam War. While much of his work, both before and after his break with mainstream American liberalism, was concerned with citizenship and government in the United States, he also came to identify much more strongly with the Vietnamese struggle for self-determination. This then extended after the war to a broader appreciation of, and solidarity with, non-American and anticolonial perspectives on international law and politics.[115] Falk suggests a common theme between the legal position of the Lawyers Committee during the Vietnam War and the *Nicaragua* judgment of 1986, whereby the International Court of Justice "repudiated a similar legal argument" to the one the United States had relied upon 20 years earlier to defend its actions in Vietnam.[116] "One of the solid successes of the Lawyers Committee and the use of international law by the peace movement in the years of the Vietnam War," wrote Falk in his foreword to the 1990 reissue of the Consultative Council's legal brief, "was to challenge the earlier notion that international law was part of the repressive side of world politics, consisting of rules and procedures made by and for the rich and powerful." Likewise, for Falk, "the *Nicaragua* judgment by the World Court was a watershed pedagogic event, teaching citizens throughout the Third World that international law fairly construed was often on their side."[117]

Falk's break with the mainstream American international law community as a result of the Vietnam War was epitomized by his intellectual trajectory regarding the Middle East conflicts. Whereas Falk initially expressed support for the idea that Israel acted legitimately in anticipatory self-defense at the outset of the Six-Day War, a reassessment of the facts of 1967 led him to label Israel's actions "a war of aggression,"[118] and his growing identification with self-determination movements around the world saw him become a vocal critic of Israel's actions regarding the Palestinian people and their territory. Further isolation followed, notes Falk, "when playing a public role as Israeli critic and supporter of the Palestinian struggle for a just and sustainable peace . . . was deemed to have crossed a *substantive* red line." In Falk's words, the "personal abuse" he received for his stated views on the Middle East "reached its climax" from 2008 to 2014, when he served as United Nations Special Rapporteur for Palestine Human Rights on behalf of the UN Human Rights Council.[119]

As with Falk, John Norton Moore's continued work of public engagement on questions of international law after the Vietnam War debate of 1965–67 led to grappling with the politics and law of the Middle East conflicts. Moore warned readers of his edited collection, *The Arab-Israeli Conflict*, that the multiple perspectives portrayed in the volumes needed to be carefully compared.[120] Warning against basing any conclusions on "history alone" or an "automatic majority" in United Nations bodies,[121]

Moore instead steered readers toward the UN Charter as "the most important source of legal rights and duties in appraising the conflict."[122] Moore implies that, when properly interpreted, the Charter can provide protection for the interests of those, such as the United States and Israel, now in a minority position within the international system's deliberative and judicial bodies. In 2017, 50 years after the public debate over the legality of the Vietnam War, Moore suggested that the legal interpretation he developed during that debate "has stood the test of time well," presumably including its deployment regarding the Middle East conflicts.[123] He is currently working with the Israeli international lawyer Yoram Dinstein on a manual on the law concerning the use of force and self-defense to, in his words, "help in restoring sanity" to that area of international law "by a return to accurate, correct, classic international law."[124] Once published, the manual will be a testament both to the enduring significance of the 1965–67 public debate over the legality of US actions in Vietnam and to that debate's connection to the conflicts in the Middle East.

Conclusion

The debate of 1965–67 was not insignificant for the development of international legal doctrine, particularly in terms of American interpretations of the UN Charter. But international law is not merely a set of doctrines. It is also a public language, its power and purpose often claimed to rely in part on public opinion. The debate over US intervention in Vietnam was particularly important, then, for its *public* nature—public in terms of its participants, its venues, and its legacies.

The public debate of 1965–67 had some effect on the US government and its consideration of international law in the context of national security policymaking. A position where the US government was relatively dismissive of international law fits with the narrative of exceptionalism that successive US governments have maintained. But the story of that exceptionalism is not a neat one, and the events of the public debate of 1965–67 make that story at least a little bit messier. Washington cared enough about international law—or at least the consequences of being perceived as a lawbreaker—to mobilize supporters to oppose the arguments of antiwar lawyers. It took from the debate, too, a renewed appreciation for the importance of public presentation in the development of its legal justifications.

The debate had an even more noticeable effect on the American legal profession's approach to international law. Unlike the more popular, or vernacular, use of international law rhetoric by the antiwar movement from 1967, the 1965–67 debate centered lawyers consciously acting in their professional capacity. As such, they were also acting as gatekeepers: first as generalists regarding the American tradition of peace through law in international affairs, then as specialists regarding the discipline of international law. Different lawyers took different lessons from the debate and moved along divergent pathways after 1967—some toward more solidarity with citizen-activist and anticolonial interpretations of international law, others toward improving the national security establishment's facility with incorporating law into policymaking—but the debate nonetheless remained an important touchstone for them.

In one sense, this analysis of a small snapshot of international law in the American public debates about the Vietnam War is unsurprising. That a government appeared to regard international law as a relatively unimportant tool of foreign policy, and that the people who cared most about international law were the international lawyers, is consistent with "realist" views of international law.[125] Our aim here, however, is to argue that a close examination of who used international law and how they used it suggest much more complexity in how international law has worked in public debates, and how the American approach to international law changed as a result of this particular public debate.

NOTES

1. See also Luke J. Stewart, "'A New Kind of War': The Vietnam War and the Nuremberg Principles, 1964–1968" (PhD diss., University of Waterloo, 2014), 69–88, 323–30; Samuel Moyn, "From Antiwar Politics to Antitorture Politics," in *Law and War*, ed. Austin Sarat, Lawrence Douglas, and Martha Merrill Umphrey (Stanford: Stanford Law Books, 2014), 154–97; Matthew Lippman, "Vietnam: A Twenty Year Retrospective," *Dickinson Journal of International Law* 11, no. 2 (Winter 1993): 325–421, esp. 344–71; Jaro Mayda, "The Vietnam Conflict and International Law," in *The Vietnam War and International Law*, ed. Richard Falk, vol. 2 (Princeton: Princeton University Press, 1969), 260–70. For accounts from participants in the public debate, see Peter Weiss, "Nuclear War in the Courts," in *Nuclear Weapons, the Peace Movement and the Law*, ed. John Dewar, Abdul Paliwala, Sol Picciotto, and Matthias Ruete (Basingstoke: Macmillan, 1986), 182–85; Richard Falk, *Public Intellectual: The Life of a Citizen Pilgrim* (Atlanta: Clarity Press, 2021), 185–219; Joseph H. Crown, "The Saga of the Lawyers Committee on American Policy Towards Vietnam," unpublished manuscript, 1976, Folder 3 (Vietnam Aftermath [1 of 2] 1965–1978), Box 43, Carey McWilliams Papers, Library Special Collections, University of California, Los Angeles. Our thanks to Simon Elliott and Molly Haigh of UCLA Library Special Collections for their assistance in accessing Crown's unpublished survey of the Lawyers Committee's work.

2. See, for example, Stephen J. Toope, "Public Commitment to International Law: Canadian and British Media Perspectives on the Use of Force," in *British and Canadian Perspectives on International Law*, ed. Christopher P. M. Waters (Leiden: Brill, 2006), 17.

3. Madelaine Chiam, *International Law in Public Debate* (Cambridge: Cambridge University Press, 2021).

4. Matthew Craven, Sundhya Pahuja, and Gerry Simpson, "Reading and Unreading a Historiography of Hiatus," in *International Law and the Cold War*, ed. Matthew Craven, Sundhya Pahuja, and Gerry Simpson (Cambridge: Cambridge University Press, 2020), 1.

5. See, for example, Martti Koskenniemi, "What Should International Lawyers Learn from Karl Marx?" *Leiden Journal of International Law* 17 (2004): 229, 244–46; Phillip Allott and Alan Dashwood, "Letter to the Editor," *The Times*, March 19, 2003, 23; Mayda, "The Vietnam Conflict and International Law," 268–69.

6. See Article 51 of the United Nations Charter, June 26, 1945 (entered into force October 24, 1945), https://www.un.org/en/charter-united-nations/

7. United Nations Security Council, "Letter dated 7 February 1965 from the representative of the United States of America to the President of the Security Council," February 8, 1965, UN Doc. S/6174.

8. William Conrad Gibbons, *The U.S. Government and the Vietnam War: Executive and Legislative Roles and Relationships*, vol. 3, *January–July 1965* (Princeton: Princeton University Press, 1989), 79n97.

9. See Brian Cuddy's chapter in this volume.

10. Gibbons, *The U.S. Government and the Vietnam War*, 3: 79n97. Much of this March 8 memo is an exact replica of the February 11 memo, but mention in the February memo of specific North Vietnamese and National Liberation Front attacks was replaced in the March memo by general claims of North Vietnamese aggression.

11. Department of State, "Legal Basis for United States Actions Against North Viet-Nam," March 8, 1965, in *Background Information Relating to Southeast Asia and Vietnam*, 3rd rev. ed., ed. United States Senate Committee on Foreign Relations (Washington, DC: US Government Printing Office, 1967), 145–48.

12. William L. Standard, *Aggression: Our Asian Disaster* (New York: Random House, 1971), 53. The 1965 US intervention in the Dominican Republic was also a spur to the creation of the Lawyers Committee, although its founders soon resolved to focus their public efforts solely on Vietnam. Crown, "The Saga of the Lawyers Committee on American Policy Towards Vietnam," 2–3.

13. Weiss, "Nuclear War in the Courts," 182.

14. Moyn, "From Antiwar Politics to Antitorture Politics," 168.

15. Lawyers Committee on American Policy Towards Vietnam, "American Policy Vis-à-Vis Vietnam, in Light of Our Constitution, the United Nations Charter, the 1954 Geneva Accords, and the Southeast Asia Collective Defense Treaty," *Congressional Record*, 89th Cong., 1st Sess. (September 23, 1965), 111: 24902–10.

16. Moyn, "From Antiwar to Antitorture Politics," 169.

17. Lawyers Committee, "American Policy Vis-à-Vis Vietnam," 24903.

18. Oscar Schachter, "The Invisible College of International Lawyers," *Northwestern University Law Review* 72, no. 2 (1977): 217–26. Compare Anthea Roberts, *Is International Law International?* (New York: Oxford University Press, 2017), 1–17.

19. Crown, "The Saga of the Lawyers Committee on American Policy Towards Vietnam," i, 2–4.

20. Crown, "The Saga of the Lawyers Committee on American Policy Towards Vietnam," 5.

21. Crown, "The Saga of the Lawyers Committee on American Policy Towards Vietnam," 4. Diem was assassinated a few weeks before Lyndon Johnson became president.

22. See, for example, Robert W. Kenney and William Standard to Lyndon B. Johnson, in *Congressional Record*, 89th Cong., 2nd Sess. (February 9, 1966), 112: 2666.

23. David L. Stebenne, *Modern Republican: Arthur Larson and the Eisenhower Years* (Bloomington: Indiana University Press, 2006), 218–20.

24. Crown, "The Saga of the Lawyers Committee on American Policy Towards Vietnam," 5; Stewart, "'A New Kind of War,'" 75–76; Weiss, "Nuclear War in the Courts," 182; Moyn, "From Antiwar Politics to Antitorture Politics," 169.

25. Gibbons, *The U.S. Government and the Vietnam War*, vol. 4, *July 1965–January 1968* (Princeton: Princeton University Press, 1995), 246n96.

26. Gibbons, *The U.S. Government and the Vietnam War*, 4: 246n96; *Congressional Record*, 89th Cong., 2nd Sess. (January 27, 1966), 112: 1312.

27. United States Senate Committee on Foreign Relations, *Hearings on S. 2793 to Amend Further the Foreign Assistance Act of 1961, as Amended*, 89th Cong., 2nd Sess., January 28–February 18, 1966 (Washington, DC: US Government Printing Office, 1966).

28. United States Senate Committee on Foreign Relations, *Hearings*, 687–713; *Congressional Record*, 89th Cong., 2nd Sess. (February 9, 1966), 112: 2665–73, introduced by Gruening; *Congressional Record*, 89th Cong., 2nd Sess. (February 25, 1966), 112: 4166–73, introduced by Morse.

29. United States Senate Committee on Foreign Relations, *Hearings*, 213–14, 511.

30. United States Senate Committee on Foreign Relations, *Hearings*, 600.

31. Crown, "The Saga of the Lawyers Committee on American Policy Towards Vietnam," 6.

32. Leonard Meeker, "The Legality of United States Participation in the Defense of Viet-Nam," *Department of State Bulletin* 54, no. 1396 (March 23, 1966): 474–89.

33. While not publicly acknowledged, the March 8, 1965, memorandum was drafted by Carl Salans, the assistant legal adviser for Far Eastern affairs, and approved by Meeker. Gibbons, *The U.S. Government and the Vietnam War*, 3: 79n97.

34. Gibbons, *The U.S. Government and the Vietnam War*, 4: 246n96.

35. *Congressional Record*, 89th Cong., 2nd Sess. (February 23, 1966), 112: 3843, introduced by Richard Russell, Democrat of Georgia.

36. John Norton Moore and James L. Underwood in collaboration with Myres S. McDougal, "The Lawfulness of United States Assistance to the Republic of Vietnam," *Congressional Record*, 89th Cong., 2nd Sess. (July 13, 1966), 112: 15518–67, introduced by Long. Senator Jacob Javits, Republican of New York, earlier entered selected excerpts of the lengthy brief into the record. *Congressional Record*, 89th Cong., 2nd Sess. (June 22, 1966), 112: 13870–74. The full text, minus the mate-

rial on the lawfulness of United States assistance under domestic constitutional processes, was republished as John Norton Moore and James L. Underwood, "The Lawfulness of United States Assistance to the Republic of Viet Nam," *Duquesne University Law Review* 5, no. 3 (1966–1967): 235–352. A shorter version was published as John Norton Moore, "The Lawfulness of Military Assistance to the Republic of Viet-Nam," *American Journal of International Law* 61, no. 1 (January 1967): 1–34.

37. Gibbons, *The U.S. Government and the Vietnam War*, 4: 246n96.

38. Cited in Lippman, "Vietnam," 347.

39. Gibbons, *The U.S. Government and the Vietnam War*, 4: 246–47n96; Lippman, "Vietnam," 347.

40. Eberhard P. Deutsch, "The Legality of the United States Position in Vietnam," *American Bar Association Journal* 52, no. 5 (May 1966): 436–42.

41. Deutsch, "The Legality of the United States Position in Vietnam," 442.

42. See, for example, *New York Times*, January 29, 1966, 1; *New York Times*, February 5, 1966, 6; *New York Times*, February 19, 1966, 3.

43. *New York Times*, February 5, 1966, 6.

44. *New York Times*, February 22, 1966, 1.

45. *New York Times*, March 10, 1966, 7.

46. *New York Times*, March 15, 1966, 3.

47. *Congressional Record*, 89th Cong., 2nd Sess. (February 9, 1966), 112: 2665.

48. Consultative Council of the Lawyers Committee on American Policy Towards Vietnam, *Vietnam and International Law: The Illegality of United States Military Involvement*, rapporteur John H. E. Fried (Flanders, NJ: O'Hare Books, 1967). An earlier version was widely circulated in manuscript form. Consultative Council of the Lawyers Committee on American Policy Towards Vietnam, "The Military Involvement of the United States in Vietnam: A Legal Analysis," October 1, 1966, https://vva.vietnam.ttu.edu/repositories/2/digital_objects/515729

49. Richard Falk, "Vietnam and International Law: The Past Recalled and the Future Challenged," in Consultative Council of the Lawyers Committee on American Policy Towards Vietnam, *Vietnam and International Law: An Analysis of International Law and the Use of Force, and the Precedent of Vietnam for Subsequent Interventions*, rapporteur John H. E. Fried (Northampton, MA: Aletheia Press, 1990), xii.

50. Stewart, "'A New Kind of War,'" 326, 329, 323.

51. Falk remains the key international legal voice on the legality of the US war in Vietnam. For a recent collection of his writings on the war, see Stefan Andersson, ed., *Revisiting the Vietnam War and International Law: Views and Interpretations of Richard Falk* (Cambridge: Cambridge University Press, 2018).

52. Crown, "The Saga of the Lawyers Committee on American Policy Towards Vietnam," 12; Weiss, "Nuclear War in the Courts," 183–85; Stewart, "'A New Kind of War,'" 329, 145.

53. For more on the Russell Tribunal, see Tor Krever's chapter in this volume.

54. Luke J. Stewart, "Too Loud to Rise Above the Silence: The United States vs. the International War Crimes Tribunal, 1966–1967," *The Sixties: A Journal of History, Politics and Culture* 11, no. 1 (2018): 17–45, esp. 19–20, 23, 31, 34.

55. Falk, "Vietnam and International Law: The Past Recalled and the Future Challenged," x; Stewart, "'A New Kind of War,'" 333.

56. Stewart, "'A New Kind of War,'" 11.

57. Mayda, "The Vietnam Conflict and International Law," 260.

58. Dean Rusk, "The Control of Force in International Relations," *Department of State Bulletin* 52, no. 1350 (May 10, 1965): 698.

59. Department of State, "Legal Basis for United States Actions Against North Viet-Nam," 145.

60. Department of State, "Legal Basis for United States Actions Against North Viet-Nam," 148.

61. Department of State, "Legal Basis for United States Actions Against North Viet-Nam," 146.

62. John Norton Moore, *Law and the Indo-China War* (Princeton: Princeton University Press, 1972), xxviii.

63. Lawyers Committee, "American Policy Vis-à-Vis Vietnam," 24904.

64. Lawyers Committee, "American Policy Vis-à-Vis Vietnam," 24905.

65. Lawyers Committee, "American Policy Vis-à-Vis Vietnam," 24905.

66. Lawyers Committee, "American Policy Vis-à-Vis Vietnam," 24907.

67. Lawyers Committee, "American Policy Vis-à-Vis Vietnam," 24905.

68. Lawyers Committee, "American Policy Vis-à-Vis Vietnam," 24907.

69. Lawyers Committee, "American Policy Vis-à-Vis Vietnam," 24905.

70. Lawyers Committee, "American Policy Vis-à-Vis Vietnam," 24908.

71. United States Senate Committee on Foreign Relations, *Hearings*, 568.

72. Meeker, "The Legality of United States Participation in the Defense of Viet-Nam," 474–75.

73. Meeker, "The Legality of United States Participation in the Defense of Viet-Nam," 476–79.

74. Meeker, "The Legality of United States Participation in the Defense of Viet-Nam," 480–81.

75. *Congressional Record*, 89th Cong., 2nd Sess. (February 23, 1966), 112: 3843.

76. Deutsch, "The Legality of the United States Position in Vietnam," 440.

77. John Norton Moore, "International Law and the United States Role in Viet Nam: A Reply," *Yale Law Journal* 76, no. 6 (May 1967): 1053.

78. Moyn, "From Antiwar Politics to Antitorture Politics," 172; *Congressional Record*, 89th Cong., 2nd Sess. (February 9, 1966), 112: 2665.

79. Richard Falk, "International Law and the United States Role in the Viet Nam War," *Yale Law Journal* 75, no. 7 (June 1966): 1139–40; see also 1134.

80. Falk and Moore were both acolytes of McDougal, the key figure in the policy-oriented approach of the New Haven school of international law.

81. Falk, "International Law and the United States Role in the Viet Nam War," 1146, 1155, 1139; Moore, "International Law and the United States Role in Viet Nam: A Reply," 1090.

82. Falk, "International Law and the United States Role in the Viet Nam War," 1122, 1135, 1159; Moore, "International Law and the United States Role in Viet Nam: A Reply," 1054.

83. John Norton Moore, ed., *Law and Civil War in the Modern World* (Baltimore: The Johns Hopkins University Press, 1974), xix–xx.

84. John Norton Moore, "The Arab-Israeli Conflict and the Obligation to Pursue Peaceful Settlement of International Disputes," *University of Kansas Law Review* 19, no. 3 (1970): 425.

85. Richard Falk, "Reply to Professor Julius Stone," *American Journal of International Law* 64, no. 1 (January 1970): 163.

86. Falk, "International Law and the United States Role in the Viet Nam War."

87. Richard Falk, "The Beirut Raid and the International Law of Retaliation," *American Journal of International Law* 63, no. 3 (July 1969): 415–43.

88. Moore, *Law and Civil War in the Modern World*, 22–23.

89. Lawyers Committee, "American Policy Vis-à-Vis Vietnam," 24906. Emphasis added.

90. Deutsch, "The Legality of the United States Position in Vietnam," 442.

91. *Congressional Record*, 89th Cong., 2nd Sess. (January 27, 1966), 112: 1312; *Congressional Record*, 89th Cong., 2nd Sess. (February 23, 1966), 112: 3843.

92. David Kennedy, *A World of Struggle: How Power, Law, and Expertise Shape Global Political Economy* (Princeton: Princeton University Press, 2016), 122.

93. Crown, "The Saga of the Lawyers Committee on American Policy Towards Vietnam," 6.

94. Harold Hongju Koh, "The Legal Adviser's Duty to Explain," *Yale Journal of International Law* 41 (2016): 189–211.

95. Lawyers Committee, "American Policy Vis-à-Vis Vietnam," 24904.

96. Stebenne, *Modern Republican*, 276. Duke did later revitalize its commitment to the study of the global rule of law but with an emphasis on the rule of law within countries rather than among them.

97. Barbara J. Keys, *Reclaiming American Virtue: The Human Rights Revolution of the 1970s* (Cambridge, MA: Harvard University Press, 2014); Samuel Moyn, *The Last Utopia: Human Rights in History* (Cambridge, MA: The Belknap Press of Harvard University Press, 2010).

98. National security law's military counterpart, operational law, was also part of this trend. See Craig Jones's chapter in this volume for more on the origins and development of operational law.

99. Peter Raven-Hansen, Stephen Dycus, and William C. Banks, "A Brief History of the Field of National Security Law," in *National Security Law: Fifty Years of Transformation: An Anthology*, ed. Jill D. Rhodes (Chicago: ABA Standing Committee on Law and National Security, 2012), 31.

100. Roberts, *Is International Law International?*, 50, 104–5.

101. John Norton Moore, "Law and National Security," *Foreign Affairs* 51, no. 2 (January 1973): 414. Moore served with both the State Department and the National Security Council at around the same time he wrote this article.

102. Eric Williamson, "Professor John Norton Moore, Former Ambassador for the Law of the Sea, to Retire," University of Virginia School of Law, January 27, 2020, https://www.law.virginia.edu/news/202001/professor-john-norton-moore-former-ambassador-law-sea-retire

103. John Norton Moore and Robert F. Turner, "The ABA Standing Committee on Law and National Security: Historic Player in the Creation and Development of the Field," in *National Security Law: Fifty Years of Transformation: An Anthology*, ed. Jill D. Rhodes (Chicago: ABA Standing Committee on Law and National Security, 2012).

104. Holly McMahon, "Reflections from the Core," in *National Security Law: Fifty Years of Transformation: An Anthology*, ed. Jill D. Rhodes (Chicago, IL: ABA Standing Committee on Law and National Security, 2012), vii.

105. Gibbons, *The U.S. Government and the Vietnam War*, 4: 247n96.

106. Eric Williamson, "The War-and-Peace Professor," University of Virginia School of Law, March 9, 2017, https://www.law.virginia.edu/news/201703/war-and -peace-professor

107. Consultative Council of the Lawyers Committee, *Vietnam and International Law*, 12–13.

108. Falk, *Public Intellectual*, 185.

109. Falk, *Public Intellectual*, 192–93, 190.

110. Falk, *Public Intellectual*, 194, 204. A meeting at the Pentagon prior to Falk's trip to North Vietnam also contributed to Falk's shift in attitude.

111. Falk, *Public Intellectual*, 199.

112. Telford Taylor, *Nuremberg and Vietnam: An American Tragedy* (Chicago: Quadrangle Books, 1970).

113. Falk, *Public Intellectual*, 200–201. See also Moyn, "From Antiwar Politics to Antitorture Politics," 177–81.

114. Falk, "Vietnam and International Law: The Past Recalled and the Future Challenged," xvi. See also Weiss, "Nuclear War in the Courts"; Falk, *Public Intellectual*, 199.

115. Richard Falk, "Foreword: Third World Approaches to International Law (TWAIL) Special Issue," *Third World Quarterly* 37 (2016): 1944; Madelaine Chiam, review of Stefan Andersson, ed., *Revisiting the Vietnam War and International Law: Views and Interpretations of Richard Falk*, H-Diplo, H-Net Reviews, December 2018, https://www.h-net.org/reviews/showpdf.php?id=52160

116. Falk, *Public Intellectual*, 192.

117. Falk, "Vietnam and International Law: The Past Recalled and the Future Challenged," xv.

118. Cited in John Quigley, *The Six-Day War and Israeli Self-Defense: Questioning the Legal Basis for Preventive War* (New York: Cambridge University Press, 2013), 135.

119. Falk, "Foreword: Third World Approaches to International Law (TWAIL) Special Issue," 1944. Emphasis in original.

120. John Norton Moore, ed., *The Arab-Israeli Conflict*, vol. 1, *Readings* (Princeton: Princeton University Press, 1974), 17.

121. John Norton Moore, ed., *The Arab-Israeli Conflict*, vol. 3, *Documents* (Princeton: Princeton University Press, 1974), vi–vii.

122. Moore, *The Arab-Israeli Conflict*, 1: 17.

123. Eric Williamson, "The War-and-Peace Professor."

124. John Norton Moore, "The Thirteenth Waldemar A. Solf and Marc L. Warren Chair Lecture in National Security Law: Defending Defense in the Law of *Jus ad Bellum*," *Military Law Review* 228 (2020): 418, 411.

125. Although note Crown's comment on Hans Morgenthau: "He originally declined to join the Consultative Council, feeling that lawyers could make little contribution towards halting the war. As the Lawyers Committee's activities came into the public eye, he asked to join and thereafter played a vigorous role, particularly in the news conferences sponsored by the Committee." Crown, "The Saga of the Lawyers Committee on American Policy Towards Vietnam," 11.

FOUR

Legality of Military Action by Egypt and Syria in October 1973

John Quigley

In the early 1970s, the United States faced delicate issues on use of force for its military action in Vietnam. The United States exited Vietnam early in 1973 only to confront new use of force issues a few months later in the Middle East. Israel in 1967 had invaded Egypt, then, almost immediately, Jordan and Syria. The United States, which regarded Israel as a virtual ally, had kept the Security Council of the United Nations from condemning Israel in 1967 despite credible claims of aggression by the three Arab countries. In the Autumn of 1973, within months of the US departure from Vietnam, Egypt and Syria sought to regain their territory, an action that raised an issue of the legality of use of force. Having just extracted itself from a military action that brought considerable international condemnation, the United States found itself protecting Israel in the face of international sentiment that favored Egypt and Syria.

With the hostilities in both Vietnam and the Middle East, serious discussion of the legalities in the Security Council never took place. The United States, using its position as a veto-wielding permanent member of the Security Council, was able to orient discussion away from legalities. In both situations—whether in regard to its own actions in Vietnam or Israel's actions in the Middle East—the United States was on thin ice from the standpoint of international legality. Both situations involved protection of national territory from outside military action. The United States had inserted itself militarily in Vietnam into what was widely regarded as a domestic civil war. Israel had seized territory of Egypt and Syria in military action that amounted to aggression, and the two Arab nations were seeking to recapture their territory. The United States had every interest in keeping the Security Council from examining the legality of Egypt and Syria's action. Its own effort to cover for Israel in 1967 could be exposed, and parallels to the legality of its own actions in Vietnam would have been aired.

For the United States, a common element was that it sought to forestall difficulties with the Soviet Union. The Soviet Union had scored major Cold War points against the United States with scathing condemnation of the United States for aggression against Vietnam. Israel's occupation of Egyptian and Syrian territory in 1967 had similarly brought a charge of aggression by the Soviet Union against Israel. Israel's continuing occupation of Egyptian and Syrian territory was similarly the target of a Soviet charge of aggression. The international context of the era was unfavorable to the United States. New states emerging from colonialism were changing the composition of the United Nations, putting the United States on the defensive with respect both to Vietnam and to the Middle East.

This chapter focuses on the 1973 Middle East episode—on the actions of Syria and Egypt to regain their territory, and on diplomatic efforts by the United States to deflect criticism of Israel and to manage its own relations with the Soviet Union.[1]

The hostilities that pitted Syria and Egypt against Israel in 1973 were raised in the Security Council of the United Nations, with Syria and Egypt on the one side and Israel on the other each claiming to be in the right. The Security Council engaged in no fact-finding. Nor did the members of the Security Council engage in serious polemics over legalities. Their orientation was to achieve a cease-fire and, beyond that, to ensure that such hostilities not recur.

The issue of legality in the situation could be framed in two different ways. A cease-fire between the parties had been mandated by the Security Council in 1967, after the hostilities that occurred in June of that year.[2] Initiation of force by either side would constitute a violation of that cease-fire. Under the Charter of the United Nations, decisions of the Security Council are binding on member states. All three states were members of the United Nations.

More broadly, the initiation of force could constitute aggression, which is also prohibited by the Charter of the United Nations. Analysis of that matter inevitably takes one back to the 1967 hostilities, which left Israel in occupation of Syria's Golan Heights and of Egypt's Sinai Peninsula, thus setting the stage for those of 1973, which were carried out in those two sectors. If Israel were the initiator of force in 1973, Israel would be the aggressor. If Syria and Egypt were the initiators of force in 1973, they would potentially have open to them an argument that they were seeking merely to reverse action of Israel in 1967, which, by the analysis of Syria and Egypt, was unlawful on Israel's part.

The Security Council, moreover, has a role under the Charter to protect the peace. States that are threatened with aggression are to seek its aid. Once peace has been broken, the Security Council is to determine what is required to restore it and to ensure against recurrence. The Security Council was at the center of action in both the 1967 and 1973 hostilities. It was engaged in efforts at peace, which continued between 1967 and 1973. Its fulfilment of that role is thus a relevant circumstance in analyzing the actions of the three states.

The issue of legality in relation to the use of force in 1973 thus requires an appreciation of the background dating back to 1967. This chapter will first recount the actions of the parties and of the Security Council, to allow an analysis of the violation *vel non* of the rules on use of force.

Arriving at a solidly based assessment is complicated by the fact that, at least in the Charter era, one is hard pressed to find precedents. Force has been used by states with respect to territory that is disputed between them, but that was not the situation in 1973. Israel did not claim sovereignty over the Sinai Peninsula or the Golan Heights. In 1981, Israel would adopt a law that applied its own legislation to the Golan Heights, a measure that came close to asserting sovereignty.[3] But this had not occurred as of 1973.

Israel Committed Aggression in 1967

It is a matter of dispute whether the 1973 hostilities qualify as a war. One analyst considers them merely a phase "in the course of a single ongoing war that had commenced in June 1967."[4] The hostilities that began in June 1967 had, to be sure, not been resolved by any treaty of peace by 1973. One author who thought Israel justified in its actions in June 1967 found its occupation of Egyptian and Syrian territory lawful as of 1973 on the rationale that the Arab states were declining to negotiate treaties of peace with Israel.[5] The 1973 hostilities took place in the context of a belligerent occupation that began in 1967, and hence relate back to the 1967 war. They are not a separate war.

Analysis of the 1973 hostilities must begin with the 1967 hostilities, to ascertain whether Israel came into occupation lawfully. Even if it did so, it can then be asked whether it was justified in continuing in occupation to the year 1973. If it acted unlawfully in 1967, its rationale for a long-term occupation is undermined.

Another element in the equation is the action of the Security Council of the United Nations. All the states involved were members of the United Nations, and under its Charter the Security Council is to deal with breaches of international peace. The contending states thus may have had obligations toward the United Nations. In 1967, the Security Council had called for cease-fires among the contending parties.[6] Those cease-fires remained in effect in 1973.

Those cease-fires were ordered after hostilities broke out on June 5, 1967, initially between Egypt and Israel. Hostilities between Israel and Syria followed on June 8, 1967. It was these two episodes of hostilities that led to Israel's occupation of Egypt's Sinai Peninsula and Syria's Golan Heights, occupations that in both instances continued in 1973.

On June 5, 1967, Israel and Egypt each claimed that the other had initiated the hostilities that began that morning. Israel, in a written message to the Security Council, claimed "that Egyptian land and air forces have moved against Israel and Israel forces are now engaged in repelling the Egyptian forces."[7] Egypt, in a written message of its own, claimed that "Israel has committed a treacherous premeditated aggression" and explained that "in repelling this aggression" it "ha[d] decided to defend itself by all means, in accordance with Article 51 of the Charter of the United Nations."[8]

When the Security Council convened, Israel gave details:

In the early hours of this morning Egyptian armoured columns moved in an offensive thrust against Israel's borders. At the same time Egyptian planes took off from airfields in Sinai and struck out towards Israel. Egyptian artillery in the Gaza Strip shelled the Israel villages of Kisufim, Nahal-Oz and Ein Hashelosha. Netania and Kefar Yavetz have also been bombed. Israel forces engaged the Egyptians in the air and on land, and fighting is still going on.

Like Egypt, Israel invoked UN Charter Article 51 to claim self-defense against an initial use of force.[9]

Elaborating on its charge of aggression committed by Egypt, Israel claimed that "approaching Egyptian aircraft appeared on our radar screens."[10] On that point, Israel asserted that Egyptian fighter jets "took off for their assigned targets in Israel, while at the same time an artillery barrage on Israel farming villages was opened from the Gaza Strip."[11] Egypt denied the truth of these claims.[12]

No Egyptian troops entered Israel, but Israeli troops entered Egypt's Sinai Peninsula, attacking Egyptian positions near the Egypt-Israel frontier, and pushing the Egyptian forces back. Three days into the fighting, Israeli troops entered Syria's Golan Heights, pushing Syrian forces out. Syria charged Israel with aggression.[13]

On June 6, the Security Council "called upon the governments concerned as a first step to take forthwith all measures for an immediate cease fire and for a cessation of all military activities in the area."[14] That resolution was criticized, however, by the Soviet Union, which said that withdrawal by Israel should also have been sought. It charged Israel with aggression.[15] Several Security Council members said it would be unproductive to focus on aggression by any of the parties to the conflict.[16]

On June 9, Syria told the Security Council that Israel was attacking into its territory through the Golan Heights. It charged Israel with aggression.[17]

The Soviet Union put forward a draft resolution to condemn Israel for aggression against Egypt and Syria.[18] Bulgaria, India, and Mali voted along with it in favor. The other eleven states abstained.[19] No abstaining member state suggested that Israel had acted lawfully, or that Egypt or Syria had not.

In the UN General Assembly, which held an emergency special session on the situation beginning June 17, 1967, Israel repeated its claim that Egypt initiated the hostilities. "[O]n the fateful morning of 5 June," Israel said, "Egyptian forces moved by air and land against Israel's western coast and southern territory."[20] Egypt again denied starting the hostilities, and the Soviet Union tabled a resolution to condemn Israel for aggression.[21]

As in the Security Council, no state backed Israel on its charge of aggression by Egypt. No investigation into the conflicting claims was being ordered, a failing that Spain thought to be a "grave mistake." Spain noted Israel's rapid troop advance into the Sinai as being inconsistent with Israel's claim that Egypt began the hostilities.[22] India said the same. It thought "that Israel struck the first blow," leaving Israel only the possibility of arguing that prior acts by Egypt short of war during the month of May 1967 might suffice to allow Israel to attack first. But, said India, "The concept of a pre-emptive strike or a preventive war is contrary to the letter and spirit of the United Nations Charter."[23] Zambia thought that if Israel felt threatened by Egypt, its recourse was to the United Nations, by which it meant to the Security Council.[24]

Although Israel had not used anticipatory self-defense as a justification, Cyprus, like India, addressed that potential issue. "No degree of military preparation by a neighbouring State, however alarming, can afford justification for the use of 'anticipatory force,'" it said.[25] Cyprus characterized Israel's conduct as "aggression: co-ordinated armed attack by air and land."[26]

When a vote was taken on the Soviet draft resolution, 36 states voted in favor, 57 voted against, and 23 abstained.[27] No state, however, said that Israel was justified. Some said that the facts had not been clarified, while others thought it better to find an overall solution to the longstanding Arab-Israeli conflict.

That was the approach taken by the Security Council when it reconvened on the issue in November 1967. Resolution 242, which it adopted, envisaged a settlement of the conflict. Resolution 242 anticipated in that connection that Israel would withdraw from the territory it occupied in June 1967. In a preamble clause that also concerned the June 1967 hostilities, Resolution 242 referred to "the inadmissibility of the acquisition of territory by war."[28] That clause, by using the term "acquisition," addressed the issue of whether Israel could claim sovereignty. The clause meant that it could not. But neither that clause nor any other provision of Resolution 242 addressed the question of whether Israel's occupations were lawful pending treaties of peace.

Even before that Security Council action in November 1967, Israel abandoned its claim that Egypt began the June 1967 hostilities. On July 7, 1967, Israeli prime minister Levi Eshkol said that once Egypt drew troops up to the Israel-Egypt frontier, as it had done in May 1967, and once it announced a plan to block shipping to Israel through the Straits of Tiran, the only issue for Israel was whether it would act "today or tomorrow."[29] In this interview about the June 1967 hostilities, Eshkol made no mention of any offensive acts by Egypt on the morning of June 5.

Eshkol's statement was taken as an acknowledgment that Israel had begun the hostilities, hence that its statements in the Security Council and General Assembly were disingenuous. France's *Le Monde* newspaper, referring to Eshkol's omission of any mention of initial acts by Egypt on the morning of June 5, wrote, "The fiction of the prior land or air attack by the Egyptian forces thus seems definitively abandoned in favor of the thesis asserted already many times that a state of war dates from the day Colonel Nasser imposed a blockade of the Straits of Tiran."[30] According to *The Times* (London), Eshkol, by his statement, "buried the often-repeated statement that Egyptian [air] and land forces attacked Israel before she launched her devastating lightning offensive on June 5."[31]

From that time, Israeli officials stopped claiming any precipitating military action by Egypt. But they did not embrace Eshkol's view that Israel's attack on Egypt was justified by Egypt's planned closure of passage through the Straits of Tiran. Shabtai Rosenne, who earlier served as legal advisor to Israel's foreign ministry and who, during the June 1967 hostilities, was Israel's deputy UN permanent representative, said that Israel was justified because Egypt had been about to attack, and that an attack in anticipation of one by an adversary was lawful. Rosenne claimed there had been a "real and urgent threat posed to Israel's very existence by the massed armies of her immediate neighbors, backed by all the other Arab states."[32]

But Itzhak Rabin, who served as chief of staff during the 1967 hostilities and was involved in the decision to attack Egypt, said that Israel's cabinet, which had voted to invade Egypt, understood that Egypt was not going to invade Israel.[33] In 1972, that assessment was confirmed by Mordecai Bentov, who served in Israel's cabinet as a government minister in 1967. Bentov said that a "story" about an expected Egyptian invasion was "invented" after the fact.[34]

Efforts by Syria and Egypt to Regain Their Territory

Hostilities ended on June 10, 1967, but thereafter not all was calm. The cease-fires called for by the Security Council in June 1967 worked to the advantage of Israel, as they left it in control of the territories it occupied in June 1967. In November 1967, Gunnar Jarring had been appointed by UN Secretary-General U Thant as his special representative to attempt to achieve peace on the basis of Security Council Resolution 242. Jarring's mission gained little traction, however. Over the next few years, attacks back and forth took place between Israel and Egypt in and across the Suez Canal. Those hostilities intensified in 1969 and finally were ended by a cease-fire between the two, signed on August 7, 1970.[35] International sentiment lay with Egypt and Syria. The UN General Assembly adopted a resolution "deploring the continued occupation of the Arab territories since 5 June 1967" and calling for a settlement based on Security Council Resolution 242.[36]

From 1970, the issue of Israel's occupations moved into the diplomatic realm. Jarring's efforts were unsuccessful, however, as he could not convince Israel to withdraw from any of the territory it occupied in 1967, and in particular from the Golan Heights or Sinai Peninsula. In negotiations with Egypt and Israel, Jarring sought a peace treaty in which Israel would vacate the Sinai Peninsula. But, as he reported to Secretary-General Thant, "Israel would not withdraw to the pre-5 June 1967 lines" as part of a potential peace treaty.[37] Jarring appealed to Israel to make such a commitment, but Israel declined to do so.[38] Considering that this refusal by Israel was the source of the "deadlock" in Jarring's efforts, Thant entreated Israel to reconsider. "I appeal, therefore," he said in his report on the situation, "to the Government of Israel to give further consideration to this question and to respond favourably to Ambassador Jarring's initiative."[39]

Israel did not reconsider. In 1973, the failure of the Jarring mission was acknowledged by Kurt Waldheim, who by then had replaced U Thant as secretary-general.[40] This failure prompted a group of nonaligned states— Guinea, India, Indonesia, Panama, Peru, Sudan, and Yugoslavia—to propose a draft resolution in the Security Council to urge a continuation of the secretary-general's efforts. At the same time, the draft resolution would have put the onus on Israel for the lack of progress. The draft recited, inter alia, that the Security Council

2. Strongly deplores Israel's continuing occupation of the territories occupied as a result of the 1967 conflict, contrary to the principles of the Charter
3. Expresses serious concern at Israel's lack of co-operation with the Special Representative of the Secretary-General

As the Security Council met on the draft resolution, Syria referred to Israel as the aggressor.[41] Egypt, referring to 1967, said,

We came to this Council in 1967, asking for what we thought—and still think—was right: an order for unconditional, immediate and total withdrawal of the forces of aggression that had invaded our lands. . . .[42]

Israel insisted that its occupation was appropriate, on the rationale that Israel was repelling Egypt as the aggressor:

For 25 years Israel has been subjected to aggression by the Arab States, with Egypt at their head. Today we have finally succeeded in repelling the aggressor, in pushing back its armies. Are we to turn the wheels of history back and restore the situation of vulnerability and chaos which invited the Arab Governments to resist peace, to continue illegitimate warfare against us for two and a half decades?[43]

Javier Perez de Cuellar, then the representative of Peru in the Security Council, explained that Peru cosponsored the draft resolution, with its language deploring the continuing occupation, in light of "the Council's responsibility for the preservation of international peace and security."[44] Perez de Cuellar thus acknowledged the failure of the Security Council to carry out its obligation to secure the peace and of Israel's continuing occupation as being inconsistent with peace.

This draft resolution was put to a vote and secured the affirmative votes of 13 of the Security Council's 15 members. The United States cast the lone negative vote, which, under Security Council procedures, constituted a veto.[45]

October 6, 1973

The hostilities that began on October 6, 1973, were immediately brought to the attention of the United Nations by Syria and Egypt. Syria claimed "that the Israeli armed forces have launched aggression against Syrian forward positions all along the cease-fire line. Our forces had to return the fire."[46] Egypt sent a letter claiming aggression by Israel:

> Israeli air formations attacked Egyptian forces stationed in the areas of El Zaafarana and El Sukhna on the Gulf of Suez, while Israeli naval units were approaching the Western Coast of the Gulf of Suez from the Egyptian territory of Sinai occupied by Israel as a result of the war it launched on 5 June 1967. Egyptian forces are at present engaged in military operations against the Israeli forces of aggression in the occupied territories.[47]

Syria and Egypt highlighted the fact that the Security Council had failed to compel Israel to withdraw from territory it had occupied since 1967. Syria complained that the Security Council was not fulfilling its function. "[O]ur organization," said Syria, referring to the United Nations, "is paralysed by the improper use of the right of veto." It said, "this veto has been utilized against justice and logic and against the will of 13 members of the Security Council."[48] That was a reference to the defeat of the draft resolution by veto of the United States on July 26, 1973.

Egypt noted that the United States was mentioning the cease-fires of 1967 as precluding use of force by any of the parties. Egypt questioned the validity of those cease-fires. It noted that Resolution 233 of June 6, 1967, "calls upon the Governments concerned to take forthwith as a first step all measures for an immediate cease-fire." Egypt noted further that Resolution 234 of June 7, 1967, demanded "that the governments concerned should as a first step cease fire." But "what was supposed to be a first step remained until it was really almost a permission and licence for the occupation of these lands."[49]

Israel's record of false claims led US officials to suspect that it had started the hostilities. James Schlesinger, who had recently served in Washington as director of the Central Intelligence Agency, and who had taken over as secretary of defense, told colleagues at the White House, "if the Israelis didn't start it it's the first time in 20 years."[50] Roy Atherton, deputy assistant secretary of state for Near Eastern and South Asian Affairs, referring to Israel's thrust into Syria in 1967, feared that "the Israelis may try to take Damascus this time."[51]

In actuality, it was the Syrian and Egyptian forces that initiated the hostilities.[52] Egypt had been planning an attack for several weeks and had drawn Syria into this effort.[53] Syria moved into portions of its Golan Heights, and Egypt crossed the Suez Canal, taking up positions Israel had held on the eastern bank of the canal.[54] The United Nations Truce Supervision Organization (UNTSO), which maintained personnel in both sectors, reported on the outbreak to the secretary-general on the afternoon of October 6, 1973:

> General heavy air and ground activity continues along all sectors. Egyptian ground forces have crossed the Suez Canal. . . . Syrian forces have crossed the area between the limits of the forward defended localities indicating the cease-fire lines in the vicinity of Kuneitra and near OP [Observation Post] November.[55]

These actions meant military activity across cease-fire lines. UNTSO informed the secretary-general: "In the field, the Chief of Staff of UNTSO addressed an appeal to the parties to cease all military activity and adhere strictly to the cease-fire."[56]

As the White House conferees charted what reaction Washington should make, they tried to guess at the public reaction in the United States to the hostilities. Atherton noted, "A lot of sympathy is with Egypt and Syria over what is seen as their patience over the last six years."[57] Kenneth Rush, deputy secretary of state, replied that "a lot of people in this country think that the first strike in 1967 was by the Arabs and the Israelis were defending themselves." Understanding that this perception was false, Rush thought that the public might sympathize with Israel.[58]

Secretary of State Henry Kissinger surmised, correctly, that Egypt and Syria had initiated the fighting, but at the same time said that the United States was using "maximum influence with the Israelis to show restraint."[59] When Kissinger consulted Soviet ambassador Anatolii Dobrynin on how to deal with the hostilities, Dobrynin told Kissinger "that the Arabs are trying to regain the lands occupied by Israel." Said Dobrynin, "for us to tell them you cannot free your land, it is ridiculous."[60]

Kissinger consulted with Israel's chargé d'affaires in Washington, Mordechai Shalev, who asked Kissinger to keep the hostilities from being discussed in either the Security Council or General Assembly for at least a few days. Shalev said he expected Israel to be in "a position of attack rather than defense" by that time, so it could withstand a cease-fire resolution without losing territory. Kissinger agreed.[61] He knew that the United States would be isolated at the United Nations in its support for Israel.[62] If the General Assembly were to take up the hostilities, feared Kissinger, that "would have meant a diatribe of the nonaligned in support of the extreme Arab position." Even the Security Council presented risks for Kissinger, because a pro-Arab resolution could be introduced, "forcing us to veto and undermining our position with the Arab moderates."[63] The United States was already on shaky footing with the Third World because of its military action in Vietnam and could ill afford more hostility.

Kissinger told President Richard Nixon that he had maneuvered to avoid a full debate in the UN General Assembly, saying it "would have been a massacre," meaning that members would have supported Egypt and Syria.[64] Kissinger's aim was to gain restoration of the cease-fire lines, which would keep Egypt and Syria from making any gains back into their territories. "The Arabs will scream that they are being deprived of their birthright," said Kissinger at a White House meeting.[65] Kissinger thus anticipated that the view of Egypt and Syria would be that they were taking back their own territory. Such a posture on the part of Egypt and Syria might be uncomfortable for the United States, which was trying to depict the Democratic Republic of Vietnam (DRV, or North Vietnam) as an aggressor against the Republic of Vietnam (RVN, or South Vietnam). The DRV, of course, regarded Vietnam as a single country and viewed its military action as being aimed at taking its own territory. Vietnam had emerged from French control in 1954 as a single state even though its territory was under two competing administrations. Vietnam was regarded as a single state both by the DRV authorities headquartered in Hanoi and by the RVN authorities headquartered in Saigon.

The United States had managed to keep the Security Council from undertaking any serious discussion of the propriety of its military intervention in Vietnam. A full-scale debate in the Security Council of Egypt's effort to retake its territory would have put *jus ad bellum* issues onto the front pages of the world's newspapers. For the United States, it was "the less said the better" as to what constituted aggression and what constituted self-defense. The United States was in jeopardy of being seen as legally responsible in each situation—in Vietnam for inserting itself in a civil conflict and in the Middle East for having covered up for Israel's 1967 aggression.

Even an embarrassing similarity in the tactics used to rationalize military action might have been exposed. In 1964, the United States falsely claimed an attack on one of its military vessels in the Gulf of Tonkin, off the Vietnamese coast, to initiate major military action in Vietnam.[66] In 1967, Israel did something similar by falsely claiming that Egypt had attacked the three Israeli settlements. In neither case had the pretense been widely revealed by 1973 within the international community. Had the Security Council undertaken serious legal analysis of the 1973 situation, a finger might be pointed at the United States for relying on manipulated facts to justify aggression.

On the ground, Egypt and Syria initially made advances against the occupying Israeli forces. Syrian troops retook a portion of the Golan Heights. Egyptian troops successfully crossed the Suez Canal and penetrated defensive installations (Bar-Lev line) that the Israeli forces had set up to thwart such an advance from the Egyptian side. Israeli forces then counterattacked, however, retaking the entirety of the Golan Heights and advancing deeper into Syria. Israeli forces managed to reclaim the territory on the eastern side of the Suez Canal and then to cross over to the western side.[67] The United States airlifted massive quantities of armaments to Israel.

Jordan stayed out of the hostilities, even though it, like Egypt and Syria, had lost territory to Israel in 1967. Egypt tried unsuccessfully to convince Jordan to open a third front against Israel on Israel's eastern side. Jordan eventually did deploy forces on the Golan Heights front. Egypt gained help from the Palestine Liberation Organization, which carried out attacks to disrupt Israel's resupply efforts.[68]

On October 22, 1973, the Security Council adopted Resolution 338, in which it called for a cease-fire in place. Fighting continued, however. A Disengagement Agreement between Israel and Egypt was reached only on January 18, 1974,[69] and one between Israel and Syria on May 31, 1974.[70] Egypt kept control of a strip of territory on the eastern side of the Suez Canal. Israel was left in control of the Golan Heights.

Use of Force to Recapture Occupied Territory

Egypt's aim in initiating hostilities against Israel in October 1973 was short of recapturing the territory held by Israel. Kissinger later wrote:

> Sadat aimed not for territorial gain but for a crisis that would alter the attitudes into which the parties were frozen—and thereby open the way for negotiations.[71]

The assessment by the US Central Intelligence Agency had been that Egypt would not try to send troops across the Suez Canal because Egypt's forces would not have the wherewithal to advance far into Sinai.[72] Egyptian president Anwar Sadat communicated with the United States during the fighting.[73] This effort by Egypt was taken by Kissinger to indicate that Egypt was seeking by its action to spur diplomacy rather than take the Sinai militarily.[74]

Egypt coordinated with Syria to coordinate a strike against Israel, thereby forcing Israel to defend from two directions.[75] Egypt did not anticipate that it could drive Israel out of the Sinai Peninsula, though it might be able to take and hold at least some Sinai territory. Doing so might invigorate the diplomatic process. Even though Egypt's military aims may have been modest, it was using military means. That requires an assessment of the legality of those means.

Syria and Egypt were attacking into their own territory that was under foreign occupation. Their use of force must be analyzed in that context. The issue of whether a state that has been invaded may use force to recapture its own territory may seem so obvious a solution as not needing to be asked.

A state that is invaded enjoys a right of self-defense.[76] That right does not dissipate with passage of time. Even apart from the right of the invaded state to recapture occupied territory, one finds in the law the right of the population of the occupied territory. In the situation in which the entirety of a state's territory is occupied, leaving that state with no government, the population is entitled to use force, within the bounds of humanitarian law, to recapture the territory. If personnel of the occupied population are captured by the occupying power in the course of such efforts, those personnel are entitled to be treated as prisoners of war, rather than as criminals.[77] If the population of occupied territory has a right to resist being occupied by force of arms, it must a fortiori be the case that if the occupied state still has a government with military capability, that government enjoys the same right.

Even if Egypt's aim was short of a recapture by military force of the Sinai Peninsula, and even if Syria's aim was short of a recapture by military force of the Golan Heights, their actions involved a use of force into territory of their own that was under belligerent occupation. And even though Egypt and Syria claimed an initiation of use of force by Israel, they both considered themselves within their rights to take military action to recapture their territory. Thus Syria, in the Security Council on October 9, 1973, stated: "Our goal can be none other than to recover usurped Arab territory." Responding to Israel's call for a return to positions held before October 6, 1973, Syria said "such positions happen to be in our national territory. And the fight we are waging now, and which was provoked by the Israeli attack, cannot be qualified as anything other than a national liberation fight, which is in conformity with the principles of the United Nations and in accordance with the norms of international law."[78]

Egypt, referring to Israel's claim of aggression against both Egypt and Syria, replied:

> The exercise of our right of self-defence is labelled aggression committed by Egypt and Syria. The representative of Israel has been hammering away on that point and constantly repeats it, imagining that he will be believed. Egypt and Syria are defending themselves. We are not in Israeli territory; we are on our territory, our national territory.[79]

Egypt depicted Israel's 1967 aggression as of a continuing character: "The Arab people have been the victim of aggression since 1967, not the aggressors."[80]

Yugoslavia pointed to a then recent declaration in support of Egypt and Syria by the Conference of Heads of State or Government of the Non-aligned Countries, which had met in Algiers a few weeks earlier.[81] The Conference adopted a resolution in which it stated that it

> Demands the immediate and unconditional evacuation by the Israeli forces of all Arab territories occupied since June 1967
>
> Reaffirms its total and effective support to the lawful efforts of Egypt, Syria and Jordan in their lawful struggle to regain, by all means, all their occupied territories.[82]

The Need to Utilize the Security Council

Article 51 of the Charter of the United Nations may pose an obstacle, however, to a state seeking to recapture territory that is occupied. Article 51 subjects the right of self-defense to the role of the Security Council as protector of international peace. "Nothing in the present Charter," recites Article 51, "shall impair the inherent right of individual or collective self-defence if an armed attack occurs against a Member of the United Nations, until the Security Council has taken measures necessary to maintain international peace and security."

Article 51 imposes, moreover, an obligation on a state using force in self-defense to report that use of force to the Security Council. Following the sentence just quoted from Article 51 comes another:

> Measures taken by Members in the exercise of this right of self-defence shall be immediately reported to the Security Council and shall not in any way affect the authority and responsibility of the Security Council under the present Charter to take at any time such action as it deems necessary in order to maintain or restore international peace and security.

Article 51 is directed at use of force across international borders. In 1973, Egypt and Syria were seeking to enter their own territory. Hence the requirement of seeking help first from the Security Council did not apply. Even though they asserted that they were entitled to recapture their occupied territories, they claimed that these new hostilities were initiated by Israel. Egypt and Syria likely decided to take this approach because they did not want to be charged with violating the cease-fire resolutions of 1967. Violation of cease-fire resolutions, however, would not necessarily constitute a use of force in violation of UN Charter Article 2(4). A cease-fire can be ordered by the Security Council without regard to the underlying rights of the contending parties. Acceptance by parties of a cease-fire is not "a free decision by the parties that they will cease to exercise a right or a privilege to employ force."[83]

In the aftermath of the 1967 war, the Security Council merely called for a cease-fire. It did not even call for a withdrawal of forces to the positions they held prior to the onset of hostilities. So the Security Council as of 1973 had not undertaken the measures required under Charter Chapter VII.

The UN Charter puts the Security Council in the role of dealing with aggression. This is the thrust of Chapter VII of the Charter. But if the

Security Council does not assume that role in a particular situation, an invaded and occupied state has the right to act on its own.

In the Security Council in 1967, no state other than Israel called Syria or Egypt out for aggression. Most avoided the issue of legal liability. In 1973, the United Kingdom counseled against "engaging now in attempts to apportion blame or attribute responsibility. The ultimate verdict," it said, "may well be that the basic factor was the frustration of the international community in its efforts to bring about that just and lasting peace in the Middle East of which the promise was held out by Security Council resolution 242 (1967) nearly six years ago."[84]

India too averted to the failure of the Security Council:

> What Egypt and Syria are doing now is nothing more than upholding the provisions of the Charter in asserting their right to self-defence and to territorial integrity. This right is inherent to every sovereign State, and if Egypt and Syria have desisted from exercising this right it was because they had hoped that the Council would find a peaceful solution.[85]

The issue of use of force to retake territory occupied by aggression was never on the table in the Security Council. Each side accused the other of initiating the hostilities, and the members of the Security Council focused on finding a solution, not on assessing blame. The view of Ibrahim Shihata, expressed in 1974, remains accurate:

> With such an intransigent Israeli position, encouraged in fact by the near total support of the U.S. Government and by the acquiescence of most other Western powers, little choice was left for Arab states to regain control over their occupied territories. Egypt and Syria finally managed, in October 1973, to exercise their territorial jurisdiction by employing forcible measures limited respectively to Egyptian and Syrian territories and aimed solely at restoring control over such territories. Governmental action taken by a state within its own territory for the restoration of legal order disrupted by unauthorized acts of others certainly falls within the inherent territorial jurisdiction of each sovereign state.[86]

An argument that Israel had a right to remain in the territory it took in 1967, hence that the 1973 attack by Syria and Egypt was unlawful, was made by Eugene Rostow.[87] He based his argument on UN Security Council Resolution 242. Rostow read Resolution 242 as requiring Israel to withdraw from the Golan Heights and Sinai Peninsula only if the Arab states made peace with Israel.[88] By 1973 no Arab state had done so.

That argument ignores the fact that Resolution 242 was not adopted in UN Charter Chapter VII, rendering it a recommendation only. But even if it could be deemed a resolution legally binding the states concerned, Resolution 242, despite its ambiguity, did not condition an Israeli obligation to withdraw on acceptance of Israel by the Arab states. Resolution 242 did expressly call for Israel's withdrawal. Resolution 242's provision that Rostow viewed as quid pro quo for an Israeli withdrawal was too vague to be deemed to reflect a legal obligation. That clause spoke of the right of all states in the area to live in peace and for acknowledgment of their statehood.

Israel's reliance on Resolution 242 was, moreover, questionable as a basis for continuing to hold the Golan Heights and Sinai Peninsula, since Israel, as we saw, had not shown itself receptive to Jarring's efforts.[89]

Whatever might have been the intent behind Resolution 242, the 1973 membership of the Security Council, in the draft resolution that was defeated only by the U.S. veto, made clear that the legal obligation in the situation was that of Israel to withdraw.

The illogicality of Rostow's view is reflected in the way in which he characterized the hostilities. He called them "the Arab attack on Israel," which of course it was not. Egypt and Syria were attacking not into Israel but into their own territory.[90]

Nathan Feinberg argued that the action of Egypt and Syria could not be self-defense. But he reached that conclusion by arguing first that Israel had itself acted in self-defense in 1967.[91] He then said that even if Israel were deemed to have acted aggressively in 1967, the action of Egypt and Syria in 1973 would still not constitute self-defense because self-defense, under Charter Article 51, is available only until the Security Council acts. Feinberg said that the cease-fire resolutions of 1967 constituted such action. That view overlooked the Security Council's inaction for seven years in dealing with the consequences of the 1967 war. Hans Kelsen had cogently argued in 1950 that states could not be expected to forego self-help if the Security Council did not effectively exercise the monopoly in use of force that the Charter gave it. "If the constitution of an international organization abolishes or restricts the principle of self-help established by general international law," Kelsen wrote, it must guarantee . . . that, to the same extent the individual Member is deprived of its right of self-help, enforcement action of the Organisation will actually take place. Otherwise the Organisation constitutes, instead of an improvement, a dangerous deterioration of the legal status under general international law.[92]

Force to Recover Territory

Security Council Resolution 338 did not condemn Egypt or Syria for aggression. It did not even condemn them for violating the 1967 cease-fire. It merely called for a new cease-fire. The majority of members of the Security Council understood the situation of Egypt and Syria and declined to place the onus on them.

A state whose territory is occupied by military force has been deemed to enjoy a right to use military force in response. In 1950, the Security Council characterized the military action that broke out in Korea as an invasion of South Korea by North Korea. In response, the Security Council cited a request from South Korea (Republic of Korea) and called on UN member states "To assist the Republic of Korea in defending itself against armed attack."[93] South Korea thus was regarded as within its rights to use force to reverse the occupation of its territory.

In 1956, Israel invaded into Egypt and occupied Egyptian territory in the Sinai Peninsula. In the Security Council, the United States proposed a resolution that, as it explained, noted "the fact that is not disputed, namely, the fact of Israel military penetration deep into Egyptian territory, and the fact that this constitutes a violation of the Armistice Agreement." This was a reference to a cease-fire dating from 1949 between Israel and Egypt.[94] Yugoslavia, supporting the US draft resolution, characterized Israel's action against Egypt as "aggression."[95] So too did the Soviet Union.[96] It was this history of Israeli aggression against Egypt that led Secretary of Defense Schlesinger, as we saw, to surmise on October 6, 1973, albeit incorrectly, that it was Israel that initiated the hostilities that began on that day.

The United States, in its 1956 draft resolution, called for a withdrawal by Israel to the 1949 armistice lines. The United States titled its request for a Security Council resolution "Steps for the Immediate Cessation of the Military Action of Israel in Egypt."[97] The draft resolution did not call for a cease-fire. Rather it called on Israel to withdraw.[98] The draft resolution did not focus on action by Egypt in response to Israel's. But by its characterization of Israel's action, the draft resolution assumed that Egypt was within its rights to oppose by force the occupation by Israel of Egyptian territory. The US draft resolution gained seven votes in the Security Council, failing only because of the vetoes cast by the United Kingdom and France, both of which were party to Israel's invasion of Egypt.[99]

The Security Council would again deal with invasion and occupation in 1990, when Iraq invaded and occupied Kuwait. Responding, the Security Council affirmed "the inherent right to individual or collective self-defence, in response to the armed attack by Iraq against Kuwait, in accordance with Article 51 of the Charter."[100] When that occupation continued for three months, the Security Council adopted a resolution reaffirming the prior resolution and "Authoriz[ing] Member States co-operating with the Government of Kuwait" to enforce that prior resolution.[101] The latter resolution reads as a recognition of Kuwait's own right of self-defense and of its right, further, to seek assistance from other states under the concept of collective self-defense.[102] The Security Council thus regarded Kuwait, by virtue of its right of self-defense, as being entitled to use military force to recover its territory that had been occupied.

Conclusion

In the Korea situation, in the 1956 Sinai situation, and in the 1990 Kuwait situation, no cease-fire, to be sure, had been ordered by the Security Council. That fact is not, however, relevant to the right of an occupied state to use force to recover its territory. The quip of Ambassador Dobrynin perhaps best characterizes the approach that was taken by the international community, as represented by the Security Council, in reaction to the 1973 hostilities.

The situation in which Egypt and Syria found themselves was not unlike that of the DRV. In both instances, the United States was impeding control of a country's territory by supporting a party that was holding a sector. In Vietnam, France had withdrawn as the colonizing power in 1954 in favor of an indigenous administration. France, with United States backing, had put in place an administration based in the southern part of Vietnam. As a condition for its withdrawal, France required the DRV to withdraw forces from south of a line along the 17th parallel, below which its favored administration would have control.[103] An additional aspect of the withdrawal agreement was that a countrywide election would be held in 1956. Thus Vietnam was deemed by all parties to be a single country, but with two administrations for a two-year period.

The southern administration, the RVN, with an army it set up called the Army of the Republic of Vietnam, refused to hold the countrywide elections, at which point the DRV, along with allied forces south of the 17th parallel, undertook to take over the southern sector by force.[104] The DRV thus was in a posture similar to that of Egypt and Syria in that a sector of their territory was being held by force of arms. In each instance, the United States stood behind the party that was impeding control. In each instance, the United States kept the UN Security Council from condemning the party that was blocking the retaking of territory (Israel in the case of the 1973 war, the United States in the case of Vietnam). In each instance, the international community regarded the use of force as lawful, as an effort to retake territory being held, directly or indirectly, by a foreign element.

It is difficult to tell a state whose territory is occupied that it cannot recapture it, particularly if the Security Council has shown itself unable to deal with the situation. Here the Security Council, as result of a veto cast by the United States, had only two months earlier shown itself unable to adopt even a resolution condemning Israel's occupation, much less a resolution calling for international action to reverse the occupation. In these circumstances, one can only conclude that Egypt and Syria were justified in their action. If one state invades another and the Security Council calls for a cease-fire but does not effectively reverse the invasion, the victim state can hardly be required to sit on its hands in perpetuity.

NOTES

1. For an overview, see Ahmad Abu al-Ghayt, *Witness to War and Peace: Egypt, the October War, and Beyond* (Cairo: American University in Cairo Press, 2018).

2. UN Security Council Res. 234, June 7, 1967, UN Doc. S/RES/234.

3. Israel, Knesset, Golan Heights Law, December 14, 1981. In 2019, Israel would add Jewish habitation of the Golan in ancient times. UN Security Council, Verbatim Record March 27, 2019, 18, UN Doc. S/PV.8495. Victor Kattan, "US Recognition of Golan Heights Annexation: Testament to Our Times," *Journal of Palestine Studies* 48, no. 3 (Spring 2019): 79, 83.

4. Yoram Dinstein, *War, Aggression and Self-Defence* (New York: Cambridge University Press, 2017), 61.

5. Barry Feinstein, "Self-Defence and Israel in International Law: A Reappraisal," *Israel Law Review* 11 (1976): 562.

6. Resolutions 233, 234, 235, 236, June 1967.

7. UN Security Council, Verbatim Record June 5, 1967, 1, UN Doc. S/PV.1347.

8. UN Security Council, Verbatim Record June 5, 1967, 1, UN Doc. S/PV.1347.

9. UN Security Council, Verbatim Record June 5, 1967, 4, UN Doc. S/PV.1347.

10. UN Security Council, Verbatim Record June 6, 1967, 15, UN Doc. S/PV.1348.

11. UN Security Council Verbatim Record June 13, 1967, 21, UN Doc. S/PV.1358.

12. UN Security Council Verbatim Record June 13, 1967, 30, UN Doc. S/PV.1358.

13. UN Security Council Verbatim Record June 9, 1967, 13, UN Doc. S/PV.1352.

14. UN Security Council Res. 233, June 6, 1967, UN Doc. S/RES/233.

15. UN Security Council Verbatim Record June 6, 1967, 5–6, UN Doc. S/PV.1348.

16. UN Security Council Verbatim Record June 6, 1967, 6–7, UN Doc. S/PV.1348.

17. UN Security Council Verbatim Record June 9, 1967, 2–3, UN Doc. S/PV.1352.

18. UN Doc. S/7951/Rev.2. The draft also condemned Israel for aggression against Jordan.

19. UN Security Council Verbatim Record June 14, 1967, 18, UN Doc. S/PV.1360.

20. UN General Assembly Verbatim Record June 19, 1967, 12, UN Doc. A/PV.1526.

21. UN General Assembly Verbatim Record June 19, 1967, 6, UN Doc. A/PV.1526.

22. UN General Assembly Verbatim Record June 28, 1967, 9, UN Doc. A/PV.1539.

23. UN General Assembly Verbatim Record June 21, 1967, 15, UN Doc. A/PV.1530.

24. UN General Assembly Verbatim Record June 27, 1967, 9, UN Doc. A/PV.1538.

25. UN General Assembly Verbatim Record June 21, 1967, 6, UN Doc. A/PV.1530.

26. UN General Assembly Verbatim Record June 29, 1967, 7–8, UN Doc. A/PV.1541.

27. UN General Assembly Verbatim Record July 4, 1967, 15–16, UN Doc. A/PV.1548.

28. UN Security Council Res. 242, November 22, 1967, UN Doc. S/RES/242.

29. Ariyeh Tzimuki, "We will let the Vatican have some control over the holy places in Jerusalem," *Yediot aharonot* (Tel Aviv, July 7, 1967): 1.

30. "Une nouvelle interview de M. Eshkol fait apparaître l'existence de divergences entre le général Dayan et lui: Le premier ministre admet que les Israëlis ont tiré les premiers," *Le Monde* (Paris, July 9–10, 1967): 2.

31. "Admission on Attack," *Times* (London, July 8, 1967): 3.

32. Shabtai Rosenne, "Directions for a Middle East Settlement—Some Underlying Legal Problems," *Law and Contemporary Problems* 33 (1968): 55.

33. Eric Rouleau, "Le général Rabin ne pense pas que Nasser voulait la guerre," *Le Monde* (February 29, 1968): 1.

34. Mordecai Bentov, "For Whom and Why Are the Settlements Necessary?,"

Al-Hamishmar (Kibbutz Artzi, April 14, 1972): 3, translated in Amnon Kapeliouk, "Israël était-il réellement menacé d'extermination?" *Le Monde* (June 3, 1972): 4.

35. "Suez all quiet as Egypt, Israel cease fighting," *Boston Globe* (August 8, 1970): 1.

36. The Situation in the Middle East, UN General Assembly Res. 2628, November 4, 1970, UN Doc. A/RES/2628.

37. Further Report by the secretary-general on the activities of the special representative to the Middle East, March 5, 1971, UN Doc. S/10070/Add.2, ¶12.

38. Further Report by the secretary-general on the activities of the special representative to the Middle East, March 5, 1971, UN Doc. S/10070/Add.2, ¶14.

39. Further Report by the secretary-general on the activities of the special representative to the Middle East, March 5, 1971, UN Doc. S/10070/Add.2, ¶15.

40. Report of the secretary-general under Security Council Resolution 331 (1973) of April 20, 1973, May 18, 1973, 40, UN Doc. S/10929.

41. UN Security Council Verbatim Record July 26, 1973, 15, UN Doc. S/PV.1735.

42. UN Security Council Verbatim Record July 26, 1973, 3, UN Doc. S/PV.1735.

43. UN Security Council Verbatim Record July 26, 1973, 16, UN Doc. S/PV.1735.

44. UN Security Council Verbatim Record July 26, 1973, 14, UN Doc. S/PV.1735.

45. UN Security Council Verbatim Record July 26, 1973, 10, UN Doc. S/PV.1735. China did not participate in the vote.

46. Letter dated October 6, 1973 from the permanent representative of the Syrian Arab Republic to the United Nations addressed to the president of the Security Council, October 6, 1973, UN Doc. S/11009, Security Council Official Records, 28th Year, *Supplement for October, November and December 1973*: 70.

47. Letter dated October 6, 1973, from the Ministry for Foreign Affairs of Egypt to the president of the General Assembly, October 6, 1973, 1, UN Doc. A/9190.

48. UN Security Council Verbatim Record October 9, 1973, 5, UN Doc. S/PV.1744.

49. UN Security Council Verbatim Record, October 8, 1973, 4, UN Doc. S/PV.1743.

50. Minutes of Washington Special Actions Group Meeting, White House Situation Room, October 6, 1973, 9:01–10:06 a.m., *Foreign Relations of the United States 1969–1976* 25, 295 [hereinafter *FRUS*].

51. Minutes of Washington Special Actions Group Meeting, White House Situation Room, October 6, 1973, 9:01–10:06 a.m., *FRUS 1969–1976* 25, 303.

52. Mohammed Abdel Ghani El-Gamasy, *The October War* (Cairo: American University in Cairo Press, 1993), 191–92.

53. Mohamed Heikal, *The Road to Ramadan* (New York: Quadrangle/The New York Times Book Co., 1975), 18–35.

54. Memorandum from William B. Quandt and Donald Stukel of the National Security Council Staff to Secretary of State Kissinger, Washington, October 8, 1973, *FRUS 1969–1976* 25, 366.

55. Supplemental information received by the secretary-general on the situa-

tion in the Middle East, UN Doc. S/7930/Add.2141, October 6, 1973, Security Council Official Records, 28th Year, *Supplement for October, November and December 1973*: 3.

56. Supplemental information received by the secretary-general on the situation in the Middle East, UN Doc. S/7930/Add.2143, October 6, 1973, Security Council Official Records, 28th Year, *Supplement for October, November and December 1973*: 4.

57. Minutes of Washington Special Actions Group Meeting, Washington, October 6, 1973, 9:10–10:16 a.m., *FRUS 1969–1976* 25, 304.

58. Minutes of Washington Special Actions Group Meeting, Washington, October 6, 1973, 9:10–10:16 a.m., *FRUS 1969–1976* 25, 304.

59. Transcript of Telephone Conversation between Secretary of State Kissinger and the Soviet Ambassador (Dobrynin), October 6, 1973, 9:35 a.m., referencing an earlier telephone conversation between Kissinger and Dobrynin the same day at 9:20 a.m., *FRUS 1969–1976* 25, 308.

60. Transcript of Telephone Conversation between Secretary of State Kissinger and the Soviet Ambassador (Dobrynin), Washington, October 6, 1973, 7:20 p.m., *FRUS 1969–1976* 25, 319–20.

61. Memorandum of Conversation, US Department of State, Washington DC, October 7, 1973, *FRUS 1969–1976* 25, 341.

62. Transcript of Telephone Conversation between President Nixon and Secretary of State Kissinger, October 7, 1973, 10:18 a.m., *FRUS 1969–1976* 25, 345.

63. Henry Kissinger, *Years of Upheaval* (New York: Little, Brown, 1982), 471.

64. Transcript of Telephone Conversation between President Nixon and Secretary of State Kissinger, Washington, October 8, 1973, 2:35 p.m., *FRUS 1969–1976* 25, 373.

65. Minutes of Washington Special Actions Group Meeting, Washington, October 7, 1973, 6:06–7:06 p.m., *FRUS 1969–1976* 25, 357.

66. Robert Scheer, "Tonkin—Dubious Premise for War," *Los Angeles Times*, April 29, 1985: A1.

67. David Rodman, *Israel in the 1973 Yom Kippur War: Diplomacy, Battle, and Lessons* (Eastbourne, UK: Sussex Academic Press, 2017), 41.

68. Abdallah Frangi, *The PLO and Palestine* (London: Zed Books, 1983), 135. Shaul Bartal, "Yom Kippur War Influence at the Recognition and the Palestinian Problem," *History Research* 5, no. 4 (2015): 255, 258.

69. "Pullback Accord Signed: Kissinger, Sadat Turn to Syrians," *Washington Post*, January 19, 1974: A1. Letter dated January 18, 1974, from the secretary-general to the president of the Security Council: Annex: Egyptian-Israeli Agreement on disengagement of forces in pursuance of the Geneva Peace Conference, UN Doc. S/11198 (1974), Security Council Official Records, 29th Year, *Supplement for January, February and March 1974*: 84.

70. "Israel and Syria Accept Accord for Disengaging on Golan Front," *New York Times*, May 30, 1974, 1. Report of the secretary-general concerning the Agreement on Disengagement between Israeli and Syrian Forces, May 30, 1974, Annex I: Agreement on Disengagement between Israeli and Syrian forces, UN Doc. 11302/Add.1 (1974), Security Council Official Records, 29th Year, *Supplement for April, May and June 1974*: 144.

71. Kissinger, *Years of Upheaval*, 460.

72. Kissinger, *Years of Upheaval*, 461.

73. Backchannel Message from the Egyptian Presidential Adviser for National Security Affairs (Ismail) to Secretary of State Kissinger, Cairo, October 7, 1973, *FRUS 1969–1976* 25, 347.

74. Kissinger, *Years of Upheaval*, 482.

75. Hassan el Badri, Taha el Magdoub, Mohammed Dia el Din Zohdy, *The Ramadan War, 1973* (New York: Hippocrene Books, 1978), 16–18, 45.

76. UN Charter, art. 51.

77. *Law of Belligerent Occupation* (Ann Arbor, MI: Judge Advocate General's School, 1945), 102. Convention relative to the Treatment of Prisoners of War, August 12, 1949: art. 4(A), UNTS 75, 135.

78. UN Security Council Verbatim Record October 9, 1973, 7, UN Doc. S/PV.1744.

79. UN Security Council Verbatim Record October 11, 1973, 18, UN Doc. S/PV.1745.

80. UN Security Council Verbatim Record October 11, 1973, 18, UN Doc. S/PV.1745.

81. UN Security Council Verbatim Record October 9, 1973, 2, UN Doc. S/PV.1744.

82. Resolution on the Middle-East Situation and the Palestine Issue, NAC/ALG/CONF.4/F/Res,2, September 9, 1973, in Documents of the Conference of Heads of State or Government of Non-Aligned Countries, Algiers, 5 to 9 September 1973, reproduced in UN Doc. A/9330, November 22, 1973: 35.

83. R. R. Baxter, "Armistices and other Forms of Suspension of Hostilities," Académie de Droit International, *Recueil des Cours* 1976-I (Leyden: A. W. Sijthoff, 1977), 353, 384.

84. UN Security Council Verbatim Record October 8, 1973, 6, UN Doc. S/PV.1743.

85. UN Security Council Verbatim Record October 9, 1973, 15, UN Doc. S/PV.1744.

86. Ibrahim Shihata, "Destination Embargo of Arab Oil: Its Legality under International Law," *American Journal of International Law* 68 (1974): 591, 608.

87. Curiously, Eugene Rostow was the brother of Walter Rostow, who, as President Johnson's aide during the 1967 Middle East hostilities, was aware that Israel initiated hostilities using the pretext of an Egyptian attack on three Israeli settlements. Walworth Barbour, "Telegram From the Embassy in Israel to the Department of State, June 5, 1967," *Foreign Relations of the United States 1964–1968* 19, 302 note 1. Eugene Rostow himself was under secretary for political affairs during the 1967 hostilities, which were understood within the Department of State to have been initiated by Israel without legal justification. Dean Rusk, *As I Saw It* (New York: W. W. Norton, 1990), 386. Memorandum for the Record, November 17, 1968, *Foreign Relations of the United States 1964–1968* 19, 287.

88. Eugene Rostow, "The Illegality of the Arab Attack on Israel of October 6, 1973," *American Journal of International Law* 69 (1975): 272, 276–77.

89. Alfred Hotz, "Legal Dilemmas: The Arab-Israel Conflict," *South Dakota Law Review* 19 (1974): 242, 269.

90. Rostow, "The Illegality of the Arab Attack on Israel," 272.

91. Nathan Feinberg, "The Legality of the Use of Force to Recover Occupied Territory," *Israel Law Review* 15 (1980): 160, 171.

92. H. Kelsen, *The Law of the United Nations. A Critical Analysis of Its Fundamental Problems* (New York: Praeger, 1950), 270.

93. UN Security Council Res. 84, July 7, 1950, UN Doc. S/RES/84.

94. UN Security Council, Verbatim Record October 30, 1956, UN Doc. S/PV.749: 6.

95. UN Security Council, Verbatim Record October 30, 1956, UN Doc. S/PV.749: 7.

96. UN Security Council, Verbatim Record October 30, 1956, UN Doc. S/PV.749: 8.

97. Letter dated October 29, 1956, from the representative of the United States of America addressed to the president of the Security Council, UN Doc. S/3706, October 30, 1956.

98. United States of America, draft resolution, UN Doc. S/3710, October 30, 1956.

99. UN Security Council, Verbatim Record October 30, 1956, UN Doc. S/PV.749: 31.

100. UN Security Council Res. 661, August 6, 1990, UN Doc. S/RES/661.

101. UN Security Council Res. 678, November 29, 1990, UN Doc. S/RES/678.

102. Oscar Schachter, "United Nations Law in the Gulf Conflict," *American Journal of International Law* 85 (1991): 452, 459–60.

103. Mitchell K. Hall, *The Vietnam War* (New York: Routledge, 2018), 10–13.

104. Hall, *The Vietnam War*, 14–15.

FIVE

Revolutionary War and the Development of International Humanitarian Law

Amanda Alexander

The distinction between civilians and combatants and the protection of civilians are perhaps the central precepts of international humanitarian law today. In the International Committee of the Red Cross' (ICRC) list of customary rules of IHL, the principle of distinction is Rule 1.[1] In Rule 4 combatants are defined as members of the armed forces and in Rule 5 civilians are defined as those who are not members of the armed forces.[2] Under Rule 106, combatants must identify themselves preparatory to attack to be eligible for prisoner of war status.

These Rules reflect the provisions of the 1977 Additional Protocol I to the Geneva Conventions. As such, the Protocol's provisions can now be considered customary, as well as treaty, law. Yet when they were negotiated, during the 1974–1977 Diplomatic Conferences on the Reaffirmation and Development of International Humanitarian Law Applicable in Armed Conflicts, many of these sections were highly contested. The provisions that resulted from these years of negotiations were viewed at the time by many of the parties as flawed compromises. Moreover, the ambiguous definition of combatants and civilians contained within the Protocol continues to be problematic—a cause for ongoing explanations and concerns.[3]

In this chapter, I address the way the Vietnam and Arab-Israeli wars informed some of the positions on these issues and ultimately contributed to the awkward shape of the provisions. These were not the only conflicts to influence the drafting of the Protocols, but Vietnam served as the archetype of the contemporary conflicts that had prompted the ICRC to draft new laws. When the ICRC began calling for new laws of armed conflict it was concerned by military developments, such as aviation, that had "almost wiped out" the fundamental distinctions between combatants and civilians.[4] It was also troubled by the rise of a "truly enormous tidal wave of guerrilla activity" that had not been anticipated by earlier conventions.[5] The Vietnam War was the consummate example of these concerns. Moreover, the Vietnam War informed the drafting process by challenging the traditional Western understanding of the laws of armed conflict. The revolutionary writings on people's war, put into practice in Vietnam, shaped a new language and paradigm of a just war, while advocating for the legitimacy of guerrilla warfare.

This language was adopted by Palestinian movements, which presented their struggle as analogous to the Vietnamese people's war. Support for the Palestinians and the Palestine Liberation Organization led to a series of United Nations resolutions, proclaiming the rights of national liberation movements and their fighters in a quasi-legal language that would later be repeated at the Diplomatic Conferences.

There was also growing support for the Palestinian and the Vietnamese resistance in the West. Wars against imperial powers were increasingly accepted as just and the means used to oppose them seemed shocking. Popular and academic commentary in the West questioned the lawfulness of counterinsurgency techniques, in particular attacks on civilians. These discourses were reflected in the debates at the Diplomatic Conference and ultimately in the provisions of the Additional Protocol I.

The Traditional Laws of Armed Conflict

In order to appreciate the changes wrought by the Additional Protocol I, it is necessary to understand the legal position before the conferences of the 1970s. Although the ICRC and other commentators claimed that there were longstanding principles protecting civilians and a regrettable lack of law concerning guerrilla warfare,[6] this was something of a misrepresentation of the existing state of the laws of armed conflict.[7]

Guerrilla warfare and people's wars, or "irregular warfare," were familiar concerns in both military and legal circles from the nineteenth century. The term "guerrilla" dates back to the Spanish irregular forces in the Napoleonic wars,[8] but guerrilla tactics have been used by both regular and irregular forces for much longer.[9] The German experience in the Franco-Prussian war and the British experience in the Anglo-Boer war were perhaps the most pivotal in shaping the understanding of irregular warfare in the late nineteenth century and informing the attitudes of the military states at the Hague Conferences in 1899 and 1907.[10]

Experience with these wars meant that during the Hague Peace Conferences, most delegates agreed that there was a strong likelihood that citizens would take up arms. For some delegates, in particular the representatives of Switzerland and Belgium, this was an admirable display of patriotism.[11] Colonel Künzli from Switzerland spoke proudly of his people's fight for independence and freedom in *levées en masse*. He emphasized that not "only able-bodied men but also old men, children and women took part in the battles."[12] The response of British general Sir John Ardagh was to suggest adding an article that stated that the Convention should not be read as diminishing or suppressing the right that belongs to the population of an invaded country to fulfill its duty of opposing to the invaders, by every legitimate means, the most energetic patriotic resistance.[13]

Germany and the Netherlands, however, opposed this approach. Germany acknowledged the value of patriotism, but stated that nothing prevented patriots from entering the army, from organizing themselves properly with a leader and a distinctive sign.[14] Moreover, Germany pointed out that soldiers too needed to be thought of:

> [S]oldiers also are men, and have a right to be treated with humanity. Soldiers who, exhausted by fatigue after a long march or a battle, come to rest in a village have a right to be sure that the peaceful inhabitants shall not change suddenly into furious enemies.[15]

This dispute was resolved by the Martens clause. Fyodor Martens, presiding over the Second Commission at the First Hague Peace Conference, made a declaration that while it was desirable that the usages of war should be defined and regulated, it would not be possible to agree on all cases.[16] Therefore, in cases not agreed upon, populations and belligerents should "remain under the protection and empire of principles of international law, as they result from the usages established between civilized nations, from the laws of humanity, and the requirements of the public conscience."[17]

The clause, Martens suggested, would leave the door open to patriotic acts, since "a heroic nation is, like heroes, above codes, rules, and facts."[18] This proposition allayed some of Belgium's fears about the treatment of irregular fighters. However, in practice, it meant that Germany and the other Great Powers had their way in this debate.[19] Indeed, Martens's statement suggests that any irregular fighting would take place outside law and in the face of law.

Little was added to this debate at the Second Peace Conference, besides the further insistence by Germany that members of a *levée en masse* bear arms openly.[20] The result was that the 1907 Hague Convention required that legitimate belligerents *must* distinguish themselves at all times, must carry arms openly, must follow a responsible command, and must conduct their operations in accordance with the laws and customs of war.[21] Article 2 of the Hague regulations stated that members of a *levée en masse* would be regarded as belligerents if they rose up before being occupied, carried arms openly, and respected the laws and customs of war. There was no right to resistance once occupied. This was made clear at the Conference. As Germany pointed out, occupied inhabitants could not be allowed to attack the occupier's lines of communication because without lines of communication an army cannot exist.[22] Any provisions that protected citizens would depend on their being peaceful. If not, the German delegate continued, most of the guarantees lose their reason for existence.[23] This is also made clear in Martens's writings.[24]

The 1949 Geneva Conventions did little to change these requirements, except for extending them to organized resistance movements.[25] Members of such movements still had to distinguish themselves.[26] Indeed, the ICRC commentary on the Geneva Convention stresses the importance of a distinctive sign:

> [F]or partisans a distinctive sign replaces a uniform; it is therefore an essential factor of loyalty in the struggle and must be worn constantly, in all circumstances. During the Second World War, this rule was not always respected by the resistance organizations but there should be no room for doubt on this matter.[27]

Thus irregular warfare had been comprehensively considered and regulated before the 1970s and the law was clear. Combatants were expected to distinguish themselves. Citizens who became involved in the war outside these strictures were liable to be executed, while the rest of the population could be subjected to reprisals.[28]

In contrast, the protection of civilians had not been clearly discussed or provided for. There was little protection in the Hague Convention. The only clear provision can be found in Article 25, which prohibits the bombardment of undefended towns, villages, dwellings, or buildings. Article

26 requires the attacking force to warn the besieged city of an impending bombardment if possible, and Article 27 encourages attackers to avoid damaging buildings dedicated to religion, art, science, or charitable purposes; historic monuments; hospitals; and places where the sick and wounded are collected.

Besides these provisions, the noncombatant population was exposed to the exigencies of war. There was no requirement to allow noncombatants—"useless mouths"—to leave a besieged town.[29] Civilians could be killed by bombardment or starvation.[30] Whole regions could be devastated if it was necessary for military success.[31] As aerial warfare became a possibility, it was understood that it was likely to be used to kill civilians, or at the least strike at their morale.[32] Attempts to limit the use of aerial warfare failed in the 1920s and again in the 1950s.[33] It was generally accepted that citizens of an enemy state are enemies too and if it was possible to bring a war to a speedier conclusion by harming them, then it should be done so as a necessity of war.[34]

The 1949 *Geneva Convention IV* was drafted to provide protection for civilians, but it still did little to protect civilians during warfare. It did not include any new constraints on aerial warfare, reprisals against civilians, scorched earth tactics, or the starvation of civilians. Rather it focused on the protection of civilians in occupied territories; its goal was to prohibit the more extreme depredations practiced by the Nazi regime against occupied populations. Thus the 1949 Convention insists that occupied civilians should be humanely treated, that their persons, family rights, religious practices, manners and customs should be respected.[35] This protection is dependent on civilians remaining passive. Article 5 states clearly that those who engage in hostile activities will lose the rights of protected persons. Moreover, even the protection offered to passive civilians is contingent on military imperatives. After listing the rights of protected persons, Article 27 acknowledges that the parties to the conflict may take such measures of control and security in regard to protected persons as may be necessary as a result of the war. It also, while prohibiting mass forcible transfers, accepts that an occupying power may undertake total or partial evacuation of a given area if the security of the population or imperative military reasons so demand.[36]

The 1949 Convention envisages that governments may manage their own populations in the same manner. It provides for parties to set up separate, "neutralized" zones to shelter noncombatants.[37] The commentary explains this is only for noncombatants—civilians taking part in hostilities will be naturally excluded.[38] Thus the protection offered to civilians by the

1949 Geneva Convention is predicated on a clear distinction between civilians and combatants in both legal and spatial terms.

These provisions reflect a common military strategy that had been used before and after the drafting of these provisions. The separation of "civilian" populations from the combatants that they might support—whether willingly or under duress—had been undertaken during a range of conflicts from the end of the nineteenth century onwards. The destruction of Boer farms and the relocation of their inhabitants in concentration camps is one of the most familiar examples.[39] However, there were similar movements of civilians during in the Spanish-American War in Cuba,[40] and in the Philippines during the American intervention.[41] Later, similar approaches were taken by Japan in Manchuria,[42] Portugal in Angola,[43] and Britain in Malaya and Kenya.[44] In all these cases, the aim was to separate guerrillas from any support from the population.[45] In South Vietnam, President Diem started moving rural communities to constructed agrovilles from 1959, in an attempt to separate peasants from revolutionaries.[46] Later this turned, with British and American input, into the Strategic Hamlet program.[47] Under this system, thousands of fortified hamlets were constructed. The aim, again, was to concentrate and shelter the rural population in hamlets, relocating villagers when necessary. It was hoped the program would produce villagers who actively supported the South Vietnamese government, while cutting off support to the guerrillas.[48]

This method of moving and resettling populations in camps and similar institutions has been recently described by a number of scholars as a technique of liberal empire—a biopolitical attempt to govern, domesticate, and deny political agency to colonial populations.[49] Although this description seems to rather overstate the liberal aspect of this strategy, it does seem clear that the intention of these laws was to limit political and military agency through a juridical and spatial separation of civilian and combatant.

Revolutionary War in Vietnam and Palestine

Thus despite experiences with irregular warfare, the prevailing idea of war, the theories, the war games,[50] and the laws of war were shaped by an ideal of orderly soldiers in uniform, of citizens subdued, separated, and demilitarized. Over the course of the twentieth century, however, an alternative imaginary of war and approach to law was formulated and articulated—an approach that was exemplified by the war in Vietnam and embraced by Palestinian movements.

The alternative model was a revolutionary people's war, a war where there was no separation between people and army, a war that unapologetically employed guerrilla tactics. As I have argued, guerrilla warfare was an old technique, but during this period it became associated with revolutionary ideology.[51] Mao's writings, and his success in China, were one of the main sources of this alternative approach. It provided a model for a revolutionary people's war that was referenced by a variety of movements that sought to overturn imperial or oppressive governments—even when it may not have been entirely appropriate.[52] Principles from the Maoist model were followed in Malaya, Burma, Algeria, Rhodesia, and Cuba.[53] One of the clearest associations, however, was with the communist movement in Vietnam. Truong Chinh, the secretary general of the Indochinese Communist Party, and Vo Nguyen Giáp, commander in chief of the Viet Minh and minister of the interior in the Democratic Republic of Vietnam, wrote their own accounts of people's war that showed the influence of Maoist theory.[54] The success of the Vietnamese strategy further inspired other movements, including Palestinian organizations. After the 1967 war shattered Palestinian hopes for liberation through traditional warfare,[55] Palestinian movements explicitly characterized their struggle as a revolutionary, people's war in the manner of Vietnam.[56] The communist Popular Front for the Liberation of Palestine (PFLP) followed Mao's teachings closely. Fatah took a less rigorous and more eclectic approach to revolutionary theory,[57] but it echoed the general themes of the Maoist approach.[58] This was the case even though, as was noted at the time, there were significant differences between the Chinese or Vietnamese and Palestinian conditions. Some observers also found it difficult to reconcile Palestinian tactics with the prevailing understanding of guerrilla warfare.[59] Nevertheless, by conceptualizing the Palestinian struggle as a "second Vietnam,"[60] it became situated within the global movement that was reshaping the vision of justifiable warfare. In time, the Palestinian arguments would strengthen and develop that vision.

Mao's model for revolutionary war was developed in several writings from the 1930s.[61] It adapted Marxist-Leninist theory to Chinese conditions by emphasizing the role of the peasantry in a prolonged people's war.[62] Mao's strategy moved through three phases: the mobilization of the peasantry; the gaining of their support in a people's war employing guerrilla strategies; and finally the move toward conventional warfare.[63]

Mao, his general Lin Piao, Giáp, and Truong Chinh all stressed that the first phase, the mobilization of the people, was essential for victory.[64] Lin Piao attributed Mao's victories to the support of the people—"the fullest mobilization of the basic masses as well as the unity of all the forces that can be united."[65] Giáp described the war in Vietnam in the same way:

> The war of liberation of the Vietnamese people proves that, in the face of an enemy as powerful as he is cruel, victory is possible only by uniting the whole people within the bosom of a firm and wide national united front based on the worker-peasant alliance.[66]

The importance of the population had led Mao to introduce rules and discipline to avoid alienating the people and to maintain a supportive and even symbiotic relationship between the people and the troops.[67] Mao says, "It is only undisciplined troops who make the people their enemies and who, like the fish out of its native element, cannot live."[68] Lin Piao writes:

> Our armymen strictly observed the Three Main Rules of Discipline and the Eight Points for Attention, (2) carried out campaigns to "support the government and cherish the people," and did good deeds for the people everywhere. They also made use of every possibility to engage in production themselves so as to overcome economic difficulties, better their own livelihood and lighten the people's burden. By their exemplary conduct they won the whole-hearted support of the masses, who affectionately called them "our own boys."[69]

The Palestinian movements also emphasized that the support of the population would be their greatest advantage;[70] the masses were considered to be "a revolutionary power capable of liquidating direct colonialism and occupation."[71] The overriding need to gain the support of the population meant, for the communist PFLP, overlooking class differences and engaging even the petit bourgeois class.[72]

Yet the role of the people went far beyond mere support. In this image of revolutionary war there is no necessary separation between civilian roles and combatant roles; it is possible and appropriate to be both. As Mao writes:

> [T]here are those who say: "I am a farmer," or, "I am a student"; "I can discuss literature but not military arts." This is incorrect. There is no profound difference between the farmer and the soldier. You must have courage. You simply leave your farms and become soldiers. That you are farmers is of no difference, and if you have education, that is so much the better. When you take

your arms in hand, you become soldiers; when you are organized,
you become military units.[73]

Or, as Truong Chinh puts it: "When the enemy comes, we fight, when he
goes, we plough."[74]

This approach disavows the controlled and passive population imagined by the Geneva Conventions, limited to peaceful pursuits. Such an
oppressed class, Giáp writes, citing Lenin, only deserves to be treated as
slaves if they do not choose to learn to use arms.[75] Indeed, for the Palestinian movements, the transformation of Palestinians from refugees to revolutionaries was regarded as "a therapeutic measure toward 'healing' Palestinian society,"[76] a cultural renaissance. "Armed struggle," Sayigh writes,
"was the source of political legitimacy and national identity, the new substance of the 'imagined community' of the Palestinians."[77]

A people's war will necessarily involve guerrilla warfare—at least in the
first phases. Revolutionary doctrine described guerrilla tactics as the obvious weapon of the weak against a more powerful opponent.[78] Guerrilla
warfare also allowed for the mobilization of the whole strength of the people against the enemy. By using guerrilla tactics, a people's army could wear
out its opponent until it was possible to transition to conventional warfare.

> Guerrilla warfare is the only way to mobilize and apply the whole
> strength of the people against the enemy, the only way to expand
> our forces in the course of the war, deplete and weaken the enemy,
> gradually change the balance of forces between the enemy and our-
> selves, switch from guerrilla to mobile warfare, and finally defeat the
> enemy.[79]

Thus there is no suggestion in this literature that guerrilla warfare is
ethically or legally problematic. It is described as a sensible and strategic
approach. Mao declared, "We should honestly admit the guerrilla character of the Red Army. It is no use being ashamed of this. On the contrary,
this guerrilla character is precisely our distinguishing feature, or strong
point, and our means of defeating the enemy."[80] Indeed, guerrilla warfare
is more than a pragmatic strategy in this literature. Guerrilla warfare is
depicted as a heroic and romantic enterprise, with an established history.[81]
The superhuman heroism and bravery and self-sacrifice of guerrilla fighters is emphasized.[82] This is a depiction that had resonance both among
subjugated peoples and in the West.[83]

Moreover, these guerrilla fighters were justified because they were engaged in just wars, fought against imperialism and unjust aggression. American imperialism, Lin Piao writes:

> is bullying and enslaving various peoples, plundering their wealth, encroaching upon their countries' sovereignty and interfering in their internal affairs. It is the most rabid aggressor in human history and the most ferocious common enemy of the people of the world. Every people or country in the world that wants revolution, independence and peace cannot but direct the spearhead of its struggle against U.S. imperialism.[84]

The fighters in these wars, Giáp states, stand against this to safeguard the freedom and independence of people.[85]

The Palestinian movements characterized their cause as part of this global fight against imperialism, analogous to the Vietnamese struggle.[86] Palestinian movements argued that Israel, which had previously been regarded in many quarters as a beset nation,[87] was an imperialist base, carrying out a program of colonization and dispossession.[88]

> The crux of the Palestine Problem is . . . the piecemeal conquest and continued seizure of the entire country by military force. It is the forcible dispossession and displacement of the bulk of the indigenous population, and the subjugation of the rest. It is also the massive importation of alien colonists to replace the evicted, and to lord it over the conquered. And it is, the colonization, by the foreign settlers, of both the expropriated private land and the seized national resources of the overpowered people.[89]

This particular view of imperialism, and the legitimacy of the struggle against it, achieved growing recognition and repetition in the United Nations General Assembly as the influence of decolonized nations grew.[90] A series of General Assembly resolutions asserted that all peoples have the right to self-determination,[91] especially those fighting alien domination—a term created to cover the Palestinian situation.[92] In 1970, Resolution 2649 specifically condemned the denial of that right to the people of Palestine. Resolution 3103, in 1973, reaffirmed that colonialism was a crime and that colonial peoples had the right to struggle against colonial powers and alien domination, using all necessary means at their disposal. Such conflicts were, the Resolution stated, to be viewed as international armed conflicts and combatants were to be accorded the status of prisoners of war.

This understanding of imperialism as a crime that justified the use of all necessary means of opposition was shown not only in defense of guerrilla warfare but also in the debates about terrorism at the United Nations. When UN Secretary General Kurt Waldheim tried to introduce an item entitled "Measures to Prevent International Terrorism" in the General Assembly, following events at the Munich Olympics, it was changed to include a study of "the underlying causes of those forms of terrorism and acts of violence which lie in misery, frustration, grievance and despair and which cause some people to sacrifice human lives, including their own, in an attempt to effect radical changes."[93] The discussion that ensued was described by a contemporary as a debate on the Arab-Israeli conflict—a debate that pitted the alternatives as state terrorism or individual terrorism.[94] Or, as Chamberlin puts it, a debate that revealed the growing divide between the proponents of "national liberation" and the enemies of "international terrorism."[95] The result, as shown in the General Assembly Resolution that set up the ad hoc Committee for International Terrorism, was a reaffirmation of the legitimacy of the struggle for self-determination and national liberation.[96]

The recognition of the Palestinian cause in the General Assembly culminated in 1974, when it invited Arafat to address the General Assembly and passed Resolutions 3236 and 3237, which reiterated the Palestinian right to self-determination and granted the PLO observer status at the United Nations.[97] These resolutions gave the arguments for national liberation more legitimacy and a quasi-legal appearance. Nevertheless, traditional commentators insisted that General Assembly statements were politics not law,[98] and they decried the danger that democracy in the General Assembly could derail the traditions of international law.[99] Even when a sympathetic lawyer like Abi-Saab asserted the view of decolonized states that national liberation movements were a form of self-defense and that insurgent leaders should be recognized,[100] he noted that this was a political challenge to the existing law.[101] As such, the alternative view of war had garnered a great deal of political legitimacy, but its legal status was still controversial.

Revolutionary War and the West

The theory of the people's war provided a stark alternative to the traditional view of warfare. As such, some of the fundamental aspects of the doctrine, such as the status of national liberation wars, continued to appear legally problematic and ethically suspect to Western experts. Nevertheless, these conflicts did shape a more subtle shift in the interpretation of the laws of armed conflict in the West. The bulk of the discussion around Israel tended to focus on the justice of Israeli and Palestinian claims to nationhood, territory, and belligerency.[102] Nevertheless, there was growing disapproval of Israeli counterinsurgency tactics—in particular, reprisals against individuals or states for supporting guerrilla or terrorist actions. Western international lawyers and states began to question the legality of such operations, especially when they were directed at civilian objects and when they appeared disproportionate.[103]

The anti-Vietnam War movement launched a more comprehensive attack on the way that the United States was fighting the war, arguing that it was immoral and possibly illegal. Popular protests and media reports drew attention to the violence and depravity of the war, the attacks on civilians and children.[104] Intellectuals and journalists produced inquiries into these acts; they staged trials judging the US campaign.[105] Although the influence of the protest movement has been queried,[106] it is possible to see a change in the legal discourse by the start of the Diplomatic Conferences.

Many of the critics of the war echoed the depiction of the people's war made in the revolutionary literature. The Vietnamese national resistance forces were described as being on the side of right, and even of law, defending the "principles of international law and their right to self-determination, political independence, territorial integrity and national unity."[107] "The people of Vietnam are heroic," wrote Bertrand Russell, "and their struggle is epic: a stirring and permanent reminder of the incredible spirit of which men are capable when they are dedicated to a noble ideal."[108]

The United States, in contrast, stood as the representative of imperialism or neocolonialism. It was the "universal empire of evil,"[109] its rapacious imperialism made it the "common destroyer of Peace and Justice" and the greatest threat to the world.[110] Critics frequently compared the United States to Nazi Germany,[111] or even suggested it was unprecedented in its imperialist aggression:

> In the course of history there have been many cruel and rapacious empires and systems of imperialist exploitation, but none before have had the power at the disposal of the United States' imperialists.[112]

After 1967, the characterization of Israel as an imperialist power, akin to the United States in Vietnam,[113] gave the Palestinian cause credibility as an ethical and just fight.[114] Left-wing groups and thinkers who had, until

1967, supported Israel, became supporters of the Palestinians.[115] Contemporaries partly attributed this shift to the Vietnam War, which had changed the political consciousness among many Western observers.[116]

Critics of imperialist war agreed with the revolutionary literature that the development of a people's army and the use of guerrilla warfare was the logical response to such overbearing imperialism. As Sartre explained for Russell's staged International War Crimes Tribunal,[117] colonialism kindled the hatred of the civilian population and made civilians potential rebels. This then determined the characteristics of the struggle. The colonialists had the superior weapons; the indigenous population had to make use of its advantage of number. Nor, in the minds of some critics, should a resistance movement, confronted with the power of an imperialist opponent, be expected to comply with the requirements of distinction.[118]

A people's war might be a reasonable and justified response to imperialism. Unfortunately, it led to an obvious response. . . .

> As it was the unity of an entire people which held the conventional army at bay, the only anti-guerrilla strategy which could work was the destruction of this people, in other words, of civilians, of women and children.[119]

Thus the imperialist, or neocolonial, response to a people's war of liberation could become genocidal.[120] Falk made a similar point, arguing that the battlefield tactics of high-technology counterinsurgency warfare plus the aggressive war character of the enterprise led to genocide.[121]

The strategic hamlet program, which critics also noted was a pragmatic response to a people's war, was attacked in similar terms. The strategic hamlets were presented by the administration as a way of protecting the peasants,[122] in a form not far from what might have been envisaged by the Geneva Convention. Critics acknowledged that this was a way of "protecting" the peasant masses from communism,[123] and they understood that the separation of guerrillas from their support base was a logical form of counterinsurgency.[124] Nevertheless, critics said any support in the Geneva Conventions was a juridical fiction.[125] They emphasized the depredations of the strategic hamlet program: the massive dislocation of people from their homes;[126] the presence of spikes, moats, machine gun turrets, patrols;[127] the use of forced labor.[128] These hamlets were nothing other than concentration camps,[129] designed with genocidal intent.[130]

Thus while these critiques acknowledged that these extreme forms of counterinsurgency were the result of a people's war—just as previous international lawyers had warned—the legitimacy of the people's war jux-taposed against the illegitimacy of an imperialist, Nazi-like regime, made the response immoral. It was a clear betrayal of all the principles that the United States purported to uphold:

> In the name of freedom pregnant women were ripped open, and the electorate did not rebel. Every American who voted Republican or Democratic shares the guilt of these sanguinary deeds. America, the self-proclaimed champion of freedom to torture and kill women and children for the crime of wishing to go on living in their homes.[131]

In much the same way, Israeli critics of the policy of occupation feared that it was, or would lead to, the destruction of Israeli democratic values.[132] It could only create further resistance and repression.[133]

The immorality and illegitimacy of the US campaign was elided into a strong implication, and even statement, of illegality. This claim was not always justified but, as the war continued, critics started to make techni-cal arguments that the bombing of civilians was a breach of the laws of armed conflict.[134] As I have discussed, there were no clear provisions that protected civilians from aerial bombardment before the drafting of the Additional Protocols, so this argument did require some interpretative work. In the Russell Tribunal, bombing was described as a crime of aggres-sion.[135] The use of napalm, in particular, was described as a breach of the Hague articles that prohibited causing unnecessary suffering and prohibit-ing bombardment of undefended places.[136] Franck argued that there was a principle in international law that required a distinction between combat-ants and the civilian population—a principle that the US leadership had disregarded.[137] He also argued that bombing civilians was in breach of the 1949 *Geneva Convention IV*, although he did not explain how the conven-tion prohibited this.[138]

Franck and some other commentators also referred back to the Hague distinction between defended and undefended places, to argue that the United States was in breach of the 1907 Hague Convention for attacking undefended places.[139] Another argument was that the illegality of bombing could be extrapolated from the prohibition on killing civilians face to face.[140] Finally, critics increasingly argued that the bombing was illegal because it targeted places that did not have military importance or, when they were military objectives, nevertheless resulted in disproportionate casualties.[141]

Other lawyers, even those who were against the war, were more cau-tious about these arguments. Telford Taylor pointed out that unfortunately

there was nothing in the Nuremberg principles or the laws of war to con-
firm that bombing civilians was illegal.[142] Yet toward the end of the war this
language began to be taken on by supporters of government policy as well
as critics. After the 1972 Christmas Bombing—the most concerted bombing campaign of the war—sparked outrage in Hanoi and the international
and American press, defenders of the campaign tried to show that it had
not caused excessive civilian casualties.[143] Burrus Carnahan stated that all
the targets were carefully verified to be military objectives and that one was
rejected because it was in a highly populated area.[144] He also argued that
there was an attempt to keep civilian casualties to a minimum, even when
this meant risking pilots' lives.[145] The result of these impressive efforts,
Carnahan states, was a remarkably small number of civilian casualties that
were certainly not disproportionate to military advantage.[146]

Thus the outrage over the Vietnam War shows a shift in the understanding of legitimate and lawful war. A people's war for liberation had a
certain claim to legitimacy, and the counterinsurgency techniques seemed
so illegitimate that it was becoming impossible to see them as lawful.
Attacks on civilians, even when those civilians could not be distinguished
from combatants, were becoming difficult to defend. The limited protection outlined by existing international law was starting to be understood
as requiring a distinction between military and civilian objectives and the
protection of civilians.

Revolutionary War at the Diplomatic Conferences

The shifting understanding of just war and the laws of war can be seen in
the debates at diplomatic conferences to draft the Additional Protocols in
the 1970s. These debates, in turn, left their mark on the Additional Protocol I.

The Diplomatic Conference on the Reaffirmation and Development
of International Humanitarian Law Applicable in Armed Conflicts took
place from 1974–1977 under the auspices of the ICRC. I have traced the
background to these conferences more thoroughly elsewhere;[147] but, by
the time the Conference began, it was seen as a way to bring the "new"
types of war, the kind of war that Vietnam exemplified, within the purview
of international law. The ICRC wanted the Conference to find a way to
incorporate wars for national liberation, to regulate guerrilla warfare, and
to "reaffirm" a distinction between civilians and combatants, that was being
threatened by these new wars.[148]

These aims show that, even before the Conference, conflicts like those in Vietnam and Israel had affected the understanding of the laws of war. As discussed above, there were clear existing laws dealing with (that is, prohibiting) guerrilla warfare and very few laws protecting civilians. This existing regime, however, no longer seemed appropriate once guerrilla wars became wars of national liberation—wars that had a claim to legitimacy and whose fighters had a claim to justice. At the same time, the counterinsurgency techniques directed at civilians in these conflicts now appeared immoral or illegal breaches of principles that were presumed to protect them. Specific techniques that were associated with Vietnam were considered candidates for targeted regulation. Napalm, the ICRC acknowledged, had aroused such reprobation in public opinion that, according to some jurists, the conditions would be favorable for obtaining complete prohibition.[149] Several proposals from states at this point specifically prohibited napalm and other incendiary weapons.[150] There were also some suggestions made about preventing the concentration of the population in strategic villages.[151]

The ICRC may have intended some changes to the law, but it did not foresee the extent to which the Conference would focus on and transform the rights of national liberation movements and fighters.[152] Indeed, as Abi-Saab noted, the ICRC had attempted to bypass this issue in its preparation for the conference:

> In spite of all the indications as to the great importance which a very large majority of States attached to the issues of wars of national liberation, not only in UN resolutions and reports, but also during the Istanbul and the Government Experts Conference, the draft protocols submitted by the ICRC to the Diplomatic Conference to serve as bases for discussions practically evaded the issue; an issue which was soon to dominate the work of the first session of the conference.[153]

This first session was marked by an opening speech by President Ould Dada of Mauritania, who spoke of the millions of men suffering from colonial oppression and stripped of their rights.[154] He insisted that it was undeniable that these were just wars and that the freedom fighters who engaged in them should be granted the same protection as their oppressors.[155]

The Conference then turned to the question of the inclusion of national liberation movements in the debates, including the PLO and the Provisional Revolutionary Government of the Republic of South Viet-Nam—or the Vietcong, as the Republic of South Vietnam explained.[156] The inclusion of these movements meant recognizing the legitimacy of their causes, as well as providing voices that could provide evidence of the atrocities committed by imperialists[157] and arguments for the revision of international law. Amaly of the PLO stated that he hoped to advance certain principles, such as confirmation of the international character of wars fought by national liberation movements; recognition of the prisoner-of-war status of combatants in national liberation movements; protection of the civilian population against the atrocities committed by colonialist and racist powers, such as arbitrary detention, collective reprisals, forcible displacements of persons, destruction of dwellings, or any other objects having no military value; and use of cruel weapons.[158]

Israel opposed the admission of the PLO, arguing that it was a body that had perpetrated atrocious crimes of terrorism against civilians and had no place at a conference on humanitarian law.[159] In response, states such as Pakistan, Syria, and Tanzania argued that it was Israel that was the perpetrator of terrorism, thereby replaying the United Nations' battle over terrorism as a feature of imperialist states or individual actors. This debate was won, again, by the supporters of national liberation movements, and the PLO was admitted to the conference.

The inclusion of the Vietcong was more controversial. Many states argued that the Provisional Revolutionary Government should be admitted, as the legitimate representative of the people of South Vietnam.[160] More importantly, it had been a victim of aggression; it had seen its country destroyed, its people decimated,[161] and subjected to genocide by American imperialists.[162] The response of the Republic of South Vietnam was that it was the Vietcong who were the imperialists, waging a war of communist imperialist expansion.[163] This response shows that imperialism was generally deployed as a sign of illegitimacy. Nevertheless, the vote to admit the Provisional Revolutionary Government was narrowly lost by 38 votes to 37, with 33 abstentions.

When these debates were resolved, the conference turned to the still contentious matter of the status of wars of national liberation as international armed conflicts. Despite the arguments of the Third World and revolutionary movements, the ICRC and Western international lawyers held fast to the view that such wars were internal conflicts. In the ICRC's report on the First Conference of Government Experts in 1971, the ICRC acknowledged that this was a contentious issue; nevertheless, it still placed its account of the debate in the section on internal war.[164] This account noted that some experts had pointed to the authority of the General Assembly resolutions that asserted that national liberation wars were international conflicts. Other experts, however, had responded that "the resolutions on the subject adopted by the General Assembly or other organs of the United Nations were no more than the concrete expression of certain aspirations and did not sanction a generally recognized principle of international law or reflect the practice of States."[165]

The Diplomatic Conference now provided an opportunity to inscribe these aspirational resolutions, and their vision of legitimate warfare, into law. Third World states argued that the new law of war should recognize and enable the natural rights of people to recover the security and freedom that had been denied to them by imperialism.[166] Imperialism, whether American or sometimes Soviet, was described as political, military, and economic aggression perpetrated by the two super powers against peace-loving peoples in Europe, the Middle East, Asia, Africa, and Latin America.[167] It was these imperialist, colonialist, and racist forces that were responsible for armed conflicts and for the violation of human rights and fundamental freedoms that followed.[168] The people fighting wars against such imperialism were lawfully justified.[169] They were fighting for their inalienable right to self-determination and national independence upheld in the Charter of the United Nations and in many General Assembly resolutions.[170] Moreover, the national liberation movements were the first to respect the principles of humanitarian law because they were well aware of the misery and suffering caused by the armed conflicts of which they were the victims.[171]

Since these wars were justified, it was also suggested that they should be treated differently under the laws of war. The laws of war should be drafted to distinguish between the oppressed and the oppressor, to help the oppressed and to punish the oppressor.[172]

Many Western states and commentators were appalled by these suggestions, considering that they undermined the language and values of existing international law. They argued that introducing a distinction between just and unjust wars would rupture the structure of modern international humanitarian law—a structure that appeared to be based on an apolitical, neutral legality.[173] Hess, for Israel, also made this point, arguing that any reference to the motives and cause for which belligerents were fighting was in clear contradiction to the spirit and accepted norms of international humanitarian law.[174]

Despite these concerns about the structure of international law, the amendment to recognize national liberation conflicts as international conflicts was eventually passed in committee, with 70 in favor, 21 against, and 13 abstentions.[175]

It was feared that the Western delegations might walk out of the conference after the vote, but this did not come to pass.[176] Perhaps, Lysaght suggests, they decided that the vote would not affect them significantly; the decolonization movement was essentially over and very few places would be affected by the new law.[177] One place, however, that the law *was* designed to impact, was Israel. As Amaly said, Palestine "fell within all three of the categories mentioned in paragraph 4: they were under colonial domination; their territory was under foreign occupation, despite the assertions of the terrorist Begin; and they were suffering under a racist regime, since Zionism had been recognized in a United Nations resolution as a form of racism."[178]

Israel, therefore, continued to object to the provision, rejecting the United States' attempts to have the new article adopted by consensus in 1977. By this point, however, those Western states that were uneasy about the provision had given up fighting for this issue. They did not want the Conference to fail on their account.[179] Nor, as Mantilla suggests, did they want to appear racist or to share the pariah status of Israel or South Africa.[180] The most they were prepared to do was to abstain, quietly restating their concerns about the neutrality and clarity of international law.

Thus the new provision was passed with only one vote against—a vote which could now be dismissed as being completely isolated from the civilized world.[181] This was a legal and political achievement for the Third World and national liberation movements. It was also a discursive triumph, clearly bringing the "political" language of justice from revolutionary literature into the laws of war. This language and perspective continued to be of importance in the subsequent debate about the rights of the fighters of such wars.

The debate about guerrilla fighters demonstrates again the division between traditional and revolutionary concepts of warfare. In the Draft Protocol, which the ICRC prepared for the Conference, combatant status relied on fulfilling essentially the same requirements as the 1949 Geneva Conventions: combatants must distinguish themselves during military engagements, must follow the laws of war, and must be under a responsible command.[182] To take a different approach, the ICRC stated, would be to risk destroying the essential distinction between combatant and civilian.[183] Under this system, guerrilla fighters in a people's war would be unlikely to receive prisoner of war status.

For the supporters of people's war and national liberation movements at the Conference, this result was unacceptable. They described the "guerrillas" who fought these wars as freedom fighters, fighting just wars against colonial and racist oppression. All fighters in such conflicts should be treated as prisoners of war;[184] they were deserving of equal,[185] if not more protection, than regular combatants.[186] The new laws drawn up by the Conference should reflect this; they should acknowledge the reality in which unarmed or ill-armed and underdeveloped peoples confronted an imperialistic aggressor equipped with the most up-to-date and cruel weapons.[187] Such movements were handicapped in their confrontation with imperialist power; their fighters could not be expected to distinguish themselves.[188] Indeed, North Vietnam questioned the principle of distinction itself in the new wars of liberation:

> As regards the national liberation armies, from the intrinsic original fact that they are the armies of weak and ill armed peoples fighting against a powerful and heavily armed enemy their activities and their lives are inseparable from the civilian population. That is the new law of the people's war. It is an historical material necessity of national liberation wars.
>
> All the world knows that in guerrilla warfare a combatant must operate under the cover of night in order not to be a target of the modern weapons of the adversary. In such circumstances, does the spirit of humanity compel them to wear emblems of uniforms in order to distinguish themselves from the civilian population?[189]

Aldrich, the head of the US delegation, had some sympathy for this approach. He later wrote:

> A rule that requires a guerrilla to distinguish himself at all times from the civilian population will simply make him an outlaw; he cannot respect it and hope to survive. It is like telling him to go around at all times with a bull's eye pinned to his chest.[190]

Most Western states, however, maintained that the three conditions needed to be met.[191] In particular, they felt it was important to maintain some distinction between combatants and civilians, in order to protect civilians.[192] Israel made this argument particularly strenuously. Reciting expert statements on the matter, Israel quoted Draper of the United Kingdom as saying that to bring "the man with the bomb who is a civilian in all outward appearances" within the framework of the protection given to regular armed combatants would mean that no civilian would henceforth be safe.[193] Aldrich worked hard to find a way to resolve this fundamental difference about whether combatants should distinguish themselves. After "two

years of hard work, official and unofficial contacts and prolonged discussion and mediation,"[194] he was able to present a compromise draft article
at the beginning of the fourth session. His solution was to only require
combatants to distinguish themselves during each military engagement
and during military deployment. There was no shared understanding of
what "deployment" meant—an ambiguity that, as Aldrich acknowledged,
made the term acceptable to more delegates.[195]

Many Western delegations were still skeptical about the provisions and
uneasy about granting combatant rights to guerrillas. Nevertheless, once
again, they found it more politically palatable to abstain than to stand with
Israel in voting against the new rule.[196] As a result, the provisions were
adopted by 66 votes to 2 with 18 abstentions.[197] Many of the delegates
spoke of their misgivings about the new article when explaining their
vote and referred to it as a compromise.[198] The ICRC commentary also
acknowledged that the article was a compromise but, it added, probably the
best compromise that could have been achieved at the time.[199]

Yet, through this compromise, the Diplomatic Conference had reshaped
the legal understanding and imagery of the combatant. Combatants were
no longer just the regular military in their conventional uniforms; guerrillas, revolutionaries, and peasant armies could be counted as combatants.
They did not have to be one thing; they could be a peasant by day and
a guerrilla by night—or Mao's scholar and fighter. Heroes and patriots
would no longer fight outside the law, as understood at the Hague Conferences; they were brought under its umbrella. To a large extent, the sym-
biosis of people and army in the revolutionary literature was achieved by
these new provisions.

Yet while these sections appeared to diminish the difference between
civilian and combatant, the Additional Protocol I also defined civilians, for
the first time in international law. Article 50 of Additional Protocol I stated
that a civilian was any person who was not a combatant, as described by
Article 43 and the 1949 Geneva Convention on Prisoners of War.[200] The
ICRC noted that there were many possible ways of defining civilians, but it
considered that this negative definition was the most satisfactory.[201] Article
50(3) states that the presence within the civilian population of individuals
who do not come within the definition of civilians does not deprive the
population of its civilian character. Abi-Saab later noted that this stipula-
tion was directly relevant to guerrilla warfare.[202] Yet despite this acknowl-
edgement, and despite the novelty of Article 50, these provisions did not
spark any controversy.[203]

Delegates were also happy to accept Article 51, which states that the civilian population and individual civilians shall enjoy general protection against dangers arising from military operations.[204] This section prohibits indiscriminate attacks, specifically area bombardment. Such a rule had never been stated before in international humanitarian law; Hays Parks would later argue that it was a new and unacceptable restriction on air warfare, intended to constrain the airpower of Israel and the superpowers.[205] Nevertheless, it was universally acclaimed as a codification of customary, existing rules of international law.[206] This perception of the provision suggests that the antiwar campaigns, that had highlighted the immorality of attacking civilians, had affected the understanding of the law. It had certainly affected what could be said about the law.

The delegates were less unanimous when it came to the details of civilian protection.[207] Nevertheless, the Conference did manage to prohibit many forms of warfare against civilians that were previously considered acceptable, such as the starvation of civilians or reprisals against civilians.[208] Moreover, it introduced a host of other provisions that attempted to protect civilians, such as precautions to be taken before attacks,[209] protection of the natural environment,[210] and protection of works containing dangerous forces.[211]

In this way, the Diplomatic Conference reshaped the laws regarding civilians and combatants. Civilians were defined as not being combatants, as a vulnerable population granted increased protection, while combatants were defined in a way that meant that they could also be civilians—at least some of the time. These definitions and images of the identities involved in war clearly owe much to the various discourses around revolutionary war. The result of these discourses is that the new laws were somewhat paradoxical; they introduced complexity and ambiguities into international humanitarian law.

These complexities were reflected in the subsequent reception of the Additional Protocol I. Although the US delegates left the conference feeling fairly satisfied with what they had achieved and confident of ratification,[212] their hopes were not to be realized. As Kattan shows in "The Third World Is a Problem" in this volume, the change in the US administration and the increasing influence of neoconservative international lawyers and Vietnam War veterans led to concerns about the implications of Additional Protocol I. One of those lawyers, Hays Parks, later wrote a comprehensive critique of the Additional Protocol I, arguing, among other points, that the Protocol's attempt to protect both civilians and irregular combatants was unworkable.[213] Many other military powers also initially refused to ratify Additional Protocol I, including India, Indonesia, Iran, Iraq, Israel,

Malaysia, Morocco, Pakistan, the Philippines, Singapore, Sri Lanka, Sudan, Thailand, the United States, and the Soviet Union.[214]

By the end of the twentieth century, however, opposition to the Protocol started to wane. More states began to ratify the Protocol and, despite the ongoing opposition from the United States and Israel, it became common to see the Protocol referred to as customary international law.[215] Indeed, the ICRC's study of Customary International Law cleaves very closely to the Additional Protocols, as was shown in the rules on combatancy cited above. This translation into customary international law has not resolved the paradoxes of the Additional Protocol; experts are still grappling with them, as the recent debate on "Direct Participation in Hostilities" shows.[216] It does mean, however, that these paradoxes, and the competing visions of war and law that shaped them at the Diplomatic Conferences, have become embedded in international law. In this way, a new vision of war, represented by the Vietnam and Arab-Israeli conflicts, was transformed into a law that affects all states.

Conclusion

The laws of war reflect imaginaries of war—the narratives that are told of war by strategists, humanitarians, lawyers, and politicians. For much of the history of the modern laws of warfare, the dominant image of a proper war was that of an orderly war between uniformed men. In the twentieth century, however, Mao and his followers described another form of war—a revolutionary people's war, a war that involved an entire, heroic, people, fighting for a just cause against imperialist oppression. This type of war was epitomized by the Vietnam War and then by the Palestinian struggle, as it reshaped itself according to the Vietnamese model. These causes appeared just—and not only to the colonial and postcolonial world. Western observers increasingly supported these battles against imperialism. Moreover, they decried the counterinsurgency techniques and attacks on civilians that were used to oppose people's wars. As these techniques lost legitimacy, they also started to look illegal.

The result, at the Diplomatic Conference, was a recognition of the justice of people's wars and an acknowledgment of their participants as combatants. At the same time, the Conference allowed combatants to move between civilian and combatant roles, while considerably increasing the protection owed to civilians. These developments represented a fundamental change to the rules and the understanding of warfare—a change that, despite the long resistance from military states, has now become central to international humanitarian law.

NOTES

1. Jean-Marie Henckaerts and Louise Doswald-Beck, *Customary International Humanitarian Law*, vol. 1 (Cambridge: Cambridge University Press, 2005), 3.

2. Henckaerts and Doswald-Beck, *Customary International Humanitarian Law*, 17.

3. See, e.g., Nils Melzer, *Interpretive Guidance on the Notion of Direct Participation in Hostilities under International Humanitarian Law* (Geneva: ICRC, 2009).

4. Claude Pilloud et al., *Commentary on the Additional Protocols of 8 June 1977 to the Geneva Conventions of 12 August 1949* (M. Nijhoff, 1987), 509.

5. Pilloud et al., *Commentary on the Additional Protocols*, 384.

6. See, e.g., James E. Bond, "Protection of Non-Combatants in Guerrilla Wars," *William and Mary Law Review* 12 (1970–1971): 787, 797; W. T. Mallison and R. A. Jabri, "The Juridical Characteristics of Belligerent Occupation and the Resort to Resistance by the Civilian Population: Doctrinal Development and Continuity," *George Washington Law Review* 42 (1973–74): 185, 205.

7. See Amanda Alexander, "A Short History of International Humanitarian Law," *European Journal of International Law* 26 (2015): 109.

8. J. Bowyer Bell, *The Myth of the Guerrilla* (New York: Knopf, 1971), 3.

9. Bell, *The Myth of the Guerrilla*, 3.

10. Lester Nurick and Roger W. Barrett, "Legality of Guerrilla Forces under the Laws of War," *American Journal of International Law* 40 (1946): 578–79.

11. James Brown Scott, *The Proceedings of the Hague Peace Conferences: Translation of the Official Texts: The Conference of 1899* (New York: Oxford University Press, 1920), 551; William I. Hull, *The Two Hague Peace Conferences* (Boston: Ginn and Co., 1909), 216.

12. Scott, *The Proceedings of the Hague Peace Conferences*, 551.

13. Hull, *The Two Hague Peace Conferences*, 218.

14. Scott, *The Proceedings of the Hague Peace Conferences*, 552.

15. Hull, *The Two Hague Peace Conferences*, 222.

16. Scott, *The Proceedings of the Hague Peace Conferences*, 548.

17. Scott, *The Proceedings of the Hague Peace Conferences*, 548.

18. Scott, *The Proceedings of the Hague Peace Conferences*, 547.

19. A. Cassese, "The Martens Clause: Half a Loaf or Simply Pie in the Sky?" *European Journal of International Law* (2000) 11: 197–98.

20. Scott, *The Hague Peace Conferences of 1899 and 1907*.

21. *Convention (IV) Respecting the Laws and Customs of War on Land*, The Hague, October 18, 1907, art 1.

22. Scott, *The Proceedings of the Hague Peace Conferences*, 553.

23. Scott, *The Proceedings of the Hague Peace Conferences*, 552.

24. Cassese, "'The Martens Clause,'" 198

25. *Geneva Convention (IV) Relative to the Protection of Civilian Persons in Time of War*, Geneva, August 12, 1949, art 4(2).

26. *Geneva Convention (III) Relative to the Treatment of Prisoners of War*, Geneva, August 12, 1949, art 4(2).

27. Jean Pictet, ed., *The Geneva Conventions of 12 August 1949: Commentary: Geneva Convention III Relative to the Treatment of Prisoners of War* (Geneva: International Committee of the Red Cross, 1960), 60.

28. Arnold Fraleigh, "'The Algerian Revolution as a Case Study in International Law,'" in Quincy Wright and Richard A Falk, eds., *The International Law of Civil War* (Baltimore: Johns Hopkins Press, 1971), 196, 202; Henry Wheaton, *Elements of International Law* 5th ed., revised by Coleman Phillipson (London: Stevens and Sons, 1916), 475, 480.

29. John Westlake, *International Law* 2nd ed. (Cambridge: Cambridge University Press, 1910–1913), 89; Coleman Phillipson, *International Law and the Great War* (London: T. Fisher Unwin, Sweet & Maxwell, 1915), 19.

30. William Edward Hall, *A Treatise on International Law* 4th ed. (Oxford: Clarendon Press, 1895), 575.

31. Wheaton, *Elements of International Law*, 487.

32. Amanda Alexander, "'The 'Good War': Preparations for a War against Civilians," *Law, Culture and the Humanities* (2019) 15: 227–52.

33. Alexander, "A Short History of International Humanitarian Law," 117; Amanda Alexander, "The Genesis of the Civilian," *Leiden Journal of International Law* 20 (2007): 375.

34. Wheaton, *Elements of International Law*, 479–80; J. H. Morgan, *The German War Book: Being "The Usages of War on Land" Issued by the Great General Staff of the German Army* (London: John Murray, 1915), 18; Westlake, *International Law*, 36; Phillipson, *International Law and the Great War*, 19.

35. Article 27 Geneva Protocol IV.

36. Article 49.

37. Article 15.

38. Jean Pictet, ed., *The Geneva Conventions of 12 August 1949: Commentary: Geneva Convention IV Relative to the Protection of Civilians* (Geneva: International Committee of the Red Cross, 1960), 131–32 commentary.

39. James Robbins Jewell, "Using Barbaric Methods in South Africa: The British Concentration Camp Policy during the Anglo-Boer War," *Scientia Militaria* 31 (2012): 8–9.

40. Dan Stone, *Concentration Camps: A Very Short Introduction* (Oxford: Oxford University Press, 2019), 13.

41. Stone, *Concentration Camps*, 13.

42. Anthony James Joes, *Resisting Rebellion: The History and Politics of Counterinsurgency* (Lexington: University Press of Kentucky, 2004), 111.

43. Joes, *Resisting Rebellion*, 113.

44. Stone, *Concentration Camps*, 85.

45. Andrew Mumford, *The Counter-Insurgency Myth: The British Experience of Irregular Warfare* (London: Routledge, 2011), 32; Joes, *Resisting Rebellion*, 106; Karl Hack, "The Malayan Emergency as Counter-Insurgency Paradigm," *Journal of Strategic Studies* 32 no. 3 (2009): 383–414, 388.

46. P. Busch, "Killing the 'Vietcong': The British Advisory Mission and the Strategic Hamlet Programme," *Journal of Strategic Studies* 25, no. 1 (2002): 135–62, 137;

William S. Turley, *The Second Indochina War: A Concise Political and Military History* (Lanham, MD: Rowman & Littlefield, 2008), 70.

47. P. Busch, "Killing the 'Vietcong,'" 155; Turley, *The Second Indochina War*, 71.

48. Turley, *The Second Indochina War*, 71.

49. Laleh Khalili, *Time in the Shadows: Confinement in Counterinsurgencies* (Stanford: Stanford University Press, 2012), 4; Patricia Owens, *Economy of Force* (Cambridge: Cambridge University Press, Kindle ed.), 9. Aidan Forth, *Barbed-Wire Imperialism: Britain's Empire of Camps, 1876–1903* (Oakland: University of California Press, 2017), 10.

50. Bell, *The Myth of the Guerrilla*, 4.

51. Bell, *The Myth of the Guerrilla*, 17.

52. Bell, *The Myth of the Guerrilla*, 57.

53. Ian F. Beckett, *Modern Insurgencies and Counter-Insurgencies: Guerrillas and Their Opponents Since 1750* (London: Routledge, 2001), 79.

54. Beckett, *Modern Insurgencies and Counter-Insurgencies*, 79.

55. Yezid Sayigh, *Armed Struggle and the Search for State: The Palestinian National Movement, 1949–1993* (Oxford: Oxford University Press, 1999), 200; Yoav Di-Capua, "The Slow Revolution: May 1968 in the Arab World," *American Historical Review* 123, no. 3 (2018): 737.

56. Sayigh, *Armed Struggle and the Search for State*, 176; Paul Thomas Chamberlin, *The Global Offensive: The United States, the Palestine Liberation Organization, and the Making of the Post-Cold War Order* (Oxford: Oxford University Press, 2012).

57. Hisham Sharabi, "Palestinian Guerrillas: Their Credibility and Effectiveness" (The Centre for Strategic and International studies, Georgetown University, 1970), 26–27.

58. Faris Giacaman, "Political Representation and Armed Struggle," *Journal of Palestine Studies* 43, no. 1 (2013): 26.

59. D. A. Heradstveit, "A Profile of the Palestine Guerrillas," *Cooperation and Conflict*, VII (1972): 26; Sayigh, *Armed Struggle and the Search for State*, 200.

60. Chamberlin, *The Global Offensive*, 26; Sayigh, *Armed Struggle and the Search for State*, 200.

61. Beckett, *Modern Insurgencies and Counter-Insurgencies*, 76.

62. Bell, *The Myth of the Guerrilla*, 19–21; J. L. S. Girling, *People's War: The Conditions and the Consequences in China and in South-East Asia* (London: Allen and Unwin, 1969), 52–57.

63. Brigadier General Samuel B. Griffith, "Introduction," in Mao Tse-tung, *On Guerrilla Warfare*, Brigadier General Samuel B. Griffith, trans. (Fleet Marine Force Reference Publication), 12–18, 21.

64. Lin Piao, *Long Live the Victory of People's War!* (Peking: Foreign Languages, 1967), 2.

65. Lin Piao, *Long Live the Victory of People's War!*, 12, also see 26.

66. General Võ Nguyên Giáp, *People's War, People's Army* (Ha Noi: The Gioi Publishers, 2004), 28.

67. Beckett, *Modern Insurgencies and Counter-Insurgencies*, 74.

68. Mao Tse-tung, *On Guerrilla Warfare*, 93.

69. Lin Piao, *Long Live the Victory of People's War!*, 29.

70. Sayigh, *Armed Struggle and the Search for State*, 197.

71. Giacaman, "Political Representation and Armed Struggle," 28.

72. *Basic Political Documents of the Armed Palestinian Resistance Movement*, selected, translated, and introduced by Leila S Kadi (Beirut: Palestine Liberation Organization Research Centre, 1969), 32.

73. Mao Tse-tung, *On Guerrilla Warfare*, 73.

74. Cited in Girling, *People's War*, 132.

75. Giáp, *People's War*, 110.

76. Giacaman, "Political Representation and Armed Struggle," 30.

77. Sayigh, *Armed Struggle and the Search for State*, 195.

78. Mao Tse-tung, *On Guerrilla Warfare*, 42; Giáp, *People's War*, 47–48.

79. Lin Piao, *Long Live the Victory of People's War!*, 32.

80. Cited in Girling, *People's War*, 77.

81. Sayigh, *Armed Struggle and the Search for State*, 195.

82. Lin Piao, *Long Live the Victory of People's War!*, 27–28; Mao Tse-tung, *On Guerrilla Warfare*, 85–86; Giáp, *People's War*, 22, 47–48.

83. Samuel Moyn, *The Last Utopia: Human Rights in History* (Cambridge, MA: Harvard University Press, 2010), 116.

84. Lin Piao, *Long Live the Victory of People's War!*, 52–53.

85. Giáp, *People's War*, 29.

86. Chamberlin, *The Global Offensive*, 20.

87. Di-Capua, "The Slow Revolution," 735.

88. Sayigh, *Armed Struggle and the Search for State*, 198.

89. Fayez A. Sayegh, "A Palestinian View," 2nd World Conference on Palestine, Amman, September 26, 1970, http://www.freedomarchives.org/Documents/Find er/DOC12_scans/12.palestinian.view.pdf

90. Ardi Imseis, "Negotiating the Illegal: On the United Nations and the Illegal Occupation of Palestine, 1967–2020," *European Journal of International Law* 31, no. 3 (2020): 1058.

91. Imseis, "Negotiating the Illegal," 1058.

92. Helmut Freudenschuss, "Legal and Political Aspects of the Recogntion of National Liberation Movements," *Millennium* 11, no. 2 (1982): 116.

93. Malvina Halberstam, "The Evolution of the United Nations Position on Terrorism: From Exempting National Liberation Movements to Criminalizing Terrorism Wherever and by Whomever Committed," *Columbia Journal of Transnational Law* 41 (2003): 573.

94. Luigi Migliorino, "International Terrorism in the United Nations Debates," *Italian Yearbook of International Law* 2 (1976): 116.

95. Chamberlin, *The Global Offensive*, 176.

96. Halberstam, "The Evolution of the United Nations Position on Terrorism," 573–74.

97. Chamberlin, *The Global Offensive*, 248.

98. Theodor Meron, "Some Legal Aspects of Arab Terrorists' Claims to Privileged Combatancy," *Nordisk Tidsskrift for International Ret* 40 (1970): 53.

99. Sanford R. Silverburg, "The Palestine Liberation Organization in the United Nations: Implications for International Law and Relations," *Israel Law Review* 12 (1977): 390.

100. Georges M. Abi-Saab, "The Newly Independent States and the Rules of International Law: An Outline," *Howard Law Journal* 8 (1962): 112.

101. Abi-Saab, "The Newly Independent States and the Rules of International Law," 112.

102. See, e.g., Henry Cattan, *Palestine and International Law* (London: Longman, 1973), 281; Quincy Wright and M. Khadduri, "The Palestine Conflict in International Law," in M. Khadduri, ed., *Major Middle Eastern Problems in International Law* (Washington, DC: American Enterprise Institute for Public Policy Research, 1972), 13–33.

103. See, e.g., William W. Orbach, *To Keep the Peace: The United Nations Condemnatory Resolution* (Lexington: University Press of Kentucky, 2014), 95; Richard A. Falk, "The Beirut Raid and the International Law of Retaliation," *American Journal of International Law* 63, no. 3 (1969); Derek Bowett, "Reprisals Involving Recourse to Armed Force," *American Journal of International Law* 66 (1972): 11–12.

104. N. L. Zaroulis and Gerald Sullivan, *Who Spoke Up? American Protest Against the War in Vietnam, 1963–1975* (New York: Doubleday, 1984), 56.

105. See, e.g., Frank Browning and Dorothy Forman, eds., *The Wasted Nations: Report of the International Commission of Enquiry into United States Crimes in Indochina, June 20–25, 1971* (New York: Harper & Row, 1972); Telford Taylor, *Nuremberg and Vietnam: An American Tragedy* (Chicago: Quadrangle Books, 1970); John Duffett, *Against the Crime of Silence: Proceedings of the Russell International War Crimes Tribunal* (Stockholm: O'Hare Books, 1968).

106. John E. Mueller, *War, Presidents, and Public Opinion* (New York: John Wiley & Sons, 1973), 63.

107. Hans Goran Franck, "International Law and the US War in Indochina," in Browning and Forman, eds., *The Wasted Nations*, 322.

108. Bertrand Russell, "Peace through Resistance to US Imperialism," in Bertrand Russell, *War Crimes in Vietnam* (New York: Allen & Unwin, 1967), 99.

109. Russell, *War Crimes in Vietnam*, 73.

110. Russell, *War Crimes in Vietnam*, 94.

111. Russell, *War Crimes in Vietnam*, 102, 117; Taylor, *Nuremberg and Vietnam*, 207.

112. Russell, *War Crimes in Vietnam*, 99.

113. Evyn Lê Espiritu, "Cold War Entanglements, Third World Solidarities: Vietnam and Palestine, 1967–75," *Canadian Review of American Studies* 48, no. 3 (2018): 365.

114. Di-Capua, "The Slow Revolution," 735; Sharabi, "Palestinian Guerrillas: Their Credibility and Effectiveness," 1; Di-Capua, *Palestine comes to Paris*, 23.

115. Espiritu, "Cold War Entanglements," 365; Chamberlin, *The Global Offensive*, 40.

116. Sharabi, "Palestinian Guerrillas: Their Credibility and Effectiveness," 3.

117. Sartre, "On Genocide," in Duffett, *The Crime of Silence*, 617.

118. Telford Taylor, refers to Falk and other lawyers, 137.

119. Sartre, "On Genocide," in Duffett, *The Crime of Silence*, 617.

120. Sartre, "On Genocide," in Duffett, *The Crime of Silence*, 617.

121. Falk, "Introduction," in Browning and Forman, *The Wasted Nations*, xv.

122. Theodore J. C. Heavner, "The Viet-Nam Situation" (1963). Department of State Bulletin, 49, 385, 396–97.

123. Russell, *War Crimes in Vietnam*, 61.

124. Russell, *War Crimes in Vietnam*, 46.

125. Yves Jouffe, "Report on the Laws of War," in Duffett, *The Crime of Silence*, 398.

126. "Report from Indochina," in Browning and Forman, eds., *The Wasted Nations*, 260; Franck, "International Law and the US War in Indochina," in Browning and Forman, eds., *The Wasted Nations*, 296.

127. Russell, *War Crimes in Vietnam*, 59.

128. Russell, *War Crimes in Vietnam*, 59.

129. "Report from Indochina," in Browning and Forman, eds., *The Wasted Nations*, 254, 260; Franck, "International Law and the US War in Indochina," in Browning and Forman, eds., *The Wasted Nations*, 296.

130. Lelio Basso, "Summation on Genocide," in Duffett, *The Crime of Silence*, 634; Sartre, "On Genocide," in Duffett, *The Crime of Silence*, 621.

131. Russell, *War Crimes in Vietnam*, 63.

132. Noam Chomsky, *Peace in the Middle East? Reflections on Justice and Nationhood* (New York: Vintage Books, 1974), 61.

133. Chomsky, *Peace in the Middle East?*, 61.

134. Task Force Report in Browning and Forman, eds., *The Wasted Nations*, 90.

135. Lelio Basso in Duffett, *The Crime of Silence*, 297.

136. Yves Jouffe, "Report on the Laws of War," in Duffett, *The Crime of Silence*, 326.

137. Franck, "International Law and the US War in Indochina," in Browning and Forman, eds., *The Wasted Nations*, 294.

138. Franck, "International Law and the US War in Indochina," in Browning and Forman, eds., *The Wasted Nations*, 295.

139. Fred Branfman, "Bombing in Laos—A Crime Against Humanity," in Browning and Forman, eds., *The Wasted Nations*, 74; Franck, "International Law and the US War in Indochina," in Browning and Forman, eds., *The Wasted Nations*, 294.

140. Erwin Knoll, Judith Nies McFadden, and the Congressional Conference on War and National Responsibility Washington, *War Crimes and the American Conscience* (New York: Holt Rinehart and Winston, 1970), 75.

141. See, e.g., Ekberg et al., "Task Force Report," in Browning and Forman, eds., *The Wasted Nations*, 90; Branfman, "Bombing in Laos—A Crime Against Humanity," in Browning and Forman, eds., *The Wasted Nations*, 76.

142. Telford Taylor, 142.

143. See Martin Florian Herz and Leslie Rider, *The Prestige Press and the Christmas Bombing, 1972: Images and Reality in Vietnam* (Washington, DC: Ethics and Public Policy Center, 1980), 54.

144. Burrus M. Carnahan, "'Linebacker II' and Protocol I: The Convergence of Law and Professionalism," in "Civilian Immunity and the Principle of Distinction," *American University Law Review* 31 (1981–1982): 861, 865.

145. Carnahan, "'Linebacker II' and Protocol I," 866.

146. Carnahan, "'Linebacker II' and Protocol I," 867.

147. Amanda Alexander, "International Humanitarian Law, Postcolonialism and the 1977 Geneva Protocol," *Melbourne Journal of International Law* 17 (2017).

148. Claude Pilloud et al., *Commentary on the Additional Protocols of 8 June 1977 to the Geneva Conventions of 12 August 1949* (Leiden: M. Nijhoff, 1987) 586–87;

Waldemar A. Solf and W. George Grandison, "International Humanitarian Law Applicable in Armed Conflict," *Journal of International Law and Economics* 10 (1975): 567, 569.

149. International Committee of the Red Cross, "XXIst International Conference of the Red Cross: Reaffirmation and Development of the Laws and Customs Applicable in Armed Conflicts" (Geneva, 1969), 60.

150. See, e.g., Conference of Government Experts on the Reaffirmation and Development of International Humanitarian Law Applicable in Armed Conflicts (Geneva, 24 May—12 June 1971), *Report on the Work of the Council* (Geneva, 1971); "Outline of an Instrument on the Protection of the Civilian Population against the Danger of Hostilities," working paper submitted by the experts of Mexico, Sweden, Switzerland, United Arab Republic, and the Netherlands at 97; proposal submitted by the experts of the Netherlands at 56; proposal submitted by the experts of Egypt, Finland, Mexico, Norway, Sweden, Switzerland, and Yugoslavia at 57; proposal submitted by the experts of Spain at 61.

151. See, e.g., Plaka (Albania), *Official Records of the Diplomatic Conference on the Reaffirmation and Development of International Humanitarian Law Applicable in Armed Conflicts, Geneva (1974–1977)* (Hein, 1981), vol. 5, 147.

152. Michael Bothe, Karl Josef Partsch, and Waldemar A. Solf, *New Rules for Victims of Armed Conflicts: Commentary on the Two 1977 Protocols Additional to the Geneva Conventions of 1949* (Leiden: Martinus Nijhoff, 1982), 40; Keith Suter, *An International Law of Guerrilla Warfare* (London: Pinter, 1984), 142–43.

153. Abi-Saab, 374.

154. *Official Records of the Diplomatic Conference*, vol. 5, 13.

155. *Official Records of the Diplomatic Conference*, vol. 5, 13–14.

156. *Official Records of the Diplomatic Conference*, vol. 5, 47.

157. *Official Records of the Diplomatic Conference*, vol. 5, 63.

158. *Official Records of the Diplomatic Conference*, vol. 5, 205.

159. *Official Records of the Diplomatic Conference*, vol. 5, 57.

160. See, e.g., *Official Records of the Diplomatic Conference*, vol. 5, Balken (Federal Republic of Germany). Seuk Djoun Kim (Democratic People's Republic of Korea), Cristescu (Romania) at 46; Chowdhury (Bangladesh), Witek (Poland) at 45.

161. See, e.g., Lechuga (Cuba), Gribanov (Union of Soviet Socialist Republics) at 15; Plaka (Albania) at 21, *Official Records of the Diplomatic Conference*, vol. 5.

162. Plaka (Albania), *Official Records of the Diplomatic Conference*, vol. 5, 21.

163. Le Van Loi (Republic of Viet-Nam), *Official Records of the Diplomatic Conference*, vol. 5, 47–48.

164. See Conference of Government Experts on the Reaffirmation and Development of International Humanitarian Law Applicable in Armed Conflicts (Geneva, 24 May—12 June 1971), paras 312–56.

165. Conference of Government Experts on the Reaffirmation and Development of International Humanitarian Law Applicable in Armed Conflicts (Geneva, 24 May—12 June 1971), 53.

166. Boudjakdji (Algeria), *Official Records of the Diplomatic Conference*, vol. 5, 38.

167. Plaka (Albania), *Official Records of the Diplomatic Conference*, vol. 5, 146.

168. Dugersuren (Mongolia), *Official Records of the Diplomatic Conference*, vol. 5, 191.

169. Plaka (Albania), *Official Records of the Diplomatic Conference*, vol. 5, 146.

170. Dugersuren (Mongolia), *Official Records of the Diplomatic Conference*, vol. 5, 191.

171. Mishra (India) *Official Records of the Diplomatic Conference*, vol. 5, 198.

172. Mishra (India) *Official Records of the Diplomatic Conference*, vol. 5, 198; Namibia, Mishra (India), *Official Records of the Diplomatic Conference*, vol. 5, 204; Boudjakdji (Algeria), *Official Records of the Diplomatic Conference*, vol. 5, 38.

173. See, e.g., Forsythe, "The 1974 Diplomatic Conference on Humanitarian Law," 80; R. R. Baxter, "Humanitarian Law or Humanitarian Politics? The 1974 Diplomatic Conference on Humanitarian Law," *Harvard International Law Journal* 16, no. 1 (1975): 17; John F. DePue, "The Amended First Article to the First Draft Protocol Additional to the Geneva Conventions of 1949—Its Impact Upon Humanitarian Constraints Governing Armed Conflict," *Military Law Review* 75 (1977): 75, 97.

174. *Official Records of the Diplomatic Conference*, vol. 6, 41.

175. Bothe, Partsch, and Solf, *New Rules for Victims of Armed Conflicts*, 43.

176. Charles Lysaght, "The Attitude of Western Countries," in Antonio Cassese, ed., *The New Humanitarian Law of Armed Conflict* (Naples: Editoriale Scientifica, 1979), 354.

177. Charles Lysaght, "The Attitude of Western Countries," 354.

178. *Official Records of the Diplomatic Conference*, vol. 6, 53.

179. Giovanni Mantilla, *Lawmaking under Pressure: International Humanitarian Law and Internal Armed Conflict* (Ithaca: Cornell University Press, 2020), 151.

180. Mantilla, *Lawmaking under Pressure*, 150. Hays Parks makes much the same argument, W Hays Parks, "Air War and the Law of War," *Air Force Law Review* 1 (1990): 79.

181. El Fattal (Syrian Arab Republic), *Official Records of the Diplomatic Conference*, vol. 6, 51.

182. *Draft Additional Protocols to the Geneva Conventions of August 12, 1949: Commentary* (Geneva, October 1973), 47.

183. *Draft Additional Protocols to the Geneva Conventions of August 12, 1949: Commentary* (Geneva, October 1973), 49.

184. Moun Seun Jang (Democratic People's Republic of Korea), *Official Records of the Diplomatic Conference*, vol. 5, 368.

185. Dugersuren (Mongolia), *Official Records of the Diplomatic Conference*, vol. 5, 191; Chowdhury (Bangladesh), *Official Records of the Diplomatic Conference*, vol. 5, 187.

186. Dugersuren (Mongolia), *Official Records of the Diplomatic Conference*, vol. 5, 191.

187. Abada (Algeria) *Official Records of the Diplomatic Conference*, vol. 5, 148.

188. *Official Records of the Diplomatic Conference on the Reaffirmation and Development of International Humanitarian Law Applicable in Armed Conflicts, Geneva (1974–1977)* (Hein, 1981) vol. 14, at 344, 324, 531. North Vietnam, Nigeria, North Korea, Pakistan, Ghana, and Lesotho.

189. *Official Records of the Diplomatic Conference*, vol. 14, at 466.

190. George H Aldrich, "Guerrilla Combatants and Prisoner of War Status," *American University Law Review* 31 (1981–1982): 872.

191. *Official Records of the Diplomatic Conference*, vol. 14. See the United States at 475, Brazil at 507, Switzerland at 508, Federal Republic of Germany at 515, Australia at 525, United Kingdom, Israel, and the Netherlands at 526. Belgium was an exception.

192. *Official Records of the Diplomatic Conference*, vol. 14, 477. Reed (US) speaking.

193. *Official Records of the Diplomatic Conference*, vol. 14, 535.

194. *Official Records of the Diplomatic Conference*, vol. 15, above n74, 155; H. Sultan (Egypt) speaking.

195. Aldrich, "Guerrilla Combatants and Prisoner of War Status," 878–79.

196. Mantilla, *Lawmaking under Pressure*, 161.

197. Brazil and Israel voted against. New Zealand, Nicaragua, Spain, Thailand, United Kingdom, Uruguay, Argentina, Australia, Bolivia, Canada, Chile, Colombia, Denmark, Guatemala, Holy See, Ireland, Italy, Japan abstained from the vote. *Official Records of the Diplomatic Conference*, vol. 15, above n74, 155.

198. *Official Records of the Diplomatic Conference*, vol. 15, see respective states at 177, 180, 182, 185.

199. Pilloud Claude Pilloud et al., *Commentary on the Additional Protocols*, 522.

200. *Convention (III) relative to the Treatment of Prisoners of War*, Geneva, August 12, 1949.

201. Claude Pilloud et al., *Commentary on the Additional Protocols*, 610.

202. Georges Abi-Saab, "Wars of National Liberation in the Geneva Conventions and Protocols," *Recueil des Cours: Collected Course of the Hague Academy of International Law*, vol. 165 (Leiden: Brill, 1979), 429.

203. Amanda Alexander, "International Humanitarian Law, Postcolonialism and the 1977 Geneva Protocol," *Melbourne Journal of International Law* 17 (2017): 30.

204. Alexander, "International Humanitarian Law," 30.

205. Hays Parks, *Air War and the Law of War*, 164.

206. *Official Records of the Diplomatic Conference on the Reaffirmation and Development of International Humanitarian Law Applicable in Armed Conflicts, Geneva (1974–1977)* (Hein, 1981), vol. 6, see Mexico at 193; *Official Records of the Diplomatic Conference*, vol. 6, 164. Freeland (United Kingdom); Claude Pilloud et al., *Commentary on the Additional Protocols*, 615.

207. See Alexander, "International Humanitarian Law," 30–35.

208. George H. Aldrich, "New Life for the Laws of War," *American Journal of International Law* 75 (1981): 778.

209. *Additional Protocol I*, above n3, art 57.

210. *Additional Protocol I*, art 55.

211. *Additional Protocol I*, art 56.

212. Aldrich, "New Life for the Laws of War," 778.

213. W. Hays Parks, "Air War and the Law of War," *Air Force Law Review* 1 (1990): 140.

214. Alexander, *A Short History of International Humanitarian Law*, 127.

215. Alexander, *A Short History of International Humanitarian Law*, 137. See also the rules cited above from the ICRC study on customary international law, Henckaerts and Doswald-Beck, *Customary International Humanitarian Law*.

216. This can be seen in the recent spate of works on direct participation in hos-

tilities, e.g., Nils Melzer, *Interpretive Guidance on the Notion of Direct Participation in Hostilities under International Humanitarian Law* (ICRC, 2009); W. Hays Parks, "Part IX of the ICRC Direct Participation in Hostilities Study: No Mandate, No Expertise, and Legally Incorrect," *N.Y.U. J. Int'l L. & Pol.* (2010): 42, 769; A. P. V. Rogers, "Direct Participation in Hostilities: Some Personal Reflections," *Mil. L. & L. War Rev.* (2009): 48, 143.

SIX

The War Against the People and the People's War

Palestine and the Additional Protocols to the Geneva Conventions

Ihab Shalbak and Jessica Whyte

In a keynote address at the 2017 "Israel Defense Forces International Conference on the Law of Armed Conflict," the "founding father of international law studies in Israel," Yoram Dinstein, argued that the biggest contemporary challenge for international law is the direct participation of civilians in hostilities.[1] Dinstein argued that the revolving door of "farmers-by-day, fighters-by-night" is an area still shrouded in doubt. Rejecting the position of the International Committee of the Red Cross, according to which civilians lose protection against direct attacks only for the duration of a specific act of direct participation in hostilities, Dinstein argued for a "continuum" approach that would deny civilian status to members of armed groups who "serve as cooks, drivers, administrative assistants [and] legal advisers" as well as to members of the political wings of armed groups. It was illusory to expect that fighters and support staff could be distinguished in "the thick of the battle," he contended. Moreover, in a context in which "irregular fighters" undermine the distinction between civilians and combatants, he argued that adapting the laws of armed conflict to what he called "new modes of fighting," like the direct participation of civilians in hostilities, is crucial.[2]

Although Dinstein framed this as a new problem, the question of the relation between irregular fighters and the civilian population had long been a central area of dispute in international lawmaking forums, and was the controversy that almost upended the drafting of Additional Protocol I to the Geneva Conventions (1977).[3] In 1974, as the Vietnam War raged, the Swiss Federal Council, working alongside the International Committee of the Red Cross, convened a "Diplomatic Conference on the Reaffirmation and Development of International Humanitarian Law Applicable in Armed Conflicts" in Geneva. The conference became a key site of contestation over what the Vietnamese military strategist General Vo Nguyen Giáp called the "people's war." While delegates from newly independent states and national liberation movements sought privileged belligerent, and thus prisoner of war, status for national liberation fighters, those from major powers argued that granting the right to use violence to irregular fighters would blur the distinction between combatants and civilians and expose the latter to harm.

Additional Protocol I (API) has typically been seen as a significant victory for national liberation movements, both by their opponents and by representatives of these movements themselves. Not only did it recognize that the situations to which the protocol applies "include armed conflicts in which people are fighting against colonial domination and alien occupation and against racist régimes in the exercise of their right of self-determination," it also significantly relaxed the conditions for combatant status enshrined in the 1949 Geneva Conventions, which had granted such status to certain resistance fighters under a responsible command on the condition that that they carried arms openly, wore a distinguishing insignia, and "distinguished themselves from the civilian population." In contrast, API explicitly recognized that "there are situations in armed conflicts where, owing to the nature of the hostilities an armed combatant cannot so distinguish himself." In a significant (though not unqualified) victory for national liberation movements, Article 44 of Additional Protocol I states that a fighter will retain combatant status in such situations provided "he" carries his arms openly: "(a) during each military engagement, and (b) during such time as he is visible to the adversary while he is engaged in a military deployment preceding the launching of an attack in which he is to participate."[4]

The belatedness of the struggle of the Palestine Liberation Organization (PLO), as one of the few national liberation movements that had not achieved statehood by the end of the Diplomatic Conference, gave Palestine a central place in the discussions about how international law should regulate anticolonial conflicts. During the final session of the conference, the PLO legal advisor and delegate to the conference, Chawki Armaly, expressed "deep satisfaction" that the "international community had re-confirmed the legitimacy of the struggles of peoples exercising their right to self-determination."[5] Armaly told the conference that, while his delega-tion was "not fully satisfied" with the "compromise text" on combatants and prisoners of war, it nonetheless constituted a basis for further improve-ment of humanitarian law.[6] While Armaly declared victory on behalf of the PLO, Israel ultimately became the only state to vote against the extension of combatant status to national liberation fighters, and then against Addi-tional Protocol I in its entirety.

At the Diplomatic Conference, Israel, alongside the United Kingdom and various European powers, depicted themselves as the guardians of a "traditional" understanding of humanitarian law, according to which the protection of civilians required that wars were fought by the soldiers of regular states.[7] Although, as a US military lawyer noted at the time, in the two decades leading up to the conference, the number of armed conflicts that fell within this "traditional model"—in which trained and uniformed soldiers fought along fixed battle-lines far from the civilian population—could be "counted on the fingers of a single hand," these delegations continued to argue that any concession to the rights of irreg-ular fighters would blur the principle of distinction between combatants and civilians.[8] This, the Israeli delegate claimed, "would expose the latter to serious risks and was contrary to the spirit and to a fundamental prin-ciple of humanitarian law."[9]

In contrast, the Palestinians, along with the North Vietnamese delega-tion, among others, argued that such a model, which assumed that tradi-tional forces aimed to spare the civilian populations of their adversaries, had little bearing on their own conflicts. Charging Israel with "daily crimes against humanity," Armaly's first speech had argued that the "protection of the civilian population against the atrocities committed by colonialist and racist powers" must be a key concern of the conference.[10] Here he singled out Israel's violence against civilians, including arbitrary detention, collec-tive reprisals, forcible displacement, the destruction of homes and other objects without military value, and the use of cruel weapons. Following the vote on the extension of POW status to national liberation fighters, Armaly argued that Israel's "solitary vote" of opposition had been based on "the fallacious pretext of protecting the civilian population."[11] The North Vietnamese delegate Nguyen Van Huong similarly framed what he termed wars of "pacification" as indiscriminate wars against the people, which aimed "to force the civilian population to give up the struggle for self-determination."[12] In such wars, he contended, "the adversary to be crushed was the entire civilian population."[13] From this perspective, he argued that, far from serving humanitarian ends, the attempt to distinguish civilians from combatants was part of a counterinsurgency strategy that consisted in "draining the pool to catch all the fish."[14]

To this day, what Dinstein calls "the 'Great Schism' between Contracting and non-Contracting Parties" to Additional Protocol I has continued to play out, as the latter, notably Israel and the United States, depict API as a license to terrorism and a threat to civilians.[15] Israel's 2006 "Manual on the Rules of Warfare" states that the Additional Protocols were adopted as a result of "pressure from Third World countries" and "substantially expanded the definition of a fighter to guerrillas and terrorists," ensuring that "Israel (and even the United States) did not sign them and does not recognise them."[16] Echoing the position of the Israeli delegation at the Diplomatic Conference, the manual contends that the distinction between legitimate and illegitimate fighters is necessary to prevent civilians taking part in military actions and to stop soldiers "hiding among the civilian population."[17]

Although this "schism" over the Additional Protocols has led to much technical legal argumentation, the stakes of such arguments were not merely legal but concerned the central existential question of the "corporate character of popular sovereignty"—or who constituted a people.[18] Writing soon before the final session of the Diplomatic Conference, the US military lawyer cited earlier suggested that the ambiguities of the amended API arose from attempts "to define precisely what constitutes peoples struggling against 'racist regimes.'"[19] During the final session of the Diplomatic Conference, this matter pitted the PLO against the Israeli delegation. The Arab people of Palestine fell within all three categories to which API now applied, Armaly told the conference: "they were under colonial domination; their territory was under foreign occupation . . . and they were suffering under a racist regime, since Zionism had been recognized in a United Nations resolution as a form of racism."[20] The Israeli delegate, on the other hand, argued that this article had a "built in non-applicability clause, since [in order for it to apply] a party would have to admit that it was either racist, alien or colonial—definitions which no State would ever admit to."[21] As the US military lawyer noted at the time, however, the other aspect of this definition—who constituted a *people*—was also a matter of ambiguity. Although he suggested that API appeared to refer to "the native inhabitants of a well-defined but externally-governed territory," he worried that its lack of specificity "allows the term 'peoples' to acquire infinite permutations"—possibly enabling "even" the Oglala Sioux militants of Wounded Knee, South Dakota to "assert that they constitute a people, and therefore a distinct polity."[22]

In what follows, we show that, as for the Oglala Sioux and other peoples subjected to settler colonial regimes, much was at stake for the Palestinians in the claim to be a people. Drawing on the record of the ICRC Diplomatic Conference, and on the archives of the Palestinian national movement held at the Institute for Palestine Studies in Beirut, we situate the PLO's position during the drafting of the Additional Protocols against the backdrop of Palestinian attempts to affirm themselves as a people, or a "distinct polity," and to counteract their prior negation by international law. We show that armed struggle played a central role in this attempt to assert a Palestinian political identity, which gave the question of the distinction between the national liberation fighter and the civilian population a particular significance for the Palestinian movement. In the period leading up to the diplomatic conference, this movement's key task had been to affirm the unity of these two figures, the farmer and the fighter, as a means to reconstitute a Palestinian people. This task was existential and political before it was legal.[23] At stake was the very existence of a Palestinian people, with a right to self-determination and a right to return to their land. Yet, however much Palestinians succeeded in asserting their rights to make law and war at Geneva, the attempt to fight this battle on the terrain of international law inscribed this struggle within a framework that was ultimately designed for states. Paradoxically, in acquiring state-like juridical recognition and status, Palestinians were increasingly forced to forgo the existential dimension of their struggle. In line with this trajectory, as Riccardo Bocco observes, "Palestinians as a stateless nation began to witness the formation of nationless state."[24]

International Law and the Undoing of Palestine

In his 2006 self-elegy, *In the Presence of Absence*, the Palestinian national poet Mahmoud Darwish asks, "What does it mean for a Palestinian to be a poet and what does it mean for a poet to be Palestinian?" He answers, "In the first instance: it is to be the product of history, to exist in language. In the second: to be a victim of history and triumph through language." For Darwish "both are one and the same and cannot be divided or entwined."[25] Darwish, as a former member of the Executive Committee of the Palestine

Liberation Organisation and a drafter of some of its most eloquent statements, did not simply express his own predicament as a poet; rather he articulated the historical and existential conditions of the modern Palestinian experience. Darwish's questions and answers formed the conceptual and political backbone of the Palestinian understanding of both their existential situation and their political vocation.

In the period prior to the Diplomatic Conference, the revolutionary Palestinian project had to range itself against existing institutions, vocabularies, and practices that failed and diminished the Palestinian people. Historically, Palestinians were reluctant to use the language of international law, but they were often compelled to participate in its operations. They feared that the ways in which they were written in and out of international legal texts precluded from the outset the very possibility of achieving their political aspirations. As early as the British Mandate period, Palestinians, as Natasha Wheatley notes, remained "aloof from the very name ascribed to them" in the League of Nations Mandate's terms of reference.[26] Wheatley cites a 1930 petition to the League of Nations in which the Arab Executive Committee, representing Palestine's Arab population, attempted to show that "His Majesty's Government had violated the rights of the Arabs which were recognized even by the Mandate," while at the same time stating that the petition "should not be considered as an expression on the part of the Executive Committee of their acceptance of the Mandate."[27] Acutely aware of the discursive and geopolitical limitations that shaped its speaking position, the Executive Committee sought to hold the Mandate authority responsible to its own terms of reference without accepting the juridical categorizations it ascribed to the Palestinian people. In other words, it made a concession to the overpowering regulative force of the Mandate but rejected its constitutive force and refused to be conscripted by it. For the Palestinians, the Mandate was not the "sacred trust of civilization" it claimed to be; rather it was an outright instrument of British colonial rule.

In 1972, Fayez Sayegh, a former member of the Executive Committee of the PLO, compiled an inventory of what he called "the international infringements on the rights of Palestinian people and the international aggression on its dignity and existence over fifty years."[28] Sayegh noted that each of these occurred in November: on November 3, 1917, Britain issued the Balfour declaration, which was later incorporated into the text of the British Mandate in Palestine. On November 29, 1947, the United Nations General Assembly partitioned Palestine against the will and the interest of the Palestinian people, giving 55 percent of the land to the Jewish minority. And finally, on November 22, 1967, the UN Security Council adopted

Resolution 242, following the Israeli victory over Egypt, Syria, and Jordan. For Sayegh, Resolution 242 was a particularly flagrant aggression because, while the Balfour Declaration referred to "the civil and religious rights of existing non-Jewish communities in Palestine" (albeit without "specifying explicitly the Palestinian identity" of these communities), and the partition plan gave the Palestinian majority a portion of the land, Resolution 242 "completely ignored the Palestinian people."[29] In Sayegh's inventory, over a 50-year period, parallel to their displacement and dispossession, Palestinians were recast in international law; from being included by exclusion, as communities without political and national rights, they became merely nameless refugees.

The statements of the incipient Palestinian resistance movement after 1948 viewed international legitimacy and law with suspicion. A Fatah pamphlet on "The Structure of Revolutionary Construction" published 10 years after the Nakba indicted "international conscience" for having "disposed of all notions of justice, right and fairness" and ignored "the principles of human rights and the UN charter."[30] The first edition of the *Sarkht Filastinnana* (*Cry of Our Palestine*) bulletin, which the Fatah movement published in Algeria in 1964, declared that the reality of the past 16 years attested "that the solution to our cause is neither through the United Nations, which has been unified over our victimization. Nor through the still born resolutions of the Arab league."[31] A similar stance was expressed by Ibrahim al Abd, a senior editor of the analytical and theoretical journal of the Palestinian Liberation Organization *Shu'un Filastiniyya* (*Palestinian Affairs*). In a 1971 review of the veteran Palestinian jurist Henry Cattan's book *Palestine: The Road to Peace*, al Abd argued that "appealing to humanitarian justice and international law [was] idealistic and unrealistic" and criticized Cattan for proposing a solution for the question of Palestine that focused on "the legal aspects" instead of highlighting "the struggle of the Palestinian people."[32] These statements expressed a prevailing Palestinian sentiment that the law was, at best, a tool of the powerful. In contrast, revolution or "armed resistance" was conceived as a means of self-annunciation and representation, in contradistinction to the external structure of recognition provided by international law.[33]

Resolution 242 was a literal translation of the balance of forces after the Arab defeat in the 1967 war with Israel. For the Palestinian movement, Resolution 242 represented the crowning of what the Palestinian anthropologist Esmail Nashif describes as a structure of annulment "wherein the Palestinian collective (since 1948) becomes superfluous, a legacy from the past that no one needs anymore."[34] In rendering the Palestinians nameless,

Resolution 242 contributed to what Nashif calls "the practice of the Pal-estinian's death by the Zionist procedure"—a term he uses to designate an attempt to disarticulate the relation between the Palestinian individual and the Palestinian collectivity. Such a procedure sought to dissolve the social "nexus of his or her time and space" and turn Palestinians into indiffer-ent "individuals who no longer need their collective in order to survive."[35] This took a particularly stark form in the areas occupied by Israel after the 1967 war; in the West Bank and Gaza, as Neve Gordon notes, "Palestin-ian national symbols were outlawed, Palestinian history was banned and erased, and any attempt to produce a national narrative that could unite and help mobilize Palestinian society was censored."[36]

Repatriation, moving "from *being* in exile to *becoming* a Palestinian once again," as Edward Said puts it, required forging a nexus to stand in for the missing space-time coordinates of Palestinian life and to enable a reart-iculation of the relationship between individual biographies and collective history.[37] Echoing the 1964 *Cry of Our Palestine* bulletin's pleas for a "pop-ular Palestinian revolution," Palestinians increasingly ranged themselves against the annulment structure that had rendered the Palestinian collec-tive superfluous. For Sayegh, looking back in 1972, what the realpolitik of Resolution 242 had failed to take into consideration was "the full meaning of the appearance of the Palestinian resistance with its future prospects."[38]

Farmer by Day, Fighter by Night

As the scale of the Arab states' defeat in 1967 became apparent, the mod-ern Palestinian national liberation movement emerged to announce the reemergence of the Palestinians as a political subject after two decades of "a political living death" in refugee camps across the Levant.[39] In a matter of a few years, the guerrilla movement institutionalized itself through the Palestine Liberation Organization, which came to embody a national political identity capable of making claims for repatriation and self-determination.[40] The figure of the guerrilla fighter, the *Fida'i*, at once symbolized the emergent Palestinian identity and the assertive Palestin-ian agency. The *Fida'i* came into being as an "annunciatory figure" who deployed the language and practice of armed resistance to restage the Palestinian as a sovereign figure with the prerogative to narrate.[41] The audibility of the fighter reestablished the visibility of the farmer. "Etymo-logically," as Helen Kinsella notes, "*visibility* is both a condition or state of *being* and the capacity to be seen."[42] In the Palestinian experience, the refugee gave birth to the annunciatory figure of the fighter, who in turn made the refugee visible *as Palestinian*. The intimate relation, rather than the distinction, between the farmer and the fighter became central to the reconstitution of a Palestinian people. The moment the figure of the *Fida'i* distinguished the Palestinian was the same moment all Palestinians became indistinguishable from the *Fida'i*.

Edward Said was one of the many individuals who "the shock" of the 1967 war drove "back to where it had all started, the struggle over Palestine." After 1967, Said explained, "I was no longer the same person."[43] He arrived in Amman in the late 1960s to join the incipient Palestinian "effort at repatriation."[44] Said's return to "where it had all started" exemplified the rearticulation of Palestinian biographies and collective history of the period. In his landmark 1969 article "The Palestinian Experience," Said opted to link the personal and the public in order to "reduce the difficulty of writing about the Palestinian experience in a language not properly its own."[45] This link served not only to reestablish Said's relationship with the collective Palestinian repatriation project but also to establish his prerogative to narrate. Said meditated on the multiple expressions of the link that reestablishes the Palestinians' relationship to their own history and to their potential destiny. In particular, he observed that in Amman of the late 1960s "two ways of life enclose all other ways, which finally connect the two. These two being a refugee in a camp and being an active member of one of the resistance groups."[46] To echo Darwish, the two "are one and the same."

The year 1967—as a new beginning, rather than as an end, of the Israeli Palestine conflict—marked a resumption of the direct confrontation between what Nashif calls "the practice of the Palestinian's death by the Zionist procedure" and a resurgent Palestinian identity. Critically, this was an identity that self-consciously perceived existence not as a product of an immutable essence but rather as an outcome of human actions.[47] As Said put it, the Palestinian "has only himself to consider now, and what he discovers, by whatever technique he uses, is how he is a Palestinian—or rather, how he has already become a Palestinian and what this must mean for him."[48] Throughout the 1970s, much of the PLO's effort went into articulating the moral, political, and aesthetic connections between the refugee and the resistant (or, put differently, between the farmer and the fighter). Having lost faith in existing institutions, ideologies, and practice after two decades of "living death" in refugee camps, armed struggle functioned as a resource in a process of national repatriation. The "imagery and language of armed struggle," as Yazid Sayigh argues, "gave new substance to the imagined community of the Palestinians."[49]

Referring to armed struggle as "a central, comprehensive and multidimensional process," the assassinated senior Fatah commander Khalil al-Wazir (Abu Jihad) remarked, "this is how we have proceeded to rebuild our people and reassert its national identity, in order to achieve its aim of return, and liberation of the land."[50] Armed struggle, in al-Wazir's formulation, was conceived as a political and pedagogical project that linked agency with insurgency. This project conditioned reclaiming Palestine, as a physical space, on reclaiming the Palestinian as revolutionary political subject. This understanding of the function of armed struggle animated both the politics and aesthetics of the Palestinian movement in the period after the 1967 war. A 1969 cover illustration of a Fatah bulletin captures the multidimensional process that al-Wazir alludes to. Over an illustration depicting the mutual embrace of a Palestinian fighter and an elderly Palestinian woman in front of a refugee camp, with children playing in the background, the caption reads: "The Palestinians: refugees 1948, revolutionaries 1965."[51]

Although the Palestinian armed resistance never posed any serious military threat to the Jewish state, Israeli reprisal attacks against various Palestinian communities were conceived by Palestinians neither as defensive nor simply as punitive but as eliminative by intent. For the Palestinians, the military actions of the Israeli state stemmed not from military necessities but rather from the Zionist logic of the state. Already in 1965, Fayez Sayegh's *Zionist Colonization in Palestine* had argued that the Zionist settler state was characterized by three features: its racial complexion and racist conduct; its addiction to violence; and its expansionist stance, which manifested in a passionate zeal for the "expulsion of native populations across the frontiers of the settler state."[52] Israeli attacks on Palestinian civilians, from this perspective, were attacks against the growing visibility and audibility of the Palestinian people as agents of their own destiny. To illustrate this point, the PLO revolutionary filmmaker, Mustafa Abu Ali, took the 1969 remarks of the former Israeli prime minister Golda Meir that the Palestinians "did not exist" as the title of his makeshift documentation of the Israeli Air Force's 1974 obliteration of the Nabatieh refugee camp in South Lebanon.[53] For Israelis and Palestinians alike, the disassociation between the *Fida'i* and the refugee was not a simple matter of distinction; it was a matter of the decimation of a militant, collective Palestinian identity.

An Arab Hanoi

Having refused to rely on the categories assigned to them in the crevices of international law, and having divested themselves of the ailing Arab anticolonial project, the Palestinian movement commenced a search for universal political vocabularies that could name their experience without diminishing it. Following the 1967 war, when "the state would fail to liberate both people and land," a new generation, as Yoav Capua notes, turned to thinkers such as Frantz Fanon and Che Guevara to articulate a "state free liberation exercise."[54] In August 1967, in the immediate wake of the 1967 war, Fatah published 14 pamphlets in the series "Revolutionary Studies and Experiences," including one on the Vietnamese revolution and a shorter study of the Algerian revolution. These positioned the Palestinian struggle within what Paul Thomas Chamberlin calls a "new global political geography" that united the "forces of liberation" (Palestine, Cuba, Vietnam, China, and Algeria) against the forces of imperialism (the United States, Rhodesia, South Africa, and Israel).[55] In Algiers, Hanoi, and Havana the newly re-constituted Palestinian movement found a new "commonality of aspirations and fate"—and new political and military models.[56] It was within this community of fate and action that Palestinians represented their struggle as a Third World liberation movement and reimagined themselves "as a stateless nation of liberation fighters rather than a group of Arab refugees."[57]

Just as General Giáp stressed that the Vietnamese struggle had "known how to apply creatively the experiences gained in the recent revolutionary struggles in the world such as in Cuba and Algeria," the Palestinians sought to apply the lessons of these struggles, and that of the Vietnamese themselves, to their own situation.[58] In March 1970, when Arafat and his deputy Salah Khalaf travelled to Hanoi for a two-week tour, General Giáp told them, "The Vietnamese and the Palestinian people have much in common [. . .] just like two people suffering from the same illness."[59] One aspect of that illness, both parties believed, was that they were faced with adversaries who refused to spare their civilian populations. The Fatah newspaper greeted the 1968 My Lai massacre, for instance, by explicitly linking it to the most infamous massacre that took place during the founding of Israel as a state: "Vietnam has its Deir Yassin," the headline read, referring to a 1948 massacre in a town whose name had come to epitomize Zionist atrocities.[60]

Just as the PLO learned from the North Vietnamese and the Vietcong, the Israelis learned from the US counterinsurgency operation in Vietnam.

In 1966, four years before Arafat's visit to Hanoi, Moshe Dayan, who would become Israel's defense minister, toured South Vietnam to study the American war effort.[61] Although he concluded that, for all their military superiority, the United States could not eradicate support for North Vietnam's independence struggle, Dayan refused to view the Palestinian *fedayeen* as a similar *political* threat. Palestinian nationalism was a fabrication, Dayan believed, as there was no authentic Palestinian political identity.[62]

As the Israeli response to the reemergence of the Palestinian movement embraced a logic that sought to negate the very notion of Palestinian people, the various Palestinian factions echoed the Algerians and the Vietnamese in conceiving their struggle as a "people's war." This designation lacked the political and strategic precision that it had in Vietnam, where Giáp defined the people's war as a "long and vast guerrilla war" in which the people as a whole took part.[63] In the Palestinian context, the "people's war" did not simply designate a specific mode of strategic conduct; rather it named the antagonistic and existential nature of the Palestinian struggle to reconstitute a Palestinian people. "A people's war" (or a war of the revolutionary masses), a 1970 Fateh pamphlet contended, "is the end result of a combination of two types of struggle—armed struggle and political struggle."[64] The idioms of armed struggle and people's war established a congruence between how the Palestinians represented and understood themselves and how they were represented by the struggling people of the world.

Along with Hanoi, Algiers—which Elaine Mokhtefi so vividly portrays as the "Third World Capital" of freedom fighters and revolutionaries—played a major role in the evolution of the Palestinian revolutionary worldview, offering inspiration, training, and communication.[65] In 1963, Khalil al-Wazir (Abu Jihad) arrived in Algiers to head the Palestine Office, enabling him to forge relationships with the various anticolonial missions that dotted the Algerian capital. In a joint 1964 communiqué, the Palestine Office and the Viet Cong mission hailed Algeria as a role model "that believed in armed revolution to achieve freedom and independence." The communiqué praised Algeria for its support of "the struggle of peoples fighting to achieve their independence" and it exposed "the barbaric actions of colonialism that aim to dismember/dismantle [colonized] peoples, subjugate and enslave them." It ended with a call to "end all criminal savage action against both the Palestinian and Vietnamese peoples."[66] The joint call from Algiers addressed itself to a community of suffering and overcoming that included both the Palestinians and the Vietnamese.

Palestinians were now part of a counter universal project of solidarity and identification based on the principles of self-determination and equality, whose actors were endowed with a moral and ethical standing that licensed their international advocacy and underpinned their solidarity. Buoyed by two decades of successful decolonization campaigns, these actors dreamed not simply of challenging the status quo but of changing the very logic and authorities that governed international relations. In a 1971 exchange with the Organization of Solidarity of the Peoples of Africa, Asia and Latin America (OSPAAAL), Shafiq al-Hout, a leading PLO activist, expressed a new logic and embrace of new authorities. Al-Hout claimed that when it comes to Palestinian legitimate rights, "it is very important to know who is speaking of them."[67] Referring to a recent speech in which the Cuban Foreign Minister Raul Roa spoke of "the legitimate rights of the Palestinians," al-Hout noted that "Raul Roa represents the Cuban Revolution and his concept of legitimate rights is different from 'legitimate rights' according to the way the North Americans in Washington understand them."[68] For al-Hout, Palestinians were "not a company asking for legitimate rights" but "a nation fighting for national rights, for liberty, for the reunification of the homeland."[69] Palestinians, in al-Hout's estimation, were not simply conventional rights claimers; they were a revolutionary people in the company of new lawmakers.

The new political geography within which al-Hout positioned the question of Palestinian rights soon made itself felt in the rarefied realm of international law. In 1968, the United Nations Conference on Human Rights was held in Tehran, in the wake of the 1967 war and two weeks after the Tet Offensive. Both conflicts left their marks on the proceedings. "Arab states and their supporters used the conference as a weapon to attack Israel," an observer writes, and the "shadow of the Vietnam conflict" hung over both the Conference and the subsequent development of the laws of armed conflict.[70] Most significantly, the Conference passed a resolution on human rights in armed conflicts that created the momentum that led to the Diplomatic Conference on the Reaffirmation and Development of International Humanitarian Law Applicable in Armed Conflicts in Geneva in 1974. As well as calling on the UN to consider the need to develop international humanitarian law, the resolution noted that "minority racist or colonial régimes . . . frequently resort to executions and inhuman treatment of those who struggle against such régimes," and considered that, if detained, such persons should be treated as prisoners of war.[71]

For the Palestinians, however, the "people's war" waged on the diplomatic front was not matched by military or political success on the ground. As Palestinian fighters, particularly left-wing factions, dreamed of their own Arab Hanoi from which to launch their own people's war, Arab host states reconsolidated themselves after the flux of the 1967 war and brutally brought this dream to a halt. In September 1970 and August 1971, the Jordanian monarchy crushed the Palestinian guerrilla movement. In Syria Hafez al-Assad ousted the leftist faction that supported the Palestinian movement. And in Iraq, the Bath regime increased its grip on the state. Across the Levant, Arab states turned on the Palestinian movement, forcing it to seek sanctuary in Lebanon. The limited 1973 October war between Israel, Egypt, and Syria revealed that, in the battle between states, there is little space for a stateless people. United Nations Security Council Resolution 338 called for a cessation of hostilities and affirmed Resolution 242. In the new situation, the rhetoric and the practice of armed struggle and people's war continued to provide unbending inspiration, but the Palestinian movement had to contemplate new options to measure up to the wall-to-wall consolidation of states across the region. These new developments reconfigured the already existing tension in the PLO between the imperatives of nation-building and those of state-building.

At a roundtable meeting of the leadership of the main Palestine factions, held in February 1974, the same month the Geneva Diplomatic Conference got underway, Nayef Hawatmeh, the secretary general of the Democratic Front for the Liberation of Palestine, argued that the PLO needed to adopt "a new formula to outmanoeuvre the expected new situation when the war between Israel and the Arab [states] formally ends."[72] In June of the same year, a simple majority of the Palestinian National Council supported the Ten Point Program that stated that "[t]he Liberation Organization will employ all means, and first and foremost armed struggle, to liberate Palestinian territory and to establish the independent combatant national authority for the people over every part of Palestinian territory that is liberated."[73] Despite its reference to armed struggle, the Ten Point Program at once downgraded its dominant role as the sole instrumental means of liberation and implicitly accepted a limited territorial compromise instead of collective national repatriation. Overall, the statist drive shifted the PLO's focus from solidarity and identification to an obsessive search for international recognition. It was these imperatives of admission and recognition that drove the PLO's participation in the drafting of the Additional Protocols to the Geneva Conventions.

States in Exile

In his encyclopedic book *Armed Struggle and the Search for State: The Palestinian National Movement, 1949–1993*, Yazid Sayigh describes the years of 1967–1972 as "years of revolution" and the years of 1973–1982 as "the state-in-exile" years. While in the first period armed struggle reasserted Palestinian identity and demarcated a common Palestinian political space distinguished from the surrounding Arab space, in the second period (which covers the entire period in which the Additional Protocols were drafted) the role of armed struggle was to secure a Palestinian state among a system of states and further "the internal processes of Palestinian state building, even if they took place in exile."[74] This "acceptance of a state-centric global order," as Noura Erakat notes, entailed significant risks for the Palestinian struggle—not least of which was that of accepting Israeli sovereignty in exchange for a truncated Palestinian state.[75]

In this statist imaginary, Algeria again provided the PLO with a role model, a contact and a strategy. In a visit to Algeria, Arafat embraced a suggestion by the Algerian president, Houari Boumediene, that "it is time for the revolution, Fatah, to start its international activity from Europe."[76] For this task Arafat sent Mahammed Abu Mayzar to Paris. To support Abu Mayzar in his mission, Boumediene dispatched the veteran Mohammad Yazid, a principle architect of what Matthew Connelly describes as Algeria's "diplomatic revolution."[77] According to Connelly, the main achievement of the Algerian revolution was diplomatic rather than military. In 1955, Mohammad Yazid headed the FLN's mission in New York, where he lobbied members of the United Nations, the American administration, and Western public opinion to support the Algerian struggle. From 1958 to 1962, Yazid served as information minister of the interim Algerian government.[78] In Paris, Yazid introduced Abu Mayzar to the many connections he had made at the United Nations. And later Boumediene appointed Yazid as Algerian ambassador in Beirut where the Palestinian movement was based.

The Palestinian delegation at the Geneva Diplomatic Conference also learned from the Algerians about how to engage on the terrain of international humanitarian law. The pressure of participating in an international lawmaking body required that the language of national liberation be translated into the language of international law and put a new premium on legal expertise. This work of translation was largely undertaken by what Umut Özsu refers to as a "small but ambitious group of mid- to late-twentieth-century jurists who hailed from Asia, Africa, and Latin America, received elite training in Europe and the United States" and subsequently established themselves as leading figures in the world of international law.[79] At the Geneva Diplomatic Conference, the PLO legal advisor Chawki Armaly—a Palestinian Christian from the Galilee who received a law degree from Beirut's Jesuit St Joseph's University in the early 1960s—learned from jurists who had already paid substantial attention to the field of international humanitarian law. Here the key figures were the Algerian jurist Mohammed Bedjaoui, whose seminal text *Law and the Algerian Revolution* crystallized the issue of the denial of privileged belligerency to national liberation fighters, and the Egyptian Georges Abi Saab, who played a central role, both at the UN and at the Diplomatic Conference, in working to secure combatant status for national liberation fighters.

In his 1961 book *Law and the Algerian Revolution*, Bedjaoui, Algerian foreign minister and ambassador to France during the Algerian War, challenged a legal order in which colonial governments could treat national liberation fighters as domestic terrorists or criminals who could be "tried, sentenced to death and executed."[80] The Algerian *Front de Libération Nationale* (FLN) was central to the campaign to grant privileged belligerent status to national liberation fighters. Along with the practical military advantages this would entail, the Algerians had recognized early that the laws of armed conflict and the international humanitarian system offered another battleground for their struggle against the French. While on the ground the FLN fought a guerrilla war on its own terms, Yazid and his team in New York fought the French on their own terms; in this contest, the French humiliatingly came up short of their own standard of civilization.

In 1957, the Algerian Red Crescent was established both to monitor French violations of the Geneva Conventions and to gain international recognition by establishing a direct relationship with the ICRC in Geneva.[81] As the French depicted Algerians as "savages" who "neglect all the laws and customs of law," the FLN newspaper regularly discussed French violence and torture as barbarous violations of the laws of war.[82] Drawing explicitly on the language of "civilization," the FLN depicted French refusals to apply the laws of war as contrary to the "humanitarian principles of justice and compassion" that must "govern and determine the treatment of man by man if *our* civilization is to be worthy of the name."[83] Mobilizing this language and the humanitarian system against the French, the Algerians released a "White Paper on the Application of the Geneva Conventions" (1960) and formally acceded to the Geneva Conventions.[84] The aims of this strategy were not only humanitarian; as Helen Kinsella notes, accepting the laws of war facilitated FLN claims that "Algeria was competent, rational, and, most importantly, civilized enough to demand and deserve self-rule."[85]

International admission and recognition similarly became a main objective of the mainstream leadership of the Palestinian movement. Symbolically, when Yasser Arafat, the chairman of the Palestine Liberation Organization, addressed the United Nations General Assembly in 1974, he was given the floor by Algeria's then-foreign minister, Abdelaziz Bouteflika, who had accepted the presidency of the General Assembly one year earlier on behalf of "generations of freedom fighters who contribute to making a better world with weapons in their hands."[86] In his speech, which was the most significant achievement of this Palestinian drive for recognition, Arafat depicted the strategy of what he called Israeli "settler colonialism" as an attempt to reduce the Palestinians to "disembodied spirits, fictions without presence, without traditions or future."[87] Speaking "in the name of the people of Palestine," Arafat began by acknowledging Bouteflika's place in what he termed the "vanguard of the freedom fighters in their heroic Algerian war of national liberation." Yet if Algeria was once the inspiration for anticolonial guerrilla fighters, it was now also a model for postcolonial states. Appealing to those statesmen who had once stood in the position of the rebel that he now occupied, Arafat asked that, having converted their own dreams into reality, they now share in his revolutionary dream. But the United Nations was not a place for revolutionaries. The belatedness of the Palestinian national liberation movement inscribed Arafat's dream within a clear teleology—from the rebel to the statesman, from the people to the state.

"The New Law of the People's War"

At the Geneva Diplomatic Conference, the Palestinian delegation framed itself as a state in waiting. Recognizing that national liberation movements had a right to fight, Abi Saab noted in retrospect, meant recognizing their "embryonic sovereignty."[88] Armaly told the conference that the PLO would sign the conference's Final Act, "not only for the protection of the civilian population of Palestine but also for the greater good of its adversaries," since it was ready to comply with all principles of the Protocols.[89] Just as the Algerians had mobilized the ICRC and the humanitarian system to facilitate international recognition, Armaly contended that the PLO "had always offered its co-operation to international humanitarian bodies and the Palestinian Red Crescent worked in close collaboration with the ICRC."[90]

The PLO's recourse to international mechanisms and international law was far removed from the earlier suspicion expressed by the *Cry of Our Palestine* bulletin. For the PLO, Abi Saab recalls, "the primary concern was achieving legitimacy of their organisation and their cause, rather than the technical aspects of it."[91] Yet, for the Palestinians, the significance of the question of the distinction between the farmer and the fighter went far beyond its technical legal significance. The critical question was whether the Palestinians could participate in the realm of international humanitarian law without disavowing the work of the previous decade in knitting together the revolutionary and the refugee. The Palestinians were well aware that they faced an adversary who, in the words of Israel's Colonel Shlomo Gazit, head of intelligence coordination in the Occupied Territories, aimed to "isolate the terrorist from the general population and deny him shelter and assistance, even though the natural sympathy of that population is with the terrorists and not the Israeli administration."[92]

In a 1974 interview, Armaly highlighted the PLO's emphasis in the drafting process on the "legal situation of prisoners of war . . . who are facing the cruellest forms of treatments, not worthy of human beings" and whose struggles "should receive the same international protection as members of regular armies."[93] In contrast to those who depicted such demands for privileged belligerent status as a threat to civilians, Armaly stressed that the PLO delegation had focused "on the protection of the civilian population from the arbitrary methods and action of the Zionist entity. . . ." From such a perspective, the demand that national liberation fighters be recognized by international humanitarian law was not a distraction from civilian protection but a means toward it. It is "important," Armaly told his interviewer, "to reaffirm the articles related to [civilian] protection, add new ones, ensure their application and prevent Israel from continuing its violation of the 1949 Geneva Convention."[94]

Throughout the ICRC Diplomatic conference, the question of the relation between national liberation fighters and civilian populations was among the most sensitive question for many delegations. It was the North Vietnamese delegate Nguyen Van Huong who argued most forcefully against the separation of the two. Throughout the proceedings, the North Vietnamese defended an amendment that would grant prisoner of war status to *any* captured members of a liberation movement, regardless of whether or not they fulfilled the conditions outlined in the 1949 Geneva Conventions, and carried arms openly, wore a distinguishing insignia, and "distinguished themselves from the civilian population."[95] According to Nguyen, these conditions presupposed conflicts between relatively equal parties each of whom could retaliate on the other's territory, and assumed that the activities of militias or volunteer corps remained "completely distinct from the life of the civilian population."[96] Conflicts between profoundly unequal powers, like the US war in Vietnam, he argued, required a different set of rules that would allow the weaker party to mobilize its key advantage: its proximity to the people. In contrast to the image of the passive civilian that animated the advocacy of the Western states, Nguyen stressed that national liberation armies are "inseparable from the civilian population." "This," he told the conference, "is the new law of the people's war."[97]

In retrospect, Abi Saab stressed that, in asymmetric conflicts, guerrilla fighters lack advanced weaponry and therefore "have to follow the 'fish in the water' theory of Chairman Mao, and rely for all their support systems, whether logistical, political or otherwise, on the local population."[98] Traditionally, Abi Saab noted, major powers have resorted to two tactics to reduce the advantages of invisibility and mobility held by guerrillas who operate in the midst of the civilian population: either they have sought to cut them off from their mass base, often through forced relocation of civilians in what amount to "concentration camps," or they have determined "to treat every civilian as a potential combatant or a hidden guerrilla fighter to avoid taking any chances."[99] In both cases, he stressed, the implications for civilians are "ominous": in the first scenario, areas from which civilians have been relocated are then treated as "free-fire zones" and attacked without discrimination, destroying the "very possibility and the natural bases of life and economic activity in such zones."[100] In the second scenario, civilians are tortured, interned, expelled, and subjected to collective reprisals, extending to the destruction of houses and villages. In highlighting the violence military powers used to separate civilians from combatants, Abi Saab challenged those who argued that only a clear distinction between the two protected civilians from harm.

By the end of the Diplomatic Conference, when a new article on combatant status and prisoners of war was adopted (now Article 44 of API), most Third World delegates were prepared to support it in what Abi Saab's Egyptian colleague Mohammad Talaat Al Ghunaimi called "a spirit of compromise."[101] Along similar lines, the Algerian delegate gave special thanks to the US delegate George Aldrich and Nguyen Van Luu (by then head of the delegation of the Socialist Republic of Vietnam) for the particular work they had done on the draft article, which he depicted as a "symbol of the genuine cooperation" that had produced it.[102] Nonetheless, in line with the previous Vietnamese objections to the requirement that national liberation fighters distinguish themselves, Al Ghunaimi spoke for many Third World delegations when he clarified that his delegation believed that a "guerrilla fighting for a just cause was a legitimate incognito combatant" and should be given the benefit of the doubt "whenever freedom of movement required disguise at any stage."[103] Nguyen Van Luu similarly expressed "great satisfaction" that the new article established the legal status of people's wars and ensured that under certain circumstances, combatants fighting for their "national and social emancipation" were now "allowed to fight without distinguishing themselves from the civilian population."[104]

According to these interpretations, international humanitarian law had now vindicated guerrilla warfare and affirmed the right of guerrillas to fight without distinguishing themselves in all circumstances. However controversial these interpretations were at the time, and have remained since, Article 44, as Amanda Alexander notes, brought about a more fluid understanding of the combatant, who "can now be a peasant by day and a guerrilla by night."[105] Alexander suggests that while "it might be expected that acknowledging that a civilian could also be a guerrilla would make their position more precarious," instead "the opposite happened" as API enshrined a new imperative to protect the civilian population.[106] For the Israeli delegate, Ruth Lapidoth, in contrast, explaining her delegation's lone vote against Article 44, the thrust of the article was indeed to allow guerrilla fighters to fight without distinguishing themselves from the civilian population. It thereby threatened, she argued, "the only way in which the civilian population could be effectively protected."[107] In 1977, though many other states shared similar reservations, Israel's delegation was alone in voting against both Article 44 and API as a whole. The Palestinians were on the winning side of the legal battle, but they did not win the war.

Conclusion

The Pakistani intellectual Eqbal Ahmad once remarked that "at the dawn of decolonization, Palestine was colonized."[108] As Indonesia and India paved the way for the global wave of decolonization in the late 1940s, Palestine fell into the hands of a colonial settler project. And at the dusk of decolonization, as the conclusion of both the Vietnam War and the Portuguese colonial empire ended a major sequence of anticolonial liberation struggles, Palestinians relaunched their own national liberation struggle. By the end of the Geneva Diplomatic Conference, most of the delegations that supported applying API to "armed conflicts in which people are fighting against colonial domination and alien occupation and against racist régimes in the exercise of their right of self-determination" recognized that their own armed struggles lay in the past. The Palestinians were more future-oriented, seeking to use the force of law to protect their civilians and secure their rights.

Explaining why the Israeli delegation had not supported Article 44 of API, Lapidoth had argued that, not only would it increase the risk of terrorism, it would also make the civilian population "an object of suspicion" to "the regular combatant who would have to search for and fight his enemy in the midst of the civilian population."[109] Israel, as we have seen, has not ratified API, nor has it applied Article 44 to its conflict with the Palestinians. Its military forces have nonetheless continued to treat the civilian population of Palestine with suspicion. Rather than a dangerous side effect of extending combatant status to national liberation fighters, such suspicion has been a constant feature of colonial wars and, in Israel's case, has resulted in significant death and destruction—from the massacres that accompanied the Nakba in 1948 to the 2014 decimation of the Shujaya district of Gaza.[110] This suspicion has an obvious foundation; as Yoram Dinstein acknowledges, Israel's regime of occupation is "not derived from the will of the people" and is "not designed to 'win the hearts and minds' of the local inhabitants"; "its foundation," rather, "is the 'power of the bayonet.'"[111] Founded on violence, this regime of occupation has therefore faced regular resistance; "every time an IDF [Israel Defense Force] force enters an Arab village," Military Advocate General Yahav complained during the First Intifada, "the soldiers encounter resistance from local villagers."[112]

In 1982, Ariel Sharon, then Israeli defense minister, besieged Beirut, the base of the PLO, for almost three months in an attempt to enforce the separation between the fighter and the refugee once and for all. The PLO ultimately agreed to leave Beirut to spare the lives of Palestinian and Lebanese civilians, after the American administration provided assurances that Palestinian civilians in the refugee camps would face no harm. Weeks later, Israel allowed the Lebanese right-wing forces into the Palestinian refugee camps, where they committed the infamous Sabra and Shatila massacre.[113] While the PLO was forced once more into exile, Israel continued to fight a war not just against Palestinian fighters but against the Palestinian people. The starkest expression of this came in 2015, from Israel's then-justice minister Ayelet Shaked. On Facebook, she posted a long quote from Uri Elitzur, the former advisor and speechwriter to Israel's prime minister Benjamin Netanyahu. Though written 12 years ago, Shaked wrote, Elitzur's statement "is as relevant today as it was at the time."[114] "The Palestinian people," the statement read, "has declared war on us, and we must respond with war."

Not an operation, not a slow-moving one, not low-intensity, not controlled escalation, no destruction of terror infrastructure, no targeted killings. Enough with the oblique references. This is a war. Words have meanings. This is a war. It is not a war against terror, and not a war against extremists, and not even a war against the Palestinian Authority. These too are forms of avoiding reality. This is a war between two people. Who is the enemy? The Palestinian people.[115]

In the eyes of the Israeli state, it appears, the Palestinians acquired people-hood only at the moment they appeared as an enemy to be annihilated.

NOTES

1. For the description of Dinstein, see "Introduction to Keynote Address: A Tribute to Yoram Dinstein," Vanderbilt University, accessed December 2, 2018, https://wp0.vanderbilt.edu/jotl/2018/05/introduction-to-keynote-address-a-tribute-to-yoram-dinstein/

2. Yoram Dinstein, "The Recent Evolution of the International Law of Armed Conflict: Confusions, Constraints, and Challenges Special Issue: The Law of Armed Conflict: Keynote Address," *Vanderbilt Journal of Transnational Law* 51 (2018): 711.

3. Karma Nabulsi notes that the "challenge of formulating the distinction between lawful and unlawful combatants drove most aspects of the legal controversy at conferences between 1874 and 1949." Karma Nabulsi, *Traditions of War: Occupation, Resistance, and the Law* (Oxford: Oxford University Press, 1999), 15. And Amanda Alexander notes that despite the consensus during the drafting of the Additional Protocols that there was a gap in the law that needed to be filled, "guerrilla warfare was not virgin legal territory at the Diplomatic Conference." Amanda Alexander, "International Humanitarian Law, Postcolonialism and the 1977 'Geneva Protocol I,'" *Melbourne Journal of International Law* 17, no. 1 (2016): 7.

4. ICRC, "Treaties, States Parties, and Commentaries—Additional Protocol (I) to the Geneva Conventions, 1977—44—Combatants and Prisoners of War," 1977, https://ihl-databases.icrc.org/applic/ihl/ihl.nsf/ART/470-750054?OpenDocument

5. Chawky Armaly, in International Committee of the Red Cross, "Official Records of the Diplomatic Conference on the Reaffirmation and Development of International Humanitarian Law Applicable in Armed Conflicts" (Geneva, 77 1974), 53 (CDDH/SR.36).

6. International Committee of the Red Cross, vol. VI, 147.

7. As Karma Nabulsi notes, this "rosy and somewhat utopian" picture of the impact of "traditional" wars on civilians ignored the violence wielded against civilians by occupying powers in the course of the nineteenth century. Nabulsi, *Traditions of War: Occupation, Resistance, and the Law*, 36.

8. John F. Depue, "The Amended First Article of the Draft Protocol Additional to the Geneva Conventions of 1949—Its Impact Upon Humanitarian Constraints Governing Armed Conflict," *Military Law Review* 75 (1977): 72.

9. Ruth Lapidoth, International Committee of the Red Cross, "Official Records of the Diplomatic Conference on the Reaffirmation and Development of International Humanitarian Law Applicable in Armed Conflicts," vol. VI, 121.

10. International Committee of the Red Cross, vol. V, 204–5.

11. International Committee of the Red Cross, vol. VI, 147.

12. International Committee of the Red Cross, vol. XIV, 237.

13. International Committee of the Red Cross, vol. XIV, 237.

14. International Committee of the Red Cross, vol. XIV, 237.

15. Dinstein, "The Recent Evolution of the International Law of Armed Conflict," 708.

16. Cited in ICRC, "Customary IHL—106. Conditions for Prisoner-of-War Status," accessed March 17, 2020, https://ihl-databases.icrc.org/customary-ihl/eng/docs/v2_cou_il_rule106. This account is not accurate. The United States did sign API but did not ultimately ratify it. On the US position, see Victor Kattan's chapter in this volume, "'The Third World Is a Problem': Arguments about the Laws of War in the United States after the Fall of Saigon."

17. ICRC, "Customary IHL—106. Conditions for Prisoner-of-War Status."

18. Paul W. Kahn, "Imagining Warfare," *European Journal of International Law* 24, no. 1 (February 1, 2013): 217. Kahn notes that the distinction between combatants and noncombatants "is quite inconsistent with the revolutionary tradition of modernity." For good discussion of the existential stakes in modern warfare see Sibylle Scheipers, *On Small War: Carl Von Clausewitz and People's War* (Oxford: Oxford University Press, 2018). Also at stake is what Neve Gordon and Nicola Perugini have described as the *"evisceration of one of [international law's] foundational figures— the civilian."* Nicola Perugini and Neve Gordon, "Distinction and the Ethics of Violence: On the Legal Construction of Liminal Subjects and Spaces," *Antipode* 49, no. 5 (November 1, 2017): 1387, https://doi.org/10.1111/anti.12343

19. Depue, "The Amended First Article of the Draft Protocol Additional to the Geneva Conventions of 1949—Its Impact Upon Humanitarian Constraints Governing Armed Conflict," 93.

20. Chawki Armaly, in International Committee of the Red Cross, "Official Records of the Diplomatic Conference on the Reaffirmation and Development of International Humanitarian Law Applicable in Armed Conflicts," vol. VI, 53.

21. International Committee of the Red Cross, vol. VI, 42.

22. Depue, "The Amended First Article of the Draft Protocol Additional to the Geneva Conventions of 1949—Its Impact Upon Humanitarian Constraints Governing Armed Conflict," 96.

23. Victor Kattan provides a compelling legal argument that, upon the termination of the British Mandate in May 1948, "sovereignty was vested in the Palestinian people." Victor Kattan, *From Coexistence to Conquest: International Law and the Origins of the Arab-Israeli Conflict, 1891–1949* (London: Pluto Press, 2009), 137. Here our focus is instead on the existential processes of self-constitution undertaken by the Palestinian national movement in the period following the 1967 war, and the ways in which that process impacted on the PLO's position during the drafting of Additional Protocol I. As Neve Gordon notes, particularly in the wake of World War II, the struggle of the colonized for self-determination, whether in Algeria or India, was "intricately tied to and informed by the colonized inhabitants' identification as Algerians and Indians and the emergence of national movements." Neve Gordon, *Israel's Occupation* (Berkeley: University of California Press, 2008), 93.

24. Riccardo Bocco, "UNRWA and the Palestinian Refugees: A History within History," *Refugee Survey Quarterly* 28, no. 2–3 (January 1, 2009): 241, https://doi.org/10.1093/rsq/hdq001

25. Mahmoud Darwish, *In the Presence of Absence*, trans. Sinan Antoon (Brooklyn, NY: Archipelago Books), 77.

26. Natasha Wheatley, "New Subjects in International Law," in Patricia Clavin and Glenda Sluga, eds., *Internationalism: A Twentieth-Century History* (Cambridge: Cambridge University Press, 2017), 283.

27. Memorandum on the Palestine White Paper of October 1930 by the Arab Executive Committee, prepared by Aouni Abdul-Hadi, December 1930, LNA R2286, 6A/23373/224, cited in Wheatley, "New Subjects in International Law," 283.

28. Fayez Sayegh, "Remarks on the Security Council Resolution 242," *Shu'un Filastiniyya*, no. 15 (1972), 5 (authors' translation). Maktabah al-Mu'assasat al-Dirasat al-Filastiniyyah [Library of the Institute of Palestine Studies (IPS)], Beirut.

29. Sayegh, "Remarks on the Security Council Resolution 242," 11.

30. The Palestinian National Liberation Movement (Fatah), "Haykal Al-Bina' al-Thawri [The Structure of Revolutionary Construction]," 1958, http://learnpalestine.politics.ox.ac.uk/uploads/sources/588d709cc0cd4.pdf

31. A 1964 copy of the second edition of the *Sarkht Filastinnana* (*Cries of Our Palestine*) reproduced in Khalil al-Wazier, *Harakat Fateh: al-Bidyat* ("Fateh Movement: The Beginnings"), *Majallat al-Dirasat al-Filastiniyya*, no, 104 (Autumn 2105), 81 (authors' translation).

32. Ibrahim al Abd, "Reviews: Cattan, Henry. *Palestine: The Road to Peace*," *Shu'un Filastiniyya*, no. 2 (July 1971), 184 (authors' translation). *Maktabah al-Mu'assasat al-Dirasat al-Filastiniyyah* [Library of the Institute of Palestine Studies (IPS)], Beirut.

33. This is not to discount Lori Allen's argument that, throughout the history of the Palestinian national movement, and especially in the period of decolonization, sections of that movement held out what she describes as "false hope in a political solution organized by international law." We regret that, as Allen's excellent account of the history of Palestinian engagement with international law was published after this chapter had been finalized and was in production, we were unable to engage with her provocative argument in further detail. See Lori Allen, *A History of False Hope: Investigative Commissions in Palestine* (Stanford: Stanford University Press, 2021), 154.

34. Esmail Nashif, "The Palestinian's Death," a catalogue essay for *Ahlam Shibli: Phantom Home*. Exh. cat. *Museu d'Art Contemporani de Barcelona* (MACBA), *Jeu de Paume*, Paris, and *Museu de Arte Contemporânea de Serralves*, Porto. Ostfildern: Hatje Cantz Verlag, 2013, 173.

35. Esmail Nashif, "The Palestinian's Death," 156 and 173.

36. Gordon, *Israel's Occupation*, 94.

37. Edward Said, "The Palestinian Experience," in *The Edward Said Reader*, ed. Moustafa Bayoumi and Andrew Rubin (London: Granta, 2001), 16.

38. Fayez Sayegh, "Remarks on the Security Council Resolution 242," 7 (authors' translation).

39. Said, "The Palestinian Experience," 32.

40. The Arab League initiated the creation of the PLO in 1964. In early 1969,

militant factions assumed control of the PLO turning it into the principle arena of Palestinian politics. On the history of the PLO and armed struggle see Yezid Sayigh, *Armed Struggle and the Search for State: The Palestinian National Movement, 1949–1993* (Oxford: Clarendon Press, 1997). For a critical account of the place of armed struggle in the reconstitution of Palestinian national identity, see Rashid Khalidi, *Palestinian Identity: The Construction of Modern National Consciousness* (New York: Columbia University Press, 1997).

41. Esmail Nashif, "The Palestinian's Death," 178.

42. Helen Kinsella, *The Image Before the Weapon* (Ithaca: Cornell University Press, 2011), 148.

43. Edward Said, *Out of Place: A Memoir* (New York: Vintage Books, 2000), 290.

44. Said, "The Palestinian Experience," 16.

45. Said, "The Palestinian Experience," 16.

46. Said, "The Palestinian Experience," 20.

47. The assassinated Palestinian militant novelist Ghassan Kanafani, in his two much-read novellas *Rijal fil-Shams* (*Men in the Sun*), 1963, and *'Aid ila Haifa* (*Return to Haifa*), 1969, expressed the growing Palestinian understanding that existence is a product of human actions and political choices. For a wider discussion of the political and intellectual questions of existence and essence among Arab and Palestinian intellectuals, see Yoav Di-Capua, *No Exit: Arab Existentialism, Jean-Paul Sartre, and Decolonization* (Chicago: University of Chicago Press, 2018).

48. Edward Said, "The Palestinian Experience," 21.

49. Yezid Sayigh, *Armed Struggle and the Search for State: The Palestinian National Movement, 1949–1993* (Oxford: Clarendon Press, 1997), 668.

50. Khalil al-Wazir, a cofounder of Fatah, was assassinated by the Israeli special reconnaissance unit Sayeret Matkal in Tunisia in 1988. See Yezid Sayigh, *Armed Struggle and the Search for State: The Palestinian National Movement, 1949–1993* (Oxford: Clarendon Press). The assassination of al-Wazir is described in some detail in Ronen Bergman, *Rise and Kill First: A Secret History of Israel's Targeted Assassinations* (New York: Random House, 2018), 317–22.

51. 1969 issue of *Hisad al-Asifa* cited in Paul Thomas Chamberlin, *The Global Offensive: The United States, the Palestine Liberation Organization, and the Making of the Post-Cold War Order* (New York: Oxford University Press, 2012), 23.

52. Cited in Di-Capua, *No Exit*, 192.

53. Mustafa Abu Ali, *Laysa Lahum Wujud* (*They Do Not Exist*), Palestinian Cinema Institution, 1974. https://www.youtube.com/watch?v=2WZ_7Z6vbsg

54. Di-Capua, *No Exit*, 179.

55. Chamberlin, *The Global Offensive*, 21.

56. Robert Malley, *The Call from Algeria: Third Worldism, Revolution, and the Turn to Islam* (Berkeley: University of California Press, 1996), 8.

57. Chamberlin, *The Global Offensive*, 20.

58. Giáp, "The South Vietnamese People Will Win," in Giáp, *The Military Art of People's War: Selected Writings of Võ Nguyên Giáp*, 214.

59. Chamberlin, *The Global Offensive*, 1.

60. Chamberlin, *The Global Offensive*, 27.

61. "Rare Photos: When Moshe Dayan toured Vietnam and called out US arrogance," Haaretz.com, February 14, 2017, https://www.haaretz.com/israel-news

/MAGAZINE-photos-when-moshe-dayan-toured-vietnam-called-out-u-s-arroga
nce-1.5433374

62. Chamberlin, *The Global Offensive*, 34.

63. Keith Suter, *An International Law of Guerrilla Warfare: The Global Politics of Law-Making* (New York: St. Martin's Press, 1984), 24.

64. The Palestine National Liberation Movement Fateh, *Political and Armed Struggle*, undated (circa 1970), 5. A copy with the authors.

65. Elaine Mokhtefi, *Algiers, Third World Capital: Freedom Fighters, Revolutionaries, Black Panthers* (London: Verso Books, 2018).

66. A copy of the communique is reproduced in Khalil al-Wazir, Sarkht Filastinnana "Fateh Movement: The Beginnings," *Majallat al-Dirasat al-Filastiniyya*, no. 104 (Autumn 2105), 121 (authors' translation).

67. A reproduction of Shafik al Hout, "History and Future of a Right," *Tricontinental Magazine* 24 (May–June 1971), in *Arab Palestinian Resistance* (Palestine Liberation Army-People's Liberation Forces), vol. 3, no. 12, 60. See https://www.freedomarchives.org/Documents/Finder/DOC12_scans/12.arab.palestinian.resistance.Dec-1971.pdf

68. Al-Hout, "History and Future of a Right."

69. Al-Hout, "History and Future of a Right."

70. Suter, *An International Law of Guerrilla Warfare*, 24.

71. "Treaties, States Parties, and Commentaries—Tehran Resolution on Human Rights in Armed Conflict, 1968—Resolution-," accessed March 18, 2020, https://ihl-databases.icrc.org/applic/ihl/ihl.nsf/Article.xsp?action=openDocument&documentId=378384ED19F0CFEAC12563CD0051D2B4

72. Nayef Hawatmeh in a transcript of the special forum "Palestinian Resistance: New Challenges," *Shu'un Filastiniyya*, no. 30 (February 1974), 14 (authors' translation). *Maktabah al-Mu'assasat al-Dirasat al-Filastiniyyah* [Library of the Institute of Palestine Studies (IPS)], Beirut.

73. "Political Program for the Present Stage Drawn Up by the 12th PNC, Cairo, June 9, 1974," *Journal of Palestine Studies* 3, no. 4 (Summer 1974): 224.

74. Yezid Sayigh, "Armed Struggle and State Formation," *Journal of Palestine Studies* 26, no. 4 (Summer 1997): 27.

75. Noura Erakat, *Justice for Some: Law and the Question of Palestine* (Stanford: Stanford University Press, 2019), 98.

76. Interview with Mohammed Abu Mayzar (2011), trans., *The Palestinian Revolution*, http://learnpalestine.politics.ox.ac.uk/uploads/sources/58e777d335f04.pdf

77. Matthew Connelly, *A Diplomatic Revolution: Algeria's Fight for Independence and the Origins of the Post-Cold War Era* (Oxford: Oxford University Press, 2002).

78. On the diplomatic role of Mohammad Yazid, see Connelly, *A Diplomatic Revolution*; and Elaine Mokhtefi, *Algiers, Third World Capital: Freedom Fighters, Revolutionaries, Black Panthers* (London: Verso Books, 2018).

79. Umut Özsu, "Determining New Selves: Mohammed Bedjaoui on Algeria, Western Sahara, and Post-Classical International Law," in *The Battle for International Law: South-North Perspectives on the Decolonization Era*, ed. Jochen von Bernstorff and Philipp Dann, The History and Theory of International Law Series (Oxford: Oxford University Press, 2019), 342.

80. Mohammed Bedjaoui, *Law and the Algerian Revolution* (Brussels: International Association of Democratic Lawyers, 1961), 218.

81. Jennifer Johnson, *The Battle for Algeria: Sovereignty, Health Care, and Humanitarianism* (Philadelphia: University of Pennsylvania Press, 2016).

82. Cited in Johnson, *The Battle for Algeria*, 107–8.

83. Kinsella, *The Image Before the Weapon*, 131.

84. Jabhat al-Taḥrīr al-Qawmī, *White Paper on the Application of the Geneva Conventions of 1949 to the French-Algerian Conflict* (Algerian Office, 1960).

85. Kinsella, *The Image Before the Weapon*, 131.

86. Cited in David E. Graham, "The 1974 Diplomatic Conference on the Law of War: A Victory for Political Causes and a Return to the Just War Concept of the Eleventh Century," *Washington and Lee Law Review* 32 (1975): 43.

87. Yasser Arafat, "Question of Palestine, A/PV.2282 and Corr.1 of 13 November 1974," 1974, https://unispal.un.org/DPA/DPR/unispal.nsf/0/A238EC7A3E13EED18525624A007697EC

88. Cited in Erakat, *Justice for Some*, 109.

89. Armali in International Committee of the Red Cross, "Official Records of the Diplomatic Conference on the Reaffirmation and Development of International Humanitarian Law Applicable in Armed Conflicts," vol. VII, 257.

90. International Committee of the Red Cross, vol. V, 204.

91. Cited in Erakat, *Justice for Some*, 110.

92. Chamberlin, *The Global Offensive*, 36.

93. Chawki Armaly, "Harakat al-Taḥrīr al-Waṭanī Tafrid Wjwdha Fy Mu'tamar al-Huqooq al- Insaniah" ("National Liberation Movements Make Their Presence felt at the Humanitarian Law Conference"), *Filastin al-Thawra*, no. 88 (Palestine Liberation Organisation, April 1974), 17 (authors' translation). Maktabah al-Mu'assasat al-Dirasat al-Filastiniyyah [Library of the Institute of Palestine Studies (IPS)], Beirut.

94. Armaly, "National Liberation Movements."

95. International Committee of the Red Cross, "Official Records of the Diplomatic Conference on the Reaffirmation and Development of International Humanitarian Law Applicable in Armed Conflicts," vol. XIV, 464.

96. International Committee of the Red Cross, vol. XIV, 465.

97. International Committee of the Red Cross, vol. XIV, 466. On the civilian as a passive figure, see Alexander, "International Humanitarian Law, Postcolonialism and the 1977 'Geneva Protocol I.'"

98. Georges Abi-Saab, "Wars of National Liberation in the Geneva Conventions and Protocols," *Collected Courses of the Hague Academy of International Law* 165 (1979): 417.

99. Abi-Saab, "Wars of National Liberation in the Geneva Conventions and Protocols," 426.

100. Abi-Saab, "Wars of National Liberation in the Geneva Conventions and Protocols," 427.

101. International Committee of the Red Cross, "Official Records of the Diplomatic Conference on the Reaffirmation and Development of International Humanitarian Law Applicable in Armed Conflicts," vol. VI, 145.

102. Abada, International Committee of the Red Cross, vol. VI, 127.

103. International Committee of the Red Cross, vol. VI, 145.

104. International Committee of the Red Cross, vol. VI, 153.

105. Alexander, "International Humanitarian Law, Postcolonialism and the 1977 'Geneva Protocol I,'" 13.

106. Alexander, "International Humanitarian Law, Postcolonialism and the 1977 'Geneva Protocol I,'" 13. This was, as Neve Gordon and Nicola Perugini put it, the high point of the recognition of "civilian value." Gordon and Perugini provide an incisive account of the process by which the people's war came to be seen through the lens of "the human shield," thereby depoliticizing and criminalizing this political strategy. Neve Gordon and Nicola Perugini, *Human Shields: A History of People in the Line of Fire* (Oakland: University of California Press, 2020), 79

107. Ruth Lapidoth, International Committee of the Red Cross, "Official Records of the Diplomatic Conference on the Reaffirmation and Development of International Humanitarian Law Applicable in Armed Conflicts," vol. VI, 122.

108. Eqbal Ahmad, *The Selected Writing of Eqbal Ahmad*, ed. Carollee Bengelsdorf, Margaret Cerullo, and Yogesh Chandrani (New York: Colombia University Press, 2006), 378.

109. International Committee of the Red Cross, "Official Records of the Diplomatic Conference on the Reaffirmation and Development of International Humanitarian Law Applicable in Armed Conflicts," vol. VI, 122.

110. Ilan Pappé, *The Ethnic Cleansing of Palestine* (Oxford: Oneworld, 2006).

111. Cited in Markus Gunneflo, *Targeted Killing: A Legal and Political History* (New York: Cambridge University Press, 2016), 55.

112. Cited in Gunneflo, *Targeted Killing*, 66. Drawing on the work of Walter Benjamin, Gunneflo provides an excellent account of the relation between the law-founding violence of the Nakba and the law-preserving violence that enforces Israel's occupation of the West Bank and Gaza.

113. Bayan Nuwayhed Al Hout, *Sabra and Shatila: September 1982* (London: Pluto Press, 2004), https://trove.nla.gov.au/work/8660264?; Seth Anziska, *Preventing Palestine: A Political History from Camp David to Oslo* (Princeton: Princeton University Press, 2018), 219.

114. Ben Norton, "Netanyahu Appoints Ayelet Shaked—Who Called for Genocide of Palestinians—as Justice Minister in New Government," Mondoweiss, accessed April 3, 2020, https://mondoweiss.net/2015/05/netanyahu-palestinians -government/

115. Ishaan Tharoor, "Israel's New Justice Minister Considers All Palestinians to Be 'the Enemy,'" *Washington Post*, accessed April 3, 2020, https://www.washington post.com/news/worldviews/wp/2015/05/07/israels-new-justice-minister-considers -all-palestinians-to-be-the-enemy/

SEVEN

"The Third World Is a Problem"

Arguments about the Laws of War in the United States after the Fall of Saigon

Victor Kattan

Following the fall of Saigon in 1975, debates on the laws of war among lawyers serving in the US government shared a common theme: the Third World,[1] which had mostly supported North Vietnam throughout that war, and which had sought to introduce the Soviet doctrine of national liberation wars into the corpus of international law,[2] was a problem. Prominent lawyers in the Carter and Reagan administrations did not like the look and orientation of the United Nations after decolonization, because in their view it had become anti-American and pro-Soviet. Accordingly, the United States refused to ratify the 1977 Additional Protocols to the 1949 Geneva Conventions (API), which is one of the core instruments on the regulation of armed conflict in international law.[3] Moving away from the UN Charter's provisions on the use of force and from lawmaking in multilateral fora, the United States began to advance new rules for employing force in conversations with smaller subgroups of "like-minded states."

In 1985, US Secretary of State George Shultz went so far as to call the UN Charter a "suicide pact."[4] The political discourse on the use of force by Reagan administration officials shifted markedly.[5] It was now argued that international law had to be reformed if it was to remain credible. How did this shift, in which the UN Charter was no longer viewed as fit for purpose occur? And why did the United States and Israel withdraw their optional clause declarations with the International Court of Justice (ICJ) within weeks of each other in 1985, and refuse to ratify AP1, following the ICJ's decision in the first phase of the *Nicaragua* case?

While most international lawyers tend to produce doctrinal studies that focus on the rules between states, in order to answer these questions it is necessary to look at the diplomatic battles waged within states and the individuals and groups that attempt to influence the foreign policy of a state to obtain a more realistic appreciation of the practice of international law. Accordingly, this chapter explores the ideological connections between the neoconservatives and Vietnam War veterans who opposed the development of International Humanitarian Law (IHL) during the Cold War due to the emergence of a Third World bloc in the UN during decolonization that supported the struggles of the national liberation movements in the Middle East and Southeast Asia. These included neoconservatives like Allan Gerson, Abraham Sofaer, Jeane Kirkpatrick, George Shultz, Frederick Iklé, Eugene Rostow, and Douglas Feith, and Vietnam War veterans like Robert McFarlane, John Poindexter, Oliver North, John W. Vessey, and W. Hays Parks.[6] All these individuals held prominent positions in the Reagan administration at the UN, the Department of State, the Department of Defense, including the Joint Chiefs of Staff, and at the National Security Council, where they helped formulate US foreign policy on countering terrorism.

In 1977, the only state that voted against Article 1 of AP1 was Israel, because it claimed that the provision broadened the scope of IHL to include "armed conflicts in which peoples are fighting against colonial domination and alien occupation and against racist régimes in the exercise of their right of self-determination."[7] At that time, the United States was one of more than 40 states that signed AP1 when it was opened for signature in December 1977. George H. Aldrich, the chairman of the US delegation, had even described their adoption by the Diplomatic Conference as representing "a major advance in international humanitarian law."[8]

Yet a decade later, the United States would espouse the Israeli view and oppose ratifying AP1. This chapter explores the reasons behind this shift, which it attributes to a convergence of interests between the neoconservatives, who had a close relationship to right-wing figures in the Israeli government,[9] and Vietnam War veterans who wanted to overcome the "Vietnam syndrome," which President Richard Nixon argued had "weakened the nation's capacity to meet its responsibilities to the world, not only militarily, but also in terms of its ability to lead."[10] It explains that following the fall of Saigon, much of the UN's activity took on an anti-American tone, and the Carter administration, rather than confront this activity, appeared to acquiesce to it. In addition, the Soviet Union questioned Washington's resolve by sending troops into Afghanistan and supporting communist insurgencies in Africa and Latin America. For neoconservatives and Vietnam War veterans, it looked like the Carter administration had lost the will to fight the Cold War.

Carter's perceived support for Third World causes at the UN would be sharply reversed by Reagan administration officials, who strongly rejected the idea that American power was dangerous to the world.[11] In their view, the Carter administration had allowed the Diplomatic Conference on the Reaffirmation and Development of International Humanitarian Law Applicable in Armed Conflict at Geneva (1974–77) to legitimize the Soviet doctrine of national liberation, giving succor to many of the national liberation struggles that were undermining the United States' allies in the Third Word.[12] One of the casualties of this struggle between Carter and Reagan administration officials was the decision by Reagan not to ratify AP1. Another casualty was the decision to withdraw the United States' optional clause declaration with the ICJ.

In this connection, the fallout from *Nicaragua v United States of America* played a major role in the reversal of US policy.[13] This was because the decision was made on the basis of customary international law, which had been shaped by events in the 1970s, which had recognized the legitimacy of national liberation movements and their struggles at the Diplomatic Conference in Geneva. In rejecting the United States' collective self-defense argument the Court had based its reasoning on UN resolutions, declarations, and treaties that had been adopted during the height of decolonization, and which recognized the right of peoples to fight "against colonial domination and alien occupation and against racist régimes in the exercise of their right of self-determination."

In summary, this chapter revisits the critiques of IHL in the years 1977–1987, which, it is argued, influenced the Reagan administration's decision to withdraw from the ICJ and refrain from sending AP1 to the Senate for advice and consent to ratification. It explains that officials in the Reagan administration viewed certain provisions of AP1 as too constraining on US power in the global confrontation with the Soviet Union, and too accommodating to the interests of the national liberation movements that were supported by the Soviet Union in undermining US interests in the Third World. These lawyers rejected the changing structure of international law brought about by the decolonization process, and they rejected the inviolability of the sovereignty of the postcolonial state. To win the Cold War, the United States wanted to go on the offensive, and in order to accomplish this objective international law needed to be interpreted flexibly.

1. Ambassador Aldrich Takes on His Critics

In 1991, after the Cold War had drawn to a close with the dissolution of the Soviet Union, Ambassador Aldrich, who had led the US delegation to the Diplomatic Conference on the Reaffirmation and Development of IHL in Geneva, penned two articles expressing his frustration at the United States' continued refusal to ratify AP1, especially as the Soviet Union had done so. The first article was published in the *American Journal of International Law*[14] and the other article was published in a festschrift in honor of Frits Kalshoven.[15] These articles drew upon similar arguments that Aldrich had advanced in the 1980s when he defended the Carter and Ford administrations' records at the Geneva Conference on Humanitarian Law.[16]

Due to the untimely deaths of his colleagues, professor (later judge) Richard R. Baxter and Waldemar Solf, who had both served in the US Army during the Second World War, and in Solf's case also in the Korean War, Aldrich had, by default, become one of the last lawyers who was still living after the dissolution of the Soviet Union who had been involved in the drafting of the Additional Protocols at the Geneva Conference. Although Aldrich was not alone in voicing criticism of the Reagan administration's stance toward AP1,[17] he was one of the most prominent, persistent, and prolific. It was not so much a question of taking sides, as Aldrich had also represented the United States for the Ford (Republican) administration before Carter and had been a senior advisor to the Nixon administration during the Vietnam War.

1.1. Ratification of AP1 Delayed

In the festschrift, Aldrich explained that when the United States signed the Protocols in 1977, the Carter administration supported the decision as a whole including the Office of the Secretary of Defense and the Joint Chiefs of Staff.[18] Upon signature, the United States even submitted a statement expressing its understanding of certain provisions of AP1, which Aldrich hoped would form the basis for the statement the United States would make when it came to ratifying the Protocol, which he thought would only be a matter of time.[19] The delay, Aldrich explained to the annual meeting of the American Society of International Law in April 1980, was because the executive had not yet finished its preparatory work, which involved an article-by-article analysis, and because he had become preoccupied with work on the law of the sea.[20] Aldrich expressed his hope that "the next Congress would have more time to devote to treaty matters than had the past several Congresses, which had been preoccupied with a few major treaty issues."[21]

In September 1982, despite opposition from Hays Parks in the Pentagon, who had served as a marine in Vietnam,[22] the J-5 to the Joint Chiefs of Staff for the Secretary of Defense completed their initial review of API and APII.[23] The review was completed without prejudice to a final assessment of the Joint Chiefs, which provided language that could be used in the form of declarations, reservations, and statements of understanding upon ratification—precisely as Aldrich had envisaged. Frederick Iklé, under secretary of defense for policy, had requested the review.[24] (NATO had also completed a review of the Protocols and concluded that they would have no adverse impact on alliance operations.)[25] The initial review by the Joint Chiefs observed that while some states, such as France and Israel, had indicated that they would not accept the protocols, other US allies had indicated that they would accept them with reservations and statements of understanding.[26] The review also observed that Norway had accepted the protocols without any reservations or statements of understanding.[27]

However, when in October 1984 Mike Matheson, the State Department's deputy legal adviser for political-military affairs, was preparing a cable to instruct the US mission to the UN to vote in favor of a UN resolution by which the United States would express its intention to ratify API in the sixth committee of the UN General Assembly, alarm bells started ringing.[28] Douglas Feith, deputy assistant secretary of defense for negotiations policy, called Allan Gerson, acting legal counsel at the US mission to the UN, on the telephone to warn him what was happening, and to oppose the vote in the sixth committee. In addition, Fred Iklé sent a cable to Gerson, explaining that the Pentagon was still considering its position and did not necessarily support ratification of API.[29] The alarm bells began to ring even louder when a "top-secret" memorandum favoring US ratification of the Additional Protocols was submitted to President Reagan by Davis Robinson, the State Department legal adviser, in November 1984.[30]

1.2. The Joint Chiefs Oppose Ratification

By May 1985, the Joint Chiefs of Staff had come out against ratification. It was now argued that the military problems created by the Protocol could not be remedied except by taking an unusually large number of reservations and understandings—27 in all.[31] It was also claimed that the problems with API "outweighed any probable military benefit from ratification."[32] The memorandum that made this recommendation was signed by John

W. Vessey, who had been appointed chairman of the Joint Chiefs of Staff by President Reagan in 1982. Vessey had a distinguished career in the US military in Vietnam, where he received the Distinguished Service Cross for heroism during the Battle of Suoi Tre (March 21, 1967).[33]

A comparison between the preliminary review on September 13, 1982, and the final review that rejected ratification on May 3, 1985, is revealing. While the preliminary review had raised concerns about the implications of ratifying API for the ability of the United States to fight in situations of guerrilla warfare, it did not reject API outright or take the view that the Protocol was so problematic that its faults could not be remedied through issuing reservations and statements of understanding. Nor did the initial review take exception with the extension of IHL to cover wars of national liberation. The only concerns expressed in the 1982 review concerned US views on belligerent reprisals, human shields, the status of mercenaries, POW status for guerrilla fighters, strategic bombing of certain kinds of critical infrastructure through the granting of special protection against attack to certain facilities even when the objects concerned were military objectives, and the standards applicable to military commanders in combat situations—which could be addressed with reservations and statements of understandings, drafts of which were provided.[34] While concern was expressed in the 1982 review that an "unscrupulous adversary" could invoke some of the language of API to turn every violation of the laws of war into a war crime—as occurred in Vietnam—this concern was not enough to support an outright rejection of API, and the Joint Chiefs reserved their view.[35] It was only in 1985 that the view was taken that API was *so disadvantageous* to the United States that no reservation or statement of understanding could overcome or remedy its intrinsic flaws.

In the 1985 review, it was argued categorically that the Diplomatic Conference had injected "the political concerns of particular blocs of states into the administration of the Geneva Conventions."[36] A rebel group "would gain a degree of international status, prestige, and legitimacy."[37] By linking the legal rights of individual combatants "to the justice of the cause for which they fight," Article 1, paragraph 4, of API created "a very bad precedent and politicize[d] what should be an objective determination and reverses several hundred years of practice."[38] "In the Korean and Southeast Asian conflicts," the review explained, "Communist governments claimed that everyone fighting against them was an 'aggressor,' and, therefore, a war criminal not entitled to prisoner of war status of treatment."[39] It was also asserted that the new standards provided for in Articles 43 and 44 on Armed Forces, Combatants, and POW status favored guerrilla forces.

"There is little military advantage for the United States armed forces in recognizing improved status for guerrilla fighters."[40] With regard to the impact of the new rules on the protection of the civilian population in situations of belligerent occupation, the Joint Chiefs complained that Articles 48–79 of AP1 were framed in such vague and subjective language that they "would oblige governments to give a broad construction to these rules during low-intensity or unpopular conflicts [such as Vietnam], to bring civilians losses to the lowest possible level."[41] The review also raised objections to the presumption of civilian status for objects that were not considered a military objective in Article 50 and 52 of AP1, "since it could adversely impact on American military operations and personnel."[42] It explained that: "'War crimes' accusations have been a principal means used to deny prisoner of war status to Americans in both Korea and Southeast Asia; the existence of a rule that everyone and everything is civilian in case of 'doubt' could be used to prove such charges in the future, or at least lend credence to them for propaganda purposes."[43] Given the many problems with AP1, the review concluded that "as a practical matter, there is a serious question whether the United States can, in good faith, ratify the Protocol with the many reservations and understandings necessary to correct the Protocol's numerous ambiguities and defects."[44] Accordingly, the review did not recommend ratification.

Whereas Hays Parks's concerns appeared not to have been sufficient to overturn the 1982 review, by 1985, when Vessey was in charge, and after Parks had joined forces with neoconservative officials like Iklé, Feith, and Gerson, who were also opposed to US ratification of AP1 (albeit for their own reasons), their concerns won the argument, as explained below. It is also suggested that a spate of high-profile terrorist attacks against US citizens between 1983 and 1985 likely tipped the balance in favor of these arguments in the administration as ratification could now be portrayed as being contrary to the government's policy of countering terrorism.

1.3. President Reagan Refuses to Send AP1 to the Senate

As Aldrich observed, in January 1987, 18 months after the 1985 review of the Joint Chiefs, President Reagan informed the Senate that he would not submit AP1 to the Senate for its advice and consent to ratification.[45] The reason advanced by Reagan for his refusal to send the Protocol to the Senate was because of problems that he described as "so fundamental in character" that they could not be remedied through a reservation or interpretative declaration.[46]

Reagan echoed the 1985 review when he explained that AP1 gave "special status to 'wars of national liberation,'" which he described as "an ill-defined concept expressed in vague, subjective, politicized terminology."[47] This, he said, as well as the extension of combatant status to irregular forces, would "endanger civilians among whom terrorists and other irregulars attempt to conceal themselves."[48] Reagan explained that he would have ratified the Protocol if it were "sound," but, "We cannot allow other nations of the world, however numerous, to impose upon us and our allies and friends an unacceptable and thoroughly distasteful price for joining a convention drawn to advance the laws of war. In fact, we must not, and need not, give recognition and protection to terrorist groups as a price for progress in humanitarian law."[49]

Instead of ratifying AP1, the Reagan administration explained that the United States would only consider itself legally bound by the rules contained in the Protocol "to the extent that they reflect customary international law, either now or as it may develop in the future."[50]

1.4. The View of the State Department Legal Advisor

In explaining the rationale for the decision not to ratify AP1, Abraham Sofaer, the State Department legal adviser, who had replaced Davis Robinson in 1985, advanced reasons that were strikingly similar to those advanced by Israel at the Diplomatic Conference in 1977.[51] These included the claim that AP1 granted legitimacy to groups like the Palestine Liberation Organization (PLO) by treating "terrorists as soldiers" by conferring upon them "POW status," and by allowing them to make a unilateral declaration under Article 96(3) of AP1 rendering the Protocol applicable to an international armed conflict in which a state was engaged in hostilities with a national liberation movement. In his explanation, Sofaer did not mention that the US delegation had actually voted in favor of this provision at the Diplomatic Conference in 1977.[52] In Sofaer's reading of the diplomatic records of the Geneva Conference, the Third World states (which he emphasized numerically dominated the conference), "were not interested in applying the rules of international armed conflict to ordinary civil wars, but insisted on applying these rules to civil wars that involved causes they favored—the so-called wars of national liberation, specifically those being conducted by the Palestine Liberation Organization and the liberation movements of southern Africa."[53]

A 1986 profile in the *Washington Post* described Sofaer as "far more of an activist and key player on policy decisions than any of his recent predecessors. He is one of those rare people in Washington who has become more important than the post he fills. Sofaer is more controversial at Foggy Bottom and in the legal community than is usual for a State Department lawyer."[54] Before he became legal adviser, Sofaer was a federal judge. In that capacity, he presided over former Israeli defence minister Ariel Sharon's libel case against *Time* magazine regarding his role in the Sabra and Shatila massacres.[55] The *Post* observed that Sofaer was impressed with the Reagan administration, so much so that he followed the path trod by many neoconservatives in switching his allegiance to the Republican Party. The *Post* thought it necessary to mention that "Sofaer, born in India to a Jewish family that originated in Iraq, frequently vacations in Jerusalem, where his wife's family own an apartment."[56]

1.5. Aldrich Responds to the Reagan Administration

In Aldrich's view, the Reagan administration had, "willfully distorted the meaning of several articles in order to declare the Protocol unacceptable."[57] For it was not the case that API automatically extended combatant status to irregulars groups, since they had to submit a declaration stating that they would abide by AP1 and had to assume the same obligations as High Contracting Parties.[58] He thought that it was virtually impossible for an irregular group to assume these obligations if they did not have the appropriate institutions in place, such as a functioning legal system and police force that could enforce the law.[59] While there were concerns regarding some provisions of AP1 from the Pentagon's perspective, such as its prohibition of belligerent reprisals and using nuclear weapons that would damage the environment, Aldrich thought these could be dealt with by way of issuing interpretive declarations[60]—and this is precisely what France and the United Kingdom did when they acceded to AP1.[61] Aldrich argued that "political and ideological considerations were determinative" in the Reagan administration's decision.[62] AP1 did not provide any solace or support for terrorists, in his view, and assertions that ratification of the Protocol by the United States would give aid or enhance the status of any terrorist group was "errant nonsense."[63]

This is strong language coming from a former deputy legal adviser to the State Department who had advised Henry Kissinger during the Vietnam peace negotiations. Although Aldrich was acquainted with the machinations of Washington, he lamented not pressing for ratification sooner, as he had not anticipated or foreseen that "those in both [the US State and Defense] Departments who had negotiated and supported the

Protocols would be replaced by skeptics and individuals with a different political agenda."[64]

1.6. Douglas Feith's Critique Makes the Front Page of the New York Times

Those skeptics and individuals with a different political agenda included Reagan administration officials like Douglas Feith, a longstanding supporter of Israel's settlement policy.[65] Feith, after a short period at the National Security Council in 1980–1981, moved to the Pentagon where he lobbied against US ratification of AP1, disparaging the protocol as "a pro-terrorist treaty that calls itself humanitarian law."[66] Significantly, Feith advanced this view of AP1 when he was deputy assistant secretary of defense for negotiations policy, before Reagan decided not to recommend ratification to the Senate. Feith attacked AP1 in the very first issue of *The National Interest*, an international affairs magazine, which was founded by Irving Kristol, the "godfather of neoconservatism."[67] The inaugural issue also featured articles by foreign policy heavyweights Zbigniew Brzezinski, Peter Rodman, Jeane Kirkpatrick, Richard Perle, Martin Indyk, Michael Ledeen, and Daniel Pipes.[68] Feith's critique of AP1 received widespread press coverage appearing on the front page of the *New York Times*,[69] and on the third page of the *Washington Post*.[70] In his memoir, Feith explained that he and Sofaer brought Caspar Weinberger, the secretary of defense, and George Shultz, the secretary of state, to agreement on not recommending ratification of AP1 to President Reagan in 1987.[71]

What Feith did not say is *how* he and Sofaer were able to persuade President Reagan to oppose AP1. Like many of the neoconservatives who rose to prominence in the Reagan administration, Feith and Sofaer were disturbed by developments at the United Nations in the 1970s when Israel was compared to apartheid South Africa and when Zionism was described as a form of racism. These views were also shared by Vietnam War veterans like Hays Parks, who complained that the Diplomatic Conference was dominated by the Third World and that the PLO was not a national liberation movement but a transnational terrorist organization sponsored by the Soviet Union that had committed terrorist attacks against the West.[72]

2. Why the Third World Was Viewed as a Problem

To appreciate why the influence of the Third World in the United Nations had become a problem in the eyes of the neoconservatives and Vietnam

War veterans, it would be helpful to take a step back at this juncture and remind ourselves of what happened during the course of the debates at the Diplomatic Conference on Humanitarian Law at Geneva (1974–77). The Diplomatic Conference that met to review and modernize the 1949 Geneva Conventions was a motley crew of radical dictatorships, liberal democracies, communist one-party states, oil-producing Arab sheikhdoms, and national liberation movements hailing from all parts of Africa, Asia, and Latin America. That decisions of the conference had to be taken by consensus made it all the more remarkable that these states and liberation movements were able to reach agreement, but their anticolonialism and opposition to the US war in South East Asia united them.[73]

As former US president Richard Nixon recognized, the Soviet Union had taken advantage of the international situation after the Second World War when it "fished assiduously in the troubled waters left in the wake of the dismantlement of the old colonial empires."[74] This included training and subsidizing guerrilla forces in the Third World. Communism's anti-imperialist message was, he explained, "a clever front for totalitarian parties, and many genuine nationalists were hoodwinked by this seemingly legitimate patriotic response to European colonialism."[75] This view would be repeated by General John W. Vessey, chairman of the Joint Chiefs of Staff, in his February 1984 speech to the House Armed Services Committee where he complained that the Soviets sought "to gain from international turmoil. Together with clients and surrogates, the Soviets are attempting to weaken the ties between the United States and its allies and to establish their own patterns of influence throughout much of the Third World."[76]

What incensed neoconservatives and Vietnam War veterans was not only the sympathy that was extended to the communist bloc by well-meaning, albeit naïve, anti-Vietnam war protestors but also the invitations extended to the national liberation movements to participate in the Diplomatic Conference, including a proposal to invite the Vietcong, which had killed thousands of American soldiers; the proposal was only narrowly defeated by 38 votes to 37, with 33 abstentions.[77] From the start of the debate, the Palestinian and Vietnamese struggles had become entwined with liberation struggles elsewhere in Africa and Asia, despite acts of terrorism by the Vietcong against thousands of civilians in South Vietnam during the war,[78] and terror attacks by PLO splinter groups like Black September in Munich (1972), Ma'alot (1974), and Entebbe (1976).[79] As Hays Parks complained, "the effort of the ICRC to develop a new law of war treaty became inextricably intertwined with the Arab war against Israel and of other conflicts supported by the Third World."[80] The demand that IHL apply equally to "freedom fighters" as well as to conventional forces was viewed by these critics as an attempt to confer legitimacy on these armed groups and to provide an international status for the PLO.[81]

While Israel and South Africa had legitimate concerns with AP1,[82] as the PLO and Umkhonto we Sizwe, the African National Congress's paramilitary wing, had committed numerous acts of terrorism in Israel and South Africa in the 1970s and 1980s, it is not clear why the liberation struggles in Africa and Asia were a specific concern of the Reagan administration, given that the United States was not engaged in such struggles, although, as we shall see, it would become embroiled in a very controversial guerrilla war in central America in the 1980s.[83] Indeed, Charles Lysaght, a member of the Irish delegation to the Diplomatic Conference, commented that most of the Western delegations "knew that no vital interest of theirs was affected. With colonial disengagement almost complete, they were unlikely to be involved in wars of self-determination, as defined, in the future. South Africa and Israel were the last frontiers."[84]

However, for officials in the Reagan administration like Feith who had strong links with the Likud party,[85] Article 85.4(a) of AP1 was of concern, as it had been drafted with a specific case in mind: "the settlement of Israelis on the Golan Heights and on the West Bank of Jordan."[86] In Likud's revisionist ideology, the Palestinians were not a people with a right of self-determination but part of the wider Arab nation that had exercised self-determination in some 20 Arab countries. In the view of Israeli prime minister Menachem Begin, the only genuine national liberation movement in Palestine had been the Irgun that drove the British out of Palestine following a series of spectacular terrorist actions.[87] Begin's view of the PLO was made demonstrably clear in Likud's 1977 election manifesto: "The so-called Palestinian Liberation Organization is not a national liberation movement but a murder organization which serves as a political tool and military arm of the Arab States and as an instrument of Soviet imperialism. The Likud government will take action to exterminate this organization."[88]

Gerson complained that the changes to IHL that had been introduced at the Diplomatic Conference in Geneva had been brought about as a result of the efforts of the Arab bloc at the United Nations that had succeeded in forging an alliance with African states; in exchange for Arab support against apartheid, the African states supported the struggle against Zionism.[89] Writing in the early 1980s, Thomas Franck observed that following the 1967 war, when Israel occupied more Arab lands, many African and Asian states analogized the Jews "to the white European settlers of Rhodesia and South Africa, denying equal economic, social, and political rights to the inhabitants of the West Bank and Gaza 'Bantustans.'"[90] Daniel Patrick Moynihan, the widely respected academic, diplomat, senator, and author,[91] who was appointed by President Ford as US ambassador to the United Nations in 1975, criticized the naivety of those in the US administration and diplomatic corps like Aldrich who believed they could "moderate" the policies of the UN majority. He pointed to the General Assembly resolution describing "zionism [with a small "z"] as a form of racism and racial discrimination" as emblematic of that body's anti-Americanism.[92] In his view, the United States would have been better off abandoning its attempt to reach out to the new nations of Africa and Asia altogether.

For neoconservatives and Vietnam War veterans, the UN had been transformed into a Third World bloc that espoused a different value system to the UN's original founding members and was changing the structure of international law through majority voting in UN forums. This included furthering the Soviet doctrine of wars of national liberation with the aim of overthrowing "colonialist, racist, and alien regimes" as expressed in AP1.[93] Not only had the Vietcong almost been invited to attend the Diplomatic Conference in Geneva, but the head of the PLO Yasser Arafat was given a standing ovation after a keynote speech to the UN General Assembly, and his organization had been granted observer status in the UN.[94] All the while, the Soviet Union was imprisoning Jewish dissidents and supporting the PLO in international forums against Israel. These developments prompted Leo Gross to express his fear that the "unbridled majoritarianism" of the UN General Assembly might soon have an impact on the work of the Security Council where serious decisions could be made.[95] This concern was echoed by Prosper Weil who complained about the emergence of an "international democracy," in which a majority or a representative proportion of states from the Third World would be able to "speak in the name of all and thus be entitled to impose its will on other states."[96]

To the veteran Israeli diplomat and lawyer Shabtai Rosenne, the 1970s "coincided with the radical change in the very texture of the UN, as a direct result of the decolonization process, and its exploitation by the Arabs as a forum for anti-Israel activities."[97] From his office on Second Avenue, Rosenne observed "intensive Arab efforts, since 1968, in the organs dealing with human rights no less than elsewhere, to create a general association of ideas between Israel and *apartheid* and racial discrimination, however impalpable the association may be, as part of the broader political operation of winning over African support for the Arab thesis and the isolation of Israel at the UN."[98] Indeed, an attempt to expel Israel from the organization preceded the adoption of the infamous "zionism is racism" resolution.[99] This, in turn, followed the adoption by the General Assembly of a score of resolutions drawing parallels between the struggle against colonialism in Africa and Israel's oppression of the Palestinians.[100]

US president Jimmy Carter had also taken a strong stand against Israel's settlement policy at the UN and had supported several Security Council resolutions describing their construction as a "flagrant violation" of international law.[101] These included voting in favor of Security Council resolution 465 that called on Israel to "dismantle the existing settlements and in particular to cease, on an urgent basis, the establishment, construction and planning of settlements."[102] For Moynihan, the Carter administration had committed a mortal sin by voting for this resolution in the Security Council as it had allowed the Security Council "to degenerate to the condition of the General Assembly."[103] Carter's decision to veto a draft Tunisian Security Council resolution calling for the establishment of an independent Palestinian state in the West Bank and Gaza a few weeks later[104] did not placate the neoconservatives. He was never forgiven.[105]

Carter's perceived support for Third World causes made him very unpopular not only with neoconservatives but also Vietnam War veterans. This was because Carter appeared to think that American power was dangerous and needed to be reined in following the Vietnam War—precisely what the neoconservatives and Vietnam War veterans were opposed to.[106] Or, as Moynihan put it, Carter represented "The view that had emerged during the Vietnam War to the effect that the United States, by virtue of its enormous power, and in consequence of policies and perhaps even national characteristics that were anything but virtuous, had become a principal source of instability and injustice in the world."[107] Following a series of setbacks in Afghanistan, Angola, and Iran, the Soviet Union—in the eyes of the neoconservatives and Vietnam War veterans—appeared to be winning the Cold War. It had to be stopped.

3. "Going Rambo": Taking the Battle to the Third World

This offensive found expression in the "Reagan Doctrine," which was described by Kirkpatrick and Gerson as being opposed to the "traditional isolationism and post-Vietnam assumptions about the illegitimacy of US intervention."[108] The doctrine, they claimed, emerged in response to the Soviet Union's quest for a global empire and its support for the national liberation movements in the Third World: "the Reagan administration articulated, in the wake of the Vietnam War, the moral and legal right to provide aid to indigenous resistance movements in countries around the globe, and justified it in terms of traditional American conceptions of legitimacy," they wrote.[109] They explained that the doctrine was formulated in response to the emergence of "Leninist dictatorships" in South Vietnam, Cambodia, Laos, Mozambique, Angola, Ethiopia, Nicaragua, and Afghanistan in the 1970s and 1980s, which the Reagan administration would roll back by providing anti-Soviet indigenous armed insurgencies with US support and training.[110]

Given the Soviet Union's manipulation, as they saw it, of lawmaking at the UN, Reagan administration officials often disparaged international governmental institutions and widely held assumptions about the sovereign inviolability of the postcolonial state. Following a spate of terrorist attacks in Beirut, Rangoon, Kuwait, London, and Rome, Robert McFarlane, the assistant to President Reagan for national security affairs and a veteran of the Vietnam War, expressed "the chilling feeling that the world [was] somehow at war even though there [were] no formal declarations and no fixed lines of battle."[111] He explained that the Reagan administration was "engaged in a new form of low-intensity conflict against an enemy that [was] hard to find and harder still to fix and destroy in the common military sense."[112] Given this "chilling feeling" and the belief that the Soviet Union was behind these attacks, the Reagan administration adopted what Burns Weston called a "Rambo-style" approach to international affairs (named after the US action film hero John Rambo, a US Army veteran traumatized by the Vietnam War, who used the skills he gained there to fight corrupt police officers, enemy troops, and drug cartels).[113] Weston referred to several actions taken by the Reagan administration that deserved this disparagement; including the Reagan administration's decision to withdraw from UNESCO; the refusal to ratify AP1 and the Law of the Sea Convention; the mining of the harbor in Nicaragua and the announced refusal to comply with the merits of the Nicaragua case, followed by the reversal of a 39-year foreign policy commitment to the ICJ's compulsory jurisdiction; the invasion of Grenada; the "sky jacking" of an Egyptian civilian aircraft following the *Achille Lauro* attack and the dispatching of a Delta force to capture the attackers in Italian territory; the bombing of the Libyan coastal cities of Benghazi and Tripoli; and so on.[114]

The bombing of the Libyan coastal cities of Benghazi and Tripoli represented a paradigm shift. It came on the heels of the *Achille Lauro* affair when members of the Palestine Liberation Front, a PLO splinter group, murdered Leon Klinghoffer, a 69-year-old Jewish American man in a wheelchair and threw him overboard. This notorious event, which was made into a film and a musical, inspired Sofaer to write an article for *Foreign Affairs* where he complained that the existing laws on counterterrorism were not only flawed but "perverse."[115] (The Italian government had refused to extradite the suspect, Abu Abbas, and let him go, after he and the hijackers had been intercepted by F-14 Tomcat Fighters in an Egyptian airplane over the Mediterranean and forced to land at a NATO airbase in Sicily.) Despite conventions criminalizing acts of terrorism, including hundreds of extradition treaties between states, the law of self-defense, in Sofaer's opinion, was inadequate, because it did not enable armed force to be used against terrorists in self-defense. The UN Charter was effectively handicapping the awesome power of the United States to enforce international law. Sofaer took specific aim at the PLO and complained that AP1 legitimized terrorism.[116] Sofaer's article was published a few weeks before Shultz's speech to the National Defense University on low-intensity warfare in January 1986, where he expressed his opinion that when the law failed, the use of force was necessary to combat terrorism, or else the UN Charter would become nothing more than "a suicide pact."[117]

When Shultz gave this speech, the ICJ was deliberating the merits of a case that Nicaragua had brought before the Court over the United States' support for the Contras, a right-wing paramilitary force of Nicaraguan rebels who were conducting covert actions against the leftist Sandinista regime in Nicaragua. The case was viewed with apprehension by the US government as it provided the ICJ with an opportunity to pass judgment on the laws of war in customary international law that had been transformed as a result of decolonization process that had provoked so much disquiet amongst neoconservatives and Vietnam War veterans.

4. The Vietnam War, the Arab-Israeli Conflict, and the *Nicaragua* Case

Central America may appear far removed from the conflicts in Vietnam and the Middle East, but for neoconservatives and Vietnam War veterans, Nicaragua was a Soviet client aligned to Cuba's fiercely anti-American revolutionary leader Fidel Castro and the PLO. There was also a direct parallel between Israel's support for the Lebanese Forces (founded by the anti-communist *Kataeb* or Phalange party) during the civil war in Lebanon (1975–90), and US support for the Contras (an anti-communist counter-revolutionary group made up of ex-guardsmen that had supported the Somoza dynasty) during the civil war in Nicaragua (1979–90), which were both justified in collective self-defense. And, of course, the US intervention in the Vietnam War had also been justified in collective self-defense.[118] Pillorying the PLO was not difficult to do as it was aligned with United States' enemies in Iran, Cuba, Vietnam, and the Soviet Union. In an article for *Commentary* magazine, the veritable "bible" of neoconservatism,[119] Kirkpatrick alleged that the PLO had made common cause with the Sandinistas in Nicaragua.[120]

The Vietnam and Arab-Israeli conflicts also affected developments in neighboring El Salvador, where the Salvadoran Communist Party leader, Jorge Shafik Handal, the son of Palestinian Arab immigrants from Bethlehem in what was then part of the British Mandate of Palestine, visited Moscow and Hanoi in search of arms. Following his visit, Vietnam agreed to ship 60 tons of weapons left behind by the Americans to Salvadoran guerrilla fighters.[121] Although the Iran-Contra scandal that damaged the careers of McFarlane, Pointdexter, and Oliver North had not yet become known, both Israel and the United States were selling weapons to Iran to fund the Contras in Nicaragua—even though they accused Iran of sponsoring international terrorism. Israel also provided the US government with weapons that Israel had confiscated from the PLO in Lebanon to send to the Contras in Nicaragua.[122]

The stakes were high in the *Nicaragua v United States* case because the ICJ was viewed as an important factor in the court of world public opinion. The Sandinistas were calculating that the United States would not be able to sustain its support for the Contras if American public opinion turned against the government as had happened during the latter stages of the Vietnam War when Congress "pulled the rug" on its contributions to the war effort following an effective political warfare offensive directed by Hanoi among antiwar groups in the US media, college campuses, and church groups.[123] The campaign succeeded in turning public opinion against the war hastening the fall of Saigon that was forever seared in the collective American consciousness by the image of hundreds of southern Vietnamese clamoring to board the last US Marine helicopter evacuating the US embassy.

4.1. The Nicaragua Case: The First Phase

Things started badly for the United States at the ICJ, when the Court ruled that it had jurisdiction to examine the merits, even though Shultz had submitted a reservation to the United States' Optional Clause declaration, which sought to prevent the Court from exercising jurisdiction.[124] Despite this reservation, the ICJ decided it had jurisdiction because the

State Department had not observed its own six-month notice period before attempting to modify its optional clause declaration.[125] The decision blindsided State Department lawyers who thought that their arguments had been airtight.[126] The decision was viewed with derision because it meant the ICJ had to decide the case on the basis of customary international law since the US multilateral treaty reservation prevented the Court from applying the UN Charter and other multilateral treaties.[127]

As customary international law on the use of force had been shaped by events in the UN in the previous decade, when the UN had recognized the legitimacy of national liberation movements and their struggles at the Diplomatic Conference in Geneva, even the ICJ's staunchest defenders in the State Department realized that were they to proceed to the merits of the case, they were likely to lose.[128] Reflecting on this moment decades later, Davis Robinson, the State Department's legal adviser, described the ICJ's decision in the first phase of the *Nicaragua* case as the "most disillusioning experience" of his life.[129] "The long love affair between the United States and the Court [had] c[o]me to an end," mused Gerson, then Kirkpatrick's counsel at the UN.[130]

On October 7, 1985, the United States terminated its optional clause declaration with the ICJ.[131] Six weeks later, Benjamin Netanyahu, then Israel's ambassador to the United Nations, followed the US lead, in what appeared to be a carefully calibrated move, by signing Israel's declaration terminating its 1956 acceptance of the compulsory jurisdiction of the ICJ.[132]

In justifying the US government's decision to terminate its optional clause declaration, Sofaer complained that a great many of the states that had emerged from decolonization since 1945 could "not be counted on" to share US views of the "original constitutional conception of the UN Charter," particularly with regard "to the special position of the permanent members of the Security Council in the maintenance of international peace and security."[133] Although the government of Israel provided no explanation for the termination of its optional clause declaration, Robbie Sabel, who was counselor for political affairs in Israel's embassy to the United States in the 1980s, later explained that Israel was wary of submitting disputes to the ICJ as the judges of the Court were appointed by the UN General Assembly that "has an automatic anti-Israeli majority."[134]

4.2. The Nicaragua Case: The Second Phase

On June 27, 1986, six months after Shultz had referred to the UN Charter's provision on the use of force as akin to a "suicide pact," the ICJ handed down its decision on the merits of the *Nicaragua* case. In a lengthy decision, the Court rejected by 12 votes to three the US government's central contention: that its support for the Contras was consistent with its right of collective self-defense under international law. By 12 votes to three, the Court also found that the United States had breached its legal obligations not to interfere in the affairs of another state by training, arming, equipping, financing, and supplying the Contra forces in Nicaragua.[135]

This decision particularly infuriated Eugene Rostow, the highest-ranking Democrat in the Reagan administration, who was also the first chairman of the Committee on the Present Danger and a leading neoconservative.[136] In addition to his directorship of the Arms Control and Disarmament Agency in the Reagan administration, Rostow penned many articles on the Arab-Israeli conflict, always siding with Israel and defending Likud's settlement policy in the Occupied Palestinian Territories.[137] Like Feith and other neoconservatives, Rostow had close connections to leading right-wing figures in Israeli politics.[138] Unsurprisingly, given his hawkish views, which he shared with his brother Walt, who was the first to advise President Kennedy to deploy US combat troops in South Vietnam,[139] Rostow claimed that the ICJ's decision on the merits in *Nicaragua* ranked "in folly with that of the Supreme Court of the United States in *Dred Scott v. Sandford* as an act of hubris and an abuse of power."[140]

What particularly upset the neoconservatives and Vietnam War veterans in the Reagan administration were the implications of the *Nicaragua* judgment for the ability of the United States to *legitimately* project its military power in overseas conflicts in the Third World unless it could demonstrate that its use of armed force was consistent with interpretations of the UN Charter and customary international law, which included the views of Third World states that had joined the UN during decolonization. This was because in rejecting the United States' collective self-defense argument, the Court had based its reasoning on UN resolutions, declarations, and treaties that had been adopted during the height of decolonization, which recognized the right of peoples to fight "against colonial domination and alien occupation and against racist régimes in the exercise of their right of self-determination" as Article 1 (4) of AP1 expressed it. If the United States did not have a right of self-defense in Nicaragua (because attacks on El Salvador and Honduras from the Sandinistas did not reach the level of an "armed attack" triggering a response in collective self-defense), then the PLO and other liberation movements could legitimately make similar arguments to justify attacks on Israel and other US allies that would not have a right of collective self-defense either. As Gerson observed, the ICJ

stipulated that acts of violence by armed bands must "occur on a significant scale before the right of self-defense could properly be invoked."[141]
Moreover, the Court excluded from armed attacks, "assistance to rebels in
the form of provision of weapons or logistical or other support."[142] This
led Gerson to complain that a government targeted by another for low-
intensity attack, in the form of supply of weapons or logistical support
for guerrillas seeking to topple its regime, was deprived of any means to
defend itself. It could not go to the UN, as it would be condemned for acting against groups struggling for political freedom. "The victim therefore
became the villain; the state daring to respond to guerrilla attacks became
itself the aggressor."[143]

5. Conclusion

Neoconservative and Vietnam War veterans in the Reagan administration—
some of whom were also international lawyers—played a crucial role in
scuttling US ratification of AP1. The reasons why they opposed ratification of AP1 varied, but in general it was based on the belief that the Soviet
Union and its friends in the Third World had succeeded in modifying
IHL in a way that was inimical to the policy goals being persuaded by
the Reagan administration in the Third World. Many US officials serving in the Reagan administration still felt chastened by the Vietnam War.
There was little military advantage for the US armed forces in recognizing an improved position for guerrilla fighters. Many of the neoconservatives had either studied in Israel or were connected to individuals in the
Likud party, and were on the record as supporters of Israel's settlement
policy, which was classified in AP1 as a "grave breach" of the 1949 Geneva
Conventions. They also viewed the PLO as "a murder organization which
serves as a political tool and military arm of the Arab States and as an
instrument of Soviet imperialism" to quote from Likud's 1977 election
manifesto.[144] Accordingly, given these strong views, there was much substance to Aldrich's claim that ideological and political considerations were
the primary reasons for the failure of the Reagan administration to ratify
AP1 in 1987. This conclusion has been borne out by subsequent events,
with the United States' closest allies during the Cold War, including many
members of NATO, as well as Australia and New Zealand, having ratified
AP1, albeit with reservations and statements of understanding. The United
States could have done the same, as Aldrich had suggested in 1977, and the
Joint Chiefs had prepared reservations and statements of understanding

in their 1982 review. In 1989, the Soviet Union even ratified AP1 without a reservation or a statement of understanding even though it is a nuclear weapon state. The irony is that the United States, by refusing to ratify AP1, has found itself in the "good company" of states like Turkey, Pakistan, Myanmar, and most glaringly of all Iran—which is still designated by the United States as a state sponsor of terrorism.

An enduring legacy of these debates is that they continue to influence contemporary debates on the law of armed conflict, by redefining traditional understandings of non-intervention and self-defense, whereby the United States and Israel continue to espouse a very broad right of self-defense in top-secret conversations among smaller groups of likeminded states.[145] In their attempts to reinterpret the *jus ad bellum* in this way, these states continue to privilege the *opinio juris* of the most technologically advanced and powerful of states and ignore the views of the Third World, even though they represent the largest bloc of states at the UN, thereby undermining the development of customary international law.[146] Sofaer, for example, continued to espouse a very broad notion of self-defense even before the attacks on the United States on 9/11.[147] After the Clinton administration (in the midst of the Monica Lewinsky scandal) bombed Afghanistan and Sudan in retaliation for attacks on US embassies in Kenya and Tanzania in 1998 in "Operation Infinite Reach," (the attacks did not emanate from those countries—the Al-Shifa plant, which produced over half of Sudan's pharmaceuticals, did not produce chemical weapons, as alleged, and bin Laden was not in the camps that were attacked), Sofaer claimed that "[a]rmed attacks permitting self-defense can occur anywhere, not just on US territory."[148] This was an argument that legitimized the US practice of targeted killings globally that became a central feature of America's endless wars.[149] Sofaer also claimed that the United States, as a permanent member of the UN Security Council, had the power "to block adoption of any measure aimed at forcing it to abide by any standard whatever, or even the enforcement of any decision of the international court that concludes the United States has behaved illegally or attempts to impose any sanction on the United States concerning its use of force."[150] It had apparently not occurred to lawyers, like Sofaer, that these arguments could be used by the other permanent members of the UN Security Council. And this is precisely what happened in February 2022, when Russian president Vladimir Putin took advantage of American arguments in formulating the Russian Federation's rationale for invading Ukraine, by referring to "precedents," such as NATO's aerial bombardment of Serbia in 1999 and US support for regime change in Iraq, Libya, Syria, and so on (states that—

coincidentally—happened to all be close allies of the Soviet Union during the Cold War, and that maintained close ties to Russia).[151]

Ultimately, however, it was Aldrich, Matheson, Robinson, and the other veteran lawyers who served in the State Department and the Pentagon during the Carter and Reagan administrations who had the last laugh. For they understood that bringing the United States into compliance with the provisions of the *jus in bello* pioneered in the 1970s was more legitimating for American war than constraining—as Amanda Alexander shows in her chapter in this volume. So while the neoconservatives won the political battle in the 1980s, it was the old school liberals long employed in government service who understood that the United States could still become bound by the consensus provisions of API, even without ratifying the protocols, through the development of customary international law.[152]

NOTES

An early draft of this chapter was first presented at the Seventh Annual Junior Faculty Forum for International Law at the University of Melbourne on May 28, 2018. The author would like to thank Anne Orford for her written comments on his paper, as well as additional feedback provided by Joseph H. H. Weiler, Martti Koskenniemi, Dino Kritsiotis, Dianne Otto, and Dan Bodansky. A revised draft was subsequently presented at a workshop organized by the Transsystematic Law Research Cluster at the Middle East Institute (MEI) at the National University of Singapore on December 6, 2018, where additional feedback was provided by the other contributors to this book. The author would especially like to thank Reviewer A for the anonymous feedback provided to him through the University of Michigan Press peer review process. Finally, a word of thanks is due to the late Peter Sluglett, director of MEI, and Charlotte Schriwer, deputy director, who provided funding for the research he undertook for this chapter in the state of Virginia and Washington, DC, where he interviewed former Reagan administration officials, and at the Ronald Reagan Presidential Library in Simi Valley, California, in November 2015 where he reviewed government documents.

1. During the Cold War, references to the "Third World" referred to those states that became members of the Non-Aligned Movement that were not aligned with either the capitalist or communist blocs. Many of these states were non-European societies that had been colonized from the sixteenth century by the European Empires, and which gradually acquired political independence since the 1940s. See Antony Anghie, *Imperialism, Sovereignty and the Making of International Law* (Cambridge: Cambridge University Press, 2004, 2007 ed.), 3.

2. See Edwin Brown Firmage, "The 'War of National Liberation' and the Third World," in John Norton Moore, ed., *Law and Civil War in the Modern World* (Baltimore: Johns Hopkins University Press, 1974), 304–47.

3. The focus of this article is on API, rather than APII, because the Reagan administration did not oppose ratification of APII, although it appears that no deci-

sion was taken in the Senate on ratification of APII because it had become too closely associated with AP1. See Gary D. Solis, *The Law of Armed Conflict: International Humanitarian Law in War* (Cambridge: Cambridge University Press, 2010), 133.

4. George Shultz, *Turmoil and Triumph: My Years as Secretary of State* (New York: Charles Scribner's Sons, 1993), 678.

5. See Richard Falk, "The Decline of Normative Restraint in International Relations," *Yale Journal of International Law* 10 (1984–85): 263–70.

6. These individuals have been identified as neoconservatives either because they were members of the Committee on the Present Danger or because they have identified themselves as such in their own writings and in interviews. While many of the names on the list are uncontroversial, some might baulk at the inclusion of Shultz. However, see his interview with Daniel Henniner, "George Shultz, Father of the Bush Doctrine," *Wall Street Journal*, April 29, 2006, reprinted on the website of the Hoover Institution here: https://www.hoover.org/research/george-shultz-fa ther-bush-doctrine. On how the neoconservatives shaped American politics in the 1970s–2000s, see Peter Steinfels, *The Neoconservatives: The Men Who Are Changing America's Politics* (New York: Simon and Schuster, 1979). Stefan Halper and Jona-than Clarke, *America Alone: The Neoconservatives and the Global Order* (Cambridge: Cambridge University Press, 2004). Gary Dorrien, *Imperial Designs: Neoconserva-tism and the New Pax Americana* (New York: Routledge, 2004). Murray Friedman, *The Neoconservative Revolution: Jewish Intellectuals and the Shaping of Public Policy* (Cambridge: Cambridge University Press, 2005). Jacob Heilbrunn, *They Knew They Were Right: The Rise of the Neocons* (New York: Doubleday, 2008). Jesús Velasco, *Neoconservatives in US Foreign Policy under Ronald Reagan and George W. Bush: Voices behind the Throne* (Baltimore: Johns Hopkins University Press, 2010). Justin Vaïsse, *Neoconservatism: The Biography of a Movement* (Cambridge, MA: Harvard University Press, 2011). Identifying Vietnam War veterans was much easier as this is a question of fact. For a book that explores the role of Vietnam War veterans in the Reagan administration, see Robert Timberg, *The Nightingale's Song* (New York: Simon & Schuster, 1995).

7. See the statement by Hess (Israel) in *Official Records of the Diplomatic Confer-ence on the Reaffirmation and Development of International Humanitarian Law Appli-cable in Armed Conflicts* (1974–1977), vol. VI, at 39–42, paras. 39–64. The records of the Diplomatic Conference can be accessed at the Library of Congress online at https://www.loc.gov/rr/frd/Military_Law/RC-dipl-conference-records.html (last visited February 13, 2020).

8. See the statement by Aldrich (United States), in *Official Records of the Diplo-matic Conference on the Reaffirmation and Development of International Humanitarian Law Applicable in Armed Conflicts* (1974–1977), vol. VI, at 293, para. 76.

9. See, e.g., the acknowledgments in Benjamin Netanyahu, *A Durable Peace: Israel and Its Place Among the Nations* (New York: Warner Books, 1993, 2000 reprint), 465 (thanking Douglas Feith for reading the manuscript and suggesting important revisions). Allan Gerson knew Yoni Netanyahu and his brother Benjamin when he studied in Israel in the early 1970s, and vacationed with them. Interview with the author, Washington, DC, November 9, 2015. Gerson died from CJD on December 1, 2019. See Katharine Q. Seelye, "Allan Gerson, Who Sought Justice for Terror Victims, Dies at 74," *New York Times*, December 4, 2019.

10. Richard Nixon, *The Real War* (New York: Warner Books, 1980), 5.

11. See Jeane J. Kirkpatrick and Allan Gerson, "The Reagan Doctrine, Human Rights, and International Law," in L. Henkin et al., *Right v Might: International Law and the Use of Force* (Washington, DC: Council on Foreign Relations, 1991, 2nd ed.), 19–36 at 21.

12. Kirkpatrick and Gerson, 30. Carter's perceived unwillingness to confront the Soviet Union in the Third World may be questioned on account of his administration's massive increase in defense spending that preceded the election of Ronald Reagan in 1980, and his support for the Mujahidin in Afghanistan before Moscow's invasion, but it was a perception largely shared by neoconservatives. See Greg Grandin, *Empire's Workshop: Latin America, the United States, and the Rise of the New Imperialism* (New York: Henry Holt & Co. 2010), 66.

13. *Military and Paramilitary Activities in and against Nicaragua (Nicaragua v. United States of America)*, Jurisdiction and Admissibility, Judgment, ICJ Reports (1984), at 392. *Military and Paramilitary Activities in and against Nicaragua (Nicaragua v. United States of America)*, Merits, Judgment, ICJ Reports (1986), at 14.

14. George Aldrich, "Prospects for United States Ratification of Additional Protocol I to the 1949 Geneva Conventions," *American Journal of International Law* 85 (1991): 1–20.

15. George Aldrich, "Why the United States of America Should Ratify Additional Protocol I," in A. J. M. Delissen and G. J. Tanja, eds., *Humanitarian Law of Armed Conflict: Challenges Ahead* (Dordrecht: M. Nijhoff, 1991), 127–44.

16. See George Aldrich, "New Life for the Laws of War," *American Journal of International Law* 75 (1981): 764–83. George Aldrich, "Some Reflections on the Origins of the 1977 Geneva Protocols," in Christophe Swinarski, ed., *Studies and Essays on International Humanitarian Law and Red Cross Principles in Honour of Jean Pictet* (The Hague: Martinus Nijhoff and the International Committee of the Red Cross, Geneva, 1984), 129–37. George Aldrich, "Progressive Development of the Laws of War: A Reply to Criticisms of the 1977 Geneva Protocol 1," *Virginia Journal of International Law* 26 (1986): 693–720.

17. Other scholars and former officials that voiced criticism of the Reagan administration's stance on AP1 included Howard Levie, who held the Stockton Chair at the US Naval War College from 1970–1971, Aldrich's colleague Waldemar A. Solf, and the ICRC's Hans-Peter Gasser. See Waldemar Solf, "A Response to Douglas J. Feith's law in the Service of Terror—The Strange Case of Additional Protocol," *Akron Law Review* 20 (1986): 261–89. Hans-Peter Gasser, "An Appeal for Ratification by the United States," *American Journal of International Law* 81 (1987): 912–25. Howard Levie, "The 1977 Protocol 1 and the United States," *Saint Louis University Law Journal* 38 (1993): 469–84. See also, Theodor Meron, "The Time Has Come for the United States to Ratify Geneva Protocol 1," *American Journal of International Law* 88, no. 4 (1994): 678–86.

18. Aldrich, "Why the United States of America should Ratify Additional Protocol I," 128.

19. Aldrich, "Why the United States of America should Ratify Additional Protocol I," 143–44.

20. See *American Society of International Law Proceedings* 74 (April 17–19, 1980): 208.

21. *American Society of International Law Proceedings* 74 (April 17–19, 1980): 208.

22. W. Hays Parks entered federal service as a commissioned officer in the Marine Corps. His initial service was as a reconnaissance officer. He served in the Republic of Vietnam (1968–1969) as an infantry officer and senior prosecuting attorney for the First Marine Division. His subsequent service included first Marine Corps Representative at the Judge Advocate General's School, US Army; congressional liaison officer for the Secretary of the Navy; and Chief, Law of War Branch, Office of the Judge Advocate General of the Navy. See W. Hays Parks, "Air War and the Law of War," *Air Force Law Review* 32 (1990): 1 at 63–111.

23. See Report by the J-5 to the Joint Chiefs of Staff on JCS Review of the 1977 Protocols Additional to the 1949 Geneva Conventions. Reference: IZ, September 13, 1982 (declassified September 30, 2013). This 45-page report produced for Fred Iklé, under secretary of defense for policy, consists of a memorandum and two annexes with suggested draft language for possible reservations and interpretative declarations in the event President Reagan agreed to send the Protocols to the Senate for advice and consent to ratification. It was signed by James E. Dalton, lieutenant general, USAF, director, Joint Staff. It would appear the Joint Chiefs of Staff, while reserving their final opinion, did not oppose ratification. Their primary concern was to avoid a situation that could lead to differing operational procedures that could adversely affect combined forces operations. They also wanted to consult with allies. The report can be downloaded from the special collections link at the Executive Services Directorate, available at http://www.esd.whs.mil/FOIA/Rea ding-Room/Reading-Room-List/Special_Collections/

24. Report by the J-5 to the Joint Chiefs of Staff on JCS Review of the 1977 Protocols Additional to the 1949 Geneva Conventions. Reference: IZ, September 13, 1982.

25. See Parks, "Air War and the Law of War," at 89, footnote 283 (criticizing the [undated] NATO review).

26. Report by the J-5 to the Joint Chiefs of Staff on JCS Review of the 1977 Protocols Additional to the 1949 Geneva Conventions (September 13, 1982), Appendix A, para. 4.

27. Report by the J-5 to the Joint Chiefs of Staff on JCS Review of the 1977 Protocols Additional to the 1949 Geneva Conventions (September 13, 1982), Appendix A, para. 4.

28. See Allan Gerson, *The Kirkpatrick Mission: Diplomacy without Apology, America at the United Nations 1981–1985* (New York: The Free Press, 1991), 250–52.

29. The cable dated October 16, 1984, is reproduced in Gerson, 252. One of the reasons why the Pentagon opposed ratification was because it did away with "the distinction between combatants and non-combatants, [and] it would be hard to square ratification of the protocols with our policy of combatting terrorism."

30. The "top-secret" memo was subsequently leaked to the *New York Times* where it was disparaged. See W. Safire, "Rights for Terrorists? A 1977 Treaty would Grant Them," *New York Times*, November 15, 1984, A31. (Criticizing Robinson for producing a memo calling on the administration to "move towards effective international humanitarian protection, consistent with Western military interests.")

31. Memorandum for the Secretary of Defense: Review of the 1977 First Additional Protocol to the Geneva Conventions of 1949. JCSM-152–85 (May 3, 1985), available on the website of the Executive Services Directorate at https://www.esd

.whs.mil/Portals/54/Documents/FOID/Reading%20Room/Joint_Staff/1985_JC
SM_152-85_Review_of_GC_AP_I.pdf

32. Memorandum for the Secretary of Defense: Review of the 1977 First Additional Protocol to the Geneva Conventions of 1949.

33. Vessey also commanded the 3rd Armored Division Artillery from 1967 to
1969, and was the division chief of staff from 1969 to 1970, before being promoted
to brigadier general.

34. Report by the J-5 to the Joint Chiefs of Staff on JCS Review of the 1977
Protocols Additional to the 1949 Geneva Conventions (September 13, 1982),
Annex B to Appendix A.

35. Strikingly, this complaint about abuse of the laws of war as "war crimes" for
propaganda purposes during the anti-Vietnam War protests was very similar to the
complaints that appeared in article written by W. Hays Parks a decade later. See W.
Hays Parks, "Exaggerated or One-Sided Claims of Law of War Violations," in John
Norton Moore, ed., *Deception and Deterrence in "Wars of National Liberation," State-
Sponsored Terrorism and Other Forms of Secret Warfare* (Durham: Carolina Academic
Press, 1997), 103–26.

36. Memorandum for the Secretary of Defense: Review of the 1977 First Additional Protocol to the Geneva Conventions of 1949. JCSM-152–85 (May 3, 1985),
2.

37. Memorandum for the Secretary of Defense: Review of the 1977 First Additional Protocol to the Geneva Conventions of 1949. JCSM-152–85 (May 3, 1985),
2.

38. Memorandum for the Secretary of Defense: Review of the 1977 First Additional Protocol to the Geneva Conventions of 1949. JCSM-152–85 (May 3, 1985),
3.

39. Memorandum for the Secretary of Defense: Review of the 1977 First Additional Protocol to the Geneva Conventions of 1949. JCSM-152–85 (May 3, 1985),
3.

40. Memorandum for the Secretary of Defense: Review of the 1977 First Additional Protocol to the Geneva Conventions of 1949. JCSM-152–85 (May 3, 1985),
36.

41. Memorandum for the Secretary of Defense: Review of the 1977 First Additional Protocol to the Geneva Conventions of 1949. JCSM-152–85 (May 3, 1985),
44.

42. Memorandum for the Secretary of Defense: Review of the 1977 First Additional Protocol to the Geneva Conventions of 1949. JCSM-152–85 (May 3, 1985),
52.

43. Memorandum for the Secretary of Defense: Review of the 1977 First Additional Protocol to the Geneva Conventions of 1949. JCSM-152–85 (May 3, 1985),
52.

44. Memorandum for the Secretary of Defense: Review of the 1977 First Additional Protocol to the Geneva Conventions of 1949. JCSM-152–85 (May 3, 1985),
97.

45. Aldrich, "'Why the United States of America should Ratify Additional Protocol I," at 129–30.

46. See the Letter of Transmittal, The White House, January 29, 1987, *American
Journal of International Law* 81 (1987): 911.

47. *American Journal of International Law* 81 (1987): 911.
48. *American Journal of International Law* 81 (1987): 911.
49. *American Journal of International Law* 81 (1987): 911.
50. See Michael Matheson, "The United States Position on the Relation of Customary International Law to the 1977 Protocols Additional to the 1949 Geneva Conventions," *American University Journal of International Law and Policy* 2 (1987): 419–36 at 420.
51. See Abraham Sofaer, "The Rationale for the United States Decision," *American Journal of International Law* 81 (1987), at 784–87. See also, the statement by Hess (Israel) in *Official Records, Vol. VI*, at 39–42. See further, the detailed explanations provided by Lapidoth in *Official Records, Vol. VI*, at 121–22, paras. 16–19 as to why Israel could not vote for Article 42 (now Article 44) of AP1. See also, the statement by Sabel as to why Israel could not vote for Article 84 (now Article 96(3)) in *Official Records, Vol. VI*, at 352–53, paras. 72–74.
52. See *Official Records, Vol. VI*, at 353, para. 75.
53. Sofaer, "The Rationale for the United States Decision," at 785. But see Levie's criticisms, "The 1977 Protocol 1 and the United States," at 475–76.
54. Don Oberdorfer, "Abraham Sofaer: Players State's Legal Adviser Deals with Policy, Then the Law," *Washington Post*, March 10, 1986, A13.
55. See Linda A. Malone, "Sharon vs. Time: The Criminal Responsibility under International Law for Civilian Massacres," *Palestine Yearbook of International Law* 3 (1986): 41–74.
56. Don Oberdorfer, "Abraham Sofaer: Players State's Legal Adviser Deals with Policy, Then the Law," *Washington Post*, March 10, 1986, A13.
57. Aldrich, "Why the United States of America should Ratify Additional Protocol I," at 133.
58. According to Solis, no liberation movement made an application under Art. 96(3). See Solis, *The Law of Armed Conflict* at 128. See also, Meron, "The Time Has Come for the United States to Ratify Geneva Protocol 1," at 683.
59. Aldrich, "Why the United States of America should Ratify Additional Protocol I," at 134–37. The United Kingdom submitted the following reservation to ensure that the Provisional IRA could not make such a declaration: "It is the understanding of the United Kingdom that the term 'armed conflict' of itself and in its context denotes a situation of a kind which is not constituted by the commission of ordinary crimes including acts of terrorism whether concerted or in isolation. The United Kingdom will not, in relation to any situation in which it is itself involved, consider itself bound in consequence of any declaration purporting to be made under paragraph 3 of Article 96 unless the United Kingdom shall have expressly recognised that it has been made by a body which is genuinely an authority representing a people engaged in an armed conflict of the type to which Article 1, paragraph 4, applies."
60. Tellingly, with the exception of Israel, the United States' closest allies (such as Canada, Australia, and the United Kingdom) submitted reservations and interpretative declarations when they ratified AP1—in some cases using language that was very similar to the language used by the Joint Chiefs in the J-5 review. For a useful analysis of these reservations, see Julie Gaudreau, "The Reservations to the Protocols additional to the Geneva Conventions for the Protection of War Victims," *International Review of the Red Cross* 849 (2003): 143–84.

61. See the declaration submitted by France upon its accession to AP1 on April 11, 2001. See also the declaration made by the United Kingdom on July 2, 2002, which stated that "It continues to be the understanding of the United Kingdom that the rules introduced by the Protocol apply exclusively to conventional weapons without prejudice to any other rules of international law applicable to other types of weapons. In particular, the rules so introduced do not have any effect on and do not regulate or prohibit the use of nuclear weapons."

62. Aldrich, "Why the United States of America should Ratify Additional Protocol I," at 133.

63. Aldrich, "Why the United States of America should Ratify Additional Protocol I," at 141.

64. George Aldrich, "Comments on the Geneva Protocols," 320 *International Review of the Red Cross (IRRC)* (October 31, 1997), available at https://www.icrc.org/eng/resources/documents/article/other/57jnv2.htm (last accessed February 24, 2020) (no page numbers provided).

65. In June 1981, Feith drafted a memorandum for Richard Allen, the national security adviser, insisting that Israel's settlements were "legal" despite the views of the State Department's legal adviser. See the advice by the legal adviser Herbert J. Hansell on the illegality of Israeli civilian settlement activity in "United States: Letter of the State Department Legal Adviser Concerning the Legality of Israeli Settlements in the Occupied Territories," *International Legal Materials* 17 (1978): 777–79. Compare this to Douglas J. Feith, "Notes on Legality of Israel's West Bank Settlements," June 16, 1981. Collection: Executive Secretariat, NSC, Near East and South Asia [Middle East]. Contents: Israel/Iraq-Israel. Box: 68. Ronald Reagan Library. Feith continued to argue in favor of the legality of Israel's settlements into the 1990s during the negotiations between Israel and the PLO. See Douglas Feith and Eugene Rostow, *Israel's Legitimacy in Law and History: Proceedings of the Conference on International Law and the Arab-Israeli Conflict* (1993). See also, Douglas Feith, "A Mandate for Israel," *National Interest* 33 (1993): 43–58, at 56.

66. See Douglas Feith, "Protocol 1: Moving Humanitarian Law Backwards," *Akron Law Review* 19 (1985–1986): 531–35, at 534.

67. See Douglas Feith, "Law in the Service of Terror—the Strange Case of Additional Protocol I," *National Interest* 1 (Fall 1985): 36–47.

68. Feith, "Law in the Service of Terror," 36–47.

69. See Leslie H. Gelb, "War Law Pact Faces Objection of Joint Chiefs: Joint Chiefs said to Oppose Revisions in War Law," *New York Times*, July 22, 1985, A1.

70. M. Weisskopf, "Geneva Convention Changes Questioned: US Fears Creation of Terrorist Safety Net," *Washington Post*, July 23, 1985, A3. Feith also appears to have influenced the views of administration officials such as Guy Roberts, assistant staff judge advocate and commander-in-chief Pacific Forces, who attended a conference on terrorism and low intensity warfare at the Fletcher School of Law and Diplomacy in 1985 and who cited Feith's article favorably in his work. See Guy B. Roberts, "The New Rules for Waging War: The Case Against Ratification of Additional Protocol 1," *Virginia Journal of International Law* 26, no. 1 (1985): 109–70 (citing half a dozen times the then unpublished copy of Feith's paper "Law in the Service of Terror" that was presented at the Fourteenth Annual Conference on Terrorism and Low Intensity Operations at the Fletcher School of Law and Diplo-

macy in April 1985). Feith's article is also cited by W. Hays Parks, "Air War and the Law of War," at 77.

71. See Douglas J. Feith, *War and Decision: Inside the Pentagon at the Dawn of the War on Terrorism* (New York: HarperCollins, 2008), at 39–40. See also, Gerson, *The Kirkpatrick Mission*, at 246–54.

72. See W. Hays Parks, "Air War and the Law of War," at 79. See also, W. Hays Parks, "Perspective and the Importance of History," *Yearbook of International Humanitarian Law* 14 (2011): 361–82 at 363.

73. As Hays Parks complained, a vote by consensus "permitted delegations to pressure other delegations to accept an article, however imperfect it may have been, rather than break consensus." See W. Hays Parks, "Air War and the Law of War," at 83.

74. R. Nixon, *The Real War*, 4.

75. R. Nixon, *The Real War*, 97.

76. Statement before the House Services Committee, February 2, 1984, in *Selected Works of General John W. Vessey, Jr., USA Tenth Chairman of the Joint Chiefs of Staff 22 June 1982—30 September 1985* (Washington, DC: Joint History Office: Office of the Chairman of the Joint Chiefs of Staff, 2008), 105.

77. See *Official Records of the Diplomatic Conference, Vol. V*, at 52–53 (no paragraph number provided).

78. According to Lewy, the Vietcong assassinated 36,725 persons and abducted 58,499 between 1957–1972. See Gunther Lewy, *America in Vietnam* (Oxford: Oxford University Press, 1987), 272–73 ("80 percent of the terrorist victims were ordinary civilians and only about 20 percent were government officials, policemen, members of the self-defense forces or pacification cadres").

79. On the connections between the PLO and Vietnam, see P. T. Chamberlain, *The Global Offensive: The United States, the Palestine Liberation Organization, and the Making of the Post-Cold War Order* (Oxford: Oxford University Press, 2012), 41–75. On the influence on popular American culture of Israel's raid on Entebbe, see Amy Kaplan, *Our American Israel: The Story of an Entangled Alliance* (Cambridge, MA: Harvard University Press, 2018).

80. See W. Hays Parks, "Air War and the Law of War," at 69.

81. Parks, "Air War and the Law of War," at 69, note 238.

82. South Africa only acceded to AP1 after the fall of apartheid.

83. See Section 5 below.

84. See Charles Lysaght, "The Attitude of Western Countries," in Antonio Cassese, ed., *The New Humanitarian Law of Armed Conflict, Vol. I* (Napoli: Editoriale Scientifica, 1970), 349–85 at 354.

85. As explained to me by Nicholas Veliotis who was assistant secretary of state from January 1981 until the end of 1983 when he was replaced by Richard Murphy. Interview with author, Metropolitan Club, Washington DC, November 19, 2015.

86. See Michael Bothe et al., eds., *New Rules for Victims of Armed Conflicts: Commentary on the Two 1977 Protocols Additional to the Geneva Conventions of 1949* (The Hague: Martinus Nijhoff, 1982), at 518.

87. See Menachem Begin, *The Revolt: Story of the Irgun* (Steimatzky, 1952, 2007 reprint), 212–30 (describing the attack on the King David Hotel).

88. Quoted in Avi Shlaim, "The Likud in Power: The Histiography of Revision-

ist Zionism," *Israel Studies* 1 (1996): 283. For a slightly different rendering of the Hebrew translation, see Walter Laqueur and Dan Schueftan, eds., *The Israel-Arab Reader: A Documentary History of the Middle East Conflict* (London: Penguin, 2016 edition), 207.

89. Interview between Allan Gerson and the author, Washington, DC, November 9, 2015.

90. Thomas M. Franck, *Nation Against Nation: What Happened to the UN Dream and What the US Can Do about It* (Oxford: Oxford University Press, 1985), 214.

91. Including, Daniel Patrick Moynihan, *On the Law of Nations* (Cambridge, MA: Harvard University Press, 1990).

92. See Moynihan, "Abiotrophy in Turtle Bay: The United Nations in 1975," *Harvard International Law Journal* 17, no. 3 (1976): 465–502. Regarding the UN debate on "Zionism is racism" resolution, see Franck, *Nation Against Nation*, 205–9.

93. See Jeane J. Kirkpatrick and Allan Gerson, "The Reagan Doctrine, Human Rights, and International Law," in Henkin et al., ed., *Right v Might*, 19–36 at 32.

94. For Yasser Arafat's keynote address, see Question of Palestine. UN doc. A/PV.2282 and Corr.1, November 13, 1974. The PLO was granted observer status in GA Res 3237, November 22, 1974.

95. See Leo Gross, "Voting in the Security Council and the PLO," *American Journal of International Law* 70, no. 3 (1976): 470–91, at 471.

96. Prosper Weil, "Toward Relative Normativity in International Law?" *American Journal of International Law* 77 (1983): 413–42, at 420. Daphné Richemond-Barak, Senior Researcher at the International Institute for Counter-Terrorism at the Lauder School of Government, Diplomacy and Strategy at the IDC Herzliya, in Israel, is the granddaughter of Prosper Weil. See W. Michael Reisman, "In Memoriam: Prosper Weil (1926–2018)," *Proceedings of the ASIL Annual Meeting* 113 (2019): 401–2.

97. See Shabtai Rosenne, "Israel and the United Nations: Changed Perspectives, 1945–1976," in Morris Fine and Milton Himmelfarb, eds., *American Jewish Yearbook 1978* (1977): 49.

98. Rosenne, "Israel and the United Nations: Changed Perspectives, 1945–1976" (emphasis in original).

99. On the decredentialization of South Africa, see GA Resolution 3207, September 30, 1974. On the attempts to expel Israel from the UN in the early 1980s, see Franck, *Nation Against Nation*, 216–18.

100. See, e.g., GA Res. A/3070, November 30, 1973.

101. See SC Res 446, March 22, 1979, SC Res 452, July 20, 1979, SC Res 465, March 1, 1980, SC Res 476, June 30, 1980. SC Res 478, August 20, 1980.

102. See SC Res 465, para 6 (adopted unanimously).

103. D. P. Moynihan, "Joining the Jackals: The US at the UN 1977–1980," *Commentary* 72, no. 2 (February 1981), available at https://www.commentarymagazine.com/articles/joining-the-jackals/ (last accessed February 24, 2020) (no page numbers given).

104. See Tunisia: draft resolution UN doc. S/13911, April 28, 1980.

105. The US vote in favor of Resolution 465 was mentioned as one reason (among others) for Carter's failure to win reelection, as it affected the New York primary in which the presidential candidate lost to his Democratic rival Ted Kennedy. See

Jack W. Germond and Jules Witcover, *Blue Smoke and Mirrors: How Reagan Won and Why Carter Lost the Election of 1980* (New York: Viking Press, 1981), at 151–56. Consider also the backlash caused by the publication of Jimmy Carter, *Palestine: Peace not Apartheid* (New York: Simon & Schuster, 2006). Even Carter's Jewish supporters in the Democratic Party turned against him. See Alan Dershowitz, *The Case Against Israel's Enemies: Exposing Jimmy Carter and Others Who Stand in the Way of Peace* (Hoboken, NJ: Wiley & Sons, 2008), at 17–48.

106. Dershowitz, *The Case Against Israel's Enemies.* See also Norman Podhoretz, *The Present Danger: Do We Have the Will to Reverse the Decline of American Power?* (New York: Simon & Schuster, 1980). Norman Podhoretz, *Why We Were in Vietnam* (New York: Simon & Schuster, 1980).

107. Moynihan, "Joining the Jackals" (no page number provided).

108. Kirkpatrick and Gerson, "The Reagan Doctrine, Human Rights, and International Law," in Henkin et al., ed., *Right v Might: International Law and the Use of Force* (1991), 19–36 at 21.

109. Kirkpatrick and Gerson, at 24.

110. Kirkpatrick and Gerson, at 23–24.

111. Robert C. McFarlane, "Terrorism and the Future of Free Society," *Studies in Conflict and Terrorism* 8, no. 4 (1986): 315–26 at 315.

112. McFarlane, "Terrorism and the Future of Free Society," 315–16.

113. Burns H. Weston, "The Reagan Administration Versus International Law," *Case Western Reserve Journal of International Law* 19 (1987): 295–302 at 296.

114. Weston, "The Reagan Administration Versus International Law," 296–97.

115. Abraham, Sofaer, "Terrorism and the Law," *Foreign Affairs* 64 (1986): 901–22 at 902.

116. Sofaer, "Terrorism and the Law," at 912–15.

117. Shultz, *Turmoil and Triumph*, at 678.

118. Public Law 88–408, August 10, 1965. See also, US State Department: "The Legality of United States Participation in the Defense of Viet-Nam," *American Journal of International Law* 60 (1966): 565–85.

119. Norman Podhoretz was the longtime editor-in-chief of *Commentary.*

120. Jeane J. Kirkpatrick, "US Security & Latin America," *Commentary* 71 (January 1, 1981), at 29.

121. See N. Rostow, "Nicaragua and the Law of Self-Defense Revisited," *Yale Journal of International Law* 11 (1986): 437–61, at 443, note 23. Rostow cites a State Department publication *"Revolution beyond our Borders" Sandinista Intervention in Central America* (July 19, 1981), at 5–6. See also, Robert F. Turner, *Nicaragua v. United States: A Look at the Facts* (Washington, DC: Institute for Foreign Policy Analysis, 1987), xii., and 55–59.

122. Amir Oren, "The truth about Israel, Iran and the 1980s US arms deals," *Ha'aretz*, November 26, 2010.

123. Turner, *Nicaragua v. United States: A Look at the Facts*, xiii, and 40–41.

124. See the reference to the Shultz letter dated April 6, 1984, in Military and Paramilitary Activities in and against Nicaragua (Nicaragua v. United States of America), *Jurisdiction and Admissibility*, 398, para 13.

125. See *Judgment on Jurisdiction and Admissibility*, 418–21, at paras 59–65.

126. See Gerson, *The Kirkpatrick Mission*, at 265.

127. See *Judgment on Jurisdiction and Admissibility*, at 424, para. 73. See also, *Judgment on the Merits*, at 31–38, paras 42–56. For a neat account of the case see Mary Ellen O'Connell, "The *Nicaragua Case*: Preserving World Peace and the World Court," in John E. Noyes, Laura A. Dickinson, and Mark W. Janis, eds., *International Law Stories* (New York: Foundation Press, 2007), 339–70.

128. Gerson, *The Kirkpatrick Mission*, at 270–71.

129. Michael P. Scharf and Paul R. Williams, eds., *Shaping Foreign Policy in Times of Crisis: The Role of International Law and the State Department Legal Adviser* (Cambridge: Cambridge University Press, 2010), at 61.

130. Gerson, *The Kirkpatrick Mission*, at 271.

131. See United States: Department of State Letter and Statement Concerning Termination of Acceptance of ICJ Compulsory Jurisdiction, October 7, 1985, 24 *International Legal Materials (ILM)* (1985), at 1742.

132. See Israel: Statement Concerning Termination of Acceptance of ICJ Compulsory, November 19, 1985, United Nations Treaty Series, C.N.318.1985.TREA-TIES-4 (signed by Benjamin Netanyahu). On the 1956 declaration, see Robbie Sabel, *International Law and the Arab-Israeli Conflict* (Cambridge: Cambridge University Press, 2002), 247–48. Prior to his appointment as Israel's UN Ambassador, Netanyahu had served as Israel's acting Ambassador to the United States in Washington, DC, a position he held for six months. Meir Rosenne, who replaced Netanyahu as Ambassador to the United States, was described by Netanyahu as "an expert in international law, [who] was among the best of the traditional diplomatic core." See Benjamin Netanyahu, *Bibi: My Story* (New York: Simon & Schuster, 2022), 170.

133. Sofaer, Schachter, and D'Amato, "The United States and the World Court," *Proceedings of the American Society of International Law (ASILPROC)* 80 (1986), at 207.

134. Sabel, *International Law and the Arab-Israeli Conflict*, 248.

135. See *Judgment on the Merits* at 146–50, para. 292.

136. Friedman, *The Neoconservative Revolution*, 142–43. Vaïsse, *Neoconservatism*, 162–63.

137. See Eugene Rostow, "'Palestinian self-determination': Possible Futures for the Unallocated Territories of the Palestine Mandate," *Yale Studies in World Public Order* 5 (1978–1979): 147–72.

138. Benzion Netanyahu, the father of Benjamin Netanyahu, introduced his son to Eugene Rostow in 1974. See Netanyahu, *Bibi*, 106. Feith and Rostow also knew each other and collaborated on a joint publication defending the legality of Israel's settlement project. See Feith and Rostow, *Israel's Legitimacy in Law and History* (1993).

139. Although Rostow was a champion of civil liberties in the United States when he was a young man and opposed the internment of Japanese Americans during the Second World War, he was a hawk when it came to foreign policy, and he was a revisionist when it came to Israel. His brother Walt Rostow, who was deputy national security adviser to McGeorge Bundy, and who was later appointed national security adviser by President Johnson, was also a hawk. Walt Rostow's staunch support for the Vietnam War attracted such infamy that when he left government in 1969, not one of America's elite universities would offer him a job. According to his biographer David Milne, Walt Rostow "was the most hawkish civilian member of the Kennedy and Johnson administrations with respect to the unfolding crisis in Viet-

nam. He was the first to advise Kennedy to deploy US combat troops South Vietnam, and the first to provide a rationale for the bombing campaign against North Vietnam that Lyndon Johnson later implemented." See David Milne, *America's Rasputin: Walt Rostow and the Vietnam War* (New York: Hill and Wang, 2008), 6–7. Like his brother, Eugene Rostow also championed the American war in Vietnam, a stance that he did not soften in his later years. When Eugene Rostow "returned to his beloved Yale after his stint in the Johnson Administration, hushed whispers of 'War Criminal' followed Rostow in the halls," Gerson recalls. "He tried to defuse student anger through teas in the faculty lounge, but was rarely able to find common ground with his detractors." See Gerson, *The Kirkpatrick Mission*, 48.

140. Eugene V. Rostow, "Disputes involving the inherent right of self-defense," in Laurie F. Damrosch, ed., *The International Court of Justice at a Crossroads* (New York: Transnational Publishers, 1987), 264–87, at 278. In *Dred Scott* (1856), the US Supreme Court's infamously decided that an African American could never become a citizen of the US: "The opinion thus entertained and acted upon in England was naturally impressed upon the colonies they founded on this side of the Atlantic. And, accordingly, a Negro of the African race was regarded by them as an article of property, and held, and bought and sold as such, in every one of the thirteen colonies which united in the Declaration of Independence, and afterwards formed the Constitution of the United States." See *Dred Scott v. John F.A. Sandford in Reports of Cases Argued and Adjudged in the Supreme Court of the United States*, December Term, 1856, ed. Benjamin C. Howard, Vol. XIX (Washington, DC: William Morrison & Co., 1857), 393 at 407–8.

141. Gerson, *The Kirkpatrick Mission*, at 274.

142. Gerson, *The Kirkpatrick Mission*, at 274.

143. Gerson, *The Kirkpatrick Mission*, at 274.

144. Shlaim, "The Likud in Power," at 283.

145. See Christine Gray, *International Law and the Use of Force* (Oxford: Oxford University Press, 2018), 170–75, 233–37, 248–53. See further Daniel Bethlehem, "Principles Relevant to the Scope of a State's Right of Self-Defense Against an Imminent or Actual Armed Attack by Nonstate Actors," *American Journal of International Law* 106 (2012): 770–77; and the critique in Victor Kattan, "Furthering the 'war on terrorism' through international law: How the United States and the United Kingdom resurrected the Bush doctrine on using preventive military force to combat terrorism," *Journal on the Use of Force and International Law* 5, no. 1: 97–144. On the ideological origins of the Bush doctrine, see Victor Kattan, "'The Netanyahu Doctrine,' the National Security Strategy of the United States of America, and the Invasion of Iraq," in Satvinder Juss, ed., *Human Rights and America's War on Terror* (New York: Routledge, 2019), 1–28.

146. Kattan, "Furthering the 'war on terrorism.'" See also, the US reaction to the ICRC's customary international law study (arguing in favor of privileging the practice of the United States and its allies) in *American Journal of International Law* 101 (2007): 639–41. See further, the letter by Bellinger and Haynes in *International Legal Materials* 46 (2006): 514–31.

147. Abraham D. Sofaer, "US Acted Legally in Foreign Raids/US Acted Legally on Terrorists," *Newsday*, October 19, 1998, A29.

148. Sofaer, "US Acted Legally in Foreign Raids," A29.

149. Sofaer remained close to Shultz after he left government service, when he became a fellow at Stanford University's Hoover Institution, where Sofaer continued to articulate a very broad right of self-defense. See, for example, Abraham D. Sofaer, "On the Necessity of Pre-emption," *European Journal of International Law* 14, no. 2 (2003): 209–26. Abraham D. Sofaer, *The Best Defense? Legitimacy and Preventive Force* (Stanford: Hoover Institution Press, 2010).

150. Sofaer, "US Acted Legally in Foreign Raids."

151. See the Address by the President of the Russian Federation, February 24, 2022, at http://en.kremlin.ru/events/president/news/67843

152. Matheson understood the United States could become bound by the provisions of AP1 by way of restating customary international law, which allowed the United States to accept the main body of substantive provisions of AP1, while rejecting those provisions the Third World had succeeded in including in the Protocol during the Diplomatic Conference. See the statement by Matheson in 1987 in "The United States Position on the Relation of Customary International Law."

EIGHT

Operationalizing International Law

From Vietnam to Gaza

Craig Jones

Israel's military today goes to great pains to represent its military operations in Gaza as being scrupulously legal and meticulously moral. It has put in place an extensive adjudicative apparatus that is prided on precision legality and live legal advice: soldiers and pilots receive training in the laws of war; targets are reviewed by specialist military lawyers in the Military Advocate General Corps; weapons are carefully calibrated to minimize unnecessary harm; and, *"where possible*," civilian casualties are avoided. More fundamentally, the Israel military also retains an overwhelming power over the definitions, thresholds, and boundaries between what constitutes the im/permissible, the un/necessary, and the dis/proportionate in its ongoing war against Gaza. The legal masters of Israeli warfare in the twenty-first century tell us that sometimes mass harm *is* necessary, or that it is *not* possible to avoid civilian casualties.[1] More law might mean more protection for those wielding this lethal definitional power, but for Gazans—and for targeted populations elsewhere—more law often means more exposure to increasingly sophisticated and putatively "humanitarian" modalities of later modern war.

In this chapter I suggest that Israel's approach to targeting law in Gaza today is indebted to—and has borrowed from—the lessons that the US military learned in the Vietnam War. The Vietnam War led to the estab-

lishment of the US Law of War Program in the 1970s, a program designed
to inculcate law of war principles across the US military. Alongside the
Law of War Program, a parallel yet seldom commented upon development took place: the invention and development of a new military-legal
discipline called "operational law." Operational law, a mix of domestic and
international law, was designed specifically to furnish military commanders
with the tools they required for "mission success." It was at the same time
a concerted "domestication" of international law that sought to emphasize
US military rights over and above legal responsibilities, and it explicitly
sought to overcome the negativity toward the laws of war that was felt by
US commanders who had fought in Vietnam. The legal restraints of the
past were proactively reimagined, and military lawyers were tasked with
convincing the military that law could be a "force-multiplier." The first
true test of this aggressive "hands on" approach came when US military
lawyers were drafted to write the rules of engagement and give legal advice
on lethal targeting operations in Panama (1989) and the First Gulf War
(1990–1991), but this chapter focuses instead on the import of operational
law principles into and by the Israel military.

The Israel military has employed military lawyers since the foundation
of the state of Israel in 1948, but it was not until 2000 that they became formally involved in military targeting decisions.[2] The outbreak of the Second
Intifada in September 2000 became the pretext for a host of war and war-
like policies toward occupied Palestine, but some of the legal inspiration—
and particularly the use of military lawyers in lethal targeting operations—
came directly from the US playbook. Just months after the Second Intifada
began, Israel announced a policy of assassination (which it renamed "targeted killing"), and while at first the United States thought it a breach of
international law, the events of 9/11 profoundly changed their political and
legal views of the world, and within a year the United States began its own
overt assassination campaign, fist in Yemen and later in Pakistan, Somalia,
and elsewhere.[3]

These examples show some of the circuits between the United States
and Israel militaries, but most of all they point to a creative, if not entirely
new, reimagining and reinterpretation of international law. Jens David
Ohlin has characterized the US approach as an "assault on international
law," but I argue first that this is a US *and* Israeli approach and, second,
that it signals an assault *through* international law.[4] The assault through
international law does not dispense with international law; instead it strategically employs and deploys its vocabulary and content in order to *wage
and win wars*. This approach, seen most clearly today in Israel's wars on

Gaza in 2009, 2012, 2014, 2018–2019, and 2021 has its roots not only in the 50-year occupation of Gaza and the West Bank but crucially also in the US experience in Vietnam.

The Ghosts of Vietnam

The US war in Vietnam (1955–1975) continues to matter in places and times seemingly far removed from the immediate contexts in which it was fought. One legacy that has only recently received sustained attention is the way that US invocations of international law during and after the Vietnam War continue to haunt interpretations of international law and military practice today.[5] This chapter focuses on a particular aspect of Vietnam's long shadow on international law: the invention and development of operational law and the concomitant employment by the United States and later Israel of military lawyers in lethal targeting operations.

Legal issues were legion during and after the US war in Vietnam but two in particular would become important in ushering in an era that, if not entirely new, would nevertheless place an unprecedented emphasis on the centrality of law to the conduct of lethal targeting operations. The first issue was the widespread perception among commanders who served in Vietnam that US military action, and particularly the major bombing campaigns, were seriously and unfairly restrained by the laws of war and overly restrictive rules of engagement. The second issue was born out of the My Lai massacre of 1968 and the realization by the US military in general, and military lawyers in particular, that flagrantly illegal behavior by US troops brings with it a heavy moral and military cost—one that would ultimately turn US and international publics against US actions in South East Asia and ferment disillusionment among the troops left fighting what would become understood as an illegal and illegitimate war.[6]

There were two major aerial bombing campaigns in the Vietnam War, as well as intermittent bombing operations that were carried out between them.[7] The first campaign was Operation Rolling Thunder (1965–68), and its main military objective was to interdict the flow of material supplies and troops from North to South Vietnam by targeting both the source of the supplies in North Vietnam and the supply routes themselves. In March 1972 negotiations between the North and South stalled and almost immediately North Vietnamese forces launched the "Easter Offensive" on South Vietnam. In an attempt to halt the offensive and get North Vietnam back to the negotiating table, the United States then launched what would

become the most intensive bombing campaign of the war—Operation
Linebacker (May–October 1972) and Operation Linebacker II (December
18–29, 1972).

Conventional understandings of the two campaigns go something
like this: Rolling Thunder was a gradualist campaign controlled largely
by civilian leaders in Washington with many—and some argue *too many*—
restrictions on what could be targeted.[8] This is contrasted with the "gloves
coming off" in Linebacker, which was executed by military men in Vietnam with less interference from civilian leaders in Washington. This narrative, and the distinction between what happened in each of the bombing
campaigns, is instructive because it reveals something important about the
relationship between politics, law, and restraint. Hays Parks, who served
as a Marine infantry officer and military lawyer in Vietnam, and who subsequently became an important commentator on international law issues
concerning the Vietnam War, insists on a categorical separation between
law and politics, and this enables him to make a series of extraordinary
claims about the air wars in Vietnam. For Parks, Rolling Thunder was ham-
pered not by the laws of war but by political restraints imposed by a civilian
leadership lacking military conviction. This led him to conclude that had
the US Air Force been able to conduct the bombing campaign according to
their "rights" under the laws of war, "Rolling Thunder undoubtedly would
have concluded in a manner favourable to the United States and at a substantially lower cost."[9]

Linebacker shared some of the same goals as Rolling Thunder but was
markedly different in its execution.[10] The main difference was that, unlike
Rolling Thunder under President Johnson, the military—and especially
the Air Force and Navy—were given day-to-day control by President
Nixon.[11] According to Parks, there was a further distinction: Linebacker
was "planned and executed with a conscious consideration of the law of
war."[12] Specifically, he claims that targeting guidance "for the first time
reflected accurate application of the law of war."[13] Linebacker was not
without its restrictions,[14] but for Parks those restrictions were appropriate
partly because he saw them originating in the laws of war (rather than from
"politics") and also because they were not *overly* restrictive.

The problem, for Parks and for military lawyers once the war was over,
was that the commanders who fought in Vietnam cared very little about
the distinctions between law and politics and came to view restrictions and
the laws of war as one and the same thing. As Parks explains: "Lots of
people came out of Vietnam thinking things were illegal when they were
not."[15] Major General William Moorman, a former judge advocate general,

had similar recollections of this period: "The senior officers on the staff having grown up in the Vietnam/post-Vietnam era had it so inculcated that there were these legal restrictions out there that they were subconsciously constraining their own range of options."[16] Previous poor instruction and training was partly to blame, according to Parks, who laments how past schooling in the laws of war "suffered [. . .] a heavy dose of negativism" where instructors "tended to emphasize that which was prohibited, and were reluctant to acknowledge that anything was permitted."[17] Military lawyers were seen as obstructing operations.[18] Col. Bridge of the US Air Force recollected: "[M]any of the initial efforts at training the front line personnel met with apathy—or worse [. . .] they could not easily accept being told how to do their jobs by lawyers."[19] I shall return to the solution that the US military came up with to solve this problem of the perceived illegitimacy of the laws of war among commanders in the following section. Here I want to briefly reflect on the implications of the My Lai Massacre for the subsequent rise of operational law.

On March 16, 1968, nearly a hundred US soldiers entered the Village of Son My on the coast of central Vietnam on a search and destroy mission.[20] They faced no enemy forces when entering the village, nor were they fired at.[21] Around four hours later well over 300 civilians lay dead.[22] Most of those killed were women and children, and many were raped before being murdered.[23] A little over a mile away another unit killed close to a hundred civilians in the neighboring hamlet of My Hoi. Those who partook in the massacres, along with their superiors, subsequently covered up their crimes.[24] It was not until over a year later that what would become known in Vietnam as the Son My Massacre—and in the United States, the My Lai Massacre—would come to US and international public attention.[25] Twenty-five years later, two Judge Advocate General Corps majors reflected on My Lai as "the greatest emblem of American military shame in the twentieth century."[26] US war crimes in Vietnam were far more frequent than conventional histories have suggested, and as new archives have become available in recent years it has become apparent that My Lai was no aberration; in fact, it was part of a pattern of US violence.[27]

The Army commissioned an investigation led by Lieutenant General William Peers, which was published in 1970. According to the Peers Report, as it became known, lack of proper training in the laws of war was one of the many factors that led to the massacre.[28] My Lai served as a wakeup call to the US military and became a lightning rod for the antiwar movement in the United States. After My Lai the US military could no longer afford *not* to provide all of its service members with training in the laws of war and rules of engagement. Indeed, Stephen Myrow argues that the significance of the Peers Report is not—as the reports itself implied—that the My Lai Massacre could have been avoided by giving those who committed it more training in the law of war "but rather that it served as a catalyst for a complete review of the U.S. Armed Forces' commitment to the law of war."[29]

According to Colonel David Graham, the Judge Advocate General's Corps began addressing the criticisms of the Peers Report "[a]lmost immediately." In May 1970, a key Army regulation governing Law of War training was revised to ensure that soldiers received adequate instruction in the laws of war. Significantly, the revised regulation required that this instruction be given by both military lawyers and commanders—preferably with combat experience, ensuring that training would be grounded in "real world experience."[30] The most important doctrinal change would come several years later, in November 1974, when the DOD published a directive that mandated the establishment of the first Law of War Program of its kind.[31] And so began a renewed institutional reorientation to "learn lessons" from the illegalities of the Vietnam War. But the language and praxis of the program would not become mired in the questionable "pasts" of that era; instead the law of war for the US military would be proactive and positive, a way of looking back in order to overcome the past and ensure victory in the future.

Inventing "Operational Law"

The Law of War Program was not the only institutional change to have come out of the Vietnam War. Inside the US military a quieter and more subtle legal-cultural shift began to take place in the late 1970s and 1980s under what would eventually become known as "operational law," or "OPLAW." Colonel David Graham provided the first widely accepted definition: "OPLAW is that body of law, both domestic and international, affecting legal issues associated with the deployment of U.S. forces overseas in peacetime and combat environments."[32]

To operationalize something is to put it to use. So what "use" did operational law serve? In the literature operational law is generally conceived of as a feature of military training and instruction in the laws of war that helps to improve discipline and compliance.[33] But operational law is not simply or only about enhancing military governance in the sense of narrowly defined compliance-building, especially where compliance is understood as limitation. The invention and development of operational law allowed the US military to *domesticate* the laws of war in two key senses: it allowed them to "nationalize" the international laws of war (and therefore advance claims of ownership to and dominance over the laws of war), and it permitted the US military to "tame" the laws of war, rendering them ever more pragmatic, practitioner-oriented, and military-friendly.

A key strand of this domestication involved an organized and positive assertion of US military rights under the laws of war.[34] The US bid to operationalize the laws of war was never a straightforward process of translation; it involved an active reconstitution of their content. In short, operational law put the laws of war to work for the US military—not for the first time, but to a then unprecedented degree. The raison d'être of operational law is to specify that which cannot be articulated by international law, transforming the abstract and general to the specifics of what is militarily "necessary." The move from the laws of war to operational law is not a neutral or purely technical exercise of rescaling but rather represents an *interpretation, transformation, and "worlding" of the laws of war*. As I have argued elsewhere, this worlding is done through a specifically military register and is designed to shape and reshape the laws of war in the US image:

> Operational law [is] the tip of the international law spear, space far away from the sites and institutes commonly associated with the treaty making of international law—the UN, ICC, or the International Committee of the Red Cross—but nonetheless working on the same project of defining and rewriting the power and purpose of law in war, albeit from a radically different direction.[35]

The United States of course has a long history of contributing to and helping define the laws of war. The Lieber Code of 1863 is an early example of how domestic US military law became incorporated into and informed the regulation of hostilities and laws of war treaties.[36] But the emergence of operational law in the 1970s and 1980s placed a burgeoning emphasis on the laws of war and created the institutional structures to ensure that law would become—and would remain—a key pillar of US war, *and not just US war*. Operational law helped to "fix" some of the governance and perception problems that emerged in Vietnam by fostering a law of war culture internally and projecting a culture of compliance externally.

Operational law was not just a new name; it was also a rebranding of the laws of war. The rationale was affirmative, in direct opposition to mainstream thinking at the time: "emphasis was placed on the use of the law as a planning tool that set forth the legal rights of the client (such as the right of self-defense) as well as his responsibilities."[37] The explicit emphasis on the right to employ force was natural, Parks insisted, because "[i]n fact, the law of war permits more than it prohibits"—and teaching and training should therefore reflect this.[38] In inventing operational law, the choice of name was deliberately to settle on familiar territory for the military commander. The acronym "OPLAW" further discursively distanced the military from the laws of war, transforming them into a familiar *military* language and an abstract shorthand. Directives from Washington drove "OPLAW"— Pentagon interpretations of the US military's legal rights and responsibilities. If this was law from Geneva or The Hague, it was first filtered through the US-owned and US-dominated space of OPLAW, and thus imbued with trustworthiness. Operational law was thus an assertion of US military proprietary over the laws of war. Like the Lieber Code more than a century earlier, this way of thinking about the laws of war would emphasize the contiguities between legal regulation and military violence.

By furnishing the military commander with information about the full range of possible legal options and the zone of permissibility, operational law and operational lawyers would become "force multipliers." The language of force multiplication vis-à-vis operational law comes from Brigadier General Pitzul, a very senior Canadian military lawyer who used the term in his opening remarks for the United States Air Force Judge Advocate General School's Operations Law Course in 2001. Making a case for the future of operational law and celebrating the involvement of military lawyers in reviewing targets for the NATO aerial campaign in Kosovo two years earlier, Pitzul assured his audience of trainee US military lawyers, "[t]he law is a force multiplier for commanders."[39] Other prominent military figures, including Major General David Petraeus, have since employed this language, describing military lawyers who served in Iraq as "true combat multipliers."[40]

Perhaps more importantly, operational law defers in no small part to military principles. As Michael Smith has argued: "Operational legality is fundamentally shaped by strategic considerations; in other words, the mission objectives dictate to a substantial degree what is authorized."[41] Corn and Corn frame the military-operational shaping of law as imperative to those who use it: "Allowing the law to develop without consideration of *operational reality* will undermine its ultimate efficacy because the constituents who must embrace the law will view it as inconsistent with their *operational instincts*."[42] To be effective, operational law must conform in part to the military "facts on the ground" as well as with the military imaginations of those fighting the war. To "operationalize law" implies not only that the law must be simplified for the commander but also that the commander and his military exigencies have some say in what goes. Operational law, therefore, is informed by the very military apparatus that it is purportedly designed to regulate.

Early proponents and practitioners of operational law emphasized the specifically *military* orientation of their new practice and placed *combat* operations at its center. Colonel Dennis Coupe, former JAG and director of national security law at the Army War College, went as far as to admit, "The job of the [operational] lawyer is to get involved with all the operational stuff, with the targeting—all the stuff involved with breaking things and killing people." Coupe also clarifies that JAG "involvement" does not mean getting in the way of military operations: "You don't want to stick your nose in where it doesn't belong."[43] Such a remark implies that law and military lawyers belong to a sphere that is separate from, and should not intrude upon, the real business of executing military operations. That may well not have been an entirely new phenomena for the US military at the time, but there is little doubt that the ghosts of Vietnam haunted conversations about law and military practice in the postwar period. Operational law was one of the key, yet underappreciated, institutional responses by the US military to their legal shortcomings in Vietnam. The next major US war—the First Gulf War—would demonstrate operational law's capacity to legislate large-scale infrastructural violence. Military lawyers were deployed in unprecedented numbers to provide legal advice on the targeting of Iraq and helped create and widen the scope of what was considered a legitimate military target.[44] The Israel military took note of these developments and would expand its own operational legal capacities when the time was right.

The Second Intifada and Legally Sanctioned Violence

In September 2000, Palestinians began protesting against the Israeli occupation in what would become known as the Second Intifada. Israel's military response to the popular uprising has been well documented but only recently have scholars excavated the careful legal interpretive work that made such a response possible.[45] Three developments in particular are instructive to my argument and help to lay important foundations for the legal conduits that continue to nourish and connect the US and Israel militaries and state policies: these conduits run both ways and represent a concerted attempt to turn sui generis policy preferences and sometimes also controversial legal opinion into "law."

The first development was a legal innovation by the Israel military's Military Advocate General (MAG) Corps that sought to conceive of the Second Intifada as precipitating and belonging to a paradigm of war. The structure of war that Israel has and continues to maintain over Gaza might seem readily apparent today, but it is the result of once deeply controversial legal imaginings. Less than two months after the Intifada began, the Israel Ministry of Foreign Affairs released a press briefing describing a series of new military regulations. The speaker who conducted the briefing was Colonel Daniel Reisner, the head of the International Law Department of the Israel military (a subdivision of the Military Advocate General Corps). He announced:

> The rules of engagement for the IDF [Israel Defense Force] in the West Bank and Gaza Strip have been modified in accordance with the change in the situation. Prior to the violent events, "police rules of engagement" were applied. [. . .] the situation has now changed. The Palestinians are using violence and terrorism on a regular basis. They are using live ammunition at every opportunity. As a result, Israeli soldiers no longer are required to wait until they are actually shot at before they respond.[46]

Here we witness the transfer of risk away from Israeli soldiers (who used to be able to fire only in self-defense but who henceforth could fire preemptively and unprovoked) to the Palestinian population, a trend that was later incorporated into Israel military doctrine and written into the military's "code of ethics."[47] The legal contention was that Israel had entered what MAG lawyers termed an "armed conflict short of war."[48] This was a deliberate act of juridical creation and innovation. The purpose was twofold: (1) to create a third category that was neither international armed conflict (IAC) nor non-international armed conflict (NIAC) in order to avoid the unwanted responsibilities that that these legal regimes would impose on Israel and the unacceptable rights they would grant to Palestinians;[49] (2) placing the Intifada in the context of war (or a war that is not quite a war)—rather than civil unrest or police operations—would override other, more restrictive legal regimes and, in particular, International Human Rights Law (IHRL).[50] IHRL and the traditional law enforcement (police) paradigms generally place far greater restrictions on the use of lethal force than the laws of war, and would not permit the kind of expansion of the definition of what constitutes a legitimate military target that Israel was advocating for.[51]

The second and related development is the assertion of a legal right to kill and an expansion what constitutes a legitimate military target. Sometime shortly after the start of the Intifada, the Israel military chief of staff, Shaul Mofaz, placed a telephone call to the office of the MAG asking Commander General Menachem Finklestein (the head of the MAG) and Reisner: "Am I allowed, if I identify a terrorist leader on the other side, am I allowed to kill him—*publicly*, not using clandestine '007' techniques? Can I kill him, and if so under what conditions?"[52] Reisner's response to Mofaz demonstrates the power of the operational law in achieving military outcomes: "[W]e came up with a legal opinion which [said] that on the basis of our understanding of the law [. . .] we think that you can target an enemy terrorist, intentionally target an enemy terrorist if you fill five conditions."[53] I have documented these conditions elsewhere, but their detailed content is far less important than the overarching new military-legal policy that they gave rise to.[54]

In November 2000, Israel publicly announced that it had targeted and killed Hussein Abiyat, a senior member of Fatah. Paramilitary Jewish groups had carried out political assassinations during the British Mandate period (1939–1947) and state-sponsored assassination continued under the structure of the Israeli state from 1948 to the 1990s.[55] What was different about the assassination of Abiyat, was that the Israel military was asserting a legal right to kill Palestinian leaders and individuals in a way that it had not done before. So began Israel's long-standing policy of targeted killing.

Though it may now seem difficult to believe, the EU and the United States condemned the policy and rejected Israel's legal justification. An international fact-finding mission, established by President Clinton and led by former US senator George Mitchell, refused to accept Israel's view that the threshold of "armed conflict" had been crossed. As far as Mitchell was concerned, the Intifada constituted civil unrest—a domestic *police* issue—and not war. The Mitchell Report dismissed the idea of war as being "overly broad" and noted that the "IDF should adopt crowd-control tactics that minimize the potential for deaths and casualties," further urging that "an effort should be made to differentiate between terrorism and protests."[56] The message was clear: terrorism could not legitimately be dealt with via recourse to war, and Israel should revert back to the law enforcement approach, a legal regime that places far greater restrictions on the use of lethal force than does the laws of war.[57] The criticism, however, was short-lived and after the events of 9/11, the United States sent delegations

to Tel Aviv, and within a year the United States began its own targeted killing program.[58]

These two developments—the invention of the paradigm of war and
the concomitant expansion of the definition of what constitutes a lawful
target via a newly asserted right to kill—might seem tangential to the rise
of operational law that I have so far traced, but they are actually closely connected. The United States borrowed both the paradigm of war and some
of the legal justifications for assassination/targeting killing from Israel, but
the apparatus that made those legal creations possible—the incorporation
of military lawyers in Israeli targeting policy by way of a beefed-up Military Advocate General—was in many ways indebted to the US invention
and development of operational law. Again, these circulations of law and
policy are bidirectional and reinforcing.

The third and final development, then, was the decision taken by the
Israel military in the early 2000s to employ military lawyers in targeting
operations and seek their legal advice on everything from broad targeting
policy to specific targeting operations. As I noted above, military lawyers
have served in Israel since—and even before—1948 and they have been an
important part of the institutional apparatus of occupation ever since.[59] It
was not until the outbreak of the Second Intifada, however, that military
lawyers began to provide day-to-day legal advice on targeting operations.
According to Reisner, the inspiration to do so came directly from the US
military and, in particular, the US experience in Panama in 1989, where
operational lawyers sharpened their newfound skills in preparation for the
First Gulf War.[60] But much more than mimicking US military practice in
employing military lawyers in targeting operations, the Israel military also
mimicked the ideological and instrumentalist logic of operational law—the
law as "force multiplier." Borrowing from the US lessons learned during
the 1970s and 1980s, it too would take a proactive and preemptive approach
to the laws of war, ensuring that its principles were aligned with and would
make space for increasingly aggressive military operations against Gaza.

Destructive Habits: Putting Operational Law to Work in Gaza

Israel has launched successive major aerial and ground assaults in Gaza
over the last two decades and has done so while also enacting and enforc-
ing a siege against the territory and its people.[61] Laleh Khalili has called
the recent rounds of violence visited upon Gaza a settler-colonial "habit
of destruction."[62] In what remains of this chapter I show how the destruc-

tive habits of the Israel military are enabled, extended, and legitimized by operational-legal logics that habitually slate Gaza and Gazans as targetable. With military lawyers sitting at the sides of commanders in both planned (deliberate) and unplanned (dynamic) targeting operations, the shape and direction of military operations in Gaza over the last two decades has been shaped in no small part by a particular, and particularly aggressive, operationalization of the laws of war.

In 2002, the Israel military laid the foundations for the attacking of civilian and government infrastructure. During that war, dubbed "Operation Defensive Shield," the Israel Air Force struck a variety of targets including the Ministry of Education, the Ministry of Civil Affairs, the Palestinian Legislative Council, the Central Bureau of Statistics, and the al-Bireh Municipal Library.[63] A MAG legal memo (which remains classified) defined these as legitimate targets, preemptively constructing them as targetable. In 2006, in Lebanon, the Israel military demonstrated that the targeting of the civilian population and civilian infrastructure was not an anomaly but would henceforth become a policy. The logic was to bomb the civilian population into rejecting Hezbollah and in turn deter Hezbollah fighters from taking up arms against Israel. This was a form of morale bombing, and it is exactly what the United States had done in the First Gulf War a decade earlier in order to put pressure on Iraqis to reject Saddam Hussein's leadership (a policy that conveniently overlooked the fact that Saddam Hussein was a dictator).

Two years after the war with Lebanon, Maj. General Gadi Eisenkott unveiled what became known as the "Dahiya Doctrine":

> In the Second Lebanon War we used a great deal of bombs. How else were 120,000 houses destroyed? [. . .] What happened in the Dahiya Quarter of Beirut in 2006, will happen in every village from which shots are fired on Israel. We will use disproportionate force against it and we will cause immense damage and destruction. From our point of view these are not civilian villages but military bases. [. . .] This is not a recommendation, this is the plan, and it has already been authorized.[64]

This is a radical reinterpretation of the laws of war, and it departs from majority interpretations of the principle of proportionality. Yet just two months before the outbreak of the next major military operation— "Operation Cast-Lead"—in December 2008, the Institute for National Security Studies, a think tank at the Tel Aviv University, which reflects mainstream military thinking, published an article by Dr. Gabriel Siboni, a colonel reservist who claimed that "[t]his approach is applicable to the Gaza Strip as well."[65]

The planning for "Operation Cast-Lead" began six months in advance, and military lawyer David Benjamin boasted that military lawyers were "intimately involved [in the] approval of targets."[66] On the opening day of the assault the Israel Air Force bombed a police cadet graduation ceremony, killing nearly 50 police personnel. By the end of the three-week assault, the Israel military had killed a total of 248 civilian police officers who were not directly participating in hostilities. An ex post facto investigation by the Israel Ministry of Foreign Affairs revealed that the MAG had approved the targeting of police on the basis that the "police are part of the armed forces" of Hamas.[67] This conveys some of the power of predefining targets through legal categories and it is not difficult to see how a single legal opinion—"the police now constitute a military target"—conditions and sets in motion a series of subsequent individual targeting operations. Two weeks into the operation, Israel military spokesman Captain Benjamin Rutland confirmed that the military had started using an expanded definition of who constitutes a legitimate target. Rutland told the BBC: "our definition is that anyone who is involved with terrorism within Hamas is a valid target. This ranges from strictly military institutions and includes the political institutions that provide the logistical funding and human resources for the terrorist arm."[68]

As documented by a major UN fact-finding investigation in 2009, the expansion of the definition of what constitutes a legitimate target led to mass destruction and death of persons and objects that should have been immune from attack, including, inter alia, civilians attempting to evacuate their houses; whole families who were in no way directly participating in hostilities; homes and whole residential areas; food and energy production facilities; medical facilities and medical vehicles; and UN buildings and mosques.[69] To justify each of these strikes the MAG offered two legal innovations: first, it defined civilian infrastructure as "dual use," meaning that when a given facility or building is also used for military purposes it loses its protected status thus rendering it a "legitimate target."[70] The same principle was later used to restrict imports into Gaza: materials that could be used for military purposes—which includes supplies like concrete that are vital to everyday life and reconstruction after military bombardment—were prohibited or severely limited from entering Gaza from 2006 onwards. Many of these restrictions remain in place today. Second, and as documented by Eyal Weizman, the Israel military made extensive use of "technologies of warning," which were used as a carte blanche to target civilian areas after they had received warnings to evacuate.[71]

In 2012, when Israel launched yet another aerial assault on Gaza ("Operation Pillar of Defense"), media and communications facilities were hit, and Palestinian and foreign journalists were killed. A military spokesperson justified the attacks thus:

> [W]hen terrorist organizations exploit reporters, either by posing as them or by hiding behind them, they are the immediate threat to freedom of the press. Such terrorists, who hold cameras and notebooks in their hands, are no different from their colleagues who fire rockets aimed at Israeli cities and cannot enjoy the rights and protection afforded to legitimate journalists.[72]

Again, we witness the enlargement of the scope of the legitimate target, but even this pattern of violence could not prepare UN Secretary General Ban Ki-moon for what he would witness in 2014 at the end of so-called Operation Protective Edge. The destruction, he told journalists, was "beyond description."[73] The Israel military struck some 5,266 targets in Gaza and the air force also carried out 840 strikes in support of troops on the ground.[74] The Israel military reported that they supplied 5,000 tons of munitions to the fighting forces,[75] while the Gaza Bomb Disposal Team estimated that the figure was between 18,000 and 20,000 tons.[76]

Reports from human rights organizations suggest that the overly permissive approach adopted by legal advisers in Operation Cast-Lead were readopted and even extended in preparation for Operation Protective Edge. Medical facilities and medical workers were targeted,[77] as were UN shelters and schools,[78] acts that were condemned by the White House as "totally unacceptable" and "totally indefensible."[79] In a letter to the MAG, B'Tselem suggested that legal and military directives had been given "to attack the homes of operatives in Hamas and other organizations as though they were legitimate military targets."[80] B'Tselem's investigations also found a "proliferation of incidents in which many civilians were killed in a single incident—more than in previous operations—in terms of both the number of casualties in each incident and the overall number of such instances."[81]

The Israel military has been conducting investigations into what the MAG call "Exceptional Incidents" that occurred during Operation Protective Edge. In one aerial strike, the Israel military targeted a residential building in order to kill a senior Hamas commander. The intelligence assessment found that "no civilians were present in the structure," and that the "entire structure" (rather than a particular part of it) must be struck in order to attack the commander. After issuing no warnings, 35 civilians were killed and a further 27 injured, the MAG found.[82] In another strike, a family home in Al-Bureij was hit because it was allegedly being used as an active Hamas command and control center. This time the intelligence assessment showed that civilians were "likely to be present in the building," but the anticipated "collateral damage" was not expected to be "excessive." Again, no warnings were issued because this may have "frustrated the objective of the attack." The strike killed 19 or 20 civilians, a figure that the MAG concede is "substantially higher" than what the intelligence assessment had anticipated.[83]

In each of these cases—and many more—the MAG took no disciplinary or criminal proceedings on the basis that the actions reviewed "accorded with Israeli domestic law and international law requirements." Key law of war principles are summoned in order to defend Israel's military action: the attacks were against *military* targets; civilian casualties were *proportional* (and often unforeseen); steps were taken to *minimize* civilian casualties; and though strikes often led to "difficult and regrettable" results, civilian harm "does not affect the legality of the attack[s] *ex post facto*."[84] It is difficult to meaningfully engage with, let alone dispute, these conclusions because the relevant information is not in the public domain and remains classified. Even if we were to accept at face value the MAG's assertions that Israel aerial action in "Operation Protective Edge" was overwhelmingly lawful (qua procedurally compliant), serious doubts remain about the quality of intelligence and the standards required in order to authorize a strike. For Cohen and Shany there are:

> [D]ifficult questions regarding the amount and quality of intelligence a military commander should gather prior to ordering an attack, particularly against buildings used by enemy combatants that might contain civilians. [. . .] the MAG suggests that, at least in relation to criminal law, the burden on military commanders to gather substantial amounts of quality intelligence is low.[85]

But more to the point, military lawyers "were constantly present and available to commanders [. . .] to provide ongoing operational legal advice" during the operation.[86] Even the most lethal and large-scale violence went through legal review. Much like in the United States in the First Gulf war, successive Israeli military operations in Gaza over the last two decades

have witnessed widespread infrastructural and human destruction by operational legal design. Much of this destruction might have taken place without the intimate involvement of military lawyers, but their presence in the
operational war rooms in both the United States and Israel has provided
vital legitimacy, and has also lifted some of the political and moral weight
of the decision to kill.[87]

The Assault through International Law

The United States and Israel have been at the forefront of efforts to shape
the international law on targeting. They have done so in no small part
through the invention and development of operational law, a seldom commented upon and yet increasingly important legal regime that blurs the
boundaries between international and domestic law and seeks to operationalize law as an extension of and means of realizing military ends. In
close cooperation and exchange, both states have adopted targeting tactics
and policies that have proved controversial and that push at the boundaries
of international law. The United States and Israel have actively and deliberately sought to widen the scope and space of what constitutes a permissible target, and this has been achieved not by ignoring or circumventing
international law but by domesticating it through the space of operational
law and via the creative and everyday interpretive legal work of military
lawyers.

In his book *The Assault on International Law*, Jens David Ohlin argues
that, "International law is under attack in the United States."[88] Ohlin is concerned in particular with a "small group of legal scholars" he calls the New
Realists who, in the wake of 9/11, set about undermining international law
and asserting the supremacy of presidential power and US sovereignty.[89]
The assault was based on an assumption that international law *impinges*
on US sovereignty and would thus *hamper* the ability of the United States
to fight its enemies in the "war on terror." Ohlin argues that this portrait
of international law is misleading, and the assault thus advanced on a mistaken premise. As a corrective he proffers:

> In the war on terror, international law is our best friend, not our
> worst enemy. [. . .] In reality, the laws of war provide the United
> States with all the tools it needs to aggressively fight al-Qaeda [. . .]
> and other jihadist organizations. [. . .][90]

The language of assault is appropriate, but my argument has been that this is not so much an assault "on" international law as it is an assault *through* international law via the interpretive space of operational law. There are two advantages to seeing legal strategy thus. First, an assault on international law assumes an essentialist conception of law—and especially the liberal idea that international law is ultimately a force for good—whereas an assault *through* the architecture of international and operational law refuses such a conception in favor of indeterminacy (i.e., international law is what states and state militaries operationalize it to be). Second, an assault *through* international law implores us to identify the ways in which, alongside its constraining function, international law also serves as a *vector* of violence. International law and the laws of war have long histories of violence and have been implicated in the pursuit of colonial conquests, imperialism, slavery, and the imposition of capitalist and (neo)liberal orders the world over, so it makes more sense to think of the ways in which violence operates *through* law rather than "on" it.[91] The assault through international and operational law does not dispense with law; instead it strategically employs and deploys its vocabulary and content in order to *wage and win wars*.

The controversial interpretations and attempts to shape the laws of war both vis-à-vis operational law and targeting that I have documented in this chapter should be seen in a broader context of the United States' and Israel's strategic investment in international law. Highlighting a distinct overlap between US and Israeli preferences for flexible juridical forms of warfare, Laleh Khalili argues: "The two powers converge on their use of overwhelming force alongside a discourse of legality. In both cases, the law has been innovatively interpreted and deployed to allow a fairly unfettered freedom of action for the military."[92] Two states alone cannot change customary international law, but they can have an outsized impact on the direction of travel if their actions are unopposed and, especially, if other states adopt similar practices.

In an important paper on the use of preventive military force in *jus ad bellum*, Victor Kattan usefully distinguishes between two different approaches to the forging of customary international law. The first approach, embodied by the International Court of Justice, is based on consensus and sovereign equality: changes in law require consent from many (though it is not clear how many) states, and violation of the norm is not an advisable way to change the norm because doing so undermines the very foundations of the law.[93] But according to Kattan, a second approach has emerged in recent decades, and especially on the heels of the NATO intervention in the former Yugoslavia, that he usefully refers to as "*hegemonic law*."[94]

Drawing on the work of Ian Brownlie, Kattan argues that the hegemonic approach "facilitates the transition of the difference in power between states in to specific advantages for the more powerful actor."[95] Kattan is principally interested in how Bush-era interpretations of preventive military force early in the war on terror have been subsequently employed not only by the Obama administration but also the United Kingdom, Israel, and Australia, despite the fact that these interpretations depart radically from the United Nations Charter. This is some distance from the areas of international and operational law that I have been documenting in this chapter, but Kattan's analysis offers some important cautionary warnings for the forging of customary law vis-à-vis targeting. Lubricating the policy transfers between the United States and Israel is a new way of forging customary law, one that departs from the democratic model of sovereign equality and consent in favor of a trailblazing custom forged by the hegemonic few and largely unopposed by asymmetrically "weaker" and legally unequipped states.[96]

It is doubtful whether many of the more brazen legal assertions I have detailed in this chapter today amount to customary international law, but that determination is governed in no small way by what model of customary international law we follow. My concern here is that powerful nations like the United States and Israel are not only forging ahead with aggressive interpretations of international law but are seeking also to make their sui generis policy preferences into law, and meanwhile those outside the operational war rooms and policy forums are shouting but are ultimately not listened to in this new paradigm. Operational law provides a shared lexicon and space for hegemonic militaries to continually reimagine the boundaries and content of international law—or at least it does for those militaries who have enough resources to think about and engage with such issues in a variety of legal, policy, academic, and intergovernmental fora. Many militaries, of course, do not: international law is disproportionately shaped not just by powerful militaries but by *juridically* minded militaries.

Few experts and commentators would likely have foreseen the extent to which their interpretive projects in the years after the Vietnam War would ripen into something so far-reaching so many years later. Nevertheless, when we look to contemporary US and Israel targeting operations in and not limited to the Middle East, we are witnessing the realization of a concerted 50-year effort to avoid patently illegal behavior on the battlefield (the legacy of My Lai) and to make the laws of war relevant once again to the warfighting commander (the legacy of the post-Vietnam War perception that the laws of war were synonymous with, and only with, restraint).

NOTES

1. Craig Jones, "Frames of Law: Targeting Advice and Operational Law in the Israeli Military," *Environment and Planning D: Society and Space* 33, no. 4 (2015): 676–96; Eyal Weizman, *The Least of All Possible Evils: Humanitarian Violence from Arendt to Gaza* (London: Verso, 2011).

2. The MAGC was formed in 1948 out of the legal service of the *Haganah*, a Jewish paramilitary organization in what was then the British Mandate of Palestine (1920–1948). Maayan Geva, "Military Lawyers Making Law: Israel's Governance of the West Bank and Gaza," *Law & Social Inquiry* 44, no. 3 (August 2019): 704–25.

3. Craig Jones, "Travelling Law: Targeted Killing, Lawfare and the Deconstruction of the Battlefield," in *American Studies Encounters the Middle East* (Chapel Hill: University of North Carolina Press, 2016).

4. Jens David Ohlin, *The Assault on International Law* (New York: Oxford University Press, 2015).

5. Brian Cuddy, "Wider War: American Force in Vietnam, International Law, and the Transformation of Armed Conflict, 1961–1977" (PhD diss., Cornell University, 2016), https://ecommons.cornell.edu/handle/1813/45131

6. David Delaney, "What Is Law (Good) For? Tactical Maneuvers of the Legal War at Home," *Law, Culture and the Humanities* 5, no. 3 (2009): 337–52; Samuel Moyn, "From Antiwar Politics to Antitorture Politics," in *Law and War*, ed. Austin Sarat, Lawrence Douglas, and Martha Merrill Umphrey, The Amherst Series in Law, Jurisprudence, and Social Thought (Stanford: Stanford University Press, 2014), 154–97.

7. Often forgotten is the fact that the United States launched relentless bombing campaigns in Laos and Cambodia for much of the 1960s and 1970s. These campaigns were particularly brutal. Neta C. Crawford, "Targeting Civilians and U.S. Strategic Bombing Norms," in *The American Way of Bombing: Changing Ethical and Legal Norms, from Flying Fortresses to Drones*, ed. Matthew Evangelista (Ithaca: Cornell University Press, 2014), 64–86.

8. W. Hays Parks, "Rolling Thunder and the Law of War," *Air University Review* 33, no. 2 (1982): 11–13.

9. Parks, "Rolling Thunder and the Law of War."

10. Mark Clodfelter, *The Limits of Air Power: The American Bombing of North Vietnam*, new ed. (Lincoln: Bison Books, 2006), 158.

11. "President Nixon gave the Seventh Air Force Commander considerably more latitude and flexibility in directing the aerial operation than previously permitted. [. . .] Now, the Seventh Air Force Commander usually set his own priorities, selected targets, and determined the strike. This allowed him to consider such important factors as military priorities, weather, enemy defences, and operational status of the target. The theatre air commander also had the authority to restrike or divert strikes based on his assessment of post-strike reconnaissance. This fundamental change in management returned a portion of the process of prosecuting the war to the professional military commander in the field." Paul Burbage et al., "The Battle for the Skies Over North Vietnam: 1964–1972," in *The Tale of Two Bridges and The Battle for the Skies Over North Vietnam* (Collingdale, PA: DIANE Publishing, 1976), 150.

12. W. Hays Parks, "Linebacker and the Law of War," *Air University Review* 34, no. 2 (1983): 2–30.

13. Parks, "Linebacker and the Law of War."

14. Crawford, "Targeting Civilians and U.S. Strategic Bombing Norms."

15. Quoted in Keeva, "Lawyers in the War Room," 56.

16. Moorman, Interview.

17. W. Hays Parks, "Teaching the Law of War," *Army Law*, 1987, 9.

18. W. Hays Parks, "The Gulf War: A Practitioner's View," *Dickinson Journal of International Law* 10 (1992–1991): 397.

19. Robert L. Bridge, "Operations Law: An Overview," *Air Force Law Review* 37 (1994): 2, emphasis added.

20. For a description of what happened at My Lai see Greiner, *War without Fronts*, 181–238, and in particular 211–29.

21. William Raymond Peers, *Report of the Department of the Army Review of the Preliminary Investigations into the My Lai Incident: The Report of the Investigation*, vol. 1 (Washington, DC: The Department of the Army, 1974), 5–16, http://www.loc.gov/rr/frd/Military_Law/Peers_inquiry.html

22. Kendrick Oliver, *The My Lai Massacre in American History and Memory* (Manchester: Manchester University Press, 2006), 1. Reliable facts and statistics are still difficult to ascertain, as Bernard Greiner explains: "As no soldier in C Company had an overview of the entire action, the Criminal Investigation Division of the Army consulted population statistics and compared these equally unreliable details with the statements of survivors and the tax registers of the provincial administrators. This yielded an overall figure of between 400 and 430 victims in Xom Lang and Bihn Tay—the villages known as My Lai (4)." Greiner, *War without Fronts*, 212. Gary Solis puts the number at approximately 345. Gary D. Solis, *The Law of Armed Conflict: International Humanitarian Law in War*, 1st ed. (Cambridge: Cambridge University Press, 2010), 236. Nick Turse claims, "Over four hours, members of Charlie Company methodically slaughtered more than five hundred unarmed victims." Nick Turse, *Kill Anything That Moves: The Real American War in Vietnam* (New York: Metropolitan Books/Henry Holt and Co., 2013), 3.

23. Greiner, *War without Fronts*, 221.

24. Joseph Goldstein et al., *The My Lai Massacre and Its Cover-Up: Beyond the Reach of Law? The Peers Commission Report* (New York: Free Press, 1976); Michael Bilton and Kevin Sim, *Four Hours in My Lai*, Rpt. ed. (New York: Penguin Books, 1993).

25. Jeffrey F. Addicott and William A. Hudson, "The Twenty-Fifth Anniversary of My Lai: A Time to Inculcate the Lessons," *Military Law Review* 139 (January 1993): 156.

26. Addicott and Hudson, 154.

27. Bernd Greiner, *War Without Fronts: The USA in Vietnam* (New Haven: Yale University Press, 2009); Turse, *Kill Anything That Moves*.

28. Peers, *Report of the Department of the Army Review of the Preliminary Investigations into the My Lai Incident*, 1: 8–13.

29. S. A. Myrow, "Waging War on the Advice of Counsel: The Role of Operational Law in the Gulf War," *USAF Acad. J. Legal Stud.* 7 (1996): 133.

30. David Graham, "Operational Law: A Concept Comes of Age," *Army Law* 175 (1987): 3.

31. US Department of Defense, "Department of Defense Directive: 'DoD Law of War Program,'" July 10, 1979, 2, http://handle.dtic.mil/100.2/ADA272470. According to Army historian Frederic Borch, the Law of War Program was "a direct result of My Lai [. . .] the Defense Department recognized that preventing similar incidents required a new approach to ensuring obedience to the Law of War." Frederic L. Borch, *Judge Advocates in Combat: Army Lawyers in Military Operations from Vietnam to Haiti* (Washington, DC: Government Printing Office, 2001), 318.

32. Graham, "Operational Law: A Concept Comes of Age," 10.

33. Parks, "Teaching the Law of War"; David E. Graham, "My Lai and Beyond: The Evolution of Operational Law," in *The Real Lessons of the Vietnam War: Reflections Twenty-Five Years after the Fall of Saigon*, ed. John Norton Moore and Robert F. Turner (Durham: Carolina Academic Press, 2002); Laura Dickinson, "Military Lawyers on the Battlefield: An Empirical Account of International Law Compliance," *American Journal of International Law* 104, no. 1 (2010): 1–28.

34. Parks, "Teaching the Law of War"; W. Hays Parks, "Rules of Engagement: No More Vietnams," in *The U.S. Naval Institute on Vietnam: A Retrospective*, ed. Thomas Cutler (Annapolis, MD: Naval Institute Press, 2016), 150–55.

35. Jones, "Frames of Law," 691.

36. John Fabian Witt, *Lincoln's Code: The Laws of War in American History* (New York: Free Press, 2013).

37. Parks, "Gulf War," 398 emphasis added.

38. Parks, "Teaching the Law of War," 9.

39. Jerry S. T. Pitzul, "Operational Law and the Legal Professional: A Canadian Perspective Speeches and Comments," *Air Force Law Review* (2001): 321.

40. Major General David H. Petraeus, commander 101st Airborne Division (Air Assault) 2003–2004 quoted in:

United States Joint Chief of Staff, "Legal Support to Military Operations" (Washington, DC: Joint Chiefs of Staff, August 2, 2016), II–6, http://www.dtic.mil /doctrine/new_pubs/jp1_04.pdf

41. Michael Smith, "States That Come and Go: Mapping the Geolegalities of the Afghanistan Intervention," in *The Expanding Spaces of Law: A Timely Legal Geography*, ed. Irus Braverman et al. (Stanford: Stanford Law Books, 2014), 152.

42. Geoffrey S. Corn and Gary P. Corn, "The Law of Operational Targeting: Viewing the LOAC through an Operational Lens," *Texas International Law Journal* 47 (2011): 344.

43. Quoted in Steven Keeva, "Lawyers in the War Room," *ABA Journal* 77 (1991): 57.

44. Craig Jones, *The War Lawyers* (Oxford: Oxford University Press, 2020).

45. Noura Erakat, *Justice for Some: Law and the Question of Palestine* (Stanford: Stanford University Press, 2019), 178–83; Lisa Hajjar, "The Counterterrorism War Paradigm versus International Humanitarian Law: The Legal Contradictions and Global Consequences of the US 'War on Terror,'" *Law & Social Inquiry* 44, no. 4 (November 2019): 922–56, https://doi.org/10.1017/lsi.2018.26

46. Israel Ministry of Foreign Affairs, "Press Briefing by Colonel Daniel Reisner," November 15, 2000, http://www.mfa.gov.il/MFA/MFAArchive/2000_2009 /2000/11/Press+Briefing+by+Colonel+Daniel+Reisner-+Head+of.htm?DisplayMo de=print

47. James Eastwood, *Ethics as a Weapon of War: Militarism and Morality in Israel* (Cambridge: Cambridge University Press, 2017).

48. George Mitchell et al., "Sharm El-Sheikh Fact-Finding Committee Final Report," *Washington, DC: International Information Programs* 5 (2001): 2002. Reisner, interview.

49. Noura Erakat expertly summarises why Israel was reluctant to classify the Second Intifada as either an IAC or NIAC: "Israel refused to recognize its confrontation with Palestinians as a civil war, or NIAC, because that would unravel the false partition separating Israel from the Occupied Territories. Such recognition would acknowledge Israel's maintenance of a singular, discriminatory government, thus exposing it to more pointed claims of pursuing a policy of creeping annexation and overseeing an apartheid regime. [. . .] If Israel recognized the conflict as an IAC, that would confer belligerent status on Palestinian militants, and Palestinian fighters would have the right, under an international legal regime, to use lethal force against Israeli military targets and installations. [. . .] This status would also permit other states to legally intervene, with military and/or financial assistance, upon a request by the Palestinian leadership. [. . .] [Instead] Israel insists that any Palestinian use of force is terroristic and criminal." (Erakat, *Justice for Some: Law and the Question of Palestine*, 179–80).

50. This position is deeply controversial. Nils Melzer points out the applicability of one legal regime—the *lex specialis* (in this case, International Humanitarian Law)—does not preclude the applicability of another legal regime—the *lex generalis* (for example, IHRL). Nils Melzer, *Targeted Killing in International Law* (New York: Oxford University Press, 2009).

51. Melzer, *Targeted Killing in International Law*; Philip Alston, "Report of the Special Rapporteur on Extrajudicial, Summary or Arbitrary Executions," *United Nations Human Rights Council*, 2010, http://www.unhcr.org/refworld/pdfid/4c0763 5c2.pdf

52. Reisner, interview, emphasis in original.

53. Reisner, interview.

54. There were actually six conditions. In summary these were: (1) targeting must comply with the rule of proportionality under international humanitarian law; (2) only combatants and those directly participating in hostilities may be targeted; (3) suspects must be arrested rather than killed *where possible*; (4) suspects who are located in areas under Israeli security control should not be targeted; (5) individual targeting operations each require ministerial approval; (6) the focus of a targeting operation must be aimed at preventing future attacks rather than being carried out in retribution for past events. Jones, "Frames of Law," 682–83.

55. Nachman Ben-Yehuda, *Political Assassinations by Jews a Rhetorical Device for Justice* (Albany: State University of New York Press, 1993); Ronen Bergman, *Rise and Kill First: The Secret History of Israel's Targeted Assassinations* (London: John Murray, 2018); Markus Gunneflo, *Targeted Killing: A Legal and Political History* (Cambridge: Cambridge University Press, 2016); Yossi Melman, "Targeted Killings—a Retro Fashion Very Much in Vogue—Features," Haaretz.com, March 24, 2004, http://www.haaretz.com/print-edition/features/targeted-killings-a-retro-fashion -very-much-in-vogue-1.117714; Dan Raviv and Yossi Melman, *Every Spy a Prince: The Complete History of Israel's Intelligence Community* (Boston: Houghton Mifflin, 1990).

56. George Mitchell, Suleyman Demirel, Thorbjoern Jagland, Warren B. Rudman, and Javier Solana, "Sharm El-Sheikh Fact-Finding Committee Final Report," *Washington, DC: International Information Programs* 5 (2001): np.

57. Mitchell et al., "Sharm El-Sheikh Fact-Finding Committee Final Report." See also Daniel Reisner, "International Law and Military Operations in Practice—III—Jerusalem Center For Public Affairs," Jerusalem Center for Public Affairs, accessed May 30, 2013, http://jcpa.org/article/international-law-and-military-oper ations-in-practice-iii/

58. Jones, "Frames of Law"; Jones, *The War Lawyers*.

59. Lisa Hajjar, *Courting Conflict: The Israeli Military Court System in the West Bank and Gaza*, 1st ed. (Oakland: University of California Press, 2005); Maayan Geva, *Law, Politics and Violence in Israel/Palestine* (Cham, Switzerland: Palgrave Macmillan, 2018).

60. For a full account of the legal exchanges between the United States and Israel, see Jones, *The War Lawyers*.

61. Ron J. Smith, "Isolation Through Humanitarianism: Subaltern Geopolitics of the Siege on Gaza," *Antipode* 48, no. 3 (2016): 750–69, https://doi.org/10.1111 /anti.12224

62. Laleh Khalili, "A Habit of Destruction," *Society and Space—Environment and Planning D* (blog), 2014, http://societyandspace.com/material/commentaries/laleh -khalili-a-habit-of-destruction/

63. Jessica Montell, "Operation Defensive Shield," *Tikkun* 17, no. 4 (2002): 33–41; B'Tselem, "Operation Defensive Shield" (Jerusalem, July 2002), http://www.bts elem.org/download/200207_defensive_shield_eng.pdf

64. Quoted in Public Committee Against Torture in Israel (PCATI), "No Second Thoughts: The Changes in the Israeli Defense Forces' Combat Doctrine in Light of "Operation Cast Lead'" (Jerusalem: PCATI, November 2009), 20, http:// www.stoptorture.org.il/files/no%20second%20thoughts_ENG_WEB.pdf

65. Quoted in Public Committee Against Torture in Israel (PCATI), 21.

66. Quoted in Gwen Ackerman, "Israel Deploys Lawyers to Head Off War-Crimes Charges," Bloomberg.com, January 22, 2009, http://www.bloomberg.com /apps/news?pid=newsarchive&sid=aMvUB8w9xphM&refer=home. See also Barak Ravid, "IAF Strike Followed Months of Planning," Haaretz.com, December 28, 2008, http://www.haaretz.com/print-edition/news/iaf-strike-followed-months-of -planning-1.260363

67. Israel Ministry of Foreign Affairs, "The Operation in Gaza-Factual and Legal Aspects" (www.mfa.gov.il: IMFA, July 29, 2009), 89, http:// www.mfa.gov.il/MFA/ForeignPolicy/Terrorism/Pages/Operation_in_Gaza- Factual_and_Legal_Aspects.aspx

68. Quoted in George E. Bisharat, "Violence's Law," *Journal of Palestine Studies* 42, no. 3 (2013): 77.

69. United Nations, "Report of the United Nations Fact Finding Mission on the Gaza Conflict," 2009, 199–217, http://www2.ohchr.org/english/bodies/hrcoun cil/docs/12session/A-HRC-12-48.pdf

70. Israel Ministry of Foreign Affairs, "The Operation in Gaza-Factual and Legal Aspects," 55.

71. Eyal Weizman, *Lesser Evils: Scenes of Humanitarian Violence from Arendt to Gaza* (London: Verso, 2011); Eyal Weizman, "Gaza Attacks: Lethal Warnings," *Al*

Jazeera, July 14, 2014, http://www.aljazeera.com/indepth/opinion/2014/07/gaza-at tacks-lethal-warnings-2014713162312604305.html

72. Quoted in Bisharat, "Violence's Law," 77.

73. Peter Beaumont and Hazem Balousha, "Ban Ki-Moon: Gaza Is a Source of Shame to the International Community," *The Guardian*, October 14, 2014, sec. World news, http://www.theguardian.com/world/2014/oct/14/ban-ki-moon-visits -gaza-views-destruction-of-un-school

74. Ben Hartman, "50 Days of Israel's Gaza Operation, Protective Edge—by the Numbers," *Jerusalem Post*, August 28, 2014, http://www.jpost.com/Operation-Prot ective-Edge/50-days-of-Israels-Gaza-operation-Protective-Edge-by-the-numbers -372574

75. United Nations Office for the Coordination of Humanitarian Affairs, "Key Figures on the 2014 Hostilities," UNOCHA—Occupied Palestinian Territory, June 23, 2015, https://www.ochaopt.org/content/key-figures-2014-hostilities

76. Al Jazeera, "Unexploded Munitions Add to Gaza Risks," August 10, 2014, https://www.aljazeera.com/video/middleeast/2014/08/unexploded-munitions-add -gaza-risks-201481003251688388.html

77. Amnesty International, "Evidence of Medical Workers and Facilities Being Targeted by Israeli Forces in Gaza," August 7, 2014, http://www.amnesty.org/en/li brary/asset/MDE15/023/2014/en/c931e37b-a3c2-414f-b3a6-a00986896a09/mde 150232014en.pdf; Derek Gregory, "Destructive Edge," *Geographical Imaginations* (blog), August 8, 2014, http://geographicalimaginations.com/2014/08/08/destruc tive-edge/; Derek Gregory, "Gaza 101," *Geographical Imaginations* (blog), July 21, 2014, https://geographicalimaginations.com/2014/07/21/gaza-101/

78. Human Rights Watch, "Unlawful Israeli Attacks on Palestinian Media," December 20, 2012, http://www.hrw.org/news/2012/12/20/israelgaza-unlawful-is raeli-attacks-palestinian-media

79. Paul Lewis and Ian Black, "Gaza Conflict: US Says Israeli Attack on UN School Was 'Totally Unacceptable,'" *The Guardian*, July 31, 2014, http://www.theg uardian.com/world/2014/jul/31/gaza-conflict-us-israeli-attack-un-school

80. B'Tselem, "Investigation of Incidents That Took Place during Recent Mili tary Action in Gaza: July-August 2014," September 4, 2014, 2, https://www.btselem .org/download/201400904_15390_letter_to_mag_corps_regarding_protective_ed ge_investiations_eng.pdf

81. B'Tselem, "Investigation of Incidents That Took Place during Recent Mili tary Action in Gaza: July-August 2014," 3.

82. Military Advocate General, "Decisions of the IDF Military Advocate Gen eral Regarding Exceptional Incidents That Allegedly Occurred During Operation 'Protective Edge,'" August 15, 2018, 24–26, https://www.idf.il/en/minisites/milita ry-advocate-generals-corps/releases-idf-military-advocate-general/mag-corps-pre ss-release-update-6/

83. Military Advocate General, "Decisions of the IDF Military Advocate Gen eral Regarding Exceptional Incidents That Allegedly Occurred During Operation 'Protective Edge,'" 26–28.

84. Military Advocate General, "Decisions of the IDF Military Advocate Gen eral Regarding Exceptional Incidents That Allegedly Occurred During Operation 'Protective Edge,'" 26.

85. Amichai Cohen and Yuval Shany, "Israel's Military Advocate General Termi-

nates 'Black Friday' and Other Investigations: Initial Observations," *Lawfare* (blog), August 27, 2018, https://www.lawfareblog.com/israels-military-advocate-general -terminates-black-friday-and-other-investigations-initial

86. Military Advocate General of the Israeli Defense Force, "Operation 'Pillar of Defense' 14–21 November 2012" (MAG: International Law Department, December 19, 2012), 5, http://www.mag.idf.il/163-5398-en/patzar.aspx

87. Janina Dill, *Legitimate Targets? Social Construction, International Law and US Bombing* (Cambridge: Cambridge University Press, 2014); Jones, *The War Lawyers*.

88. Ohlin, *The Assault on International Law*, 8.

89. Ohlin, *The Assault on International Law*, 8.

90. Ohlin, *The Assault on International Law*, 155.

91. Antony Anghie, *Imperialism, Sovereignty and the Making of International Law* (Cambridge: Cambridge University Press, 2007); Lauren A. Benton, *Law and Colonial Cultures: Legal Regimes in World History, 1400–1900*, Studies in Comparative World History (Cambridge: Cambridge University Press, 2002); Lauren A. Benton, *A Search for Sovereignty: Law and Geography in European Empires, 1400—1900* (Cambridge: Cambridge University Press, 2010); Laleh Khalili, *Time in the Shadows: Confinement in Counterinsurgencies* (Stanford: Stanford University Press, 2012); Helen M. Kinsella, *The Image Before the Weapon: A Critical History of the Distinction Between Combatant and Civilian* (Ithaca: Cornell University Press, 2011); China Mieville, *Between Equal Rights: A Marxist Theory of International Law* (Chicago: Historical Materialism, 2006).

92. Khalili, *Time in the Shadows*, 64.

93. Victor Kattan, "Furthering the 'War on Terrorism' through International Law: How the United States and the United Kingdom Resurrected the Bush Doctrine on Using Preventive Military Force to Combat Terrorism," *Journal on the Use of Force and International Law* 5, no. 1 (2017): 124–25.

94. Kattan, "Furthering the 'War on Terrorism' through International Law," 125.

95. Kattan, "Furthering the 'War on Terrorism' through International Law," 126. Quoting Ian Brownlie "International Law at the Fiftieth Anniversary of the United Nations" (1995–I) 255 *Recueil des Cours* 49, quoted in Michael Byers and Simon Chesterman, "Changing the Rules About Rules? Unilateral Humanitarian Intervention and the Future of International Law," in J. L. Holzgrefe and Robert O Keohane, eds., *Humanitarian Intervention: Ethical, Legal and Political Dilemmas* (Cambridge: Cambridge University Press, 2003), 177, 193–94.

96. "[T]he United States had, as early as the 1980s, abandoned the traditional approach to creating customary international law that had been based on consensus-building efforts. Those 'halcyon days', which produced the Declaration on Principles of International Law concerning Friendly Relations (1970), the Definition of Aggression (1974), the Additional Protocols to the Geneva Conventions (1977) and UNCLOS [UN Convention on the Law of the Sea] (1982), were over" (Kattan, "Furthering the 'War on Terrorism' through International Law," 129–30, footnotes removed).

NINE

From Vietnam to Palestine

Peoples' Tribunals and the Juridification of Resistance

Tor Krever

"Overwhelming evidence besieges us daily of crimes without precedent. Each moment greater horror is perpetrated against the people of Vietnam. We investigate in order to expose. . . . We arouse consciousness in order to create mass resistance. This is our purpose and the acid test of our integrity and honour."[1] With these words, the philosopher and antiwar activist Bertrand Russell opened the first session of the International War Crimes Tribunal for Vietnam. A conscientious objector in the First World War, Russell had a long history of antiwar activism and was outspoken in opposition to US aggression in Vietnam. In a 1963 letter to the *New York Times*, Russell wrote that American conduct in Vietnam was "reminiscent of warfare as practiced by the Germans in Eastern Europe and the Japanese in South East Asia."[2] In June 1966, Russell issued an "Appeal to American Conscience," announcing that he was approaching "eminent jurists, literary figures and men of public affairs" from around the world to constitute a tribunal to investigate.[3] Russell, by then in his mid-90s, would serve as honorary president, while the French philosopher Jean-Paul Sartre would take on the role of executive president, and the Yugoslav historian Vladimir Dedijer that of chairman and president of sessions. They were joined by an international assortment of prominent figures—Simone de Beauvoir, Lelio Basso, James Baldwin, Isaac Deutscher, Mahmud Ali Kasuri, Peter Weiss, Lázaro Cárdenas, Lawrence Daly, and others.

Given the eventual size of the antiwar movement, it is easy to forget just
how complacent much of the US and European public still was in the mid-
6os, as the Johnson administration unleashed Operation Rolling Thunder.
The obfuscations of the Western media kept the worst of US aggression
away from the news and a large majority of Americans favored further
escalation.[4] A tribunal documenting and publicizing that aggression might,
Russell believed, go some way to raising consciousness in "the smug streets
of Europe and the complacent cities of North America."[5] By providing "the
most exhaustive portrayal of what has happened to the people of Vietnam,"
he hoped, the tribunal would galvanize opposition to the war and mobilize
resistance to US imperialism.

Political mobilization through appeals to public consciousness was hardly
new. What was strikingly original, however, was the use by private citizens of
a tribunal—a body modeled on a legal court—to judge and condemn state
behavior with reference specifically to international law. Only two years
before the Vietnam tribunal, Henry Cabot Lodge Jr., then US ambassador in
Saigon, had told reporters: "As far as I'm concerned, the legal aspect of [the
war] is of no significance."[6] A handful of legal challenges had been mounted
in the United States by conscientious objectors opposing the draft, but these
had focused largely on the conscience of the objector, not the legality of US
actions. With Russell's tribunal, legality and international law were thrust to
the fore, the privileged frame by which US aggression was to be judged and
through which resistance was to be mobilized.

The Vietnam tribunal proved disappointing in the short term, with little
immediate impact on *bien pensant* opinion. Nonetheless it provided a model
and inspiration for numerous further "peoples' tribunals." Subsequent tribunals have focused on repression and the violence perpetrated by military juntas across Latin America (1973), rights violations in West Germany
(1978–79) and, with respect to native Americans, in the United States (1980),
and responsibility of Japanese political and military authorities for sexual
slavery and rampant sexual violence in Asia and the Pacific during the 1930s
and 1940s (2000). More recently, similar tribunals have been organized on
issues ranging from the 1965 Indonesian politicide to the Canadian mining
industry in Latin America. In 2005, a World Tribunal on Iraq challenged the
United States' imperial intervention in Iraq, while in 2009, in the wake of
Israel's 2009 assault on Gaza, a Russell Tribunal on Palestine was launched
to investigate and confront the occupation of Palestine.

While each differed in its particular focus and specific institutional
makeup, all bore Russell's stamp and reproduced the model of the peoples' tribunal established in 1967.[7] These tribunals, I argue in this chap-

ter, represent a political practice of resistance—to imperialism, to war, to injustice. Focusing on two examples—the original Vietnam tribunal and the more recent Palestine tribunal—I suggest that the novelty of this practice lies in its embrace of law and legalism as the primary form through which resistance is expressed and enacted. As such, I argue that peoples' tribunals are defined by a structural antinomy. Set up by private citizens, political activists, and civil society organizations, these tribunals enjoy no official legal authority. While adopting the form of a legal tribunal, they do not seek to emulate formal courts of law. "The point," Jacques Derrida observed, "is not to reach a verdict resulting in sanctions but to raise or to sharpen the vigilance of the citizens of the world."[8] The peoples' tribunal is a vehicle for mobilizing resistance to systemic injustice: a political practice with no pretence of neutrality or impartiality. At the same time, however, it is a model that rests, in its very adoption of the *tribunal* form, on law and legalism. As Luis Moita writes, "the formalism of the [tribunal's] public sessions reproduces the model of a court hearing."[9] For supporters like Moita, the very legitimacy of peoples' tribunals lies in their hewing closely to such formalism and the purported apolitical neutrality of liberal legalism.

In short, there is an apparent tension between the form and name these bodies choose to take—the tribunal—and their avowedly political nature. In this chapter, I show how in the case of both the Vietnam and Palestine tribunals this tension resolved itself concretely into the question of these bodies' relationship with international law. In both cases, international law and legality were foregrounded as the privileged frame of analysis and condemnation. Yet the two tribunals also differed in important respects, reflecting a shift over time in how the constitutive tension between law and politics was balanced. The embrace of international law by the Vietnam tribunal in the 1960s, at the height of the Third World movement and anticolonial internationalism, can, I suggest, be understood as an instance of "principled opportunism"—legalism mobilized in aid of the tribunal's broader practice of resistance against imperialism.[10] By the time a peoples' tribunal for Palestine was constituted in 2009, however, both Third World and workers' movements had collapsed, the language of international law and human rights displacing other emancipatory frameworks in the political imagination of internationalism. This can be seen, I argue, in the even greater prominence awarded legalism by the Palestine tribunal, international law now not merely invoked tactically but celebrated as the tribunal's very raison d'être. In this way, peoples' tribunals both reflect and contribute to the juridification of resistance.

A War Crimes Tribunal for Vietnam

In November 1966, five months after Russell's "Appeal to American Conscience," preparations for the Vietnam tribunal were underway and a preliminary meeting held in London. The tribunal, Russell told the gathered members, was to be convened "so that we may investigate and assess the character of the United States' war in Vietnam." There was "no clear historical precedent," although the Nuremberg Tribunal, flawed as it was, offered an example: an expression of outrage at the actions of the Nazis and an attempt to devise criteria against which such actions could be judged and according to which they might be condemned. Nonetheless, the Vietnam tribunal, if inspired by similar sentiments, would be markedly different. Lacking the backing of any state, it could not hope to compel individuals to stand accused or to impose sanctions. These, however, were not limitations, Russell insisted, but rather virtues: unencumbered by reasons of state, the tribunal was free to undertake its "solemn and historic investigation" impartially and "record the truth in Vietnam."[11]

Earlier that year, Russell had written to President Johnson inviting him to appear before the tribunal to defend US actions and answer the evidence of US atrocities.[12] The invitation went unanswered. When a further invitation was extended, by Sartre to Secretary of State Dean Rusk, the latter remarked glibly to reporters that he had no intention of "playing games with a 94-year-old Briton."[13] In private, though, US officials expressed concern about the tribunal and its potential impact. In July 1966, an interagency group chaired by Under Secretary of State George Ball and composed of officials from the State Department, CIA, US Information Agency, and Department of Defense was charged with discrediting Russell and the tribunal and, if possible, preventing its meetings.[14] The next month, Ball reported to the president that the group was "quietly exploring with the British and French available legal steps that could be taken to forestall this spectacle. We also plan to stimulate press articles criticizing the 'trials' and detailing the unsavory and leftwing background of the organizers and judges."[15]

The propaganda campaign was successful in the United States, where a deferential media rehearsed State Department aspersions: the tribunal was "a farce" whose members were "not interested in peace," a group of anti-Americans spreading communist propaganda.[16] According to the *New York Times*, Russell was "a full-time purveyor of political garbage indistinguishable from the routine products of the Soviet machine" who had "sunk to defending—not just denying or minimizing, but actively defending—the atrocities of the Viet Cong in Vietnam."[17] The White House, Under Secretary of State Nicholas Katzenbach happily reported to President Johnson, had provided the background for the smear.[18]

Less hyperbolic was the claim that the tribunal was biased, its members hostile to US policy, and their conclusions predetermined. In the face of such reproach, Russell remained unapologetic. We must reject the view, Russell insisted at the tribunal's London meeting, "that only indifferent men are impartial men." Open minds were not to be confused with empty ones. Every day brought new prima facie evidence of crimes in Vietnam and the tribunal's members could not help but have feelings about them. Quite the contrary: "[n]o man unacquainted with this evidence through indifference has any claim to judge it."[19]

For Sartre, too, such complaints misconstrued the nature of the tribunal. "There is no question of judging whether American policy in Vietnam is evil," he told *Le Nouvel Observateur* in November 1966. Of this, "most of us have not the slightest doubt." The task of the tribunal was narrower: not simply to condemn US policy in moral terms but to determine the *legality* of that policy and its concomitant actions—do they fall, specifically, "within the compass of international law on war crimes?" On this question, Sartre insisted, "our judgements cannot be given in advance, even if we are committed, as individuals, in the struggle against imperialism. . . . This war is certainly contrary to the interests of the vast majority of people, but is it *legally* criminal? That is what we will try to determine."[20]

The task of the tribunal, then, was not merely to provide an "exhaustive portrayal" of US violence but to judge that violence in legal terms. Here, then, was the strikingly original aspect of Russell and Sartre's venture: private citizens would use the form of a legal tribunal, applying international legal norms, to judge state behavior. This was both novel and controversial. Russell and Sartre had initially planned to hold their tribunal in Paris, only for the French to deny its members visas. "Justice of any sort," stated French President de Gaulle, "in principle as in execution, emanates from the State." The tribunal, he insisted, "through its very form . . . would be acting against the very thing which it is seeking to uphold."[21] Not at all, shot back Sartre in April 1967: "Real justice must draw its force both from the state and the masses." The tribunal did not claim, whatever de Gaulle affected to believe, to substitute itself for any existing court. It was precisely the institutional vacuum left by self-interested states and a cowed UN that required people of conscience to carry forward the Nuremberg legacy.[22]

De Gaulle was not to be moved, however unconvincing his dissembling: the Palais de l'Élysée had already assured the US embassy the previous month that the tribunal would be banned from French soil.[23] In Britain, Harold Wilson's government, faithfully subservient to Washington, followed suit, refusing visas to North Vietnamese witnesses and condemning the tribunal as one-sided. Russell and Sartre eventually found a reluctant host in Sweden, Prime Minister Tage Erlander confiding to his British counterpart that despite the "considerable political embarrassment" caused by the tribunal, he simply lacked the legal power to prevent it.[24]

The tribunal's first session opened finally on May 2, 1967, in Stockholm. Age and ill health prevented Russell from attending, but his opening statement, a passionate indictment of the war and a call for the tribunal to work diligently to record the truth of Vietnam, was read by his secretary, Ralph Schoenman. Eight days of hearings followed with testimony heard from Vietnamese witnesses as well as a potpourri of experts: lawyers, doctors, biochemists, agronomists, sociologists, historians, journalists. A second session was convened between November 20 and December 1 in Roskilde, Denmark.

To read the tribunal record today is to read a catalogue of atrocity—"a litany of pain," as one contemporary observer put it.[25] There are the sober reports of weapons experts, doctors, and scientists on the fragmentation or cluster bombs designed specifically to maim; on the medical effects of napalm; and on the use and consequences of chemical weapons and defoliation and the destruction of dykes and irrigation systems. There are the reports from members of the tribunal's fact-finding missions to North Vietnam, firsthand accounts of the ravages of napalm—"his ears just melted"—and evidence of deliberate targeting of civilians—village after village obliterated; hospitals, schools, and churches bombed, far removed from any military target. And then there is the testimony of survivors: the prisoner of war tortured; the young school teacher, Ngo Thi Nga, asleep with her pupils in a small village classroom when the American bombs fell; the nine-year-old Do Van Ngoc, herding cattle under a rain of napalm— "on my right hand, the thumb is stuck to the other fingers; large scars remain on my stomach and my thighs."[26]

At the close of the Stockholm session, after considering this and other testimony and submissions, the tribunal issued a verdict finding that the US had committed "acts of aggression against Vietnam under the terms of international law." The tribunal further found that US government and armed forces' "deliberate, systematic and large-scale bombardment of civilian targets, including civilian populations, dwellings, villages, dams, dikes, medical establishments, leper colonies, schools, churches, pagodas, historical and cultural monuments" amounted to war crimes.[27] In Roskilde, the tribunal's findings were similarly damning: the United States was guilty of using illegal weapons, maltreatment of prisoners of war and civilians, and genocide.

Russell and Sartre had hoped to arouse anger in the West and galvanize opposition to the war. In October, between the tribunal's two sessions, 100,000 protestors marched on the Pentagon. But how many of them knew of the tribunal and its vast catalogue of US excesses? Media coverage in the United States was fleeting and deeply unfavorable, largely indistinguishable from official efforts to delegitimize the hearings. As the Stockholm session drew to a close, the CIA happily reported to President Johnson that the tribunal "has gone rather badly," in part due to lack of "good press."[28] Outside the United States, press coverage was greater—negative in Britain, more positive in France and Italy—but still limited.[29] The Roskilde session attracted even less media attention. "The distressing side of it all," lamented de Beauvoir, "was that because of the negligence of the press there were so few of us to profit from this impressive collection of documents, evidence, and explanations."[30] Indeed, awareness of the atrocities visited on Vietnam remained low in the United States where opposition, when it did grow, centered largely on the balance sheet of American lives.

Still, the tribunal would leave its mark, if not in immediately mobilizing mass opposition to the war and US imperialism, then in the new practice of resistance for which it would provide the model. This practice took the form of a tribunal, placing international law center stage and presenting its conclusions in terms of the legality of US policies and practices. For anti-imperialists, this was a strikingly novel form of resistance, one rooted in law and legality as both the frame of analysis and the grounds for condemnation. If, in Kenneth Tynan's words, the tribunal propagated "a symbolic and demonstrable truth," that truth was a rather narrow one, that the United States had violated international law.

Between Law and Politics

Here, then, was a practice of resistance that sought, through a process of documenting and publicizing violent policies and practices, to mobilize opposition to systemic injustice. As such, it was an avowedly *political* body, as are peoples' tribunals more generally. Their ultimate goal is not an impartial, evenhanded analysis of opposing claims but a forceful intervention in international politics. Yet the form that this political practice takes is that of the tribunal, an institution rooted squarely in the tradition of liberal legalism with its commitment to the ostensibly *apolitical* application of formal legal process. This structural antinomy at the heart of the peoples' tribunal gives rise, in turn, to a fundamental tension between clashing conceptions of juridical and political legitimacy.

For supporters who value juridical legitimacy, peoples' tribunals are to be celebrated for their ability to "harness the power and legitimacy of law."[31] It is their "emphasis on law, international law in particular, and a deliberative process of evaluation of evidence in the light of law," Andrew Byrnes and Gabrielle Simm argue, that sets tribunals apart from mere "speech at a public rally" or a "political show trial." For Byrnes and Simm, the difference between a legitimate process rooted in law and one tarnished by overt politics "lies in the extent to which the forms and procedure of a legal proceeding are observed, as well as in the cogency of the analysis and reasoning that is adopted."[32] Many participants in peoples' tribunals share this view. In her recent book on the World Tribunal on Iraq, Ayça Çubukçu describes how a significant number of organizers of that tribunal insisted that its legitimacy could only stem from its foundation in law. For these organizers, law was to be "the sole mother tongue" of the tribunal: "what was perceived as the self-evident legitimacy of international law would and could be appropriated by the [Iraq tribunal] through the adoption of its procedures." In short, if the tribunal sought legitimacy, it would have to "base itself in the fabric of international law" and defer to the "expertise of international lawyers as its competent technicians." Otherwise, it risked becoming "a mere political campaign."[33]

The value placed on legalism is also shared by critics of peoples' tribunals, for whom these bodies lack legitimacy precisely because they deviate from a strict facsimile of legal process. Richard Goldstone, whose 2009 UN Fact Finding Mission on the Gaza Conflict had identified the commission of war crimes and possible crimes against humanity during Israel's "Cast Lead" operation,[34] complained in the *New York Times* that the Palestine tribunal was in fact "not a 'tribunal'" at all. "The 'evidence,'" he complained, was "one-sided and the members of the 'jury' are critics whose harsh views of Israel are well known."[35] Others echoed criticisms of Russell and Sartre, dismissing the Palestine tribunal as "political theatre," its convenors using "a legal façade to create an image of neutrality and credibility" while really pursuing their partisan political agenda.[36] These supporters and detractors differ in their evaluation of these institutions' fidelity to legalism, but both are agreed on the *source* of legitimacy.

Other supporters of peoples' tribunals, however, are happy to present their projects as openly political. Russell had warned against fetishized notions of impartiality: of course we're biased, he happily acknowledged; how can one know anything about what is going on in Vietnam and not be biased? Only the wilfully ignorant could be unaware of the suffering of the Vietnamese people, only the most callous indifferent to it. What of even-handedness in evaluating the acts of all sides to the conflict? For Sartre, such a notion rang hollow, the implicit equation of US and Vietnamese actions nonsensical. "I refuse to place in the same category the actions of an organization of poor peasants, hunted, obliged to maintain an iron dis-cipline in their ranks, and those of an immense army backed up by a highly industrialized country of 200 million inhabitants."[37] Russell was no less impatient with false equivalences. "Who would compare the 100,000 tons of napalm with a peasant holding a rifle," he would soon ask the tribunal. "Who can fail to distinguish the power which destroys the hospitals and schools of an entire people from the defenders who attack the aeroplanes carrying napalm and steel fragmentation bombs?"[38] Four decades later, supporters of the Palestine tribunal would also have no truck with claims of bias or tortured attempts to draw an equivalence between Israeli aggres-sion and Palestinians' desperate acts of resistance.

On this view, then, the motive behind peoples' tribunals is not an abstract commitment to legalism and impartiality. While law provides a useful analytical frame and vocabulary, tribunals' goals should be ulti-mately political: to resist and mobilize opposition against US imperialism, as for Sartre and Russell, or Israeli settler colonialism, as for supporters of Palestinian liberation. For these activists, then, knowledge and disapproval of imperial or settler-colonial violence and oppression could not detract from the legitimacy of a tribunal created to condemn it. For some, like Arundhati Roy, it is its very source. Speaking at a session of the World Tri-bunal on Iraq in June 2005, Roy rooted that tribunal's legitimacy precisely in its partisan nature:

> I would like to briefly address as straightforwardly as I can a few questions that have been raised about this tribunal. The first is that this tribunal is a kangaroo court. That it represents only one point of view. That it is a prosecution without a defense. That the verdict is a foregone conclusion. . . . Let me say categorically that this tribunal is the defense. It is an act of resistance in itself.[39]

For Roy, the tribunal, in giving a voice to the otherwise silenced vic-tims of US imperialism, was an act of resistance and a small, if impotent, defence to a prosecution waged not in courtrooms but in the bloody streets of Baghdad and Fallujah. And yet the Iraq tribunal, no less than the Vietnam tribunal before it and the Palestinian tribunal after it, still embraced the juridical form, its findings framed by international law, its condemnation couched in the language of legality. The United States and United Kingdom, it concluded, were guilty of "planning, preparing and waging the supreme crime of a war of aggression in contravention of the United Nations Charter and the Nuremberg Principles."[40]

The point is that these modes of legitimacy—legal and political—are mutually exclusive. If something is partisan, it cannot appeal to juridical neutrality, and vice versa. If the purpose of a people's tribunal is political, part of a practice of resistance, why adopt the form of a tribunal at all? What is to be gained by privileging international law and the language of legality? Alternatively, if it seeks to claim the juridical legitimacy attaching to the tribunal form and international law, how can it remain political?

International Law and Principled Opportunism

While peoples' tribunals are marked by this irresolvable tension between the juridical and political, they must, in practice, make something of a choice. Concretely, the tension reveals itself—and is temporarily "resolved"—in how these bodies characterize their relationship to *international law*. Like the Iraq tribunal, and later the Palestine tribunal, the Vietnam tribunal had foregrounded international law and legality as its frame of analysis and condemnation: the United States was found to have violated international law, its actions denounced for their illegality. Organizers differed, however, in their rationales for privileging legalism.

For Russell, international law could serve as the basis against which US policy and actions were to be judged, but there was no pretence of the tribunal as a formal legal proceeding. As he put it in his opening statement to the Roskilde session: "We are not judges. We are witnesses. Our task is to make Mankind bear witness . . . and to unite humanity on the side of justice in Vietnam."[41] Tariq Ali, who traveled to North Vietnam on a fact-finding mission for the tribunal and later testified, recalls much the same: it was an "act of resistance to a war," the aim "to open the eyes of the world—to say look, here is the evidence we have brought: study it, see what you think, do something about it. . . . We were screaming. It was a scream of rage to the world: look, are you going to do something or not."[42]

Sartre, in contrast, was far more concerned that the tribunal should operate specifically on the terrain of international law. For him, the tribunal's task was to determine not the moral character of the war—no hearing was necessary to condemn US imperialism—but rather specifically the legality of US policies and actions. By the time the tribunal met in Stockholm in May 1967, a split had formed between a Paris-based "Sartre group" and a London-based "Russell group."[43] The split was in part about personalities—Dedijer, close to the Parisians, and Schoenman, in London, were both polarizing figures. But contrasting perspectives on the tribunal's goals, and the role of law in those goals, also played its part. Both groups were equally opposed to US imperialism in Southeast Asia, yet, as Arthur and Judith Klinghoffer write, the Paris group "stressed international law" and "focused on procedural matters."[44] The Londoners, however, along with the American members of the tribunal, looked to a broader horizon and "wanted to use the tribunal as part of [a] revolutionary agenda."[45] A commitment to legalism might offer a "salve for European radicals," but it was hardly going to end the war. Some, like Julius Lester, who had traveled to North Vietnam and testified in Stockholm, felt that the legalistic approach that dominated the proceedings had little "practical validity"—"spotlighting illegalities could not transform political realities."[46] The concern of the tribunal, they felt, should not have been to identify the existence or otherwise of war crimes but "to prevent the defeat of Vietnam's revolution."[47]

Sartre, for his part, was not blind to these criticisms. As he explained already in his *Le Nouvel Observateur* interview in November 1966, "we have been reproached with petit bourgeois legalism." The charge, he conceded, was not misplaced. "It is true, and I accept that objection." He, too, was under no illusions that international law and legality were going to end the war or imperialism. His use of legalism, he suggested, was tactical, not principled.

> [W]ho are we trying to convince? The classes who are engaged in the struggle against capitalism and who are already convinced (crimes or no crimes) that it is necessary to fight to the bitter end against imperialism? Or that very broad fringe of the middle class which, at the moment is undecided?

The Vietnamese certainly did not need their struggle framed in legal terms in order to oppose US aggression, nor others in the Third World movement fighting against imperialism. Likewise, those in the workers' movement in Europe and North America were already committed to anti-imperialist internationalism. Rather, Sartre was adamant, "[i]t is the petit

bourgeois masses which must today be aroused and shaken." This depoliticized segment of society had no existing commitment to anticapital-
ism or anti-imperialism. How might their opposition to the war, then, be
mobilized? "[I]t is by means of legalism," with its sheen of objectivity and
legitimacy, Sartre insisted, and the seemingly apolitical, objective standards of international law "that their eyes can be opened," their opposition
mobilized.[48]

If political action might be spurred on by international law and its violation, the goal of that action, Sartre was clear, was not to be found on any
legal terrain. The United States was committing war crimes, even genocide.[49] Might the tribunal's condemnation of such crimes, and the public
outcry many hoped it would provoke, convince the United States to wage a
more humane war? To even pose the question was to miss the point. Asked
whether there is "a way of waging war which is to be condemned, and
another which is not," Sartre responded with a resounding no. The war,
Sartre insisted, was inseparable from the context in which it was rooted,
namely the "onslaught of American imperialism against the countries of
the Third World which attempt to escape its domination."[50] For Sartre, the
war in Vietnam was an attempt to quash a national liberation struggle, but
also "an example and a warning" to others tempted to resist neocolonial
subsumption—to "all of Latin America . . . and all of the Third World"—
that such struggle "does not pay." The choice was simple: "submission [to
imperialism] or radical liquidation."[51]

We might then see the Vietnam tribunal as an instance of what Robert
Knox has called principled opportunism, the use of international law as
a tool within a wider political strategy. On this approach, law is "not to
be used on its own terms, but rather in furtherance of a strategic goal."[52]
Crucially, for both Knox and Sartre, the deployment of international
legal argument and the language of legality should not displace or sup-
plant politics. On this Sartre was clear, his horizon extending well beyond
legal judgment as an end in itself. "It is on the basis of the results of our
inquiry," he insisted, "that it will be possible to organize demonstrations,
meetings, marches, signature campaigns." Law was merely a tool in the aid
of a broader *political* mobilization.

From Vietnam to Palestine

As Vietnam tribunal delegates gathered in Stockholm in May 1967, and
Russell condemned the "arrogant brutality" of the United States and its

"enormous new onslaught against the people of Vietnam,"[53] war planners in Tel Aviv were preparing for their own war of aggression. Arrogance and brutality were not uniquely American traits: in June, Israel invaded and occupied East Jerusalem, the West Bank, the Gaza Strip, and the Golan Heights, continuing its policy of dispossession and ethnic cleansing inaugurated with the Nakba of 1948. In 1970, two days before his death, Russell would write of the "tragedy of the people of Palestine." "How much longer," he asked, "is the world willing to endure this spectacle of wanton cruelty?"[54] All too long, it is painfully apparent, some seven decades after the expulsion of the Palestinian people, as an apartheid regime of walls, checkpoints, house demolitions, bombings, blockades, targeting killings, and torture grows ever more brutal, Israeli political leaders ever more brazen.

Already in the 1960s, clear parallels could be drawn between Vietnam and Palestine. National liberation movements in both, delegates at the 1966 Tricontinental Conference in Havana urged, should be supported in their resistance against imperialism and colonial oppression. Three years later, PLO chairman Yasser Arafat praised "the alliance of the Arab and Palestinian national liberation movement with Vietnam" and other liberation movements in Asia, Africa, and Latin America. While each struggle had its own peculiarities, all were engaged, Arafat insisted, in the same broader confrontation with "imperialism, injustice and oppression."[55] Affirming the affinities between their struggles, Vietnamese general Vo Nguyen Giap would tell a visiting Palestinian delegation in March 1970: "The Vietnamese and Palestinian people have much in common, just like two people suffering from the same illness."[56]

While Russell wrote and spoke of Palestine with the same passion and clarity as Vietnam, no similar peoples' tribunal would engage with the violence of Israeli settler colonialism in his lifetime. Only in 2009, in the wake of Israel's assault on Gaza—"Operation Cast Lead," in the jargon of Israeli war planners—would a Russell Tribunal on Palestine be launched. Like its namesake, the Palestine tribunal gathered a jury of eminent personalities including the Nobel laureate Mairead Maguire, diplomats such as the French ambassador and one-time resistance fighter Stéphane Hessel, former government ministers including Ronald Kasrils and Aminata Traoré, political activists such as Angela Davis, and legal authorities including John Dugard, Michael Mansfield, and José Antonio Martin Pallin. From 2010 to 2014, the tribunal held sessions in Barcelona, London, Cape Town, New York, and Brussels.

In Barcelona, the tribunal heard testimony on issues such as the right of the Palestinian people to self-determination, Israel's settlements and plun-

dering of natural resources, the annexation of East Jerusalem, the blockade of Gaza and Israel's deadly "Cast Lead" assault the previous year, and
the construction of the infamous Wall in occupied Palestinian territory. Of
particular concern was the complicity of the EU and its member states in
violations of international law, the tribunal emphasizing in its conclusions
the EU's failure to implement both international and European law.[57]

In London, the tribunal turned to an examination of the complicity
of multinational corporations in Israel's violations of international law,
hearing evidence relating to the supply of arms to occupation forces and
bulldozers for the demolition of Palestinian homes, the construction and
maintenance of the Wall, and the provision of financial and other services
to Israeli settlements. Such activities, the tribunal found, rendered the corporations such as G4S and Caterpillar complicit in violations of international humanitarian and human rights law.[58] Traveling beyond Europe, the
tribunal considered in Cape Town whether Israeli policies and practices
affecting the Palestinian population in Israeli and occupied territory could
be characterized as a regime of apartheid.[59] Here it found that Israel does
indeed subject the Palestinian people to a "systematic and institutionalised
regime" of domination "amounting to apartheid as defined under international law."[60] With a nod to the historical significance of its location, the
Cape Town meeting also called on "global civil society" to "replicate the
spirit of solidarity that contributed to the end of apartheid in South Africa,
including by making national parliaments aware of the findings of this Tribunal and supporting the campaign for Boycott, Divestment and Sanctions
(BDS)."[61]

In New York, the tribunal took up the question of US and UN responsibility for Israel's violations of international law. In its findings, it rehearsed
the long history of US complicity in Israeli oppression, concluding that
Israel's settler colonial expansion, and the violent policies attendant on it,
would not be possible without the United States' economic, diplomatic,
and military support. The UN was likewise condemned for its failure to
take proportionate action in the face of Israeli violations.[62] At a final session
in Brussels in early 2013, the tribunal's jury summarized its findings from
each of the four previous sessions, once more mapping the violations of
international law it had attributed to Israel and the responsibility of other
parties—the United States, the UN, the EU, private corporations—in
assisting Israel in those violations.[63]

The following year, as Israel launched yet another brutal assault on
Gaza, the tribunal assembled again in Brussels for an emergency session.
Once more, in Richard Falk's words, "the enormity of the devastation and

the spectacle of horror" of Israeli attacks on Gaza was rehearsed, once more the heart-wrenching testimonies of Palestinians heard.[64] Here was the third major military assault on Gaza in six years, some 700 tons of ordinance deployed over 50 days of a relentless offensive. And once more, the tribunal was clear: Israeli actions amounted to war crimes, crimes against humanity, and other violations of international law.[65]

As with earlier tribunals, organizers of the Palestine tribunal had to once more grapple with the tension between legal form and political practice. "We had this tension at every session, at every meeting," Frank Barat, one of the tribunal's coordinators, recalls. To award the lawyers too central a role would undermine efforts to raise awareness. "If you have ten jurists talking for two days about international law, you won't reach the people." The "fine line between the tribunal as spectacle and as legal proceeding," Barat feels, "was very difficult to navigate."[66] Observing the tribunal's New York session, Christopher Federici felt that "the Tribunal appeared conflicted by stark contrasts between the desire to project a sense of procedural legality and the inescapable underpinnings of activism that drove the very desire to organize."[67]

Just as the Paris group's commitment to international law won out as the organizing principle in the Vietnam tribunal, so too in the Palestine tribunal was the tension again resolved in favor of legalism. "Quite a lot of people complained to us that [the tribunal] is just a lawyers' initiative, that we have to be an activist initiative," Barat recalls. Such criticisms are clearly exaggerated, the hand of political activists unmistakable in the undertaking. But it is equally apparent that organizers made a choice—tactical, principled, or otherwise—to privilege international law, illegality, and complicity with illegality as the tribunal's guiding concerns. This is clear from the tribunal's various published findings, cited above, but also from its official aim: "to examine the violations of international law, of which the Palestinians are victims, and that prevent the Palestinian People from exercising its rights to a sovereign State."[68]

Put this way, the problem to which the tribunal was responding was cast as a narrow issue of legality, albeit one with far-reaching consequences. Barat, writing with Daniel Machover, a legal adviser to the tribunal, expands on this formulation slightly: the tribunal was also "a response to the failure of the international community to act appropriately to bring to an end Israel's recognized violations of international law."[69] But they too frame the tribunal's very raison d'être as a commitment to legality. The Palestine tribunal, they argue, "fulfilled *a real legal function by promoting and stimulating the implementation of the rule of law*. It does not compete with other jurisdictions (domestic or international), but works in complementarity with them to enforce the law in Palestine."[70]

None of this is to suggest that the tribunal's organizers—or Barat and Machover—were not also concerned with the broader issues of Israeli settler colonialism and Palestinian liberation, or that they were not committed to extra-legal action. Indeed, it is apparent that many saw the institution and the invocation of international law and legalism, like Russell and Sartre, as the means to spur further political mobilization. Still, they made a concrete choice, tactical or otherwise, to use and privilege the language of law and legality, and the juridical form of the tribunal, as those means to frame Israel's aggression in Gaza, and the dispossession and oppression of the Palestinians more generally, as foremost a spectacular violation of international law, and one to be opposed as such.

From Principled Opportunism to Legalism

How does the choice to privilege law and legalism, albeit in the service of a political intervention, compare with that made by Russell, Sartre, and other organizers of the Vietnam tribunal? At first blush, there is little difference between the two. Organizers in both instances were confronted with the tension between law and politics central to the very nature of peoples' tribunals. Both chose to frame and analyze instances of injustice and oppression—US imperialism and its manifestation in Vietnam; Israeli settler colonialism and its continuing violence in Palestine—specifically in terms of international law. And both chose to use the juridical form and procedures of the tribunal to publicize and condemn it: US policy and actions in Vietnam violated international law, likewise Israeli policy and actions in Palestine.

Still, if the calculus was fundamentally the same, the two tribunals differed in important respects. The Vietnam tribunal gave little suggestion it was committed to international law qua international law or to legalism as the answer to, or *in and of itself* the means to end, imperialist aggression. Indeed, its organizers were openly skeptical about the emancipatory potential of international law. As Sartre put it, imperialism "is beyond the reach of any legal or moral condemnation."[71] Determining that the United States was violating international law or even stopping its violations would not affect the systemic logic of imperialism undergirding those violations: a *legal* imperialist war is still an imperialist war. That would take something else, Sartre insisted: "The only thing possible is to combat it; intellectually by revealing its inner mechanism, politically by attempting to disengage oneself from it . . . or by armed struggle."[72]

If such skepticism about the power of international law was shared by the Palestine tribunal's organizers, they were not nearly as forthright in their public statements. In fact, in sharp contrast, the later tribunal went so far as to insist on "the supremacy of international law as the basis for a solution to the Israeli Palestinian conflict."[73] More generally, international law and the question of legality or illegality became the central motif and discourse of the Palestine tribunal to a degree never reached by its earlier counterpart. While it heard from witnesses and experts who spoke to extra-legal issues, including the systemic issues of settler colonialism and imperialism, the tribunal's published textual record is far narrower. Israel's settlements are deemed illegal; likewise its annexation of East Jerusalem. War crimes are identified in Israel's Cast Lead assault on Gaza. Multinational corporations are condemned for complicity in Israel's violations of international law. But there the analysis ends. Such crimes and other unlawful acts, including the United States or multinational corporations' complicity in those crimes and acts, are abstracted from their context and the structural logics that produce those acts and complicity—settler colonialism, imperialism, capitalism. Again, this is not to suggest that the tribunal's participants were indifferent to these deeper issues. But the tribunal made a concrete decision to frame its findings squarely in terms of international legal conclusions. This is in sharp contrast with the Vietnam tribunal's published conclusions. Take, for example, its "verdict" on whether the US government was guilty of genocide against the people of Vietnam. The answer was a unanimous yes, but the tribunal sought to go beyond a formal legal condemnation, setting out an historical and political analysis of the US war against Vietnam and how this genocide "arises within the framework of the general policy of imperialism."[74]

One can speculate as to why the Palestine tribunal chose to take a more legalistic approach than its predecessor, framing its concern narrowly as Israel's violation of international law and its stated goal, likewise narrowly, to hold Israel accountable and ensure compliance with the law. But an undoubtedly significant factor was the new conjuncture in which the tribunal took shape, one which differed markedly from an earlier era. In 1967, a peoples' tribunal evaluating and applying international law was entirely novel. Yet the tactical deployment of international legal argument in aid of a broader practice of resistance against imperialism was not out of place in the 1960s, at the height of the Third World movement and anticolonial internationalism. Already at Bandung, in 1955, newly independent states had sought to use and expand the scope of legal concepts such as sovereignty and self-determination to challenge the imperial status quo.[75] Imperialism and colonialism were, to be sure, in Antony Anghie's words, "central to the constitution of international law," the latter structurally connected with relations of exploitation and domination.[76] Still, in the 1960s and early 1970s, many Third World jurists felt that, despite the legacy of colonialism in international law, the latter could be used to advance an anti-imperial agenda. The growing numerical advantage of newly independent states in institutions such as the UN General Assembly could provide such an opening. In 1960, for instance, Third World states, aided by the Eastern bloc, were able to pass UNGA Resolution 1514, Declaration on the Granting of Independence to Colonial Countries and Peoples, calling for an immediate end to colonialism and advancing an expansive conception of self-determination.[77] Anticolonial delegates to international legal conferences drew on principles of anti-imperialism and self-determination to argue for, and articulate, legal distinctions between wars of national liberation and wars of "imperialist aggression," seeking to legitimize anticolonial struggles aimed at establishing an international order free of imperial domination.[78] Crucially, however, such appropriations of international law, and principles such as that of self-determination, were embedded within a broader critique of, and struggle against, imperialism, functioning, as Adom Getachew shows, as merely the "juridical component" of a political project of "international nondomination."[79]

Within this constellation of forces, Russell and Sartre's calculation was understandable. With the Third World movement ascendant and a strong workers' movement in the North Atlantic metropoles, one could appeal to a depoliticized "middle class" on the basis of legality and hope to solicit solidarity for an anti-imperial politics from those with no prior principled commitment to anti-imperialism. Yet that calculation began to look rather different by the 1980s with the defeat of many anti-imperialist struggles, the collapse of the Third World movement, and the decline of the workers' movement, the latter's commitment to a radical internationalism giving way to more parochial concerns. Little remained of the mass anti-imperialist movements of the 1960s and early 1970s uniting and mobilizing activists and revolutionary masses in metropolitan core and periphery alike—those who, in Sartre's words, "are already convinced (crimes or no crimes) that it is necessary to fight to the bitter end against imperialism." Political mobilization increasingly depended on appeals to the depoliticized masses of late capitalist society made, as prefigured by Sartre and the Vietnam tribunal, in the language of legality and international law. But such appeals were now divorced from any mass anti-imperial movement: legality increasingly became itself the horizon of political resistance. By the turn of the century, the language of international law—and in particular of human rights—had displaced anti-imperialism, so long a mainstay of political vernacular in the twentieth century, as the primary emancipatory framework in the imagination of internationalism.

As Vietnamese peasants died at the hands of US imperialism, antiwar protestors in the United States and Europe expressed their moral and strategic opposition to the war, denouncing it as immoral and imperialist, but rarely sought to characterize that opposition in terms of the war's legality or the criminal liability of American leaders and strategic planners. This was precisely the novelty of the Russell Tribunal. Lawyers, of course, had foregrounded international law—most notably Richard Falk—but it was not the vernacular of the popular antiwar movement.[80] In contrast, as the United States prepared to invade Iraq in 2003, legality and international law were quickly cemented as the dominant frame configuring public debate about the war, especially within the antiwar movement.[81] During both the lead-up and aftermath of the invasion, much popular opposition to the war was framed in the language of legal argument—the war was an illegal use of force—including the language of international criminal law—the war was the work of war criminals and, as such, George Bush and Tony Blair should be tried in The Hague. The "illegality" of the war, in short, became, as Knox shows, "one of the central pillars of the campaign against the war." This juridification of opposition was reflected, as already noted, in the proceedings of the World Tribunal on Iraq, which proclaimed that "[t]he invasion and occupation of Iraq was and is illegal."[82] International law, deployed tactically by Sartre and the Vietnam tribunal to stir antiwar sentiment among an apolitical middle class, had become an organizing principle for antiwar activists, the politics of anti-imperial resistance now subsumed within this depoliticized vernacular.

Within this new conjuncture, it is perhaps entirely unsurprising that the Palestine solidarity activists should have turned to the tribunal form and embraced international law as the organizing principle and framework for their intervention. An anticolonial and anti-imperial politics of national liberation, although very much still alive in Palestine, no longer resonates globally as it once did. Moreover, the embrace of legalism by opponents of the US invasion of Iraq appeared to offer an example of law put to great effect in mobilizing resistance. "Even though the Iraq war ultimately went ahead," Knox writes, "the anti-war movement's message managed to mobilise millions of people, delegitimised the war and damned a number of the governments and politicians associated with it."[83] While going on to chart the pitfalls of the movement's embrace of legalism, of which he is highly critical, Knox, like Sartre, nonetheless notes the power of international legal argument in raising antiwar sentiment beyond traditional radical and antiwar political constituencies. The language of illegality was the glue that held together a diverse coalition drawn from a "range of demographics (age, class and education) and political constituencies."[84] With its aura of objectivity and legitimacy, law could unite a diverse coalition without the need for a deeper political critique.

What of Palestine? Might the language of international law and legality also help mobilize opposition to the injustices of Israeli settler colonialism? It is difficult to judge the success of the Palestine tribunal; how should success even be measured? While the tribunal's Cape Town session attracted significant attention in South African media, the same cannot be said of the tribunal or international media more widely.[85] No doubt some observers, exposed to the tribunal's legal arguments and conclusions for the first time, saw their opposition to Israeli policy harden. Certainly, support for the Palestinian cause extends beyond radical political constituencies and the mobilization of international legal arguments through fora such as the Palestine tribunal no doubt plays a role. At the same time, however, the tension between legal form and political practice at the center of peoples' tribunals remains. One cannot simply pick and choose; legalism comes with a cost.

Hilary Charlesworth has written of international law's tendency to focus attention on particular incidents and outbreaks of violence without ever systematically engaging with underlying structural forces. Legal analysis, she suggests, "concentrate[s] on a single event or series of events," but in doing so "miss[es] the larger picture."[86] In focusing on Israeli policies and practices as foremost an issue of *illegality*, the Palestine tribunal's published record reproduces this narrow analytical frame and risks obscuring or even foreclosing a deeper inquiry into the conditions and political-economic forces that lie behind, and provide the context for, unlawful acts. At its Cape Town session, for example, the tribunal considered carefully the definition of apartheid in international law and interpretation of the 1973 UN Convention on the Suppression and Punishment of the Crime of Apartheid. Its conclusions offer a careful legal analysis of the Convention and its application to Israeli policies and practices vis-à-vis the Palestinian people and leave little doubt that "Israel subjects the Palestinian people to an institutionalised regime of domination amounting to apartheid as defined under international law."[87] Why does an apartheid regime exist in Palestine? The tribunal's conclusions offer no insights. For anyone reading the tribunal's published conclusions, the settler-colonial, imperialist, political-economic, or other drivers of Israeli apartheid disappear from view. Israeli apartheid is a crime without cause or context.[88] Of course, the tribunal was seeking to generate headlines, not undertake a nuanced scholarly analysis. But that is precisely the point. The headlines and attendant public awareness the tribunal sought to generate were headlines and awareness about the illegality of Israeli policy: that Israel is guilty, for example, of the crime of apartheid. By focusing the debate on questions of law and legality, and specific instances of illegality—apartheid, occupation, war crimes—the resulting discourse deflects attention from, or even risks erasing, Israel as a colonial project.[89]

If the tribunal's findings were constrained by its focus on international law, what consequences followed from its identification of legal violations? Insofar as its case against Israeli practices and policies rested on international law, the Palestine tribunal foregrounded further international legal engagements as the desirable, even necessary, concomitant to its findings of illegality. In London, having heard evidence of "corporate complicity" in Israeli violations of international law, the tribunal advocated for actions to be brought before domestic courts to hold corporations liable under civil or criminal law, urging states to ensure there are "sufficient remedies available."[90] The tribunal's findings, its organizers observed, were "likely to form . . . the basis of legal advocacy for years to come."[91] In its Cape Town findings, the tribunal urged the prosecutor of the ICC to "initiate an investigation . . . into international crimes," while the UN General Assembly should request an advisory opinion from the ICJ on the occupation and apartheid. If international law provides the framework for identifying the problem, it also necessarily provides the solution. A single recommendation was directed at "global civil society," which was urged to support the campaign for Boycott, Divestment and Sanctions (BDS).[92] Barat and Machover argue that the tribunal was indeed interested "in empowering civil society and reinforcing the work of already existing campaigns." How would it do so? "[B]y providing additional legal arguments and ideas that will assist in future litigation and legal lobbying."[93]

Juridification and Resistance

Reviewing the Palestine tribunal and its published record, one is presented with a claustrophobic view of political possibility, further international legal interventions the horizon of the political imagination. Israel commits atrocities in Palestine? ICC investigation is the answer, the tribunal proclaims. That court's history of selective and highly politicized interventions, reproducing one-sided narratives of complex conflicts and demonizing some perpetrators while legitimating imperial military interventions, should give any anti-imperialist pause. Far from ending the impunity long enjoyed by Western states and political leaders, the ICC has helped to institutionalize it.[94] More generally, by prescribing further legal engagements as the appropriate response to Israeli domination and Palestinian suffering, the Palestine tribunal's approach risks reproducing the tendency, noted by Noura Erakat, to "attribute injustice to a failure of law or to its nonexistence and thus prescribe more law, better law, and/or stricter adherence to law as the requisite corrective."[95] As we have seen, the tribunal framed Palestinian suffering as foremost a failure to enforce international law. If only that law were enforced adequately and Israel's international legal violations ended, the tribunal implied, all would be well. Yet as scholars such as Nicola Perugini and Neve Gordon show, there is no inherent opposition between international law and domination, the former often mobilized in support of the latter, including in Palestine.[96]

Importantly, I am not suggesting that the organizers of the Palestine tribunal were necessarily blind to this. Many of the activists involved would no doubt recognize international law as itself part of the problem, deeply implicated in the production and reproduction of injustice and domination, in Palestine as elsewhere. And the tribunal's support for a *political* campaign of BDS is significant. Nonetheless, the channeling of political resistance primarily into legal avenues follows logically from the choice to foreground law and legalism as the frame of analysis and condemnation and, ultimately, as the privileged language of resistance.

This is the dilemma of all peoples' tribunals, I have suggested, caught between juridical form and political practice. If the purpose of a peoples' tribunal is political, I asked above, what is to be gained by privileging law and the language of legality? Organizers of both the Vietnam tribunal and Palestine tribunal, I argued, believed that law could be deployed tactically so as to mobilize political opposition to systematic injustice and oppression within constituencies not already committed to this cause. But in seeking to claim the juridical legitimacy attaching to the tribunal form and legalism, I also pondered, how can they remain political? In this chapter, I have argued that however one chooses to resolve these competing concerns, there are costs associated with that choice. I have focused my critique on the Palestine tribunal, but the Vietnam tribunal faced the same bind.

Where that tribunal differed was in the political context in which it operated. While embracing legalism, it operated squarely within the param-
eters of the global anticapitalist movement with a committed politics of
anti-imperialism. Whether or not its efforts to frame US imperialism as a
violation of international law were successful, there was little chance of that
politics being subsumed by legalism. That calculus, I have suggested, looks
very different today, imperialism and its settler-colonial outposts trium-
phant and workers' and national liberation movements in tatters. If international politics has become increasingly juridified, so too has political
resistance, the depoliticized language of international law displacing other
emancipatory frameworks in the political imagination of internationalism.
Peoples' tribunals, I fear, do not merely reflect but also contribute to this
shift.

NOTES

I am grateful to Teresa Almeida Cravo, Robert Knox, Brian Cuddy, and Victor Kattan for comments on an earlier version of this chapter.

1. Bertrand Russell, "Opening Statement at the International War Crimes Tribunal," *World Outlook*, May 12, 1967, 482. Due to frail health, Russell was unable
to attend the tribunal in person. Instead this statement was read at the opening of
the tribunal's first session in Stockholm on May 2, 1967, by his secretary, Ralph
Schoenman.

2. Bertrand Russell, *The Autobiography of Bertrand Russell, 1944–1969* (New
York: Simon & Schuster, 1969), 242.

3. Bertrand Russell, "Appeal to American Conscience," in *War Crimes in Vietnam* (London: Allen & Unwin, 1967), 116.

4. In mid-1966, some 60 percent of Americans favored escalation of the war.
William C. Gibbons, *The United States Government and the Vietnam War: Executive
and Legislative Roles and Relationships, Part IV: July 1965–January 1968* (Princeton:
Princeton University Press, 1995), 430–31.

5. Russell, "Opening Statement."

6. *US News and World Report*, February 15, 1965, quoted in Leon Matarasso,
"Outline of the General Introductory Report," in *Prevent the Crime of Silence:
Reports from the Sessions of the International War Crimes Tribunal founded by Bertrand
Russell*, ed. Peter Limqueco and Peter Weiss (London: Allen Lane, 1971), 76.

7. On peoples' tribunals generally, see Andrew Byrnes and Gabrille Simm, eds.,
Peoples' Tribunals and International Law (Cambridge: Cambridge University Press,
2018); Dianne Otto, "Beyond Legal Justice: Some Personal Reflections on People's
Tribunals, Listening and Responsibility," *London Review of International Law* 5, no. 2
(2017).

8. Lieven De Cauter, "For a Justice to Come: An Interview with Jacques Derrida," last modified April 5, 2004, http://archive.indymedia.be/news/2004/04/831
23.html

9. Luís Moita, "Opinion Tribunals and the Permanent People's Tribunal," JANUS.NET, *e-journal of International Relations 6*, no. 1 (2015): 41.

10. I borrow the term from Robert Knox. See Robert Knox, "Marxism, International Law, and Political Strategy," *Leiden Journal of International Law* 22, no. 3 (2009) and Robert Knox "Strategy and Tactics," *Finnish Yearbook of International Law* 21 (2010).

11. Bertrand Russell, "Speech to the First Meeting of the War Crimes Tribunal, London, 13 November 1966," in *Prevent the Crime of Silence: Reports from the Sessions of the International War Crimes Tribunal founded by Bertrand Russell*, ed. Peter Limqueco and Peter Weiss (London: Allen Lane, 1971).

12. Bertrand Russell, Letter to Johnson, August 25, 1966, cited in Harish C. Mehta, "North Vietnam's Informal Diplomacy with Bertrand Russell: Peace Activism and the International War Crimes Tribunal," *Peace & Change* 37, no. 1 (2012): 78–79.

13. Tom Wells, *The War Within: America's Battle over Vietnam* (Berkeley: University of California Press, 1994), 142.

14. Gibbons, *United States Government*, 433.

15. Memorandum for the President from Ball, August 29, 1966, quoted in Gibbons, *United States Government*, 434.

16. Wells, *War Within*, 142; Luke J. Stewart, "Too Loud to Rise above the Silence: The United States vs. the International War Crimes Tribunal, 1966–1967," *The Sixties: A Journal of History, Politics and Culture* 11, no. 1 (2018): 3–4.

17. Bernard Levin, "Bertrand Russell: Prosecutor, Judge and Jury," *New York Times*, February 19, 1967, VI.24.

18. Mehta, "Informal Diplomacy," 82.

19. Russell, "Speech to the First Meeting."

20. Jean-Paul Sartre, "Le crime," *Le Nouvel observateur*, November 30, 1966, reprinted in translation as "Imperialist Morality: Interview with Jean Paul Sartre on the War Crimes Tribunal," *New Left Review* I/41 (1967), 3.

21. "Text of de Gaulle's Letter Banning War Crimes Tribunal," *World Outlook*, May 12, 1967, 483.

22. "Sartre à de Gaulle," *Le Nouvel observateur*, April 26, 1967, reprinted in translation as "Jean-Paul Sartre's Answer to de Gaulle," *World Outlook*, May 12, 1967, 484.

23. Stewart, "Too Loud," 10.

24. Stewart, "Too Loud," 12.

25. Kenneth Tynan, "Open Letter to an American Liberal," *Playboy*, March 1968, 137. Many of the reports and testimonies presented at both sessions of the tribunal are collected in John Duffett, ed., *Against the Crime of Silence: Proceedings of the Russell International War Crimes Tribunal* (New York: O'Hare, 1968) and Peter Limqueco and Peter Weiss, eds., *Prevent the Crime of Silence: Reports from the Sessions of the International War Crimes Tribunal Founded by Bertrand Russell* (London: Allen Lane, 1971).

26. Limqueco and Weiss, *Prevent the Crime of Silence*, 143.

27. Jean-Paul Sartre, "Summary and Verdict of the Stockholm Session," in *Prevent the Crime of Silence: Reports from the Sessions of the International War Crimes Tribunal founded by Bertrand Russell*, ed. Peter Limqueco and Peter Weiss (London: Allen Lane, 1971).

28. Stewart, "Too Loud," 15.

29. See Page Arthur, *Unfinished Projects: Decolonization and the Philosophy of Jean-Paul Sartre* (London: Verso 2010), 164–66.

30. Quoted in Arthur J. Klinghoffer and Judith A. Klinghoffer, *International Citizens' Tribunals: Mobilizing Public Opinion to Advance Human Rights* (Basingstoke: Palgrave Macmillan, 2002), 157.

31. Sally Engle Merry, "Resistance and the Cultural Power of Law," *Law & Society Review* 29, no. 1 (1995): 21.

32. Andrew Byrnes and Gabrielle Simm, "International Peoples' Tribunals: Their Nature, Practice and Significance," in *Peoples' Tribunals and International Law*, ed. Andrew Byrnes and Gabrielle Simm (Cambridge: Cambridge University Press, 2018), 13.

33. Ayça Çubukçu, *For the Love of Humanity: The World Tribunal on Iraq* (Philadelphia: University of Pennsylvania Press, 2018), 22.

34. See UN Human Rights Council, "Human Rights in Palestine and Other Occupied Arab Territories: Report of the United Nations Fact Finding Mission on the Gaza Conflict," A/HRC/12/48, September 15, 2009.

35. Richard J. Goldstone, "Israel and the Apartheid Slander," *New York Times*, October 31, 2011, A27.

36. "Russell Tribunal on Palestine," NGO Monitor, last modified October 3, 2012, https://www.ngo-monitor.org/ngos/russell_tribunal_on_palestine/

37. Sartre, "Imperialist Morality," 7.

38. Bertrand Russell, "Closing Address to the Stockholm Session," in *Prevent the Crime of Silence: Reports from the Sessions of the International War Crimes Tribunal Founded by Bertrand Russell*, ed. Peter Limqueco and Peter Weiss (London: Allen Lane, 1971), 188.

39. Quoted in Çubukçu, *Love of Humanity*, 1.

40. Jury of Conscience, "Declaration of Jury of Conscience World Tribunal on Iraq: Istanbul 23–27 June 2005," *Feminist Review* 81 (2005): 97.

41. Quoted in Noam Chomsky, "Foreword," in *Prevent the Crime of Silence: Reports from the Sessions of the International War Crimes Tribunal Founded by Bertrand Russell*, ed. Peter Limqueco and Peter Weiss (London: Allen Lane, 1971), 9.

42. Tor Krever, "50 Years after Russell: An Interview with Tariq Ali," *London Review of International Law* 5, no. 3 (2017): 499. Ali has also written of his involvement with the tribunal in Tariq Ali, *Street Fighting Years: An Autobiography of the Sixties* (London: Verso, 2005). His testimony before the tribunal is transcribed in Tariq Ali, "Report from Cambodia and North Vietnam," in *Prevent the Crime of Silence: Reports from the Sessions of the International War Crimes Tribunal Founded by Bertrand Russell*, ed. Peter Limqueco and Peter Weiss (London: Allen Lane, 1971).

43. Klinghoffer and Klinghoffer, *International Citizens' Tribunals*, 129.

44. Klinghoffer and Klinghoffer, *International Citizens' Tribunals*, 129.

45. Klinghoffer and Klinghoffer, *International Citizens' Tribunals*, 129.

46. Klinghoffer and Klinghoffer, *International Citizens' Tribunals*, 130.

47. Klinghoffer and Klinghoffer, *International Citizens' Tribunals*, 130.

48. Sartre, "Imperialist Morality," 7.

49. See Jean-Paul Sartre, "Genocide," *New Left Review* I/48 (1968).

50. Sartre, "Imperialist Morality," 3.

51. Sartre, "Genocide," 19.

52. Knox, "Strategy and Tactics," 227.

53. Russell, "Opening Statement."

54. Quoted in Samih K. Farsoun and Naseer H. Aruri, *Palestine and the Palestinians*, 2nd ed. (New York: Routledge, 2018), 302.

55. Quoted in Paul Chamberlin, *The Global Offensive: The United States, the Palestine Liberation Organization, and the Making of the Post-Cold War Order* (Oxford: Oxford University Press, 2012), 22.

56. Quoted in Paul Chamberlin, "The Struggle Against Oppression Everywhere: The Global Politics of Palestinian Liberation," *Middle Eastern Studies* 47, no. 1 (2011): 25. The delegation included Arafat and his deputy, Salah Khalaf.

57. Russell Tribunal on Palestine, "Conclusions of the First International Session of the Russell Tribunal on Palestine," accessed May 10, 2020, http://www.russelltribunalonpalestine.com/en/wp-content/uploads/2010/08/CONCLUSIONS-TRP-FINAL-EN-last.pdf

58. Russell Tribunal on Palestine, "Findings of the London Session," accessed May 10, 2020, http://www.russelltribunalonpalestine.com/en/wp-content/uploads/2011/01/RTOP-London-Session-Findings.pdf. See also Asa Winstanley and Frank Barat, ed., *Corporate Complicity in Israel's Occupation* (London: Pluto Press, 2011).

59. See Barbara Harlow, "Apartheid or Not Apartheid? The Russell Tribunal on Palestine, South Africa Session, November 2011," *Law, Culture and the Humanities* 9 (2013).

60. Russell Tribunal on Palestine, "Findings of the South Africa Session," accessed May 10, 2020, http://www.russelltribunalonpalestine.com/en/wp-content/uploads/2011/11/RToP-Cape-Town-full-findings3.pdf, 20–21.

61. Russell Tribunal on Palestine, "Findings of the South Africa Session," 20–21.

62. Russell Tribunal on Palestine, "Findings of the Fourth International Session," accessed May 10, 2020, http://www.russelltribunalonpalestine.com/en/sessions/future-sessions/new-york-session-full-findings.html

63. Russell Tribunal on Palestine, "Findings of the Final Session of the Russell Tribunal on Palestine," accessed May 10, 2020, http://www.russelltribunalonpalestine.com/en/full-findings-of-the-final-session-en.html

64. Richard Falk, "Is Israel Guilty of Genocide in Its Assault on Gaza?" *The Nation*, October 6, 2014, https://www.thenation.com/article/archive/israel-guilty-genocide-its-assault-gaza/

65. Russell Tribunal on Palestine, "Extraordinary Session on Gaza: Summary of Findings," accessed May 10, 2020, http://www.russelltribunalonpalestine.com/en/sessions/extraordinary-session-brussels/findings.html

66. Frank Barat, Interview with author, June 23, 2020.

67. Christopher Federici, "Russell Tribunal on Palestine in New York: On US, UN Complicity," *Palestine Chronicle*, October 12, 2012, https://www.palestinechronicle.com/russell-tribunal-on-palestine-in-new-york-on-us-un-complicity/

68. Russell Tribunal on Palestine, "About," accessed May 10, 2020, https://www.russelltribunalonpalestine.com/en/about-rtop.html

69. Frank Barat and Daniel Machover, "The Russell Tribunal on Palestine," in *Is There a Court for Gaza? A Test Bench for International Justice*, ed. Chantal Meloni and Gianni Tognoni (The Hague: T.M.C. Asser Press, 2012), 528.

70. Barat and Machover, 531 (emphasis added).

71. Sartre, "Imperialist Morality," 4.

72. Sartre, "Imperialist Morality," 4.

73. Russell Tribunal on Palestine, "About."

74. Sartre, "Genocide," 19.

75. Luis Eslava, Michael Fakhri, and Vasuki Nesiah, "The Spirit of Bandung," in *Bandung, Global History, and International Law*, ed. Luis Eslava, Michael Fakhri, and Vasuki Nesiah (Cambridge: Cambridge University Press, 2017), 6.

76. Antony Anghie, *Imperialism, Sovereignty, and the Making of International Law* (Cambridge: Cambridge University Press, 2004), 3. See also China Miéville, *Between Equal Rights: A Marxist Theory of International Law* (Leiden: Brill, 2005).

77. UN General Assembly Resolution 1514 (XV), "Declaration on the Granting of Independence to Colonial Countries and Peoples," A/RES/1514/XV, December 14, 1960. See Victor Kattan, "Self-Determination as Ideology: The Cold War, the End of Empire, and the Making of UN General Assembly Resolution 1514 (14 December 1960)," in *International Law and Time: Narratives and Techniques*, ed. Luca Pasquet and Klara van der Ploeg (Springer, 2023).

78. See Jessica Whyte, "The 'Dangerous Concept of the Just War': Decolonization, Wars of National Liberation, and the Additional Protocols to the Geneva Conventions," *Humanity* 9, no. 3 (2018).

79. Adom Getachew, *Worldmaking After Empire: The Rise and Fall of Self-Determination* (Princeton: Princeton University Press, 2019), 74.

80. See, e.g., Richard Falk, "International Law and the United States Role in the Viet Nam War," *Yale Law Journal* 75 (1966); Lawyers Committee on American Policy Towards Vietnam, *Vietnam and International Law: The Illegality of United States Military Involvement* (Flanders: O'Hare Books, 1967); Richard Falk, *Revisiting the Vietnam War and International Law* (Cambridge: Cambridge University Press, 2017).

81. Robert Knox, "International Law, Politics and Opposition to the Iraq War," *London Review of International Law* 8, no. 3 (forthcoming). See also China Miéville, "Multilateralism as Terror: International Law, Haiti and Imperialism," *Finnish Yearbook of International Law* 19 (2008).

82. Jury of Conscience, "Declaration," 96.

83. Knox, "Iraq War."

84. Knox, "Iraq War."

85. Victor Kattan, "The Russell Tribunal on Palestine and the Question of Apartheid," *alshabaka*, November 23, 2011, https://al-shabaka.org/briefs/russell-tribunal-palestine-and-question-apartheid/

86. Hilary Charlesworth, "International Law: A Discipline of Crisis," *Modern Law Review* 65 (2002): 377. I have written about this elsewhere in the context of international criminal law. See Tor Krever, "International Criminal Law: An Ideology Critique," *Leiden Journal of International Law* 26 (2013); Tor Krever, "Ending Impunity? Eliding Political Economy in International Criminal Law," in *Research Handbook on Political Economy and Law*, ed. Ugo Mattei and John D. Haskell (Cheltenham: Edward Elgar, 2015). Knox makes much the same argument: Knox, "Iraq War."

87. Russell Tribunal on Palestine, "South Africa Session," 21.

88. More recently, Amnesty International, Human Rights Watch, B'Tselem, and the UN Special Rapporteur on human rights in Occupied Palestine have all issued reports concluding Israel's is an apartheid regime. The same criticism can be made of these reports' narrow focus on a legal conception of apartheid at the expense of an engagement with settler colonialism as the structure behind Israeli apartheid—and indeed has been made, at least of the Amnesty report, by commentators such as Lana Tatour and Nihal El Aasar. See Lana Tatour, "Amnesty Report: The Limits of the Apartheid Framework," *Middle East Eye*, February 8, 2022, https://www.middl eeasteye.net/opinion/israel-amnesty-apartheid-report-limits-framework; Nihal El Aasar, "Why Won't Amnesty Say 'Colonialism'?" *Novara Media*, February 8, 2022, https://novaramedia.com/2022/02/08/why-wont-amnesty-say-colonialism/

89. In fairness, in New York, the tribunal did in fact write of Israel's "settler-colonial expansion," while in Brussels it went so far as to declare that Palestinians are "clearly the victim of colonialism." But here again the characterization of Israeli actions as colonial served merely to affirm the unlawfulness of those actions, the tribunal emphasizing "the illegal and criminal nature of colonialism" in "denying a people their right to self-determination." Russell Tribunal on Palestine, "Final Session."

90. Russell Tribunal on Palestine, "London Session," 52–54.

91. Barat and Machover, "Russell Tribunal," 538.

92. Russell Tribunal on Palestine, "South Africa Session," 35.

93. Barat and Machover, "Russell Tribunal," 531.

94. Tor Krever, "Dispensing Global Justice," *New Left Review* 85 (2014).

95. Noura Erakat, *Justice For Some: Law and the Question of Palestine* (Stanford: Stanford University Press, 2019), 5.

96. Nicola Perugini and Neve Gordon, *The Human Right to Dominate* (Oxford: Oxford University Press, 2015).

TEN

War and the Shaping of International Law

From the Cold War to the War on Terror

Brian Cuddy and Victor Kattan

The Distinctiveness of the Wars in Vietnam and the Middle East

Drafted at the conclusion of two world wars involving direct clashes between the great powers, the Charter of the United Nations sought to save succeeding generations from the scourge of war and to discourage states from threatening or using force against the territorial integrity or political independence of any state.[1] The UN Charter lists only two exceptions to the prohibition on the use of armed force in international affairs: when force is authorized by the UN Security Council to maintain or restore international peace and security and when states, acting individually or collectively in self-defense, resort to force in response to an armed attack against their territory or military personnel.[2] As Richard Falk explained in his foreword to this volume, the UN Charter encapsulated a "war-prevention rationale" that emerged out of the carnage of the Second World War and the perceived interests of the victors in peace. It sought to prevent a Third World War.

Yet as soon as the ink on the text of the UN Charter had run dry, the world was divided into competing blocs, and its security architecture never functioned as envisaged. The atomic bombings of the Japanese cities of

Hiroshima and Nagasaki came in the wake of the adoption of the UN Charter in 1945. This was followed by the Korean War, the Suez Crisis, the wars of decolonization in Africa and Asia, the Yugoslav wars, the 9/11 attacks and the subsequent "war on terrorism," and most recently the war in Ukraine, which all implicated the United States and its allies.[3] While macro-level "peace" was still desirable for these status-quo powers, armed force became an increasingly attractive tool in situations short of direct great-power war.

So why, given all these wars, do we focus on just two? Why should we care about the Vietnam War, which is now history, and the conflicts between Israel, the Palestinians, and the wider Arab world, which could become history? How do these conflicts differ to the multitude of other armed conflicts that have occurred elsewhere in the world since the adoption of the UN Charter? In our view, these wars are worth studying because they have been particularly significant in shaping, and in the attempted remaking of, international law from 1945 to the present day. And they have achieved this significance in large part because of their impact on the politics and culture of the world's most powerful nation, the United States of America.

The Vietnam War and the Arab-Israeli conflicts are distinctive in the history of international law because of how they changed American society due to their length, their intensity, and the passions they provoked in the popular media, on university campuses, and on the street. The Vietnam War and the multiple Arab-Israeli conflicts became cultural moments that captured the public imagination in ways few other conflicts did, even those that were more lethal. They also had an oversized impact on public policy not only in North America but also in Europe and Australia. They transformed the ways in which governments speak about war and how they justify them. This can be assessed not only through studies of popular media, film, and literature but also in the number of references to these two conflicts in policy statements, political speeches, government publications, and references to scholarly publications on the law of war as demonstrated in the contributions to this volume.

Before we look at some of these documents and how the relationship between the United States and Israel was forged through fighting common enemies, let us begin by taking a closer look at American popular culture.

American Popular Culture

The influence of the Vietnam War and the Arab-Israeli conflicts on shaping the law of war was due to several factors, but a significant one that is seldom mentioned is the impact of the English-language international media, cinema, and other forms of popular culture, which all shape the views of policymakers and the wars they fight. In her groundbreaking study of the special relationship forged between the United States and Israel since the Second World War, Amy Kaplan examined news media, fiction, and film to explain how, in the aftermath of the Six-Day War of June 1967, "many Americans romanticized Israel's way of making war as a humane and muscular alternative to the American approach, which had led to the quagmire in Vietnam."[4] She made the striking observation that: "The Israeli air force accomplished in hours what Operation Rolling Thunder, the massive bombing campaign in North Vietnam, could not do in two years."[5]

America's conduct and defeat in the Vietnam War, together with Israel's lightening victory over three Arab armies in the Six-Day War, shaped the attitudes and ideas of a whole generation of international lawyers in the United States. The influence of these conflicts on the intellectual and professional context of American international law stems both from US involvement in these conflicts and opposition to that involvement beginning with the emergence of the antiwar movement following the drafting of university students by the Johnson administration in 1965, and continuing through the culture wars that ensued.[6] While the political depth of this activism was always suspect, in part because it was "closely connected to the vulnerability of these students, many from privileged backgrounds, to the military draft then in place,"[7] as Richard Falk recalled, it undoubtedly contributed to the intensity of the antiwar activism that shook America for a brief period in the 1960s and 1970s.

In her interviews with legal scholars who lived through that era, Naz Modirzadeh observed that the Vietnam War was deeply personal for many of these scholars, who "woke up to read the newspapers with headlines discussing the stunning numbers of American soldiers killed as the war progressed. They experienced firsthand the bitter differences that emerged between colleagues, families, and friends."[8] They also "watched the nightly news, which often featured astonishingly raw footage of the war, including close-up portrayals of the suffering of Vietnamese civilians."[9] This was a moment when "[d]iscussion of the war was constant, everywhere. Many professors had students who were protesting, or were going off to war, or were dedicating themselves to anti-war activism."[10] One interviewee explained that what struck them most about the debates was their intensity, and that "[n]othing has come close to that."[11]

The intensity of dissent over the Vietnam War was something the South African jurist John Dugard experienced when he spent part of 1969 teaching a course on comparative civil liberties at Princeton University, on the invitation of Richard Falk, and when he spent the remainder of the year visiting American universities across the country. Dugard recalled that "[a]ll university campuses we visited were alive with dissent over the Vietnam War, and there was an idealism and vitality among the students that I was not to encounter on subsequent visits to the United States."[12]

The Vietnam War and the multiple Arab-Israeli conflicts also affected younger generations of scholars and government advisers who did not experience the war firsthand. Some of these were the children of those who served in the war. But even those with no direct family connection were influenced in different ways, including through Hollywood, which has kept these conflicts in the public eye. Hollywood films include the multiple Academy Award winning *The Deer Hunter* (1978), *Coming Home* (1978), *Apocalypse Now* (1979), *Platoon* (1986), *Born on the Fourth of July* (1989), and *Forrest Gump* (1994). Other Vietnam War films that performed well at the box office that were nominated for Academy Awards, but did not win any, include *Full Metal Jacket* (1987), *The Quiet American* (2002), and *The Trial of the Chicago Seven* (2020)—the latter won a Golden Globe for best screenplay.[13] Then there was the multimillion-dollar *Rambo* franchise (1982–2019) starring Sylvester Stallone. More recently, PBS produced a 10-part American television documentary series about the Vietnam War that was directed by Ken Burns and Lynn Novick and broadcast in 2017 to critical acclaim.[14] The series was shown in 88 countries (including Vietnam) and was watched by 39 million unique viewers.[15] And this was before it appeared on Netflix. The Arab-Israeli conflicts have also produced a plethora of films and spy thrillers, from Hollywood blockbusters like *Exodus* (1960); *Syriana* (2005); *Munich* (2005); *Beirut/The Negotiator* (2018); *The Little Drummer Girl* (2018), based on John Le Carré's novel; and the Netflix film *The Spy* (2019). Then there was the multiple Emmy award winning television series *Homeland* (2011–2020), based on the Israeli television series *Prisoner of War*, and more recently the Israeli Netflix television series *Fauda* (2015–), which has been watched by millions of people all over the world.

Various political viewpoints motivate these different products of popular culture, but some prominent themes do emerge, such as a glorification of special operations forces and the sensationalism of foreign intelligence work that involves prying into the personal lives of ordinary people and putting them into compromising situations so that they reveal critical information about the enemy. One such common theme in some of these films is the negative portrayal of America's adversaries. "Ming the Merciless" in the film *Flash Gordon* (1980), popularized by the rock band *Queen* in their song of the same name, for example, bore a striking resemblance to the Vietnamese Communist Party leader Ho Chi Minh. In more recent productions, the enemy is the Arab and Muslim world, which continues to be vilified in the media as an enemy of Western civilization.[16] The ongoing negative portrayal of the broader Arab/Muslim world may also explain, in part, why contemporary scholarship on the American War on Terror adopts a view of the law that is "aridly technical, acontextual, and ahistorical," as compared to the passionate scholarship on the Vietnam War, when the stakes for many scholars were higher because American lives were placed directly at risk.[17]

Citations in Scholarship and Training Programs

Popular culture portrayals of the Vietnam War and the Arab-Israeli conflicts form a backdrop to their more direct influence on public policy. A sense of this influence can be gained by appreciating the quantity of literature on these conflicts. A simple search on the catalogue of The Peace Palace Library, the largest international law repository in the world, turned up 4,700 entries for the "Arab-Israeli conflict"; 2,100 entries for "Israel Palestine conflict"; and 1,200 entries for the "Vietnam War."[18] By way of comparison, a search for "Falklands War" produced 144 entries and the "Gulf War" 834 entries.[19] The only other comparable conflict was the Iraq War in 2003 that produced 2,200 entries.[20] However, the legal arguments around preemptive/preventive war produced to justify the invasion of Iraq in the United States, as encapsulated in the 2002 *National Security Strategy of the United States of America* (NSS-2002), owed much to previous Israeli policy, especially Israel's 1981 raid on an Iraqi nuclear reactor.[21]

The direct impact of the Vietnam War and the Arab-Israeli conflicts on the law of war can also be ascertained by the number of references to these conflicts in official government publications. For example, the *United States Department of Defense Law of War Manual* published in June 2015 and updated in December 2016, made multiple references to the Vietnam War and Israeli military actions and court decisions. A simple search of the manual revealed that the word "Vietnam" is mentioned 84 times and "Israel" 48 times. Strikingly, there are as many references to the war in Afghanistan, which is the longest war in US history, as there are references to Israel's conflicts with its Arab neighbors. By way of comparison, there are only 15 references to the Kosovo War and only 2 references to the war in Bosnia.[22] The United Kingdom's *Joint Service Manual of the Law of Armed Conflict* published in 2011 mentioned the Vietnam conflict 8 times and the conflicts between the Arab world and Israel 3 times. *The Australian Defence Doctrine Publication on the Law of Armed Conflict* published in 2006 mentions the Vietnam War half a dozen times, with specific examples of incidents highlighted. The International Committee of the Red Cross's Customary International Humanitarian Law study makes more than 300 references to Israel and more than 30 to Vietnam.[23]

In addition to these publications, the Vietnam War even led to the development of new branches of the law in the United States, such as "national security law" and "operational law." The former was developed by scholars such as John Norton Moore and the American Bar Association that were directly influenced by the Vietnam War as explored in the chapter by Madelaine Chiam and Brian Cuddy. After the 1990 Gulf War, Israeli military lawyers began participating in training programs on operational law in the United States, which was then employed to deal with the Palestinian situation, as explored in Craig Jones's chapter.[24] Such training programs further developed the professional networks of American and Israeli international lawyers. Key figures in these networks gained influence in both countries, including Yoram Dinstein, a professor emeritus of international law at Tel Aviv University, who earlier in his career served as an official for the Israeli government.[25] His publications on the laws of war have become essential reading in courses on the laws of war all over the world.[26] Another key figure in this network is Michael Schmitt, the Francis Lieber Distinguished Scholar at the Lieber Institute of the United States Military Academy, and a prolific law of war scholar, who is now professor of international law at the University of Reading.[27]

Not long after the establishment of these operational law training programs, as Noura Erakat has documented in her work, Israeli government lawyers sanctioned violent tactics "short of war" to kill Palestinians deemed to be terrorists by Israel during the second intifada.[28] Israel's impressive credentials as the ultimate national security state have led to the paradoxical situation that its way of fighting war is now idolized by some Arab states—such as the United Arab Emirates and Saudi Arabia—that once opposed it.[29] And where war goes, military law follows.

A Common Enemy

Israel became the model that successive US administrations, particularly right-wing Republican administrations, would emulate in searching for

monsters to destroy. During the Cold War, the Jewish state became perceived as a bastion that safeguarded Western values from a hostile world
comprised of Third World revolutionaries and communist nations that
ganged up on Israel in the United Nations.[30] The United States and Israel
had a common enemy: Third World revolutionary forces supported by
their Cold War nemeses the Soviet Union and Red China, exemplified by
Vietnamese and Palestinian groups that attacked civilian targets, such as
hotels, markets, and public buses, and kidnapped civilians in order to sow
violence and discord.[31] In 1972, the United States began vetoing Security
Council resolutions critical of Israeli policy in East Jerusalem, the West
Bank, and the Gaza Strip[32] following the kidnapping and murder of Israeli
athletes at the 1972 Munich Olympics, forever linking Palestinian nationalism with international terrorism in the media.[33]

The following year, the United States shielded Israel again at the Security Council and organized a massive airlift to Israel in the 1973 October War, after Egypt and Syria with Soviet backing sought to recapture
lands conquered by Israel in 1967—as we learned from John Quigley in his
chapter in this volume.[34] The use of force by Egypt and Syria in the October War raised the issue of whether the use of force to recapture previously
occupied lands can be considered a legitimate use of force. The legitimacy
of this type of force has implications for other longstanding occupied territories such as Nagorno-Karabakh or Northern Cyprus.

The perception that Israel and the United States were engaged in a
collective fight on behalf of the free world against international terrorists,
from Vietcong guerrillas to Palestinian freedom fighters, was dramatically
captured in the 1976 Raid on Entebbe, a counterterrorist hostage-rescue
mission carried out by Israeli commandos in Uganda that revitalized "the
portrait of Israel as an indomitable and righteous military power defending beleaguered innocents and striking a blow for civilization."[35] Kaplan
explained how news coverage of the Entebbe raid "took on mythic dimensions and became etched in American popular culture."[36] In his autobiography, Benjamin Netanyahu, Israel's prime minister, whose brother was killed
during the Raid on Entebbe, credits his father with giving him the idea to
court leading political figures and media moguls in the United States in the
1980s to adopt "a new and far more aggressive American-led approach to
combatting global terrorism."[37]

The image of heroic Israeli soldiers freeing Western civilians from
the clutches of international terrorists was shared by many government
officials in the United States who came of age in the 1970s, when Israel
was castigated as a colonial power in cahoots with the apartheid regime of
South Africa. As Kattan explained in his chapter, following the fall of Sai-

gon in 1975, neoconservative neophytes and battle-hardened Vietnam War veterans assembled to remake America by joining forces with the Reagan administration to take the fight to the enemy, whether that fight took place at the UN or in the field.[38] These individuals would come together again after 9/11, when a second war against international terrorism was declared.

The First War against International Terrorism

In June 1984, US Secretary of State George Shultz announced to the world that the United States would adopt a policy of "active defense" in preventing international terrorism.[39] The new policy was announced by Shultz following the suicide truck bombings of the American Embassy in Lebanon and US Marine Corp barracks at Beirut's International Airport in 1983.[40] The attack was widely blamed on agents of Iran's Revolutionary Guards who had begun a covert war against the United States, which Ayatollah Khomeini called the "great Satan," and the State of Israel, the "little Satan."

The term "active defense" had earlier been used by Israeli governments to justify their counterinsurgency strategy against returning Arab refugees who were displaced from their homes in 1948, as we learn from reading Brian Cuddy's chapter that traces the strategy to Israel's border wars of the early 1950s.[41] This was also when early iterations of ideas like the "accumulation of events doctrine" and the "unable or unwilling test" were first mooted by Israeli officials to get around the necessity of proving that Israel had been subjected to a prior armed attack by the Arab states, as required by Article 51 of the UN Charter.[42] Cuddy observes how, after initially being rejected by US lawyers, these ideas later circulated between Israeli and US officials during and after the Vietnam War. US lawyers justified the US incursion into Cambodia in 1970 using an "unable or unwilling" rationale, for example, before the doctrine circled back to the Arab-Israeli conflict, where the United States offered it as a rationale for Israel's Entebbe rescue operation in 1976, and then Israel reemployed the doctrine to justify its repeated incursions into Lebanon in the 1970s and 1980s.[43] Since then the "unable and unwilling doctrine," or "test," as it is sometimes called, has been invoked to justify the killing of US enemies in drone strikes far removed from traditional battlefields—including in Pakistan, Syria, Mali, Ecuador, Yemen, Georgia, and the Congo.[44]

It was during the Reagan administration when the association between the enemies of Israel and the United States was strengthened. A key moment in this process was the notorious Klinghoffer affair in 1986, when a PLO splinter group murdered a 69-year-old Jewish-American man in a wheelchair and threw him overboard off the coast of Syria, which was subsequently made into a television action drama as well as an opera. This was when Shultz wrote an influential article in *Foreign Affairs*, in which he went so far as to describe the UN Charter as a "suicide pact."[45] Shultz cited an article by Abraham Sofaer, the State Department legal adviser, who claimed that "Since the days of President James Madison, the United States has repeatedly acted against armed bands that attacked Americans and then fled, seeking sanctuary in neighboring countries unwilling or powerless to prevent or punish their acts."[46]

Gone was the US commitment, however self-interested, to their earlier vision of a rules-based liberal world order that inspired the establishment of the United Nations in 1945, which reaffirmed the equal rights of nations large and small and which prohibited any use of unilateral armed force that could not be justified under the UN Charter, in which self-defense was limited to using force in response to an armed attack on a state from another state.[47] The Reagan administration had come around to the view that there was no point in referring to the UN Charter when it was the Charter that needed reform. This was especially the case as many of the states that had emerged from decolonization since 1945, and which could now contribute to the formation of new rules of customary international law, could not be counted on to share US views of the "original constitutional conception of the UN Charter," particularly with regard "to the special position of the permanent members of the Security Council in the maintenance of international peace and security."[48] Instead the United States referred to precedents from its imperial age—from the days of James Madison's westward expansion of American territory to settle Europeans in lands stolen from Native Americans—that were cited by Sofaer as though the prohibition on the use of force in the UN Charter did not exist.

The position adopted by the Reagan administration toward the UN Charter contrasted starkly with the situation during the Vietnam War, when the US government still sought to maintain its liberal image as a champion of a rule-governed international order "when it went to great lengths to argue that its policies and practices in Vietnam accorded with international law and the UN Charter," explained Falk.[49] This is a view that is also borne out in the chapter by Madelaine Chiam and Brian Cuddy, which demonstrates that both those lawyers associated with the prowar camp and those lawyers associated with the antiwar camp felt at ease debating the merits and cons of the Vietnam War by referring to the UN Charter.[50] This was very different to the US legal justifications for employing force during the "war on terror" in which successive US governments (both Democrat and Republican) saw the UN Charter as outdated and not fit for purpose and increasingly articulated arguments justifying armed force *outside* the Charter framework. In other words, in the 1960s, the lawyers, from whatever ideological standpoint, all agreed on the terms of the debate, i.e., the UN Charter, whereas until recently US lawyers were increasingly articulating a preventive war rationale that was wholly at odds with the Charter framework. When, following Russia's premeditated attack on Ukraine in February 2022, the Biden administration vociferously demanded adherence to the "rules-based world order" envisioned by the UN Charter, it apparently forgot how previous US administrations had jettisoned this very order.

The Second War against International Terrorism

By the Reagan administration, then, the war prevention rationale that had informed the authors of the UN Charter was seen by the US government as too restrictive and outdated for the modern world. Washington argued that it needed urgent reform. The only other state to support this view at that time was Israel.[51] But in little more than a decade, the international resistance to the idea that the US could pursue terrorists overseas in endless wars was washed away following the attacks on the Twin Towers on 9/11.[52] In the words of Robert Cooper, a former foreign policy advisor to British prime minister Tony Blair, the West needed "to revert to the rougher methods of an earlier era—force, pre-emptive attack, deception, whatever is necessary to deal with those who still live in the nineteenth century world of every state for itself. Among ourselves, we keep the law but when we are operating in the jungle, we must also use the laws of the jungle."[53]

Cooper was adamant that if "terrorist syndicates" used bases in failed states "for attacks on the more orderly parts of the world, then the organized states will eventually have to respond."[54] "This is what we have seen," he wrote, "in Colombia, in Afghanistan and in part in Israel's forays into the Occupied [Palestinian] Territories."[55] Note how Israel's "forays" into the West Bank and Gaza were seen by Cooper as a model for liberal states to tackle terrorism elsewhere.

Thus we had come full circle: an Israeli military strategy that had been condemned at the UN in the 1950s for being contrary to the UN Charter, and initially rejected by US lawyers as a basis for escalating the war in Vietnam,[56] had now become an acceptable policy. Following the attacks on 9/11, the security of the whole world was at stake, so it was claimed. Article 51 of the UN Charter, which literally required a state to take a hit in the form of an "armed attack" before it could respond in self-defense, was not good law when faced with terrorism "of a suicidal variety."[57] It had become incumbent to revise the UN Charter.

In 2002, in the lead-up to the invasion of Iraq, the United States decided that the policy enunciated by Shultz in 1984, which as Shultz recalled was opposed by many American officials at the time,[58] had in fact reflected customary international law "for centuries," and was therefore binding on all states, friend and foe alike.[59] The *National Security Strategy of the United States of America* (NSS-2002), published in September 2002, went even further when it argued that the unique threats to America's security meant that the United States had to be able to respond to future threats "even if uncertainty remains as to the time and place of the enemy's attack."[60]

The claim that a state could respond in self-defense to *threats* and not just to armed attacks or attacks that were "imminent" was explicitly rejected at the UN's World Summit Outcome in 2004.[61] Rather than hinder the further development of the law, however, the categorical position adopted at the World Summit galvanized those lawyers in the United States who rejected the sovereign equality of states and who used their positions of authority to "update" the law to reflect modern threats that would enable preventive military action.[62] And the only state that had a track record of acting in self-defense to prevent future attacks prior to 9/11—and justifying these attacks by attempting to make an international law rationalization—was Israel, when it attempted to justify its bombing of an Iraqi nuclear reactor in 1981.[63] But as former IDF lawyer Daniel Reisner told Israel's *Haaretz* newspaper in 2009, even though the Security Council had condemned Israel for violating international law, "today everyone says it was preventive self-defense."[64]

Attempts at Reforming the Law

What followed the terrorist attacks on 9/11 was a concerted effort by a small group of government lawyers to transform the law to overcome resistance for the need to change the rules.[65] There appeared to be a residual fear that there might be a repeat of the Vietnam syndrome, when massive opposition to that war weakened Washington's ability to lead the world. There was concern that the malaise caused by the Iraq War might make future Western interventions more difficult given public opposition to further wars. This was dramatically captured in President Obama's decision, following a vote in the British House of Commons, not to enforce his red line in Syria after a chemical weapons attack on civilians by the

Assad regime.[66] As Guglielmo Verdirame commented: "There is no better evidence of the long shadow that the Iraq war continues to cast that, while in 2003 the British Parliament supported intervention against the mere possibility that weapons of mass destruction might be used, ten years later the British Parliament voted against it after they had actually been used."[67]

The war prevention rationale that had inspired the authors of the UN Charter had long divided legal opinion into two categories: those who strictly separated the *jus ad bellum* from the *jus in bello* and read the UN Charter as a war-prevention mechanism, and those who thought that wars were inevitable and had to be managed as though armed conflict was an extension of a state's foreign policy. Those who viewed war as an undesirable, albeit routine situation, since any international law that "seeks to prevent war but ignores power is destined to fail,"[68] read the UN Charter as a complex document that had to be interpreted in the light of other legal, political, and strategic pillars.[69] The law could not remain static but had to adapt to changing circumstances.

The belief that the law needed revising was due to a combination of threats, both real and imagined, as well as the advent of new weapons technologies: data mining and predictive analytics, precision-guided missiles, remotely piloted drones, robotics, and autonomous fighter jets.[70] It had become incumbent for responsible states to "adapt legal and institutional arrangements to the development of new strategies, which, in turn, respond to innovation in military technology."[71] Unsurprisingly, the governments calling for a change to the law of war were also the same governments that were jointly developing these new weapons systems.[72]

And again, America's experience in Vietnam and Israel's wars with its Arab neighbors were the laboratories for the development of new weapons, whether it was the HueyCobra attack helicopter or Boeing's twin-turboshaft Apache helicopter.[73] Although drones had been used in the Vietnam War to take pictures, it was only with Israel's development of weaponized drones in its numerous interventions in the Lebanese civil war in the 1970s and 1980s "that the various constituent technologies of drones had matured to the point that it became possible to watch a particular person from the sky, and then to target and kill that person."[74]

A Common Threat Perception

It appears that attempts at reforming Article 51 of the UN Charter remained limited to small circles of lawyers and secret meetings between like-minded states,[75] a process that is ongoing.[76] Although there remains resistance to these efforts at the UN General Assembly,[77] the conversations[78] are revealing for what they tell us about the importance of the Vietnam and Arab-Israeli conflicts in shaping ideas and identifying threats, as these conflicts appeared to influence the views of two of the officials that were leading those conversations.[79] This included John Bellinger III, who was the legal adviser to the National Security Council when NSS-2002 was written, and Daniel Bethlehem, who continued the work that was initiated by Bellinger when he was appointed the principal legal adviser to the United Kingdom's Foreign and Commonwealth Office from 2006 until 2011, which coincided with Israel's "second" war in Lebanon and the assassination of al-Qaeda leader Osama bin Laden in Pakistan.[80]

Apart from both holding key government positions, and being of the same generation, Bellinger and Bethlehem also have family and work connections to Vietnam and Israel. Bellinger III was the son of John B. Bellinger II, a decorated Army colonel and Defense Department official, who was born in NATO Headquarters, and did two tours of Vietnam.[81] Bellinger III, whose mother was a Russia analyst in the Central Intelligence Agency, also has history with Israel, having secured the dismissal of lawsuits filed in multiple US jurisdictions against senior Israeli officials accused of harming US citizens in military operations on civilian vessels trying to breach the blockade of Gaza that were brought under the Alien Tort Statute.[82] Bethlehem has close family connections to Israel and has advised the Israeli government on sensitive legal disputes with the Palestinians before he was appointed legal adviser of the FCO.[83] In a written submission to the United Kingdom's House of Commons Select Committee on Foreign Affairs, Bethlehem expressed support for a very wide concept of preventive self-defense that would allow states to use force in international affairs if the government employing such force reasonably foresaw the *threat* of an attack as opposed to an actual attack.[84]

While no single individual can change the policy of a government, they can contribute to new thinking that might influence government if they hold key government roles where they have direct access to decision makers and can contribute to the formation of policy. Consider the role of the Vietnam War and the Arab-Israeli conflicts in shaping the thinking of the Bush War Cabinet after 9/11, a group of people focused above all on ensuring the preeminence of American military power and rebuilding the armed forces after Vietnam.[85] The Vietnam War and the conflicts between Israel and the Palestinians also shaped the thinking of key figures in Bush's Department of Defense, as suggested by multiple references to those conflicts in confirmation hearings before the Senate Armed Services Committee for Donald Rumsfeld, Paul Wolfowitz, Dov Zackheim, and Douglas Feith.[86]

Other key figures influenced by the Vietnam and Arab-Israeli conflicts whose names appear in some of the chapters of this book were legal advisers, such as W. Hays Parks and Feith who held positions at the Pentagon in the Reagan and Bush administrations, and Shultz, Sofaer, Allan Gerson, and Eugene Rostow who held positions at the State Department in the Nixon, Reagan, and Bush administrations. These individuals had either served in the Vietnam War or had close connections to Israel.[87] The foreign policy beliefs they held in common also contributed to greater convergence in international law interpretations between the United States and Israel.[88] There was an ideological current that connected them all.

The Politics of the Additional Protocols

The convergence between American and Israeli interpretations of international law since the 1970s can be seen not only in justifications for using armed force, but also in arguments around how to use force legitimately during armed conflicts. The Vietnam War and the Arab-Israeli conflict influenced both the drafting of rules for the conduct of hostilities at the Diplomatic Conference in Geneva in the 1970s and the subsequent interpretations of those rules. Under the stewardship of George Aldrich—who as a State Department lawyer had previously handled day-to-day legal issues relating to the Vietnam War—the United States played a central role in drafting the new rules. But while the United States signed the 1977 Additional Protocols to the 1949 Geneva Conventions, it did not ratify them. The Reagan administration ultimately ended up siding with Israel, which was the only state that had remained steadfastly opposed to them in Geneva.[89]

Since that time, the United States has adopted language that is virtually indistinguishable from Israeli prime minister Benjamin Netanyahu's talking points about terrorists hiding among civilians and human shields. Indeed, to an Arab or Afghan ear, United States' claims about killing civilians in Afghanistan, Iraq, and Yemen are virtually indistinguishable from Israeli claims about the necessity of killing civilians in Gaza. Netanyahu has consistently encouraged a firmer Western response to terrorism, including being more accepting of civilian casualties, since he was a diplomat in the United States in the 1980s,[90] a claim that he repeats in his 2022 autobiography.[91] Writing in a 1986 book, he rejected the idea that "military strikes aimed at terrorists and terrorist attacks on civilians belong on the same moral plane." Arguing that this "false symmetry" arose "because of the sloppiness of the West's thinking about the use of force," Netanyahu suggested that "the rules of engagement have become so rigid that governments often straitjacket themselves in the face of unambiguous aggression." He cautioned that "an absolute prohibition on civilian casualties affords the terrorist an invincible shield."[92]

Netanyahu attributed the West's reluctance to use force against terrorists located among civilians to the Vietnam War, arguing in the same 1986 book that "America's loss of clarity in the wake of Vietnam has become a general Western malaise."[93] Yet in this analysis Netanyahu displayed his own intellectual sloppiness, for the Vietnam War was not simply the prompt for the West's reluctance to use force among civilians but also gave rise to justifications for civilian casualties—justifications that were subsequently adopted by Netanyahu and the government of Israel. As Neve Gordon and Nicola Perugini observe in their history of the use of human shields, during Operation Protective Edge (2014) the Israeli Foreign Ministry justified Israel's actions by using "language strikingly similar to the arguments used by . . . the American administration during the Vietnam War," including the claim that Palestinian tactics "violate the customary prohibition against perfidy under international humanitarian law."[94]

As Amanda Alexander explained,[95] under pre-1977 law, that is, before the Additional Protocols to the 1949 Geneva Conventions were concluded at the Diplomatic Conference in Geneva, irregular fighters, whether they were the Vietcong or Palestinian *fedayeen*, were mostly placed outside the bounds of international law. Under the 1907 Hague Convention, there was no right of resistance once occupied (there was a right for civilians to resist an occupying force *while that force was occupying territory*, known as a *levée en masse*, but not once the territory was subdued). There was a clear distinction in the law between civilians and combatants, and civilians who engaged in hostilities lost the rights of protected persons and could be lawfully killed. In other words, civilians who became involved in armed conflict were liable to be executed, while the rest of the population could be subjected to reprisals. During the Vietnam War, however, direct attacks on civilians became difficult to defend morally. Images of civilian deaths, including woman and children, shocked the conscience of mankind, filling the pages of newspapers and even provoking the establishment of peoples' tribunals to pass judgment on the actions of the United States government. The United States had lost the battle for public opinion. As Tor

Krever explained, the Russell Tribunal on the Vietnam War would become a model for subsequent peoples' tribunals, including on Israeli actions in Palestine, even if their political motivations and beliefs about the value of law differed.[96]

Attempts to use the law to condemn American actions in Vietnam, and prevent similar actions in other wars, were not limited to nonstate peoples' tribunals. A major push to reform the laws of war resulted in the 1974–1977 Diplomatic Conference in Geneva. With their growing clout in international forums, newly independent states and their supporters pushed for the protection of both civilians and guerrilla fighters in the negotiations for the Additional Protocols, as well as the recognition of wars of national liberation as international armed conflicts. As Alexander observed, their success in these measures entailed a significant change in the understanding of the law of war (or international humanitarian law): combatants were no longer defined as being limited to the regular military in their conventional uniforms, but included guerrillas, revolutionaries, and peasant armies. A civilian could, as Alexander pointed out, be a peasant by day and a guerrilla by night—Chairman Mao's scholar and fighter: "Civilians were defined as not being combatants, as a vulnerable population granted increased protection—yet at the same time combatants were defined in a way that meant that they could also be civilians, at least some of the time."[97]

This novel definition of a civilian was seen as a great victory for Third World freedom fighters and especially the PLO, as explored in the chapter by Ihab Shalbak and Jessica Whyte.[98] But the anticolonial success was bittersweet. Gaining greater protections for civilians and more legitimacy under international law for liberation fighters were somewhat illusory gains for Palestinians, allowing them to accrue more features of statehood but without the attainment of independence, and they did not prevent Israel from developing its own understandings of the laws of war that played on the now-ambiguous status of civilians, as well as using its position as a technologically advanced state to exploit the complexity of the law.

Learning the Lessons of Vietnam

The paradox was that critics of American power could not be absolutely certain that killing civilians was unlawful, if the military could prove that civilians were engaged in hostilities.[99] Under pre-1977 law, this task was easier to prove. A civilian was a civilian and a combatant was a member of the armed forces. But in post-1977 law, the definition of a civilian became ambiguous: a civilian killed in a military operation may have been a combatant. Distinguishing between civilians and combatants now became a question of fact, and answering that question was dependent on fact-checking.

Only the biggest military powers have the capacity to check facts. They control the area of hostilities, accredit journalists, and control their movements. Their governments can also prevent human rights organizations entering a country. Governments are better placed to saturate the media with disinformation and half-truths: ready-made stories about terrorists hiding among civilians, blurring the distinction between combatants and civilians, which is easily done in a densely populated city like Baghdad, Gaza, Fallujah, Kyiv, Kharkiv, Mariupol, or Saigon. The military can edit YouTube clips to show only what they want the world to see disseminated widely on social media.[100] They have the capacity to leak misleading stories to the press corps. Their security services have even created fake Facebook and Instagram accounts and deploy Twitter bots manned by Twitter "armies."[101] The military often employ spokespersons fluent in American, Australian, British, or South African English who control the war narrative on television, radio, and the internet to ensure that their story is the first to break, dominating the headlines for the first 24 hours before the story becomes stale.

The United States and Israel had learned the lesson of Vietnam: you must dominate the war narrative to ensure you win the battle of public opinion, which can be just as decisive to the outcome of a war as victory on the battlefield. Dominating the war narrative is, in turn, enabled by the deployment of historical knowledge and argument. As W. Hays Parks commented in his critique of the ICRC's customary international humanitarian law study, how and why nations fight and a good grasp of history are important to understand the development of the law of war.[102] Therefore when making a claim that a particular practice reflects the law, the historical context is important. Parks suggested that a claim in the ICRC study that a 1972 Soviet statement favoring the prohibition of particularly cruel means of warfare, like the use of napalm, was a reflection of the law was mistaken. For Parks, the Soviet statement was a reflection not of the law but of the political context in which it was made—in this instance the 1972 North Vietnamese invasion of South Vietnam (often called the Easter Offensive) and its defeat by US airpower. Accompanying the Soviet statement was "the famous photograph of the young South Vietnamese girl running down the road, naked, following a napalm strike against North Vietnamese forces."[103] Parks added that the photograph became "the centerpiece for increased opposition to the Vietnam War, and criticism of US weapons."[104]

As Parks intuitively recognized, there is always the possibility that government propaganda will influence not only the peace movement but also international lawyers responsible for formulating studies of customary international law. But absent from his criticism of such studies, which he has been articulating for more than four decades, was any admission that the US war in Vietnam might have been wrong and morally indefensible.[105]

Making and Breaking Global Rules

International law develops through precedents, but not all precedents are equal. By "precedent" we do not mean legal precedents, as in court decisions, as there is no rule of stare decisis in international law as there is in common law systems. However, when it comes to the use of force, precedents—in the form of previous conflicts—do matter; especially those conflicts that capture the public imagination. Although these precedents do not bind states, they may contribute to the formulation of global rules that fill the gaps not covered by conventions, and to the interpretation of those conventions. To quote Hays Parks again, "war is the ultimate test of law. Government-authorized actions in war speak louder than peacetime government statements."[106]

The US approach to the making of global rules is one that emphasizes the practice of the dominant powers—namely itself and a handful of other states. In the words of Olivier Corten, when US lawyers cite "major states" to support their legal interpretations, it is usually a euphemism for "the United States and some of its Allies."[107] Occasionally alternative expressions may be used, such as "Western governments," the "community of democracies," or even the "civilized world."[108]

While the formation of customary international law is technically based on the sovereign equality of all states, no matter how large or small, outside the hallowed halls of the Peace Palace it is the practice of the dominant states that matter, especially when it comes to the law of war. It is the views of the states that fight more wars, more often, that count. This creates the rather perverse situation that a lawbreaker could become a lawmaker and decide what amounts to law and what does not.[109] Preventing this hegemonic path requires other states to uphold the standards of the UN Charter and other treaties that the United States and other powerful states have ratified.

The United States began openly articulating a hegemonic approach to international law in the 1970s when Third World states came to dominate the UN General Assembly. The United States was concerned about losing control of the formation of customary international law at a time when it was in a relatively weak international position having lost the Vietnam War. It is a concern that Washington has continued to express in more recent times. Consider the American reaction to the ICRC customary international humanitarian law study mentioned above. The United States explained that it was "troubled" by the extent to which the study "relied on non-binding resolutions of the General Assembly, given that states may lend their support to a particular resolution, or determine not to break consensus in regard to such a resolution, for reasons having nothing to do with a belief that those propositions in it reflect customary international law."[110] This reasoning was striking in its similarity to that advanced by US legal advisers, like Hays Parks, when he advised the Reagan administration not to ratify AP1.[111]

This view, which dismisses majority decision-making in UN organs in favor of the minority positions of the powerful, is extremely dangerous to the concept of a global plural legal order. Scholars need to be more vigilant about the sources and origins of these arguments. For if international law is about nothing other than maintaining a Pax Americana, and if the law of war is nothing but the latest expression of US foreign policy, then there will be no standard by which to judge the actions of future states that violate international law. This, to a certain extent, is the trouble with the war in Ukraine. For the historically minded international lawyer, the Biden administration's strident criticisms of the war for violating international law appear contrived.[112]

In his criticism of the US government's legal rationale for its 1970 invasion of Cambodia, Richard Falk presciently foresaw that it would no longer be possible for the United States to make credible objections to future violations of international law.[113] Indeed, five decades after he wrote those words, there does not appear to be any anxiety, worry, or foreboding in the United States about what the legal arguments advanced to justify the never-ending war on terror might entail for future conflicts, as Modizardeh astutely observed from her many conversations with military lawyers in the United States.[114] Justifications for employing armed force outside the confines of the UN Charter, often made in the heat of the moment, have a tendency to develop a life of their own, as the Vietnam and Arab-Israeli "precedents" have demonstrated, and played into Russian president Vladimir Putin's hands when he was able to cite America's previous violations of international law to justify his country's own violations in Ukraine.[115] Efforts at unilaterally rewriting rules for employing force outside the UN Charter are even more dangerous. Not only do these efforts allow for the subjective interpretation of the law by the states employing force, and of the threats they may face, but they also tend to "assume military action and enable, rather than constrain, violence."[116] Action to address this danger will fare better if it acknowledges the Vietnam War and Arab-Israeli conflicts as key sites of production for these permissive interpretations, and if it understands the pathways of people, doctrines, and technologies that connect them.

NOTES

1. See the preamble, Art. 2(4), Charter of the United Nations, October 24, 1945, 1 UNTS XVI.

2. See Chapter VII, UN Charter.

3. For a recent collection of state practice on the use of force that reflects the mainstream view of international law in this area, but which does not consider the reasons why some conflicts have had a greater influence on the development of the law than others, see Tom Ruys, Olivier Corten, and Alexandra Hofer, eds., *The Use of Force in International Law: A Case-Based Approach* (Oxford: Oxford University Press, 2018).

4. Amy Kaplan, *Our American Israel: The Story of an Entangled Alliance* (Cambridge, MA: Harvard University Press, 2018), 7.

5. Kaplan, *Our American Israel*, 110.

6. On the draft see Laura E. Hatt, "LBJ Wants Your GPA: The Vietnam Exam," *Harvard Crimson*, May 23, 2016. On the culture wars see Andrew Martin, *Receptions of War: Vietnam in American Culture* (Norman: University of Oklahoma Press, 1993). Keith Beattie, *The Scar that Binds: American Culture and the Vietnam War* (New York: NYU Press, 1998). William S. McDonnel, ed., *The Counterculture Movement of the 1960s* (New York: Greenhaven Press, 2004).

7. Richard Falk, *Public Intellectual: The Life of a Citizen Pilgrim* (Atlanta: Clarity Press, 2021), 119.

8. Naz K. Modirzadeh, "Cut These Words: Passion and International Law of War Scholarship," *Harvard International Law Journal* 61, no. 1 (2020): 1–64, at 51.

9. Modirzadeh, "Cut These Words," 51.

10. Modirzadeh, "Cut These Words," 51.

11. Modirzadeh, "Cut These Words," 51.

12. John Dugard, *Confronting Apartheid: A Personal History of South Africa, Namibia, and Palestine* (Johannesburg: Jacana Media, 2018), 51.

13. On his second visit to Vietnam in 1972, Richard Falk traveled as part of a four-person delegation to Hanoi to repatriate three American pilots. One of the members of the delegation was David Dellinger, the oldest defendant in the trial of the Chicago Seven who features prominently in the 2020 Netflix film of the same name. See Falk, *Public Intellectual*, 221. Dugard recalled that he spent a day observing the trial in Chicago. See his recollections in Dugard, *Confronting Apartheid*, 51.

14. The series also attracted some criticism from historians. See, for example, Colleen Flaherty, "Historians MIA," *Inside Higher Ed*, January 9, 2018, https://www

.insidehighered.com/news/2018/01/09/professors-debate-role-historian-or-lack
-thereof-ken-burns-and-lynn-novicks-vietnam

15. Hanh Nguyen, "'The Vietnam War' Premiere Is the Best Performing PBS Episode Since 'Downton Abbey' Series Finale," *IndieWire*, October 13, 2017.

16. On this see Jack G. Shaheen, *Reel Bad Arabs: How Hollywood Vilifies a People* (Northampton, MA: Olive Branch Press, 2012). Mahmood Mamdani, *Good Muslim, Bad Muslim: America, the Cold War, and the Roots of Terror* (New York: Penguin Random House, 2004). Howard Friel and Richard Falk, *The Record of the Paper: How The New York Times Misrepresents US Foreign Policy* (New York: Penguin Random House, 2007). Greg Philo and Mike Berry, *More Bad News from Israel* (London: Pluto, 2007).

17. See Modirzadeh, "Cut These Words." Modirzadeh does not consider the negative portrayal of the Arab/Muslim world in her article as a possible explanation for the different styles of legal scholarship between the Vietnam War and the War on Terror, but it could be implied, given that the dehumanization of the enemy in popular media, combined with the advent of modern technology such as drones has created a cultural barrier between those responsible for formulating and executing policy (including government legal advisers and scholars of the law of war, whether they are military or civilian) and the enemy thousands of miles away who are no longer visualized as living, breathing, human beings. On this issue, see the insightful article by Ed Pilkington on US drone operators, "Life as a drone operator: 'Ever step on ants and never give it another thought?,'" *The Guardian*, November 19, 2015.

18. The search was done on the catalogue (https://peacepalace.on.worldcat.org/discovery#) in November 2022.

19. Peace Palace Library (https://peacepalace.on.worldcat.org/discovery#).

20. Peace Palace Library (https://peacepalace.on.worldcat.org/discovery#).

21. The formal legal argument to justify the invasion of Iraq was based on a series of Security Council resolutions; however, this argument was invented after the decision had already been taken to go to war. On the role of official documents setting out the purposes of the institutions of state in formulating the reasons for going to war, see the perceptive article that was authored by Anthony Carty over a decade before the findings of the Iraq War Inquiry were made public: Anthony Carty, "The Iraq Invasion as a Recent United Kingdom 'Contribution to International Law,'" *European Journal of International Law* 16 (2005): 143–51. For an assessment that takes into account the findings of the Iraq War Inquiry, documents disclosed on the drafting of NSS-2002 and Israel's raid on Osiraq see Victor Kattan, "The 'Netanyahu doctrine': *The National Security Strategy of the United States of America* and the invasion of Iraq," in Satvinder Juss, ed., *Human Rights and America's War on Terror* (New York: Routledge, 2019), 1–28.

22. The only other war that is liberally referenced is Iraq, with 238 references, but that conflict could be considered an extension of the Arab-Israeli conflict in ideological and political terms since Iraq was a direct participant in the First Arab-Israeli conflict in 1948 and given that Saddam Hussein had a long history of funding and hosting radical Palestinian factions in Baghdad, and even fired Scud missiles into Israel in 1991. His WMD capability was also considered a threat to Israel, even though it later transpired that his government had destroyed its stockpiles.

23. See Jean-Marie Henckaerts and Louise Doswald-Beck, eds., *Customary International Humanitarian Law. Volume 1: Rules* (Cambridge: Cambridge University Press, 2009).

24. See Craig Jones, "Operationalizing International Law: From Vietnam to Gaza," this volume.

25. According to an investigative report in *Haaretz*, Dinstein continued working for the Israeli government when he became head of Amnesty International's Israel section from 1974 to 1976. See Uri Blau, "Documents Reveal How Israel Made Amnesty's Local Branch a Front for the Foreign Ministry in the 70s," *Haaretz*, March 18, 2017, https://www.haaretz.com/israel-news/2017-03-18/ty-article/.pre mium/how-israel-made-amnestys-local-branch-a-front-for-the-foreign-ministry -in-the-70s/0000017f-da78-dc0c-afff-db7b23800000. Dinstein was later appointed the Charles H. Stockton Professor of International Law at the U.S. Naval War College in Newport, Rhode Island, just before and after the September 11, 2001, attacks.

26. See Yoram Dinstein, *War, Aggression and Self-Defense* (Cambridge: Cambridge University Press, 2017, now in its sixth edition). Yoram Dinstein, *The Conduct of Hostilities in the Law of Armed Conflict* (Cambridge: Cambridge University Press, 2016, third edition). Yoram Dinstein, *Non-International Armed Conflicts in International Law* (Cambridge: Cambridge University Press, 2014). Yoram Dinstein, *The International Law of Belligerent Occupation* (Cambridge: Cambridge University Press, 2009).

27. Schmitt claims that he was given unprecedented access to the Israeli operations center responsible for overseeing combat operations against Hamas. See Noura Erakat, "If Israeli Tactics in Gaza Are Legal, No One is Safe: Response to Michael N. Schmitt and John J. Merriam," *Jadaliyya*, July 18, 2015.

28. Noura Erakat, *Justice for Some: Law and the Question of Palestine* (Stanford: Stanford University Press, 2019), 178–83.

29. It has been reported in the Israeli press that Israel has trained Colombian and Nepalese mercenaries to fight on behalf of the United Arab Emirates in Yemen and both the UAE and Saudi Arabia have purchased Israeli spyware, surveillance, and monitoring systems. See Zvi Bar'el, "Yemen's War Is a Mercenary Heaven. Are Israelis Reaping the Profits?," *Haaretz*, February 17, 2019.

30. Significantly, this was a view that was shared by American, and not only Israeli, lawyers. See W. Hays Parks, "Perspective and the Importance of History," *Yearbook of International Humanitarian Law* 14 (2011): 361–82.

31. Although these actions are often thought of as being unique to Palestinian groups, it was a strategy that was also employed by the Vietcong. See Heather Stur, "The Vietcong committed atrocities too," *New York Times*, December 19, 2017. This is not to downplay the fact that American and Jewish groups have also resorted to terrorism in the past from groups like the Weathermen to Kahane Chai. In November 2022, the government of prime minister Benjamin Netanyahu formed a coalition with the Jewish Power Party (Otzma Yehudit) and appointed Itamar Ben-Gvir, a former Kahanist, minister for national security. In May 2022, the US State Department removed Kahane Chai from its list of foreign terrorist organizations: https://www.state.gov/foreign-terrorist-organizations/

32. See Robert Alden, "Policy Shift by US at UN," *New York Times*, September 12, 1972, 10.

33. Kaplan, *Our American Israel*, 127–28.

34. See John Quigley, "Legality of Military Action by Egypt and Syria in October 1973," this volume.

35. Kaplan, *Our American Israel*, 132.

36. Kaplan, *Our American Israel*, 133.

37. Benjamin Netanyahu, *Bibi: My Story* (New York: Simon & Schuster, 2022), 174.

38. See Victor Kattan, "'The Third World Is a Problem': Arguments about the Laws of War in the United States after the Fall of Saigon," this volume.

39. The policy was encapsulated in National Security Decision Directive 138, April 3, 1984, at 4, available on the website of the American Federation of Scientists at: https://fas.org/irp/offdocs/nsdd/nsdd-138.pdf. Shultz's speech calling for a policy of active defense was later republished in an influential book edited by Netanyahu. See George P. Shultz, "The Challenge to the Democracies," in Benjamin Netanyahu, ed., *Terrorism: How the West Can Win* (New York: Farrar, Straus, Giroux, 1986), 16–24. According to Shultz, President Reagan read the book on a trip to Tokyo "and had come back to the senior staff area several times from his cabin on *Air Force One* to read passages to us that he particularly liked." See George P. Shultz, *Turmoil and Triumph: My Years as Secretary of State* (New York: Macmillan, 1993), 790n5.

40. See US Department of Defense: Report of the DOD Commission on Beirut International Airport Terrorist Attack, October 23, 1983 (published on December 20, 1983).

41. See Brian Cuddy, "From Retaliation to Anticipation: Reconciling Reprisals and Self-Defense in the Middle East and Vietnam, 1949–1965," this volume. It could also be argued that preventive war was part of Israel's self-identity in that it formed a decisive moment of its history when it was established as a state following Ben-Gurion's decision to begin the war of independence earlier than planned by initiating the battle six weeks before the end of the mandate scheduled for midnight on May 14–15, 1948, when the Arab states had planned to intervene. According to Esber's remarkable study, as early as December 1947, the Zionist leadership had decided to embark on a policy of "offensive defense." See Rosemarie M. Esber, *Under the Cover of War: The Zionist Expulsion of the Palestinians* (Alexandria, VA: Arabicus Books 2008), 173.

42. Cuddy, "From Retaliation to Anticipation."

43. Cuddy, "From Retaliation to Anticipation."

44. See Ashley Deeks, "Unwilling or Unable: Toward a Normative Framework for Extra-Territorial Self-Defense," *Virginia Journal of International Law* 52 (2011–2012): 483–550. Olivier Corten, "The 'Unwilling or Unable' Test: Has It Been, and Could It Be, Accepted?" *Leiden Journal of International Law* 29, no. 3 (2016): 777–99.

45. Shultz, *Turmoil and Triumph*, 678 citing Abraham D. Sofaer, "Terrorism and the Law," *Foreign Affairs* 64 (1986): 901–22.

46. Sofaer, "Terrorism and the Law," 919.

47. See *Legal Consequences of the Construction of a Wall in the Occupied Palestinian Territory, Advisory Opinion, ICJ Reports 2004*, 194, para. 139. On the issue of whether

Article 51 can apply to attacks from nonstate actors see Christine Chinkin and Mary Kaldor, *International Law and New Wars* (Cambridge: Cambridge University Press, 2017), 157–61.

48. Quoted from Sofaer, "The United States and the World Court," *Proceedings of the American Society of International Law* 80 (1986): 207.

49. See Richard Falk, "Foreword: How International Law Evolves: Norms, Precedents, and Geopolitics," this volume.

50. See Madelaine Chiam and Brian Cuddy, "Public Discourses of International Law: US Debates on Military Intervention in Vietnam, 1965–1967," chap.3 this volume.

51. See Stephen Neff, *War and the Law of Nations: A General History* (Cambridge: Cambridge University Press, 2005), 386; Jackson Maogoto, *Battling Terrorism* (Aldershot, UK: Ashgate, 2005), 90; Tom Ruys, *'Armed Attack' and Article 51 of the UN Charter: Evolutions in Customary Law and Practice* (Cambridge: Cambridge University Press, 2013), 422; Kattan, "The 'Netanyahu Doctrine,'" 3–7; Christine Gray, *International Law and the Use of Force*, 4th ed. (Oxford: Oxford University Press, 2018), 170–75.

52. See George P. Shultz, "Hot Preemption," adapted from remarks delivered at the dedication of the George P. Shultz National Foreign Affairs Training Center in Arlington, Virginia, on May 29, 2002, available online: https://www.hoover.org/re search/hot-preemption. See also *The National Security Strategy of the United States of America* (2002), 15 at https://2009-2017.state.gov/documents/organization/635 62.pdf. A. D. Sofaer, "On the Necessity of Pre-emption," *European Journal of International Law* 14, no. 2 (2003): 209–26. John Yoo, *War by Other Means: An Insider's Account of the War on Terror* (New York: Atlantic Monthly Press, 2006).

53. Robert Cooper, "The New Liberal Imperialism," *The Guardian*, April 7, 2002.

54. Robert Cooper, *The Breaking of Nations* (New York: Atlantic Books, 2004), 17–18.

55. Cooper, *The Breaking of Nations*, 17–18.

56. Cuddy quotes Abram Chayes, who in 1961 advised that Article 51 of the UN Charter could only be invoked in response to an armed attack. See Cuddy, "From Retaliation to Anticipation," this volume.

57. Daniel Bethlehem, "International Law and the Use of Force: The Law as It is and Should Be," memorandum submitted to the Select Committee on Foreign Affairs, June 7, 2004, para. 32 at https://publications.parliament.uk/pa/cm200304 /cmselect/cmfaff/441/4060808.htm

58. See Shultz, *Turmoil and Triumph*, 645.

59. See *The National Security Strategy of the United States of America* (September 2002), 15 at https://2009-2017.state.gov/documents/organization/63562.pdf

60. *The National Security Strategy of the United States of America*, 15.

61. See A More Secure World: Our Shared Responsibility Report of the Secretary-General's High-level Panel on Threats, Challenges and Change, UN Doc. 59/565, December 2, 2004, paras. 188–92 ("we do not favour the rewriting or reinterpretation of Article 51.")

62. See Victor Kattan, "Furthering the 'War on Terrorism' through International Law: How the United States and the United Kingdom Resurrected the Bush

Doctrine on Using Preventive Military Force to Combat Terrorism," *Journal on the Use of Force and International Law* 5, no. 1 (2018): 97–144.

63. See the statement by Israel's UN Ambassador in UN Doc. S/PV.2288, June 19,1981, paras. 79–85.

64. Quoted by Yotam Feldman and Uri Blau in the Israeli newspaper *Haaretz* on January 29, 2009, at https://www.haaretz.com/1.5069101. On whether international law can really progress through violations see Kattan, "Furthering the 'War on Terrorism' through International Law," 123–30. On what really happened at the UN after Israel's 1981 raid on Iraq see Kattan, "The 'Netanyahu Doctrine,'" 24–26.

65. Kattan "Furthering the 'War on Terrorism' through International Law." See also Legal Adviser Bellinger speech, "Legal Issues in the War on Terrorism," October 31, 2006, London School of Economics at https://2009-2017.state.gov/s/l/20 06/98861.htm

66. House of Commons, August 29, 2013, cols. 1425–1547.

67. See Guglielmo Verdirame, "The Law and Strategy of Humanitarian Intervention," *EJIL: Talk!*, August 30, 2013. Verdirame's partner, Henry Newman, is a Conservative political adviser to Michael Gove MP, a British minister. Gove was founding chairman of Policy Exchange, a right-of-center think tank, and a founding member of the Henry Jackson society, a British-based neoconservative think tank that "Believes that only modern liberal democratic states are truly legitimate; and that the political or human rights pronouncements of any international or regional organisation which admits undemocratic states lack the legitimacy to which they would be entitled if all their members were democracies." Gove has expressed open support for preemptive wars, including Iraq in 2003, irrespective of the prohibition on the use of such force in the UN Charter. See Michael Gove, "The Very British Roots of Neoconservatism and its Lessons for British Conservatives," in Irwin Stelzer (ed.), *The Neocon Reader* (New York: Grove Press, 2004), 271–88, at 274. In common with his neoconservative views, Gove admires the hardline stance adopted by successive Likud governments in Israel toward the Palestinians and opposes Israel having to "give up" land (that is, land, which it must be emphasized, is not Israel's to keep) for peace with the Palestinians. See Michael Gove, *Celsius 7/7* (London: Weidenfeld & Nicolson, 2006), 51–62. In February 2020, Verdirame submitted a written observation as *amicus curiae* to the International Criminal Court, with several other lawyers, opposing the jurisdiction of the court to open an investigation into Israeli war crimes in Israeli-occupied East Jerusalem, the West Bank, and Gaza, despite Palestine being recognized as an observer state by the UN in November 2012. In the 2022 special honours list, Verdirame, who is King's Counsel, and a Professor of International Law at King's College London in the Department of War Studies, was awarded a life peerage as "Baron Verdirame, of Belsize Park in the London Borough of Camden": https://www.gov.uk/government/news/political-pe erages-2022

68. Guglielmo Verdirame, "The 'Sinews of Peace': International Law, Strategy, and the Prevention of War," *British Yearbook of International Law* 77, no. 1 (2006): 95.

69. Verdirame, "The 'Sinews of Peace,'" 83–162.

70. With regard for the need to adapt the law for drone technology, see, for example, *The Report of the Task Force on US Drone Policy* (Washington, DC: Stimson Center, second edition, 2015), https://www.stimson.org/wp-content/files/file-attac

hments/recommendations_and_report_of_the_task_force_on_us_drone_policy_se cond_edition.pdf. John Bellinger III is listed as one of the task force members, while Daniel Bethlehem is listed as a working group member.

71. Verdirame, "The 'Sinews of Peace,'" 84.

72. On the US government's failure to develop a lethal drone in the Vietnam War and Israel's success in developing such a drone in its wars in Egypt and Lebanon, see Konstantin Kakeas, "From Orville Wright to September 11: What the History of Drone Technology Says About Its Future," in Peter L. Bergen and Daniel Rothenberg, eds., *Drone Wars: Transforming Conflict, Law, and Policy* (Cambridge: Cambridge University Press, 2015), 368–74.

73. This included the Bell UH-1 Iroquois and AH-1G HueyCobra attack helicopters in Vietnam, and the remotely piloted drone pioneered by the Israeli air force. The iconic Apache attack helicopter used all over the world from Iraq to the Gaza Strip, evolved from the US Army's "earlier, abortive attempt during the Vietnam War to acquire a high-speed, heavily armed helicopter gunship—the Lockheed AH-56 Cheyenne—to provide fire support for ground combat units and protect rotary-wing aircraft transporting infantry, weapons, and supplies to forward battle areas." See Thomas C. Lassman, "Reforming Weapon Systems Acquisition in the Department of Defense: The Case of the U.S. Army's Advanced Attack Helicopter," *Journal of Policy History* 25, no. 2 (2013): 173.

74. Kakeas, "From Orville Wright to September 11," 374–75.

75. See Daniel Bethlehem, "Self-Defense Against an Imminent or Actual Armed Attack by Nonstate Actors," *American Journal of International Law* 106, no. 4 (2012): 770–77. Daniel Bethlehem, "The Secret Life of International Law," *Cambridge International Law Journal* 1, no. 1 (2012): 23–36.

76. See the statement by Australia's attorney general George Brandis QC explaining that Australia has adopted the Bethlehem Principles test of an imminent threat of attack, online at https://www.ejiltalk.org/the-right-of-self-defence-again st-imminent-armed-attack-in-international-law/#_ftn7

77. Julian Borger, "Latin Americans fear precedent set by legal justification for Syria intervention," *The Guardian*, April 2, 2019.

78. See Kattan, "Furthering the 'War on Terrorism' through International Law."

79. Kattan, "Furthering the 'War on Terrorism' through International Law," 114–23.

80. Kattan, "Furthering the 'War on Terrorism' through International Law," 114–23.

81. See Bart Barnes, "Obituary: John B. Bellinger Jr," *Washington Post*, January 10, 2012, B5.

82. See John B. Bellinger III, biography on the website of Arnold and Porter LLP at https://www.arnoldporter.com/en/people/b/bellinger-john-b

83. Bethlehem's wife, Ady Schonmann-Bethlehem, was the Deputy Head of the International Law Department in the Office of the Legal Adviser of the Israeli Ministry of Foreign Affairs in Jerusalem for many years. See her profile on the website of King's College London, where she is a Visiting Professor in the Dickson Poon School of Law and in the Department of War Studies (where her husband is also a Visiting Professor): https://www.kcl.ac.uk/people/ady-schonmann-bethl ehem. On Bethlehem's role advising Israel during the ICJ Wall proceedings (2003–

4) before he took up his FCO post, see Ewan MacAskill, "Israel adviser switches to top FO job," *The Guardian*, March 7, 2006. On Bethlehem's legal advice to the ICJ in the *Wall* advisory opinion, which he wrote with Alan Baker and Ruth Lapidoth, see the series of articles published on the website of *Haaretz* in January 2004 by Nathan Guttman, Aluf Benn, and Gideon Alon. On his advice to the Sharon government over the Jenin killings, see Chris McGreal, "Israelis dub Jenin probe 'anti-Semitic,'" *The Guardian*, April 28, 2002. Bethlehem is also on the board of Palantir, a data mining and predictive analytics company, and the company is a client of Daniel Reisner, at the law firm of Herzog, Fox, and Neeman in Tel Aviv. Reisner's other clients include Elbit systems, Boeing, Lockheed Martin, and Pratt & Whitney. Reisner's CV is available online: http://www.intjewishlawyers.org/site /wp-content/uploads/2018/01/Daniel_Reisner.pdf

84. See the written evidence submitted to the House of Commons Select Committee on Foreign Affairs by Daniel Bethlehem QC, Director of Lauterpacht Research Centre for International Law, University of Cambridge (7 June 2004), www.publications.parliament.uk/pa/cm200304/cmselect/cmfaff/441/4060808 .htm, para 35(a). See also Bethlehem's response to a questionnaire published by Elizabeth Wilmshurst when she was formulating *The Chatham House Principles on the Use of Force*, www.chathamhouse.org/publications/papers/view/108106, p. 41 (emphasis added). Bethlehem's name did not appear in *The Chatham House Principles* when they were published, indicating that he did not agree with the formulation of self-defense adopted by the other international lawyers involved in formulating the principles. See Elizabeth Wilmshurst, "The Chatham House Principles of International Law on the Use of Force in Self-Defence," *International and Comparative Law Quarterly* 55 (2006): 963.

85. See James Mann, *Rise of the Vulcans: The History of Bush's War Cabinet* (New York: Viking, 2004).

86. See Nominations before the Senate Armed Services Committee, First Session, 107th Congress, S. Hrg. 107–749 (January–December 2001), online: https:// www.govinfo.gov/content/pkg/CHRG-107shrg75903/html/CHRG-107shrg759 03.htm. Wolfowitz's connections to Israel are also addressed in Mann, *Rise of the Vulcans*.

87. Other influential individuals in the Reagan, Bush, and Trump administrations with close connections to Israel include Elliott Abrams and John Bolton. On Abrams's connections see Elliott Abrams, *Tested by Zion: The Bush Administration and the Israeli-Palestinian Conflict* (Cambridge: Cambridge University Press, 2013), at 59 where Abrams addresses his neoconservatism. On Bolton, see John Bolton, *Surrender Is Not an Option: Defending America at the United Nations* (New York: Simon and Schuster, 2008).

88. See Michael Thomas, *American Policy Toward Israel: The Power and Limits of Beliefs* (New York: Routledge, 2007).

89. See the chapter by Kattan, "'The Third World Is a Problem,'" this volume.

90. See Benjamin Netanyahu, ed., *International Terrorism: Challenge and Response* (Jerusalem: The Jonathan Institute, 1980). Benjamin Netanyahu, ed., *Terrorism: How the West Can Win* (New York: Farrar, Straus, Giroux, 1986). Benjamin Netanyahu, *Fighting Terrorism: How Democracies can Defeat the International Terrorist Network* (New York: Farrar, Straus and Giroux, 2001). Ben Caspit and Ilan Kfir, *Netan-*

yahu: The Road to Power (New York: Citadel Press, 1998). Netanyahu's influence in the United States remains enormous. Consider the standing ovation he received before both Houses of Congress in 2015 when he openly criticized a sitting US president. On Netanyahu's recollections of this speech see Netanyahu, *Bibi*, 527–39.

91. Netanyahu, *Bibi*, 151–52.

92. Netanyahu, *Terrorism: How the West Can Win*, 204–5.

93. Netanyahu, *Terrorism: How the West Can Win*, 204–5.

94. Neve Gordon and Nicola Perugini, *Human Shields: A History of a People in the Line of Fire* (Berkeley: University of California Press, 2020), 171. Gordon and Perugini also note the similarity of the Israeli language justifying Operation Protective Edge to arguments made by the Italian government during the 1935–36 war in Ethiopia.

95. See Amanda Alexander, "Revolutionary War and the Development of International Humanitarian Law," this volume.

96. See Tor Krever, "From Vietnam to Palestine: Peoples' Tribunals and the Juridification of Resistance," this volume.

97. Alexander, "Revolutionary War."

98. See Ihab Shalbak and Jessica Whyte, "The War Against the People and the People's War: Palestine and the Additional Protocols to the Geneva Conventions," this volume.

99. The difficulty of this issue has also bedeviled the ICRC. See Nils Melzer, *Interpretive Guidance on the Notion of Direct Participation in Hostilities under International Humanitarian Law* (Geneva: ICRC, 2009). But see Hays Parks, "Part IX of the ICRC 'Direct Participation in Hostilities' Study: No Mandate, No Expertise, and Legally Incorrect," *New York Journal of International Law and Policy* 42, no. 3 (2010): 769–830.

100. See, for example, Gordon and Perugini, *Human Shields*, 170–78.

101. See, for example, Yarno Ritzen, "How armies of fake accounts 'ruined' Twitter in the Middle East," *Al Jazeera*, July 15, 2019. While the Russians, Chinese, Emiratis, and Saudis are often blamed for these tactics, we know that Western democratic states also employ them. See, for example, Amanda Holpunch, "US immigration police broke Facebook rules with fake profiles for college sting," *The Guardian*, April 11, 2019. In 2015, the British Army announced the creation of the 77th Brigade, a psychological operations unit responsible for "non-lethal" warfare that reportedly uses social media to "control the narrative," as well as disseminating UK government-friendly podcasts and videos. See Laurie Clarke, "Twitter needs to start exposing the UK's murky online propaganda," *Wired*, October 8, 2019.

102. W. Hays Parks, "The ICRC Customary Law Study: A Preliminary Assessment," *Proceedings of the American Society of International Law* 99 (2005): 208–12.

103. Hays Parks, "The ICRC Customary Law Study," 209.

104. Hays Parks, "The ICRC Customary Law Study," 209.

105. Consider the political views Parks expressed in W. Hays Parks, "Air War and the Law of War," *Air Force Law Review* 32 (1990): 63–111. W. Hays Parks, "Exaggerated or One-Sided Claims of Law of War Violations," in John Norton Moore, ed., *Deception and Deterrence in "Wars of National Liberation," State-Sponsored Terrorism and Other Forms of Secret Warfare* (Durham: Carolina Academic Press, 1997), 103–26.

106. Hays Parks, "The ICRC Customary Law Study," 210.

107. Olivier Corten, *The Law against War: The Prohibition on the Use of Force in Contemporary International Law* (Oxford: Hart Publishing, 2012), 13.

108. Corten, *The Law against War*, 13.

109. See, generally, Michael Byers and Georg Nolte, eds., *United States Hegemony and the Foundations of International Law* (Cambridge: Cambridge University Press, 2003).

110. John B. Bellinger III and William J. Haynes II, "A US government response to the International Committee of the Red Cross study Customary International Humanitarian Law," *International Review of the Red Cross* 89 (2007): 443–71, at 445.

111. This is explored in the chapter by Kattan, "'The Third World Is a Problem.'"

112. Nico Krisch, "After Hegemony: The Law on the Use of Force and the Ukraine Crisis," *EJIL Talk!*, March 2, 2022, https://www.ejiltalk.org/after-hegemony-the-law-on-the-use-of-force-and-the-ukraine-crisis/

113. Richard Falk, "The Cambodian Operation and International Law," in Richard A. Falk, ed., *The Vietnam War and International Law, Volume 3: The Widening Context* (Princeton: Princeton University Press, 1972), 55–56.

114. Modirzadeh, "Cut These Words," 30.

115. President Putin referred to "precedents," such as NATO's aerial bombardment of Serbia in 1999, and US support for regime change in Iraq, Libya, Syria, and so on to justify his decision to initiate a "special military operation" in Ukraine. See Address by the President of the Russian Federation, February 24, 2022, at http://en.kremlin.ru/events/president/news/67843

116. Chinkin and Kaldor, *International Law and New Wars*, 167.

Acknowledgments

This book emerged out of a workshop, *The Vietnam and Arab-Israeli Conflicts: International Legal Migrations, Comparisons, and Connections*, hosted in Singapore on December 6, 2018. The workshop was organized by the Transsystemic Law Research Cluster at the Middle East Institute (MEI), an autonomous research institute at the National University of Singapore, in conjunction with the Department of Security Studies and Criminology at Australia's Macquarie University. We would like to acknowledge the financial support provided to the Transsystemic Law Research Cluster by the MEI, and the support of colleagues, especially Bilahari Kausikan, Engseng Ho, Michelle Teo, Carl Skadian, Ang Cheng Guan, Francesco Mancini, Sinja Graf, Sharon Koung, Jamaliah Jamal, the late Rommel Hernando, and Priyaa Vasudevan.

All the speakers who presented at the Singapore workshop are contributors to the present volume, including Richard Falk, whose comprehensive foreword is based on his keynote lecture at the workshop. We are grateful to all of them for their timely contributions and for making the workshop such a great success. In addition, following peer review we solicited two extra chapters from Craig Jones and Tor Krever. We are grateful to them for their contributions. Our thanks also go to the team at the University of Michigan Press who have supported this project through to publication, including acquisitions editor Elizabeth Demers and editorial associate Haley Winkle; Law, Meaning, and Violence series editors Martha Minow and Austin Sarat; the two external peer reviewers who provided valuable feedback on an early version of the manuscript, as well as the revised manuscript; production editor Kevin Rennells; and the supporters of Michigan's open access publishing program.

Working on an edited volume is a challenging task, made even more difficult in our case by delays associated with the Covid-19 global pandemic. We have navigated those challenges together, with each editor bringing complementary disciplinary and regional expertise to the project. While the editors' names are listed alphabetically, the book is the product of a genuine joint enterprise based on equal partnership. The same is true for each of the four coauthored chapters within the book. Finally, allow us to express our immense gratitude to our wives Jess and Amrita for their love and support, and to our children to whom we dedicate this book.

B.C. & V.K.

Contributors

Amanda Alexander is Senior Lecturer at the Australian Catholic University. Her publications include "A Short History of International Law," published in the *European Journal of International Law*, and "The 'Good War': Preparations for a War Against Civilians," published in *Law, Culture and the Humanities*.

Madelaine Chiam is Associate Dean Learning and Teaching and Associate Professor at La Trobe Law School. She is the author of *International Law in Public Debate* (Cambridge University Press, 2021).

Brian Cuddy is a historian of US foreign relations and Lecturer in Security Studies at Macquarie University in Sydney, Australia. He is the editor, with Fredrik Logevall, of *The Vietnam War in the Pacific World* (University of North Carolina Press, 2022).

Richard Falk is Albert G. Milbank Professor of International Law Emeritus, Princeton University and author of *Public Intellectual: The Life of a Citizen Pilgrim* (Clarity Press, 2021). He served as UN Special Rapporteur for Occupied Palestine between 2008 and 2014.

Craig Jones is the author of *The War Lawyers: The United States, Israel, and Juridical Warfare* (Oxford University Press, 2020) and Senior Lecturer in Political Geography in the School of Geography, Politics, and Sociology at Newcastle University. He researches the legal and medical materialities of war and conflict in the contemporary Middle East.

Victor Kattan is Assistant Professor at the School of Law in the Faculty of Social Sciences at the University of Nottingham. He is the author and editor of three books on the conflicts in the Middle East, including as editor, with the late Peter Sluglett, of *Violent Radical Movements in the Arab World: The Ideology and Politics of Non-State Actors* (Bloomsbury, 2019).

Tor Krever is Assistant Professor at the University of Warwick School of Law, where his research focuses on the theory and history of international law. He is currently completing a book on the figure of the pirate in international legal thought and is co-general editor of the *London Review of International Law*.

John Quigley is Professor Emeritus at the Moritz College of Law, The Ohio State University. His most recent books are *Britain and Its Mandate over Palestine: Legal Chicanery on a World Stage* (Anthem Press, 2022) and *The Legality of a Jewish State: A Century of Debate over Rights in Palestine* (Cambridge University Press, 2021).

Ihab Shalbak is Lecturer in the Department of Sociology and Social Policy at the University of Sydney. His research examines the relation between dominant forms of knowledge and politics, and has been published in *Postcolonial Studies* and *Thesis Eleven* among other outlets. He is currently completing a book that traces the emergence of the think tank form.

Jessica Whyte is Scientia Associate Professor of Philosophy at the University of New South Wales. She is the author of *Catastrophe and Redemption: The Political Thought of Giorgio Agamben* (SUNY Press, 2013) and *The Morals of the Market: Human Rights and the Rise of Neoliberalism* (Verso, 2019), and an editor of *Humanity: An International Journal of Human Rights, Humanitarianism and Development*.

Index

Solf, Waldemar, 176
Southeast Asia Treaty Organization
  (SEATO), 66
  act under Article 51 and 53, 69
  Meeker memorandum, 69
  Soviet Union, x, 6, 19, 33, 88, 91, 104,
    134, 175, 176, 182, 183, 185, 186,
    187, 189, 192, 193, 194, 267
State Department memorandum
  legal arguments, 66–67
  no supporting legal authorities, 67
  North Vietnam violated Geneva
    Accords, 66
Stewart, Luke, 65
Strategic Hamlet program, 117
Suez Crisis, 28
  Israel's defense, 38–39
  Israel's Sinai campaign, 38
  UN General Assembly special session,
    38
Suleimani, Qassim, 26
Swiss Federal Council, 146

Taylor, Maxwell, 39
Taylor, Telford, 77, 125
Tel Aviv, 20, 30, 31, 34, 36, 218, 245, 266
Ten Point Program, 158
"Third Worldism," 19
Traditional model of armed conflict
  Palestinian and North Vietnamese
    view on, 147
  US military lawyer's views, 147
Truman, Harry, 13
Tyler, Roger, 28, 30

United Nations Charter
  Article 51, xiv, 36, 38, 40, 41, 45, 46,
    49, 66, 68–69, 69, 70, 90–91, 101,
    103, 105, 268, 270, 272
  Article 53, 69
United Nations General Assembly, x,
    xvii, 3, 10, 14, 38, 91, 92, 93, 97,
    121, 122, 128, 129, 150, 160, 161,
    177, 185, 186, 190, 250, 253, 273,
    278, 279
United Nations Truce Supervision
  Organisation (UNTSO), 34, 96
US war in Vietnam. *See* Vietnam War

Vessey, John W., 183
Viet Minh, 13
  communist core, suspicion of, 13
  Geneva Accords, 13
  People's Republic of China, support
    to, 13
Vietnam syndrome, 174, 271
Vietnam War, 1, 16. *See also* Middle East
  conflicts
  American popular culture, 262–65
  armed conflicts, 7
  arrogant brutality of US, 244–45
  background, 12–14
  bombing campaigns, 209
  causative factors, 113
  common enemy, 266–68
  crimes tribunal for, 236–39
  critical year of 1967, 16
  Easter Offensive, 209
  First Indochina War, 13
  history connected, 8–9
  human rights politics, 6
  international law rationales, Ameri-
    cans involvement, 4
  international law scholarship, 6
  law and politics, 239–42
  law of war, impact on, 265
  legal issues, 209
  Lyndon B. Johnson administration,
    role of, 57
  My Lai massacre, 209
  Netanyahu's reasons and Western
    malaise, 275
  new rules drafting and United States,
    274
  Nicaraguan soldiers, training to, 9
  Peers Report, significance of, 212
  Rolling Thunder operation, 209, 210
  scholarship and training programs,
    citations in, 265–66
  shaping law of war, influence on,
    262–63
  shaping thinking, 273
  Son My Massacre, 211
  Viet Minh, 13
  younger generation of scholars,
    affected by, 264
Vietnam War veterans, 19, 133, 166, 174,
    175, 182, 185, 188, 268